14

7

THE
OLIVE
TREE

THE
OLIVE
TREE

A Personal Journey Through
Mediterranean Olive Groves

Carol Drinkwater

Weidenfeld & Nicolson
LONDON

First published in Great Britain in 2008
by Weidenfeld & Nicolson

1 3 5 7 9 10 8 6 4 2

A CIP catalogue record for this book
is available from the British Library.

ISBN-13 978 0 297 84774 8
ISBN TPB 978 0 297 85437 1

Typeset by Input Data Services Ltd,
Bridgwater, Somerset

Printed and bound in the UK by
CPI Mackays, Chatham ME5 8TD

Weidenfeld & Nicolson

The Orion Publishing Group Ltd
Orion House
5 Upper Saint Martin's Lane
London, WC2H 9EA

An Hachette Livre UK Company

www.orionbooks.co.uk

The Orion Publishing Group's policy is to use papers that
are natural, renewable and recyclable products and made
from wood grown in sustainable forests. The logging and
manufacturing processes are expected to conform to
the environmental regulations of the country of origin.

For Phyllis, in celebration of all the fires we have lit together and the apples we have enjoyed.

I am so fortunate to have you for my mother.

Contents

Acknowledgements

It is impossible to list the numerous folk who have been involved in this book, companions along the way or casual encounters, some who added vibrancy or occasionally irritation to my journey.

Those who cannot be forgotten, in no particular order, are Matty and Sammy Cremona, Soheila and Alex Hayek, Giorgio Ruta, Marie-Gabrielle and François L'Huillier, Hocine Diffalah, Guy Beaufoy, Salvatore Spatola, Hamzaoui Mohamed, José Gómez, Dighton Spooner, Fedcrico La Notte, The Argan families, Attilio Sonnoli, Antonio Azara, Peter Greene, Nicola Noviello, Mustafa and Nadget Bouchema and a dozen, if not more, beekeepers in Algeria.

Back at home, hearty thanks go to Frank Barrett, Wendy Driver, Susie de Carteret, Chris Brown, Carmel Lynch for the argan tips, Alan Samson, my splendid editor, Jonathan and Marion Lloyd for loyal support, Dennis Drinkwater and Hitesh Shah.

At my publishing house, Weidenfeld & Nicolson, an entire team are beavering away, all of whom are excellent, headed by Susan Lamb and ably supported by so many including Lucinda McNeile and Jessica Mead.

As always to the booksellers and buyers, a very big hearfelt thank you.

Lastly, Michel: you come first.

MY OLIVE TREE JOURNEY

Atlantic Ocean

Santander
Bilbao
Cordillera Cantabrica
Altamira

PORTUGAL

Cuacos de Yuste
Madrid
EXTREMADURA
SPAIN
CASTILLA ~ LA MANCHA
Barcelona

Coto Donana N'Park
Cordova
Jerez
Cadiz
Granada
Guadix
Algeciras
Almeria
Tangier

Mediz

Casablanca
Volubilis
Meknes
Algiers
Blida
Bej
Kabylia Mts
Setif

Marrakesh
Essaouira
Talmste
BERBER
Atlas Mts
Timg. Rui

MOROCCO

ALGERIA

FR

Ah, if we could but answer! Or if we had tree-speech!

D.H. Lawrence, *Sea and Sardinia*

Strange Fruits

It was the season of nightingales, our May songstress, diva of the Cannes Film Festival. The olive groves were aflame with red poppies while on high, in the canopies, the trees were shedding their minuscule petals, floating earthwards they were, falling like grains of sand. The days had grown so hot, so rainless, that it might have been mid-summer. Our nights, stars bright and low in the heavens. Guests were with us: business colleagues who had flown in to attend the festival. I was lost in a world of my own, preoccupied, drifting through the greater part of the days in the shade at the table beneath the *Magnolia grandiflora*, downloading photo images from my laptop on to disks. I had only days earlier returned from strife-torn Israel and Palestine, the last ports of call on the first half of a solo, round-the-Mediterranean journey. War was looming once more in those Middle Eastern territories. I had sensed the itch of it during my travels, rubbed up against its steel edge. The news coming out of Lebanon seemed to confirm the world's worst fears.

I had made good friends over that way, found perhaps the oldest living trees on the planet there. I was fretting for their safety.

The last invader on my mind was the *Bactrocera (Dacus) Oleae*.

June: wrong time of year to travel; best to sit it out, take time, relax. Days among the trees, earth-digging in the greenhouse, cane-cutting for tomatoes. Yes, pass the summer on the farm, set off again when

I

the leaves are golden, gathering the threads in the autumn. White, box-shaped monitoring traps were being unloaded. Michel had collected them from Nice. Now, they were being hung by Quashia on the outer branches, south side of the olive trees, in the lower groves. They exuded a scent, a pheromone, these inanimate boxes, masquerading as female olive flies, luring the unsuspecting male. It alerted the farmer to the insect's flight path. As soon as the first sighting was recorded, it was essential to bring out the spraying machines, go to work, zap. I stared down the terraces at the traps, motionless in the beating, windless heat. They might have been party lanterns, these traps for randy flies! I was bowing to the majority. My husband, Michel, and our loyal Algerian-Arab gardener of sixteen years, Mr Quashia, were urging me to accept the treatment of the trees.

'The olives must be protected, if we are not to lose everything again.'

Bactrocera (Dacus) Oleae, the dreaded *mouche d'olive*, the olive fruit fly (we had nicknamed it Dacus), remained an undefeated enemy. It has no natural predators in Europe.

'Feed them to the nightingales!' I joshed.

Almost invisible, these insects appeared with the first heat and laid their eggs within the soft, delicate flesh of the olive pit, the developing drupe. We had lost our entire crop two winters back due to my 'stubbornness', my refusal to kill them off with insecticides, the men reminded me. The previous season had yielded a feeble return so we had experimented with bottle traps, but these had proved unsuccessful.

It is frequently the case with olive trees that one year they deliver bumper crops and the following lesser quantities. This autumn was promising a bumper return.

'It's foolishness, Carol, to risk it.'

Michel was in the kitchen preparing lunch. I was still buried in my own shaded world beneath the magnolia when Quashia came running to tell us 'the critters have arrived!' I protested one last time, arguing the case for an insecticide-free, organic harvest.

'The flies rot the fruits, Carol.'

Michel nodded, concurring.

'I don't understand why you can't support this,' I said to him in English.

'Because Quashia's right. If there was an alternative . . . but there isn't.'

Eventually, begrudgingly, I deferred to the power of two, to the others' point of view, and the men set to spraying the *oliviers*. It was the last week of June.

'Note it down, Carol! Mark it in your diary.'

The products remained effective for a mere twenty-one to twenty-eight days. The process had to be repeated at almost monthly intervals right through to October, till the summer heat had abated and the flies had given up their begetting. Habitually, this had amounted to three, even four sprays annually but recently, due to the lengthening summers and climatic changes, spraying was becoming a five-time requisite. I was praying this would not prove the pattern this year.

I had moved indoors, out of the heat, spending my days in my den. Or I kept in the shade, watching the slick of mercury rising. Clipped up outside the greenhouse, the thermometer was registering high nineties. July. Wide-sky blueness, not a cloud in sight. Rainless, rainless days. The droning, lusty whistle of the cicadas on heat. The drone of helicopters scouting for fires. Irrigation was our all-consuming occupation. Mr Quashia donned the Panama I had given him and took control. Michel and I assumed all other farm responsibilities. The flies had punctured few fruits and the olives were fattening up splendidly.

Lebanon and Israel were at war.

Michel was called back to Paris.

Quashia and I were closing holes in the fences to keep the dogs from escaping and harassing the postgirl, jittery at the best of times but impossible in this insufferable heat. We were refilling the water basin every two days. Watering, watering. A call from Paris took me north where I joined my husband. I needed information, documentation regarding an Algerian visa for my upcoming travels. Quashia enjoyed holding the fort. He was reconstructing walls, digging paths, relentlessly energetic. Uphill tracts were required for a tractor – who was to drive it? – to access the apex of the land where several young olive groves planted a few years earlier were rising vigorously. Our new plumber had been called in to lay down coils of black piping; yard after yard snaked beside the trunk bases along baked-brittle terraces at the summit of the land. We were installing a drip-feed system for the younger groves, more difficult to access. Our water consumption had quadrupled. The *goutte-à-goutte*, drop-by-drop feeding, was healthier for the trees and consumed less water.

I spoke to Quashia on the telephone on a daily basis, listening while he bitched about the insufferable heat, *'la canicule'*. To make matters worse, Ramadan, the Islamic month of fasting, had fallen; the poor man was suffering for his faith. Our friend was working in temperatures of close to a hundred, quenching the thirst of the plants without the liberty of slaking his own.

In Paris, my Algerian visa was proving problematic. I had applied for it twice, and did not want to leave the city again without it. On both occasions it had been thrown back at me, for infuriatingly insignificant reasons. I furnished what had been requested for a third time, delivering the forms personally, and was warned by the young Algerian that I could be looking at a forty-five-day delay. A postponement of my departure seemed the only avenue open to me if I was not to risk being refused entry at the Algerian border. It was inconvenient. I had been planning to travel during the winter months when the roads and hotels were less tourist-loaded and I wanted to be back in France by late May.

September was in full-throttle, but the heat showed no signs of abating. I decided to sit out the wait at the farm assisting Quashia, releasing him to sleep during the noonday, the most taxing for his fast. It was mid-afternoon when I arrived. No sign of life besides the four dogs who thundered down the drive, leaping, slobbering over me, walking on my feet as I pulled the gates to. Quashia was occupied elsewhere, preparing his post-sundown meal, perhaps. As I followed the winding drive towards the villa, I paused to admire our crop's growth, but the trees were a sorry sight, in dire need of water, even the old fellows who always fended for themselves, but it was not their water-stressed, shrivelled condition that was shocking to me. It was the shade of the fruits: the olives were black. It was not a play of light; the olives were black.

'But it cannot be!' I cried to no one.

If the dreaded female fly manages to perforate the base of the drupe and lay her eggs, the larvae remain there, feeding off the fruit's juice and flesh. Eventually, sucked dry of oil and nutrients, the drupe turns black and drops to the ground.

This can't be happening, I moaned half audibly.

In spite of all the toxins we had rained down upon the trees, and no matter what anyone from the Chambre d'Agriculture or the garden centre had assured us, these products *were* toxic; how had the flies still prospered and penetrated the fruits?

I took a closer look, cradling several of the small olives between my fingers and I was amazed, heartened to observe that the fruits were perfectly healthy. When the fly slips her ovipositor, her tubular egg-laying organ, into the fruit, puncturing the outer layer of skin as she does so, an infinitesimal circular black bruise appears on the olive. It is frequently the first clue we farmers have of the fly's presence in the groves. I could find none. I moved between trees, up and down terraces, scrupulously examining the crops. I found no signs of infestation.

So, why were so many of the olives black? Had another rot taken hold? The explanation proved quite simple, but equally troubling.

Our olives, or more than 50 per cent in this expanse of garden where the most mature groves on the estate dominated, were ripe. It was mid-September. The ripening process of an olive is quite splendid as it passes through its spectrum of ravishing colours. It begins as a hard, pale green bead. Then, during the months of summer, it slowly develops a piebald, green-violet hue. Finally, after metamorphosing into a rich shade of prune, it turns black. This final stage rarely, if ever, takes place before Christmas, and we do not wait for that transformation. The harvest kick-off, *la cueillette*, is traditionally the third week of November. We prefer to gather the fruits at the outset when the olives are *tournant*, 'turning', between green and prune. Looking about the groves, I calculated that our crop was two months ahead of schedule.

This was a state of affairs I had not encountered before.

I deposited my luggage and hurried to telephone the mill.

'The miller's away until next week.'

When I explained the crisis to his assistant, anxious to know whether others had phoned in with the same dilemma, the gloomy girl said no one else had complained.

'Sounds as if flies've got 'em. They'll fall. You'll be losing the lot.'

Even if we dropped everything and picked the black fruits immediately, it was highly unlikely that any mill would be open. No one starts pressing in September, not even as far south as Malta. But even if one mill made the entrepreneurial decision to open their doors two months early, there was precious little to press. The fruits were ripe on the surface, but they were still too small, barely more than skin and stone. At this stage, the oil quantity within them would be minimal.

I am not an olive farmer by profession. It is my passion, but, had it also been our livelihood, this unheard-of turn of events would have been sufficient to cause financial disruption, if not ruin. As it was, we would be losing all this year's investment. We were always struggling; we ran the farm on a shoestring. Still, its viability was not my first concern. I wanted to know what was going on.

The previous autumn, during late October, early November, a spell of unseasonably hot weather had hit our coast. It had taken many farmers by surprise. The olive fly is known to breed whenever temperatures are suitably ambient. Last year, the little pest had a bonus outing. After the final spray of the year had been completed and the fruits were oleaginous and plump, Indian summer temperatures hit the coast and out came the fly, tunnelling its deadly reproductive organ into the fat offerings and, at the last moment, contaminated all unprotected crops.

The previous winter at Appassionata, our olive farm in the south of France, another incident, equally disturbing, had occurred. The orange trees, whose customary sweet-scented flowers open from bud in early spring, blossomed in November. I remembered circling the trees on several occasions and asking Michel, 'What will this mean for their cycle?'

The flowers died off before Christmas and as the new year unfolded green nubs began to appear. The trees were fruiting three months ahead of schedule. When March came round, I was away on my travels; the natural cycle of the citruses kicked in and they flowered again, and throughout this summer the orange groves have been nurturing two generations of baby fruits: one crop larger and more advanced than the other, growing simultaneously on the branches. What will this mean, I asked myself. If a woman conceived and carried a foetus for four months and then conceived again, would this be science fiction? These unnatural occurrences were the direct result of soaring temperatures; unprecedented heat waves; interminable dry spells; plant cycles out of synch: climate change, earth mismanagement.

I stood alone in the house, ranting. We had taken the advice, heeded the recommendations of experts and had invested money that I would have preferred not to spend on expensive products. Chemicals, which, in my opinion, were not fit to be sprayed on a weed-infested parking lot let alone on our delectable olives. When I failed to reach Gérard, our experienced and always helpful miller, I picked up the phone to our man at the Chambre d'Agriculture.

'Yes, the groves are ahead of schedule by one month,' he confessed.

'Here it is closer to two,' I said, determined to register accurate facts.

He was perplexed, but was unable to offer any solutions except to warn me, 'You must spray the trees again at once.'

'I don't want to do that. We have sprayed three times already this summer, and—'

'The heat is showing no signs of abating. It is imperative you spray or you will lose everything. You are legally entitled to spray five times. This will only be your fourth outing.'

I argued the point no further.

Quashia and I set to work laying nets. There was no need to cut back the grass beneath the trees because the ground was a dustbowl. There had been no rain since April. We harvested the small ripe fruits and I pickled them. No longer oil material, these early samples were destined to be winter table olives. So, they had not gone to waste. Still, the crisis has been laid at our farm door.

'I am not doing it,' I said to Michel once he had returned from Paris. 'No more spraying.'

He begged me to be less inflexible. 'We have chosen to use

pesticides this year. It does not make sense to sabotage the process midway and lose the crop at this stage.'

He and Quashia went to work and I kept out of the way, ruminating, frustrated, angry.

Michel arrived back at lunchtime, covered in sweat and leaves and debris, looking very much the worse for wear. 'It's pretty foul, that stuff, *un vrai saloperie*; you're right.'

'Exactly. There has to be something less noxious.'

'If there was, don't you think we'd know about it?'

My Algerian visa arrived, but, in the light of what had come to pass, I postponed my travel plans and stayed home to help with the harvest. I found a mill high in the hills, operating the ancient granite-stone system. It had begun pressing. I booked us an appointment. All hands to the land, to gather for this first oil of the season.

The following day I received a letter from the AOC office. '*Chers adhérents*', it began before issuing an official warning to all AOC-registered farms. NO FRUIT was to be picked or harvested during the twenty-one days that followed a spraying. It was an illegal act to do so (due to toxin residue left in the fruits, which they omitted to mention). I totted up the dates, realised that we would be within the infringement period and called to cancel the recently booked mill rendezvous. I was seething. Fruits were falling, fruits were rotting.

Gérard eventually switched on the *centrifuge* machines two weeks ahead of schedule. Now came the next challenge: *les étourneaux*, the starlings. The hungry creatures were congregating, Hitchcockian swarms blackening the skies, plunging down upon the branches and picking them clean within a matter of hours.

'Next year, the chemical companies will be marketing a vastly expensive spray aimed at the destruction of the starlings!' I bellowed to anyone within the farm's parameters who was still willing to listen to me.

With a trio of friends who descended from various points north, we swooped upon the trees ourselves, gathering the fruits at top speed and I hastened them to the mill. The ratio of oil to fruit was 7 per cent down on our previous year. We were not alone. Every farmer I spoke to told the same sorry tale, but few acknowledged that what we were looking at was a climate shift, a problem partially caused by ourselves, by the tons of pesticides and products rained down upon our agricultural lands.

I bumped into René, our silver-haired friend and erstwhile olive guru, at the weighing machines. He was in the company of the local water sorcerer. René was running Raymond's farm. Seven hundred trees, a little more than double our count and producing a ten times greater yield. They were pressing their first harvest of one and a half ton of fruits.

'It's just a freak season,' was René's explanation. 'You'll be fine next year. You should water the trees more frequently. You'll get more oil.'

'We've got four wells now and the pump is turning day and night. The fields are always irrigated. We're expecting twelve tons of fruit this year,' glowed the sorcerer.

Christmas came. We bottled our new oil and celebrated its arrival with friends, as was our tradition, though I genuinely believed its quality and taste had been compromised. Still, it was fine, I had to admit it.

It was January, unseasonably warm. From the farm's upper terraces looking west, a dense custard-yellow cloud had broken across the Fréjus promontory and Esterel. The mimosa trees were bursting into blossom, flecking and fleshing out the lower slopelands. They were three weeks ahead of season. I was finally ready to hit the road. Fortuitously, Michel was due to attend a documentary film festival in Barcelona. I set my disembarkation date to coincide with his stay there. Circumnavigating the western Mediterranean in an anti-clockwise direction, I intended to slip south from upper Spain, cross to North Africa, traverse the sea again to Sicily and, skirting the western coast of Italy via dreamed-of destinations, meander back home, returning to Appassionata.

My quest for ancient stories of the olive tree, of those who trans-ported it to remote, watery inlets within the Mediterranean, still held true. I hoped to discover a gnarled, buckled old oleaster or two, a western Mediterranean long-termer, and some fascinating folklore, but to that had now been added another dimension: the twenty-first-century olive. I was still eager to track the myths and legends of peoples residing around this sea, whose ancestors grew up with the medicinal powers and mysteries of the olive, but I was concerned now for its future. I wanted to grasp the newer picture. I wanted to comprehend the scenario unfolding before us, and how we, on our little farm, might fight the dreaded pests without chemicals, without distressing our small patch of earth and its ecosystem.

Northern Spain

In the hills surrounding Nice, for those farming *cailletier* olives the harvests had been stored. Now came pruning, and Appassionata's centuries-old groves required challenging hours of labour. We had not cut back for three years and within the trees' canopies hung clusters of dead, briared branches, but we were leaving Quashia alone so he could only handle the essentials. We could have attacked the work before Christmas, given that our vintage had been early, but I had entreated the others to hold off, anxious to lessen the disruption of the plants' cycles. I was unsure whether adhering to regularity could soften the impact of climate changes. Still, I argued for the rhythms of time-honoured seasons until we knew better.

I was booked on the Ventimiglia to Montpelier TGV train, en route for Barcelona, leaving early the following morning. A batch of forms had arrived from the oil bureaucrats, officials whose task it was to oversee the quality of oil produced by farmers, requesting details of the damage our farm had suffered at the beaks of the thieving starlings. I stuffed them into my luggage. I had months of travelling before me and was scribbling last-minute, almost-forgotten instructions for Quashia, a personal detail or two into my own notebook, before I shut down my laptop, slid it into my already straining backpack and turned out the light. This time tomorrow I would be in Spain.

I could not claim to know Spain, having visited the country on four previous occasions only, skimming its rim, dipping into its cities, but I had never infiltrated its dark and mysterious heart, never penetrated its multi-layered substance. Reflecting on those earlier excursions, recalling images, I realised that my impressions were barely more than clichés: a nation of bullfighters, flamenco dancers, overcrowded tourist resorts, Virgin Marys, *tapas*: nothing but a fistful of Spanish iconography churned out regularly for postcards.

I had embarked on my first trip when I was thirteen. Of the silver-grey olive and the sweetly scented citrus groves I had been ignorant. Totting up dates, I realised our holiday had taken place during the latter part of Franco's dictatorship, he who wrested Spain from the Republicans in 1939 after a grotesque three-year civil war and remained in power until his death in 1975. Along with my parents and younger sister, I had set out for the Costa Daurada, Spain's Golden Coast, driving from rural Kent with its gentle oasthouse scenery in my parents' Austin A60 Cambridge. Today, it would be a trip of no consequence but back then it was, not brave, but reasonably ambitious. Continental holidays were not a common event in the market-town world of my childhood. So here we were, descending France on course for the northern Spanish fishing village of Sitges. The journey itself took us the better part of three days. I sat in the front with my father, a series of maps on my lap, proudly navigating while my mother and sister dozed in the back.

Recollections of that two-week sojourn are patchy. What remained was the incident of my father's food poisoning. Our three-star establishment served the *demi-pension* meals in a vine-bowered garden. So exotic, so sweetly scented it seemed to me until my father began to interrogate the waiter, attempting to identify the meat on our plates. The fellow appeared not to understand. This caused Daddy to yell at the underling, and the more vocal my father grew the less willing was the waiter to furnish the information; the less willing, in fact, to attend to us at all.

'Please leave it, Peter,' pleaded my mother on the second or third balmy evening, but Daddy refused to.

I have a clear memory of the embarrassment I felt as he stabbed at the tablecloth with a thick finger and over-enunciated his perpetual question.

'What meat is this you're serving us? I am paying for it; I want to know what I'm eating.'

The thin-boned Spaniard, who had given up on verbal responses, stood alongside the check-clothed table, his arms hanging loosely at his side as though held together by string, and shrugged.

Eventually, patience at an end, my father lifted his plate and waved it beneath the nose of the feckless server. 'This,' he bellowed red-faced, pointing at a threadbare cut of steak. 'What is it?'

The waiter, probably in his late teens, certainly no more than early twenties, and no doubt grateful for this summer employment, even if, in my father's opinion, he showed little aptitude for his role, sighed, raised two fingers to each side of his black-haired head and emitted the sounds 'Ee-aw, ee-aw'.

'Donkey! Jesus Christ!'

Directly after dinner, my father retired upstairs to a room that reeked of Ambre Solaire, Yardley's lavender water and Brylcreem. Mummy drew the curtains while my father, supine on the bed in the crepuscular light, groaned dramatically. During the succeeding days, he refused to budge while beyond the windows the sun beat down on to melting tarmac and glimmering sea and we were obliged to entertain ourselves without him. Each morning after breakfast, when we tiptoed into the sacred darkness to give him a kiss, he rasped instructions about digging into the pockets of his shorts to extract a fistful of pesetas for ice creams.

'I told you it was better not to ask,' sighed my pretty mother, shaking her head at the condition of him.

She took us to a seaside church – Sant Bartolomeu, it must have been – to light candles for his swift recovery, but he was little changed when we returned from the beach later, arms full of soggy towels. There, a service with high mass was under way with a dozen or more newborns in neatly pressed white gowns cradled in the arms of doting parents. I had never before been present at a communal baptism and it was the closest we came to brushing shoulders with the life of the local inhabitants. I would not have understood that it was financially less taxing to employ the priest for several christenings all at once and I had certainly not been aware of the crippling poverty and oppression the Catalans were enduring. I knew nothing of the dictatorship and how would I have understood that the tourism we represented must have been a godsend to those people?

Reflecting now from the rolling train, I found myself curious about the life of that beleaguered, melancholy waiter. Where was he today? Had he dreaded the sight of us? Was the opportunity to eat donkey a blessing that he and his family with lowlier rations would have thanked God for? When we were not on the beach sunbathing, we traipsed narrow streets in search of somewhere for a cup of tea. Phyllis, my mother, was tea mad: 'I could kill for a nice cup of tea.' Back on his feet, back to his old self, my father took great delight in dragging us from beachside café to beachside café, comparing prices. It drove me crazy with boredom. Then an outing to the nearby city of Barcelona, thirty-five minutes north of Sitges, where catastrophe struck us once more when my father found himself driving the tram-lines, and in the wrong direction. Due to onslaughts of hooting traffic, he was unable to shift. Such panic when an oncoming tram approached, blasting its horn, flashing its lights, my mother yelling, 'Peter!' . . .

I was seated at a café on the terraced pavement outside the *gare*, the Montpelier railway station, recalling these paper-thin memories. Since that first, somewhat troubled adolescent visit, I had only managed whistle-stop trips to the cities of Madrid and Barcelona and what delighted me about such lack of familiarity was the realisation that I was uninitiated. It felt as though I was entering Spain for the first time.

The third week of January; sun shining; weather winter-perfect. All about me, sporting black anti-reflect sunglasses, inhaling, slow exhale, cigarette smoke rising, were Arabs, business folk, students. I had departed that morning, winding and wheeling from Cannes along the speckled coast. Now, I had two hours to kill before I picked up a Spanish express due to deliver me late into the Catalonian capital where Michel awaited me. His commitments honoured, we would weekend there. Afterwards, to Paris his itinerary led him while mine was to be local buses, coach- and island-hopping, pleasing myself, tracking olive clues, until I had descended the peninsula. Cádiz for Mardi Gras. Cádiz hosts one of the most popular of Spain's many carnivals and contains a wealth of olive history. Onwards from a neighbouring port, Algeciras or Tarifa, south to Morocco. Most of this was undiscovered territory for me. I had settled upon this loose, snake-like peregrination principally to avoid the over-constructed coast roads. Also, I had a rendezvous with an Englishman who had bought an olive and fig farm in Extremadura, a lesser known region deep in the heart of Spain, west of Madrid. Aside from a few exchanged emails, I knew very little about him. His details reached me by a very circuitous route. I had approached Friends of the Earth and from there was led to European Funding. They, in turn, suggested I contact Simon.

This Spanish train offered far fewer comforts than its French counterpart. There was nowhere to purchase coffee or sandwiches; it lacked both bar and refreshment trolley. So I settled to gazing at the passing view of rose-mirrored wetlands reflecting the setting sun. It was Friday. Dusk was rolling into evening. The world of Europe was commuting home for the weekend while I was off on a brand new adventure into forgotten epochs, southern elsewheres.

In May past, I had returned to the farm after an eight-month expedition encircling the eastern basin of the Mediterranean. Commencing in Beirut, I had ascended into the Christian hills of Mount Lebanon. There a village, Bechealeh, where the survivors from two olive groves were thriving, fruiting even, in among terraces of trees planted dozens of centuries later. What was remarkable about these ancient collosi was that they had been scientifically dated at between six and seven thousand years old. On a journey that had carried me across seas, cultures, history, war zones, time and space, I had come face to face with what might well have been the naissance of olive farming and had spent a moment of time in the presence of, possibly, the oldest living examples of life on earth. The sequoia forests in California, often cited, are the tallest but not the most aged. Some have reached 1500 years, but they are mere babies alongside those Lebanese masters.

Who planted those olive trees? Whose was the unidentified hand that had first reached up into an olive branch and picked off one small berry, firm and single-seeded? Where had that happened? Which peoples or person had first come up with the idea of taking a drupe and grinding its stoned fruit to a pulp, thus releasing its powerful, essential golden oil? Who was the man or woman – from which clan or tribe – who had first cultivated the wild ancestor of *Olea europaea*?

The answers remained mysteries.

If two small groves of olives can survive for the entire span of man's civilised history, what might we learn from their staying power? What opportunities might they offer for our future?

During those earlier travels, I had been bowled over by the ingenuity of nature, become fascinated by the wealth of history and civilisations residing at the Mediterranean's rim, bobbing about its shores, where the first alphabets were born, where the seeds of agriculture had been sown. And always, everywhere, the olive tree had played a significant role. Since Michel and I set up home on our olive farm, I had developed a profound affinity with these trees. Their longevity, mystery, medicinal powers, not to mention their gnarled and tortured beauty, set them apart. Olives are a cornerstone of the Mediterranean's traditions and cultures, but the ancestry of both the wild and cultivated varieties remain an unsolved mystery.

The answers mattered to me now more than ever, because I felt our own farm, its direction, was at risk.

Spain. Its history leads us to a remote, almost ungraspable past, even before the existence of *olea*, the wild olive tree, as far as I was aware. Some millennia before Spain and Portugal had come into existence, this peninsula had been populated by Iberians, a people, or peoples, who had crossed over from Africa by the shortest route possible. Setting sail on rafts from what today is the northern coast of Morocco, passing by Gibraltar – almost certainly some disembarked and settled there – and then continuing onwards to the foot of the mainland. I was moving in the opposite direction, towards that Iberian influx, and would, undoubtedly, encounter clues both botanical and otherwise, to their history. This African exodus is thought to have taken place somewhere around 3000 BC – a thousand and so years after the Bechealeh groves of Lebanon had been planted – and these Iberian peoples were destined to become the roots of 'Spain'. They brought the great African continent and its earliest traditions to this more northerly, river-veined, mountain-divided promontory. Did they bring with them rudimentary agricultural expertise? Did they plant olive trees? I did not know, yet.

But they were not the beginning of the story. Further north, travelling Spain's other sea borders, its blustery Atlantic coasts and elevations, Stone Age settlers or nomads had already left significant traces. Beyond Barcelona, I intended to begin there, to pay a visit to those cave dwellers, those prehistoric hunters . . .

The train slowed, wheezed and ground to a halt. I peered into the darkness. We were at Portbou station, held up at the border by frontier police. A voice from a whistling loudspeaker informed us, in Spanish and French, that disembarkation was forbidden, *interdit, prohibido*. Twenty or more officers, police and customs, boarded, snaking the carriages' central aisles, checking identity cards. Sniffer dogs accompanied them. I was obliged to show my passport three times. Visible within shadows and shafts of light beyond my windowpane were the black hands on the broad-faced station clock. They marked the hour between half-past eight to after nine. I began to feel agitated. This is Europe, I was thinking, Portbou, whose rail tracks were laid in 1929 to create easier access into Spain when the World Exposition was held for the second time in Barcelona. What was causing such a lengthy delay? Surely not routine checks? Since the Madrid bombings of 2004, when the central station of Atocha and several commuter trains, *las Cercanías*, travelling at rush hour towards the Spanish capital were blasted by a series of strategically targeted bombs leaving close to two hundred dead and almost 2000 injured, security at every port of entry must have been permanently tightened. I could only assume that nothing imminently threatening was holding us up.

Eventually our transport juddered back out of the border station. It was a quarter past nine. Beyond the windows, the deep, dark silhouettes of the January countryside were inpenetrable. I opened up the thumbed, yellowing paperback balanced on my knees: George Orwell's *Homage to Catalonia*: '. . . the red flags in Barcelona, the gaunt trains full of shabby soldiers creeping to the front, the grey war-stricken towns further up the line . . .' The Spain I was about to penetrate would be neither that of my childhood nor Orwell's from his time of service with the militia during the civil war, but where my roads would lead me, what I would find, I had little inkling.

★

Disembarking at Estaciós França, worn out after eleven hours of trains, a taxi delivered me to the attractive boutique hotel situated close to the Museu d'Art Contemporani, a couple of blocks from the Plaça de Catalunya, once the extremity of the old city walls, that stood at the head of the tree-lined Las Ramblas, where my husband awaited me. It was almost ten thirty, the perfect time to venture forth on a Friday night in search of dinner. Michel suggested we stroll Las Ramblas – the local Catalan language uses Les Rambles – and then double back to a bar, a *cerveceria*, he had discovered where they served delicious *tapas*.

The late evening air was agreeable. Flower stalls lined the pedestrian walkways. Being together was a pleasure, precious days set aside before I disappeared south.

'Rambla,' I said, as we meandered hand in hand down the avenue and I revelled in the blast and spectacle of colours, the noise and activity, 'is a derivative of the Arabic *ramla*, "a sandy or stony riverbed".'

During earlier times throughout Spain, in the dry season, the *ramlas* were access routes for packhorses and donkeys. The poet Federico García Lorca described Las Ramblas, this world-famous series of *ramlas*, as the only boulevard in the world that he wished would never end. In spite of its chaotic liveliness, its almost souk-like crush of life and commerce, I wondered why. It led directly to the port. Lorca was at home in ports with their transient encounters, the passage of itinerant peoples. He enjoyed the company of sailors, but he was not happy at sea; he was afraid of water. A son of well-heeled gentleman farmers, he was a child of the land. Earth images, olives especially, were omnipresent in his poetry and plays.

Barcelona was vibrant, gearing up for its nocturnal pastimes. Long gone was a city chipped at the edges by civil war, where blood ran down the walls and trickled through the streets. Michel talked about the films he had seen at the festival and then we mused upon Spain, quite possibly the first land mass in Europe to have been inhabited. There were so many Spains. Was there a unifying heart to this nation? Spain, whose admission into the European Union transformed the prospects of a people pinched and deprived of democracy for half a century.

'Spain is a land without a backbone,' the philosopher and writer Ortega y Gasset observed in 1922. Divided by several high and jagged mountain ranges, *las sierras*, and rivers. Over millennia, these had created distinctive peoples with their own linguistic and cultural differences. Peoples who, until the late twentieth century, were almost incapable of being harnessed into a whole, into a coherent nation. I wondered whether these social fissures accounted in part for the nation's tumultuous, fascistic history.

'What do you hope to find here?' Michel asked me.

'For five centuries from 218 BC, the Romans ruled over this peninsula. They planted leagues of olive trees and transformed this fist of land into the world's leading producer of olives and oil. They used the oil to fuel their capital, feed their armies and, for the transportation of those crops, they fired tons of clay pots, amphorae. Spanish olive oil was traded, delivered to the extremities of the Roman Empire. Yet the Spanish were never in the driving seat. Two thousand years on and the situation has changed. Spain has finally clawed itself to the position of olive oil superpower. They are farming over 300 million olive trees, producing 30 per cent of the world's oil. They have usurped the title from Italy. I am looking forward to tracing the shift that has taken place and, who knows, perhaps I'll find a Roman olive tree or two or, if I am really lucky, the oldest olive tree in the western Mediterranean.'

Retracing our steps towards Plaça de Catalunya, crossing over by an empty pizzeria, we arrived at Michel's choice of *cerveceria*, where parties of hungry men and women awaited tables in loud but good-natured fashion. We joined the queue. Once through the doors, we were directed to a pair of high stools at the bar. The noise level was staggering as though a grand fiesta were under way. Satisfied and expectant diners, families, couples, student groups, gaggles of girls, tables of silver-haired men sporting expensive suede shoes, corduroy trousers, casually elegant; black-haired women in leather and fur coats; a convivial mix. Our waiter, formal in black waistcoat and crisp white shirt, suggested a couple of beers. Glasses in hand, we pushed through the crowds, the length of the bar, inspecting wriggly, tentacly, saucy *tapas* offerings, a mouthwatering, colourful display. Sizzling in the spacious kitchen, hillocks of small fishes and other spiky, unrecognisable marine creatures were being grilled, fried, spatch-cocked. Sharp, juicy aromas hit my nostrils. *Gambas al ajillo*. 'Yes, I'll have garlicky prawns swimming in warm olive oil. But raw sea urchins, fresh from the Med? No, thanks, I'll give that black-quilled fellow a miss.' Tiredness was soon replaced by ravenous hunger.

Tapas: little dishes of *raciones*, rations, traditionally an accompaniment to aperitifs.

'Where was the *tapas* born?' I pondered.

'The Spaniards eat so late – 10 p.m. is early in the major cities – that after work they congregate in bars where these varied nibbles stave off hunger and avoid the consumption of alcohol on empty stomachs.'

'But what does *tapa* mean? What is the origin of this style of eating?'

'In olden times, in order to keep flies from falling into a glass of liquid it was covered with a chunk of plain bread. *Tapa* means cover.' Unlike mine, Michel's Spanish was fluent.

'So, the original *tapa* was an edible lid of bread?'

'Later, the plain slice was dressed with humble tasties such as anchovies or olive oil.'

We were ordering peelings of cured hams, shell and fish dishes, grilled *gambas*, octopus dressed with lemon and samphire – nothing so modest as a lid of bread! Each plate marinated or drowned in olive oil, coated in chunky nuggets of sea salt. On our high stools we guzzled, olive oil running through our fingers.

'So, Spain has been cultivating olive trees for two thousand years?'

'At least!' I cried, mouth full.

Spanish literature is rich with its symbols and folklore. I had read repeatedly that it was the Romans who brought the silvery beauty to the peninsula, but I felt certain this was not so. My guess was that it was the Phoenicians, those biblical Canaanites – originally from Israel, the Holy Land and disputed Palestinian territories – who resided along the coastline of Phoenicia – today Syria, Lebanon and Israel – who as sailors and merchants *par excellence* plied and dominated the trade routes of the Mediterranean. They, who gave us the first known written alphabet. They, who later created a powerful empire at Carthage in modern-day Tunisia and from its ports ruled the seas until the Romans destroyed them.

But I was also nursing a personal hunch that the wild olive tree, *Olea sylvestris*, had been growing pretty much everywhere round the Med basin from prehistoric times, 12,000 years ago, perhaps as part of the regrowth of forests after the melting of Europe's last Ice Age, and that if the Phoenicians did anything to kick-start the Iberian oil industry it was to transport their skills, to teach olive husbandry to the Iberians.

'Can you prove all this?'

'It depends what I find,' I grinned.

'But once the Romans conquered here, the oil industry took off at a rate of knots?'

I nodded. 'To such a degree that, centuries later, it was the Spanish who transported the olive tree to the Americas and by so doing changed irrevocably the history and cuisine of South America. In return, aside from boats loaded with gold, they returned with coffee, tomatoes, potatoes, chili peppers and tobacco as well as the small crimson cochineal insect used to dye the cotton grown in their numerous plantations.'

Their twenty-first-century position as world leader in olive oil must be sweet revenge for the Spaniards who, as far as the olive goes, have lived for many centuries in the shadow of the Italians. I was fascinated to discover these immense farming activities for myself.

During our precious weekend together, Michel and I walked for miles, *flâneurs* arm in arm, as we rarely have time to be in France, pausing for delicious, teeny cups of strong Arabic coffee in *pasticerias*, investigating wide uptown avenues where the architecture was flamboyant and fairytale-like, and he listened while I talked.

'Since the Phoenicians founded Cádiz in 1100 BC, the Iberian peninsula has been a vital crossroads for culinary and cultural exchanges.'

'That's surprising. I thought it opened up later with the Moors?'

'Certainly the Moors, who for more than seven hundred years from AD 711 ruled much of the land . . .'

'. . . particularly in Andalucía.'

'Yes, particularly in Andalucía,' I laughed, enjoying Michel chipping in. 'The Moors introduced a collection of fruits and spices: almonds, citrus, sugar cane, saffron, mint, cumin, cinnamon, and greatly contributed to the language, in particular words relating to agriculture, cooking and irrigation, but they did not bring olive oil. The Romans, Greeks and Phoenicians before them sowed the seeds of production and exchange here.'

Before Michel left, I passed him the officially stamped letter informing us that the DDAF (Direction Départementale de l'Agriculture et de la Fôret) was profoundly concerned about the starlings. An official enquiry was now under way to assess the damage caused by winter flocks. The notification had been accompanied by a form. We were obliged to make a declaration stating what percentage of our crop had been eaten by birds and what percentage had been designated AOC fruits. He promised to handle it.

After an early Monday morning *au revoir* to my man, I felt little desire to hang around the Mediterranean city we had been rediscovering together so I took a bus. I had been toying with the idea of revisiting Sitges – today a major gay resort; homosexuality in Franco's Catholic Spain had been illegal. While searching out olive clues, I discovered that Sitges in the early sixties, around the time I had holidayed there with my family, was at the heart of a thriving counterculture, one of the few mainland towns nurturing an artistic resistance to the thirty-six-year dictatorship, but I found no pointers to an ancient olive culture. Instead, my first port of call was to be Empúries, Ampurias in Spanish.

The Greeks, or, more specifically, the Phocaen-Greeks who hailed from Foça on the western seaboard of what is today Turkey, were the sailors who, around 600 BC, cruised into the harbour of Marseille, colonised it, christened it Massilia and then sailed on west, wheeling round the Gulf of Lions, to found Empúries in 575 BC. It is thought that these Phocaen-Greeks, like the Phoenicians and Etruscans, had already been trading with the indigenous people, the Indigetes, before they settled the territory. Where the Indigetes originally hailed from nobody knows, but their language was possibly Iberian.

Empúries was to become the largest Greek emplacement on the Iberian peninsula, ideally situated as it was for commercial exchanges between Massilia (Marseille) and Tartessus, a very wealthy, long since sunk-without-trace city that neighboured Cádiz in the south. The Greeks must always have intended Empúries to be a dynamic economic centre because they christened it Emporiai, 'Trading Posts', and it served them well, but they never mingled. They took no interest in the natives and their presence created enemies. The Phoenicians, who controlled Cádiz, judged them a threat, competitors to the commercial and business routes they were founding everywhere. To put a stop to these Greeks and to any ambitions they harboured about controlling this coastline or, indeed, the entire trading waters of the western Mediterranean, the Carthaginian-Phoenicians combined forces with the Etruscans, a people from ancient Italy and Corsica, to beat the Phocaens back, defeating them in 535 BC in a showdown off the southern coast of Corsica.

Sixty-five years earlier, the Carthaginians had failed to shut them out of Marseille, but the wheels of fortune in the Med were shifting once more and this vigorous skirmish, an overwhelming defeat for the Phocaens, terminated all their dreams of far-west trading posts. Emporiai proved to be the pinnacle of their incursions as well as their undoing. They had been irrevocably scuppered, leaving the scene wide open to the Carthaginians. That was until, first seen bobbing on the horizon, thirsty for expansion and wealth, the Romans rowed in.

To reach Empúries I was obliged to take an *autobus* to Girona and then another, climbing the Costa Brava towards its northern extremes. I made my way to the central *estación de autobuses*, a large and bustling terminus with a striking, if shabby, Art Deco façade. Once through hellish surburban traffic and a gunpowder-blue fog that hung like an interminable cloud, the countryside became quite lovely and frequently, around the high coastal bluffs of the Costa Brava, the 'Wild Coast', dramatic and unconstructed. I had not expected it to be so red-rock rugged and pine-green, with sheer, cragged walls plunging to the sea. Beneath, hidden bays, nestling coves. The tail end of January; almonds in blossom. Thoughts on ancient Greece, I recalled my arrival into the Peloponnesian city-state of Messini, built into headlands high above the port of Kalamata, at the foot of the village of Mauromati. Precisely one year earlier the first of the season's almond flowers had greeted me. Those soft-hued petals, delicate as an oriental watercolour, semaphored spring. Today, the weather was so mild it might already have been spring. I had not even a jacket.

Two hours after my departure, L'Escala, seaside resort, renowned throughout Spain for its anchovies. I climbed down from the bus, and asked directions from a man with bristling wheelbarrow moustache, black hat and wooden cane and began the hike north. The early haze had burned off. The light was nacreous, uplifting. Winding through country lanes set back a distance from the sea, my approach was flanked on either side by puddles of wild large-headed daisies, white clovers and a trio of wagtails feeding at the roadside.

Pausing for breath, I sighted the curved sandy bay of Empúries/ Emporiai behind which lay the ruins of the Greeks' *neapolis*, new city. A short walk further north, on what had once been an offshore islet, at the mouth of the River Fluvia, would have found me at their *palaiopolis*, their first settlement here. Five years later – by which time they had perhaps encountered less resistance from the locals? – they had crossed the slender strip of water to the mainland and constructed the *neapolis*. The ruins that remained inland of the bay I was gazing upon were the relics of that second colony and of the Roman holding that came after them. Phoenicians, Greeks, Romans, each colonised this coast, but nothing of Phoenicia or its Carthaginian empire remains. The position was well situated, secluded yet perfectly access-ible from the open sea: ideal. I was surprised to find that the bay lacked construction save for one hotel, a pure white building with clean angular, Art Deco lines nestling at the water's edge.

Apart from a woman with unruly black hair in pale blue summer dress accompanied by a younger man, the ruins were deserted. The couple were wandering about the neocropolis lower down the sloped land, closer to the beach from which the puzzle of archaeological stones had been cordoned off. Beyond the fence, a narrow, wooded pathway intersected ancient metropolis and sand and sea. People were jogging there, or walking dogs. I found the location peaceful and felt at ease; a place to retreat to, I thought, as I clambered over dry limestone walls where the skilled masonry work was shaded by umbrella pines. It was a typical Mediterranean location, well chosen by its colonisers. Occasional Hellenistic statues, bearded but lacking limbs, stood sentry over the Greek town, gazing impassively back to their mother country. The remnants of stone houses traced a design built around individual central courtyards. A temple constructed during the first century BC stood on the site of an earlier hospital, dedicated to Isis and Serapis, Egyptian deities linked to medicine and health. A sign informed that these Greeks of Emporiai were trading with Egypt and that the temple was built by a merchant venturer from Alexandria. Terracotta water pipes were stacked here and there, probably Roman, but no olive mills, no pressing stones. Had the easterners planted no olive orchards here? From the bus I had spied fields of centennial olive trees, but nothing older. I walked the upper city, the Roman remains, where the *cardo maximus* was indented with chariot tracks. The Romans constructed a fish-salting factory here. This was the first of many I was to find dotted round the western basin. Garum, a paste of fish and olive oil, was the main export. And surely the esteemed anchovy business in neighbouring L'Escala found its genesis here?

The Romans spent almost two centuries in their attempts to gain control of Iberia. Once theirs, they rechristened it Hispania and divided it into a trio of provinces: Baetica, Lusitania and Tarraconensis. Hispania Tarraconensis, the largest of the three, in which Empúries fell, was designated imperial and controlled by the emperor himself.

Leaving the museum, housed in the church of a former Servite monastery, I glanced at my watch; it was lunchtime. The museum cafeteria was closed so I strolled towards the beach and the white hotel. Although it was out of season and structural work was going full tilt, the establishment was about to serve lunch in an airy, sparsely furnished dining room with wooden tables, solid dressers and whacky cane chairs. It boasted a splendid, far-reaching view out to sea and, northwards, along the coast. The menu was handwritten in Catalan with translations into Castilian Spanish. Catalan bears similarities to Provençal; both are Romance languages. With the help of my French, I found I could grasp certain phrases, reminding me that I was at the rim of the Mediterranean where webs, tapestry threads and sources intermingled.

I ordered their fish stew with potato, *El nostre suquet de gallineta*, or, in Spanish, *Nuestro suquet de gallineta*. *Suquet* in Provençal is 'port'. Coastbound from our farm, a district of the old town of Cannes, lies Le Suquet, probably the site of the first anchorage. In French a *galette* is a pancake, originally made of buckwheat. I accompanied my dish with a glass, a *copa*, of locally produced *vino blanco* though I might have chosen a glass of Cava, Spain's answer to champagne, which I learned from my attractive auburn-haired waitress was a local Catalan wine. Also on the menu was Catalan chocolate mousse with *arbequina* olive oil and sea salt.

'Do Catalans believe that it was the Phocaens who brought the olive to this coast?' I asked her.

Dressed in black with a burnt-orange half-pinafore tied at her waist, an earthy colour that lifted the severity of her beautiful features, she replied, 'The *arbequina* olive was imported from Palestine in the eighteenth century.'

I was intrigued, but she knew no more of ancient trees.

Our conversation was a potpourri of languages, almost oriental-sounding. My waitress's English was faltering, though less so than my rusty Spanish, but we managed. She hailed from a neighbouring *pueblo*, 'born and bred'. Slender, dark, striking: high-boned with sunken cheeks and mesmerising, slightly nervous eyes, green as a cat's in the night. Her mother tongue was Catalan, she claimed with pride, though she spoke fluent Spanish.

Was she the proprietress? She laughed, shaking her head, softening, and pointed to a distinguished middle-aged gentleman on the terrace. Wearing a suit, he was orchestrating the spring-cleaning of garden furniture and seemed unperturbed when a stray hosepipe soaked his trousers and polished shoes. He was also Catalan, also born within spitting distance of his hotel.

The view beyond the window fanned out across the Golf de Roses. Beneath a luminously silver sun, the pleated sea was empty save for a single distant boat. The mighty north wind, *la Tramuntana*, was known to create havoc on this coast. Similar to our mistral, it could blow forcefully for three, sometimes five, full days. Ships, off the coast of Cadaqués, ripped by the reefs, had sunk at its bidding, but today all was calm. On shore the languorous flop of waves against the beach vied with yells from a gaggle of arriving school children bending and dipping like birds, shell-seeking. Overhead, gulls swooped and glided.

Round the headland from the fishing town of Roses lay Cadaqués and then Cap de Creus National Park. I had hoped to find one work of Salvador Dalí's that contained an olive tree, to justify a visit to that stretch of coast, but I had not been successful. Federico García Lorca, friend to both Dalí and his sister, Ana Maria, visited them at their house near Cadaqués in 1927, penning 'Ode to Salvador Dalí' in which he described the painter as master of 'an olive-coloured voice'.

Brushing at his sodden trousers, the proprietor, now with mani-cured wife, was seating himself alongside a quartet of diners. The room, noisy with clattering cutlery, was animated. Discreetly in-sinuating itself into the conviviality was the music of a stringed instrument: the Sarabande in the fourth of the six Bach cello suites, performed by Catalan cellist Pablo (Pau) Casals. A great fan, here I was listening to him, albeit a recording, on his native soil. I put down my pen and tuned in, still observing the midday comings and goings of this surprisingly good guesthouse, and I concluded that the choice of record was no accident.

Casals quit Spain in 1939 after the defeat of the Republicans, vowing never to return until Franco, Nationalist leader and future dictator, had been ousted. For a time he settled close to home in the French border village of Prades, but eventually moved to Puerto Rico, the birthplace of his cherished mother, where in 1973, at the age of ninety-six, he died, just two years before the long-awaited demise of Franco. The year of Casals' death coincided with that of another Pablo, the marginally younger, ninety-three-year-old Picasso, also in self-imposed exile from Spain. Neither artist had returned to native soil for decades. Casals endured a thirty-four-year exile, while Picasso's lasted five years longer. Living in France, the painter had last set eyes on his mother country in 1934.

In that Catalan dining room I recalled a touching tale about Casals.

One of Casals' many ambitions had been to found an orchestra, a spearhead for Barcelona, creating music with which the region could identify and be proud of. He had achieved this by 1920 and, in spite of growing international recognition and commitments, he con-tinued to perform with and conduct the orchestra on a regular basis, until 1936; then, while rehearsing Beethoven's Ninth Symphony, news arrived at the rehearsal rooms that their concert of the following evening, for which they were preparing, had been cancelled. Franco's armies were moving north, taking the country. The fighting would soon be on the streets of their capital. Casals was advised to disband immediately, definitively, to send his musicians back to their families. With heavy heart he assented but begged, before doing so, one final favour of the orchestra he had fine-tuned over sixteen years. He asked them to complete the work, to play through to the last movement before separating. It would be a dignified finale, a more elegant leave-taking, expressed through their music. All agreed. And once the final notes of the symphony had sounded, his compatriots packed up their instruments and left, each to his own home. They were never to reconvene, never to play together again.

The mood in the dining room was subdued now. The establishment had an understated elegance about it, a gentility, but I had the sense, and I think not mere fancy, that running deep within these people was a defiance, a spirit of individuality, of their hard-won Catalan identity. George Orwell wrote that in Catalonia everyone eventually took sides. Here, the choice seemed immutable.

I would have liked to linger, spend a night at the hotel *blanco*, watch the dawn come up in golden streaks across the eastward-greeting bay, tease out conversation about the little-spoken-of war years and its effects upon olive farming, but a post-prandial walk before the evening bus to Girona and onwards to Barcelona was all that was left to me.

The narrow track between beach and ruins, shaded by pines, led to the islet, now attached to the mainland, where the *palaiopolis* had once existed and where today stands the medieval village of Sant Martí d'Empúries. Along this stretch had once existed the ancient Greek harbour, long since silted up. In 1992, when the Olympic Games were held in Barcelona, it was here that the torch was brought ashore. The path I was treading at the water's edge had been laid for the occasion. Seated on a large rock, communing with the waves, was a lone mustachioed figure in a woollen hat. Clad in clingy Spandex cycling shorts, he spun his body as I passed, calling, *'buenos días'*. I nodded, continuing. He rose, treading the sand in my direction.

Sant Martí, lapped betwixt siesta and the season. End of January, mid-afternoon. The medieval town was boarded up, deserted. Even the eleventh-century church had bolted its doors. I was anxious for signs of life; the woollen-hatted fellow was on my heels. I argued that this was mere coincidence, but he was tailing me. On this deserted adjunct to the mainland, there was no one. I barely registered the walled enclave, hurrying as I was along a path in a direction I had not considered. Retracing my steps would have involved meeting him head-on. I cut inland towards fields and agricultural holdings, citrus-scented. He gained on me. I grew jittery, rounded a bend where a convergence of trees hid me for the time it took for me to make a decision. In among the stand, to the left, was an escape route. I stepped fast into what proved to be an open-air garden centre with dozens of potted lemon slips and patchwork plots of recently planted vegetables. I looked for a worker, for anyone, but in vain. I slid behind a tree while the stooped, gangly stalker strode on past my shelter. I realised then that, had he clocked my escape into this nest of plants and utensils, had he followed me in, I would have been cornered. Heart thumping, I waited until he was well out of sight, then slipped from my cover, retracing my original route, skirting Sant Martí, intent on the white hotel. I was perspiring, my heart rate was increasing when, like fire in dry grass, ten metres ahead to the right, he reap-peared. Hovering, watching, arms dangling, then pacing in my dir-ection. I had travelled through so many lands deemed dangerous for a lone woman and now, in northern Spain, pootling about a picturesque coastline where fear and physical threat had been far from my thoughts, suddenly I was alarmed.

I skipped from the path, thudded on to the beach where the sand slowed me; then, heartened, I sighted the hotel, two, three hundred yards ahead. I felt safer in the open. Thick-trunked pines obscured the path. The cries of voices. A quartet, adults and children, had joined the track; must have arrived by the shortcut the stalker had taken. He was loitering among the trees, eyes glued on me. They overtook him. I ran, heaving feet in the sand, and leapt back on to the way directly behind them. They were striding fast, power walking. I picked up pace to tag along, trying not to draw attention to myself. I glanced behind me. The stranger was still coming after me, like a surly bull. In no time our unlikely caravan had reached the hotel. The family continued on, hugging the curve of the bay. I fled inside and buried myself in the loos until I had regained composure. In the dining room, I gulped coffee while the oddball paced the bay, waiting for me to resurface. What could he possibly want? Surely not to attack or rob me in broad daylight? I asked my waitress if she had seen him before. She frowned, shook her head. One of the construction team, she offered, was finishing work. A handsome young man in overalls covered in plaster and sweat. He gave me a lift to the bus station in L'Escala.

It was close to 10 p.m. when the hotel, ours until yesterday, slid open its doors. I was exhausted, missing Michel. Worn out, unexpectedly insecure, I judged myself ill-equipped for the several months' journey that lay ahead. The knowledge that I had so recently completed the eastern circuit did little to alleviate doubts.

A late rise due to procrastination was followed by a postponement of my departure. Instead, I walked. To the waterfront, to the Olympic port, hunting the headless fish. Frank Gehry's. Fashioned out of latticed steel, I came upon it within a crowded complex of shops and blocks, plonked there as though no one at the municipality had known what to do with it. Its immense fishing-net frame shone coppery in the sunlight. I was saddened by it, not elated, this tailed torso trapped in space, nailed to its spot, unable to fly or swim. An accurate description of my own state that day. And then to Antonio Gaudí's unfinished masterpiece, his vast and exquisitely detailed basilica, the Expiatori de la Sagrada Familia, where he worked exclusively, obsessively, between 1909 until his death in 1926, and is buried within it. Gaudí, I read, spoke Catalan, refusing all his life to communicate in Spanish. I sat at a stall across the street from his temple at twilight, sipping beer, watching the rising towers light up, reminding me of organ pipes; poetic madness looming skywards.

Late that night, strolling nowhere in particular, lost within a *barrio*, the neighbourhood known in Catalan as L'Eixample, I pushed open a door to what I had thought was a restaurant and found myself staring into a bar. I asked if they served food and the bartender, a man in a suit rather than a uniform who had hurried to greet me – that, or block my entrance – shook his head. The few guests, half a dozen, bemused expressions, looked my way, as though my arrival had disrupted intimate exchanges. It was curious. The gathering, such as it was, seemed well heeled but of another era. A forties film noir, an Edward Hopper painting. A woman, long-haired, blonde, swept up to the left, hanging heavily on the right, smoking, leaning low over the table. Her cropped-haired companion sat with his back to me. Three striped suits on stools at the bar, late thirties. The space was compact, low-ceilinged. I had the idea I had walked into a private club. I was intrigued.

'May I have a glass of wine?' I was disinclined to leave until I had discovered more. Again the bartender shook his head. 'Apologies, *disculpeme*, only whisky.' With that he closed the door, shutting me out. I lingered a moment in the darkened street looking for a sign, some clue, but nothing was posted. I returned after dinner but I was unable to relocate the door. I felt as though I had glimpsed Camino Real.

I ate my last meal in Barcelona at a modest family restaurant close to where I was staying. The menu was in Catalan. The furniture was carved hardwood, heavy. Two gently spinning fans hung from a white-painted, ribbed ceiling. Square tables, white linen cloths, two or three rock-hard hams dangling from the rafters, close by the espresso machine. The waiters and waitresses wore white jackets. Frilled caps perched on the women's heads, and always aprons. It was sombre, old-fashioned, yet inviting.

My simple meal consisted of potato and onion tortilla served with an undressed salad, *ensalada*, with chunks of tuna, sausage and onion. When I requested garlic, my waiter smiled, shaking his head. 'You have onion, that's sufficient.'

'Olive oil then, please, and a glass of Rioja.'

Two bottles were delivered. The oil was Catalan from *arbequina* fruits, green, peppery, good.

Here, the waiter was more accommodating, informative.

'The *arbequina* oil business in the north is in crisis.' Vast acreages, he claimed, were being abandoned. Irrigation was the problem.

The wine label read Cune Rioja 2003 Crianza. I wondered about *crianza*.

'It's the ageing. *Crianza* is "upbringing", "breeding".'

The wine-governing body, *Denominación de Origen*, operated a standards watchdog in the way the French olive and wine institutions oversee the AOC we have been honoured with for our oil.

'A *crianza* must have aged for minimum two years. In the provinces where the rules are stricter, it is essential that at least one of those years is in oak cask. Beyond *crianza* comes *reserva* and then the highest accolade, *gran reserva*.'

Still suffering 'stage-fright', but it was time to hit the road. My tree was calling. At the *estación de autobuses nord* the following morning I bought a one-way ticket to the city of Santander, a popular tourist resort on the Atlantic coast in the north-eastern *provincia* of Cantabria. From there, a local bus to connect me to the medieval town of Santillana del Mar. I expected to arrive in time for dinner. Including one brief stop in Bilbao, the journey to Santander was a little over nine hours. I grabbed a creamy 6 a.m. *café con leche* and a croissant at the bus station cafeteria where, stamped on the paper napkins, I found an advertisement for Rentokil. I could not remember when I had last consumed such quantities of milk (with my daily shots of *café con leche*), bread, eggs and potatoes in the tortillas. Hoisting my bag into the hold, I felt a stab of regret at leaving Barcelona, at saying *adiós* to Catalonia. Where I was heading was a far cry from Spain's olive regions. It was a long shot. I was hoping to unearth some ancient plant history.

A handful of us boarding. A shrivelled old man, crutches, a Basque beret tilted sideways on his head, big as an umbrella. Allocated to me was an aisle seat, two rows from the front. The fifty-seater was almost empty. I shuffled down through the bus and chose a position halfway. After I had installed myself, arranging reading, writing material on the free place at my side, I settled by the window and began to relax. Moments later, a robust fellow with a tattoo snaking from beneath his white T-shirt and winding round his neck as though strangling him, stopped alongside my assumed position.

'You are in my spot,' he announced.

'The coach is empty,' I replied. 'Does it matter?'

'That *asiento* is mine.' He rattled a flimsy docket at me, evidence of his claim. I looked up at the overhead rack and the adjoining seat, gently insinuating the inconveniences of shifting. Unmoved, he waited, glassy-eyed beneath big, bushy eyebrows and a wild head of hair so plastered with gel it shone like coal. Eventually, I gathered up my materials and proceeded to the rear. The last of the passengers hurried aboard studying his ticket gravely, spotted his designated pew alongside the tattooed traveller and plonked himself there, leaving entire rows empty. I had not expected it of the Spanish. I had imagined a more carefree attitude.

Once through the hellish traffic circulating the outer suburbs, travelling south towards Tarragona before turning westwards in the direction of Lleida (Lérida), there unfolded a countryside carved up by jumbles of roads, concrete bridges and railway lines held high on ugly, concrete-piered viaducts traversing gullies and yet more roads.

Afterwards, pleasing images beyond the windows. South of Barcelona, first sightings of olive trees, juniors, and vines and almonds, typically Mediterranean. Pale pink almonds, one or two in each vineyard, powder puffs of colour in the wintery fields. Many Catalan farmers planted one or two in the groves, said the waitress at Empúries; it contributed a hint of almond flavour, a uniqueness to the oil. I had never heard that before.

The first days of February: gentle weather; a T-shirt, no cardigan. It was nineteen months since I had begun this trek, searching the ancient roots of the olive, its impact on Mediterranean peoples. A tapestry of cultures, living together, interwoven. I dreamed unlikely dreams: a western tree as old as the Bechealehs, an organic way of life, clues from the past to enlighten us . . .

Inland now through startling landscape; mauve-rust mountains, dramatic backdrops. Along the Costa Brava, the lovely *fincas* were sandstone. Here, white *haciendas*, ensconced within vineyards, and silhouettes of lone olives. This was not one of Spain's most renowned olive-producing regions. Quaint iron wells, built on stone, rusted wellheads; farmsteads veiled by stands of pencil-thin cypresses, a hint of Italy, of Tuscany. Alternatively, the *haciendas* stood alone, imposing, within fields of stubby wooded vine stock, soil the tones of baked biscuits, nothing to conceal them. The streams, rivulets, wadis, were dry, surprising in this winter season. Terracotta-tiled slanting roofs; backgrounds of mountains; wineries, *haciendas*. The Catalan wine industry made its mark on the international map in the late nine-teenth century when France's highly lucrative business was wiped out by the *Phylloxera*, a grape pest that feeds off the roots of vines. Native to North America, the insect had inadvertently been carried over on cargo ships transporting New World grape stock. Within a decade, the plague had spread across the European continent. France alone lost three-quarters of its wine production. Some French viticulturists grew so desperate they buried a toad at the foot of every plant in the hope that they would eat the sap-sucking aphids. Few areas were spared except those whose stock grew on sandy soils. These the bug did not infest. Catalan winegrowers, I do not know why, fared better than most though the northern areas of the Costa Brava around Cap de Creus suffered. Barcelona and its surrounding territories were already enjoying a renewed boom period and this foreign agricultural crisis gave an added kick to their economy when Catalan merchants and vintners found they were able to double the prices of their wines and ship them far afield.

Occasionally, the earth was a sharply metallic orange-red, iron-rich, sloped with olive trees, ancient terraces and oval or igloo-like stone huts that reminded me of the drystone walled *bories* in Provence, dated close to 600 BC. They are thought to have been built by the Ligurians. The coach flew by too quickly. Difficult to say whether these were the remnants of Iron Age oppida, settlements. Also a throwback to the Ligurians? Crossing from Italy by land, their route traversed southern France, ascending the Pyrenees to reach this northern section of the peninsula. The history of their presence here is obscure.

Sleeping passengers, with the Basque-bereted pensioner snoring loudly at the rear. Beyond, deserted fields and hillsides, not a soul labouring. A quiet earth, its activities taking place beneath the soil. Here, too, the narrow riverbeds lacked water, dribbles working through loose, dry pebbles. In this first week of February. Was Spain facing severe water shortages? A lack of waterways? The Guadalquivir in Andalucía and the Ebro in Cantabria, the latter Spain's longest river, flowing not far from this *autostrada*, remained the only two sufficiently water-bearing to be useful in navigation and irrigation.

Ebro: a derivative of Iberia?

Many of the passing farms were named *Mas* something or other. *Mas* – 'country house' or 'farm' in Provençal. *Vau au mas*: 'I am going to the farm'. The fruit trees beyond the walled enclosures were pruned as in southern France, Provençal fashion: central branches lopped, leaving a ring of exterior boughs reaching upwards, curving at ten to two.

The scent of pressed olives. Like a truffle dog, I was alerted to the aroma I knew so intimately. I leaned close to the window, scanning the countryside, but I saw no mills, nor drupes remaining on the passing trees. The sky was clear, watery blue. Yet threatening purple clouds hung low over the groves, rising like smoke whorls. Was it a result of spraying, of an insecticide?

The landscape grew inhospitable, uninhabitable; a desert denuded of vegetation or homesteads, only blunt-headed rocks, beige bunyons rising out of stony ground. To the right, a sign: Lleida. Somewhere here, the *pueblo* of Arbeca, population less than 2500, the village that gave its name to the *arbequina* olive. The capital of *arbequina* olive farming in northern Spain, the first to receive a DO for its oil. Here was where the *arbequina* oil business was facing crisis; where the arable lands were being abandoned. The return of fruits on trees irregularly irrigated was not a viable harvesting proposition. To install irrigation was expensive, logistically challenging. Gazing out, I saw a scrubby arid steppeland with barely a weed.

From Catalonia into Aragon. Zaragoza (Saragossa), the capital, was founded as Caesaraugusta by the Romans in 25 BC. Later, it was a Moorish stronghold attacked by El Cid. Later still, El Cid fought as a mercenary for its Moorish king. The painter Goya, born in Aragon, spent his school years and apprenticeship in this capital. So, too, the filmmaker Luis Buñuel.

The air had grown perfumed and sweet. The scents of Spain: I was alive to them. Olive groves flanked us before we became engulfed in clouds. Aragon claims the highest peaks in the Pyrenees, some reaching over 3000 metres. Fighting with the militia, George Orwell was entrenched within these ranges for months, Zaragoza and its city lights within his sight. His 'ice-cold trench' had been dug out of razor-sharp, limestone rock 'like sand-martins' nests'. He bemoaned the lack of action in 'this cock-eyed war'. It was 1937, early days of the civil war. Water was delivered to the soldiers on the backs of donkeys who, when they refused to do as bidden, were kicked by the local Aragonese in the *cojones*, the testicles.

Lunch break in the middle of high central plains; mountains white and chalky; the ground looked as if it had not known rain in centuries. We pulled off the motorway and swung into a newly constructed garage complex with a sign overhead written in large lettering and, bizarrely, only in English: WASH YOUR TRUCK. Lorries and coaches were directed to parking spaces by a bevy of short men in blue-serge overalls and orange safety vests. Our attendant was waving frantically in between pulls on a whistle chained round his neck. You could believe it was Times Square so rigorously were we regimented. Once at our stand, the driver announced a thirty-minute pause. If any passenger failed to be back on board by precisely ten past, they would be left behind. I looked out at the dust and several stacked bracelets of split tyres. What a place to be abandoned.

'Absolutely no waiting for any stray *pasajero,*' repeated the fat-bellied governor. '*El coche* will be gone and it will be *demasiado tarde!*' Three times he called the number of our bus: 2200. I grabbed my bag, muttering '*gracias*' as I stepped down. 'You've got twenty minutes,' he yelled after me.

The interior of the *cantina* was a fuggy barn with Cellophane sandwich wrappings on the floor and half-eaten plates of food scattered at many of the unoccupied, plastic tables. Cigarette butts overflowed the ashtrays. My fellow travellers were already at the counter, calling for beers, hot food. So, too, our *señor,* also engaged in bear hugs and animated conversation with fellow employees from the bus company, each clutching a generous-sized glass of beer between podgy fingers. I bought a Serrano ham baguette, a quart bottle of red wine and a bar of Toblerone and wandered out of the smoky joint into the fresh air. In spite of the altitude, the day was mild but everything was covered in a beige film as though this were a quarry. I found a solitary olive tree planted in a pot and perched beneath it on a low stone wall. I bit into my sandwich; dust ground my teeth. I had *coche* 2200 in sight so was ready to step aboard. After a swift visit to *los servicios*, I returned to my olive tree, glimpsing through the cafeteria window as I passed, our driver with lunch companions now seated at a table surrounded by a clutch of half-consumed beer and wine bottles. The first compatriot was already waiting to board, the Basque octogenarian. Hoping to glean a little inside information about the changing faces of Spain over the years, I wandered his way, smiling 'hola', but he read my intentions and hobbled off on his sticks.

It was gone two, over an hour since we had pulled in. Two of the passengers went in search of the driver. I wasn't holding out a great deal of hope and my instincts were sound. The upshot of the merry lunch was that our fellow would not be continuing on with us to Bilbao and Santander. A replacement was on his way. We hung about in the parking for another twenty minutes. I was beginning to worry about my connection to Santillana del Mar when a uniformed employee with overnight bag marched purposefully towards our bus. He met nobody's eye, determined not to get the flak for his colleague's intemperance.

And on we continued.

Through a Basque countryside of *alquerías*, farms with steadings, outbuildings – from the Arabic *al-garya*, meaning 'small town'. After a brief Bilbao stop, the coach pulled into Santander station at five to seven. My next bus was due to depart on the hour. I grabbed my rucksack and ran around the depot, arriving at the stand to see it disappearing. It was the last connection of the day to Santillana del Mar, I learned, but a coach to Torrelavega was leaving in ten minutes. Torrelavega: a neighbouring town where I would find a taxi. But this was a different company. I was obliged to buy my ticket in advance. Up stairs I flew, down escalators, dragging luggage, elbowing my way to the front of queues, wrong queues, until eventually I found the ticket office. Too late. The chubby, acne-faced girl with a scar of deep plum lipstick, ghoulish against pale skin, glanced at a monitor in her booth.

'There it goes,' she sighed.

'And the next one?' I begged.

'Tomorrow, 10 a.m. Nothing for Santillana del Mar or Torrelavega tonight. You must stay in Santander.'

The prospect of a night in this port city was not displeasing and, had I organised myself better, I would have opted for it, paying a visit to the old residential resort quarter of El Sardinero, fascinated to discover the origin of its name. Sardinero: 'black sardine'? Had there been a BC fish-salting industry here, too, or were they exclusive to the Phoenician-Roman Mediterranean?

In the city's Museo de Bellas Artes hung a portrait of Franco, the last on display in Spain. Another of Fernando VII, judged to have been a weak and cruel king, painted by Goya in 1815. This work had been achieved after the Inquisition had levelled charges of obscenity against the artist, decreeing his two fabulous Maja paintings shameless. Both canvases portrayed the same woman striking an identical pose; naked in one, clothed in the other. The charges were settled and Goya's role as First Painter to the Court reinstated but, in the wake of the scandal, Fernando reduced the status of his position.

It was a pity to miss out on these excursions, but my goal was Las Cuevas de Altamira, a series of caves first brought to the world's attention during the late nineteenth century. Entrance tickets were impossible to come by, I had been warned months earlier in Paris. A nine-month waiting list, the hotel receptionist in Barcelona had confirmed, while a guide-book had predicted a ten-month delay. Only twenty-five people a day were given access to the caves due to carbon-dioxide erosion, so I had pre-purchased my reservation some time earlier. The lags and hold-ups with the coach meant that I would lose my precious ticket, booked for eleven thirty the following morning, if I could not find an alternative means of reaching Santillana that very evening.

I hung around outside the station near the taxi rank but few vehicles of any description were passing by. An ample, middle-aged woman, gloves, hat, bags of shopping, puffed up beside me, quizzed me about my destination and then heartily dissuaded me from attempting the journey.

'Slim chance of finding a car,' she panted, dabbing her powdered forehead with her inner wrist. 'Who'll travel that distance at this hour.'

I frowned. It was not yet eight. But this was Santander not Barcelona. I was in the provinces and all had gone underground.

'Take a hotel,' she cooed, 'sample our delicious cuisine, hire a cab early tomorrow when the chappies are more cooperative, less expensive.'

I thanked her for her concern and wandered from the stand to the street's extremity, glancing at adjacent pensions. As I did so, a taxi rounded the corner beyond the station. I raised my arm, but my corpulent counsellor had already nabbed it.

Seventy euros was the fare I negotiated with the Cantabrian driver, polite and thickly accented, close to double the bus ticket from Barcelona, but what alternative had I? It was nudging eight thirty. The journey of thirty kilometres would take fifty minutes. I had no hotel booked in Santillana del Mar. In I climbed, to a cabby keen to strike up conversation.

'Where you from?'

I never know these days what to reply. 'England, Ireland, France . . .'

'England! Tony Blell your governor, hah! Some governor, take you citizens to war. And give me your opinion on Hairy Edems?'

'Who?' I was exhausted from the day's exercises.

'Like our ETA movement in neighbouring Basque region. Dialogue is the answer. Tony Blell has done right with Hairy Edems. Talk him to.'

'Ah, Jerry Adams.'

'Sí, sí. Irish music and local here very semejante.'

'Semejante, similar?'

'Sí. Flute, Celtic. What think you Rolling Stones, John Lennon, Keith Richards? Better than Cara al Sol. Every damned day singing it in school.'

I was having a hard time keeping pace. 'Cara al Sol?' Facing the Sun? Ah, the fascist anthem.

'Keith Richards, la musica pura. Fantastico guitar but loco with coca. You take drugs?'

I leaned forward and took a harder look in the rearview mirror, studying again the face of the man chauffeuring me. He was, as I had originally gauged, middle-aged, fifty-five. He did not wait for my response, which in any case was not forthcoming. Instead he began to eulogise marijuana. 'Overlooking the sea, lights twinkling, a small glass of beer out the terrace, and a hoint.'

I was struggling again. Ah, a joint.

'Perfecto relaxation. Fantastico amor, pero . . .'

Great lovemaking but the downside was he got the munchies very badly. Was this during the fantastic lovemaking, I was wondering, while attempting to glimpse a rather magnificent seaboard view passing alongside us. It was too dark. 'And your wife?'

'She smoke leettle, but happy with *fantastico amor.*'

I had not expected such conversation. I reflected upon Franco and half a century of oppressive history. 'It's illegal here, yes?'

'*Sí.*'

'Difficult to come by?'

'*Sí, sí,* but I grow weed in enclosure in *jardín.* My children come by, smoke with us, too. When they adolescent I didn't encourage, but now in their thirties, OK. We not on south *costa,* not kilometres from Moroccan *costa.* Here, north, Atlantico, so we must grow *hachís* in garden. Smoke in house privacy, of course.'

In my mind, arithmetic. He had been enjoying his indulgence for a couple of decades, perhaps longer. Had he been a joint-smoker when Franco was in power? I attempted the question but my Spanish was not sufficiently adept or my accent confused him.

'Not do coke,' he assured me. 'Turns you loco like Keith Richard. Coco loco. You smoke *hachís?*'

'My husband has never approved,' I hedged.

'But I bet he drinks whisky. Far better for his health to enhoy a hoint . . .'

And so we arrived at Santillana, a pristine medieval market town. Traversing narrow cobbled lanes, solid stone buildings embracing us, we reached a big irregular square, the central plaza. My driver pulled up in front of the imposing wooden doors of the Parador Nacional, which, because I had not made a booking, my new dope-head friend suggested was my safest bet. As we shook hands, he bowed and wished me a good stay, requesting fifty euros instead of the negotiated seventy.

'The run was quick,' he grinned. 'Enhoy the caves. They'll blow your mind.'

Over dinner, heavy boiled food with lashings of butter, in the hushed, ornate dining room, served by a waitress in a dark red and black local costume, I lifted my glass of Rioja, glanced about at the scattering of guests who looked mostly like archaeologists, and I spared a thought for the taxi driver who had recommended this conservative, state-run establishment, lounging on his terrace about now, getting gently high with his cool beer and 'hoint' and I tried to place him within my preconceived images of Spain.

I checked out the next morning before breakfast, having walked round the corner and found another hostelry, far cheaper, friendlier and offering Internet access. I had been told at the Parador Nacional that a connection did not exist anywhere in the town. Once resettled, I strolled the streets and marvelled at how extraordinarily well preserved it all was, the red-tiled houses, the flower-filled wooden balconies and galleries, here and there fancy iron grills, *rejas*, protecting the windows, but I found the neatness overly quaint; it made me claustrophobic. Traditional Spain, 'a class and mode of life that is dying', but it seemed to be thriving hereabouts, where the men were slight, fit as matadors and haughty, staggeringly rude, while the women were dumpy, middle-aged whatever their age, yet warm and accommodating. The bourgeoisie seemed to be alive and kicking in Santillana with its cumbersome wooden furniture and spruce window ledges and steps. Santillana is an abbreviation of Santa Juliana. In summer, this UNESCO World Heritage Site, settled by monks in the eleventh century bringing the saint's relics from Turkey, must be heaving with tourists, but in February it was a ghost town and I felt as though I were touring a film set on a disused lot. I was also disappointed that Santillana del Mar, or Saint Juliana of the Sea, was several kilomètres inland.

I had asked at the Parador the estimated time to walk to the caves, *las cuevas*. The slender male night clerk had replied curtly, 'twenty minutes'. In the morning, the podgy female receptionist in ill-fitting costume screwed up her face and shook her head. 'Oh, don't walk. An hour at least.'

I paid my extortionate bill and said farewell to the Parador Nacional. It was time for the caves. Hard to describe my excitement and sense of anticipation.

In 1875, Don Marcelino Sanz de Sautola, a Cantabrian landowner, lawyer and amateur anthropologist who lived in a rambling country estate not far from Vispieres and the rolling countryside I was now striding across with its farmsteads and *alquerías*, learned from a hunter, one Modesto Cubillas (great name!), that in a neighbouring district, while quarrying for stone, locals had blasted the rocks with gunpowder and had unearthed some unusual caves. Don Marcelino, whose hobby was local history, decided to pay the quarry a visit.

There, he discovered a pencil-thin aperture, released after millennia by the rockslides. This slender crevice allowed him entry into what, from the outside, appeared to be a vestibule. The cave of Altamira is 270 metres long, a little more than a quarter of a kilometre. It was damp within and must have smelt like hell after thousands of years without sunlight and fresh air. Negotiating his passage through dark, labyrinthine tunnels and spaces, he penetrated. From its principal chamber, the tunnels wound and turned, descending drastically in height in places from twelve to two metres. Remarkably, given the twilight conditions, he observed black markings on several of the rock surfaces. Don Marcelino had no idea what they were and certainly did not realise the profound significance of what he had stumbled upon.

In 1878 he travelled to France for Paris's third World Fair, a far grander show than the two previous. While in the Anthropological Sciences pavilion he noticed a display of prehistoric tools. Falling into conversation with researchers and scientists, he learned that they had come from caves in France. It inspired him to take another look at the Cantabrian offerings. The following year he retraced his steps to Altamira and began digging about, close by the original entrance, where he uncovered tools and spears along with shells and bones. He knew he was on to something and returned regularly. On one of these visits he was accompanied by his eight-year-old daughter, Maria. As the story goes, Maria looked towards the ceiling, oil lamp in hand, and noticed the artwork. Her reported response has become a cute, over-quoted line. Still, it is history. 'Look, Daddy, at the oxen!'

In fact, the figures the girl was pointing to, and which her father had to crouch low to see because the paintings had been achieved in one of the shallowest chambers, represented not oxen but a herd of prehistoric bison. The upshot of this remarkable father-and-daughter outing was that the following year Don Marcelino published a booklet recounting his explorations and findings in these caves, as well as others in the area, in which he claimed that these drawings were from the Upper Palaeolithic period – in other words 14,000 years old, and therefore the earliest human artwork to have been unearthed anywhere.

And guess what?

The scientific community of the day rejected the findings,

ridiculing Don Marcelino internationally, claiming that prehistoric man was not capable of such exquisite artistry, or on such a scale. The Church, keen to discredit an ancient treasury of such sophistication for fear it threatened the omnipotence of God and put the question of evolution uncomfortably into the spotlight, became involved. The cave paintings were proclaimed forgeries. Don Marcelino died in 1888, before his conclusions and the brilliance of his investigative work was acknowledged. Not until 1902 did scientists, in particular Émile Cartailhac, an eminent French prehistorian, whose voice had been one of the most vociferous denouncers of Marcelino, publicly admit that an injustice had been perpetrated and that the world of science needed to rectify that error. Altamira was genuine. Even more mind-blowing, later excavations revealed the existence of two periods of human occupation. The first was somewhere in the region of 18,500 years ago while the second was between 15,500 and 14,000 years ago.

More than twice the age of the olive trees in Bechealeh.

My walk from the manicured town led me to its outskirts before I began to ascend a gentle incline that curved and then hugged the lip of a forested elevation. With the pine-tree vegetation and the chalet-style houses, I could have believed I was in Switzerland or southern Germany. I tried to find somewhere for coffee, having quit the hotel before breakfast, but everywhere was closed. I passed local people engaged in neighbourly conversations at the roadsides, but nothing open. It was off season. The few folk who were about remarked on my passage with stares or indifference.

The road had straightened out. I knew I was on the right track and fast approaching the museum and caves when I spied a tourist bus stationed within a secured parking lot ahead to the left. It was only five to eleven. I paused, gazing down into the valley. I was ahead of my schedule. I caught the distant barking of dogs, a rook's screech echoing in the morning's stillness. Echoing. Echoes, in time and space. I stared at cattle grazing long-range, tiny as miniature toys down in the flat lowerlands. Altamira is Spanish for 'high view' and the caves are situated at 156 metres above present sea level. I was a long way from the Mediterranean. I had made a detour that seemed to be taking me drastically off course. The vegetation here was alpine rather than meridional. Traces of olive trees were slender possibilities. But I was hoping that from here my story would flip backwards in time to a beginning that was earlier than the magnificent groves of Bechealeh.

In Anatolia, in central Turkey, at Çatal Hüyük, I had tracked down what are thought by scientists to be clues to the earliest examples of fruit pressing, of almond and cherry farming. Those communities had settled, had created a fixed, organised society. They, too, had painted in their huts. They had travelled distances for berries and fruits, they had traded with distant neighbours. But they were an agricultural civilisation. Here, at Altamira, existed flourishing hunter communities.

I was beginning to think that the discovery of olive pressing was way older than I had imagined. The olive had been my link, my connecting point, to the countries that circle the shores of a sea, an inner sea, but in stitching those links together what was emerging was the birth of the Mediterranean landscape itself, its botanical journey, too. I had wanted to discover the historical roots of the olive to understand the evolution of the gnarled and twisted shapes begetting fruits on our farm. I wanted to get to grips with its chemical make-up, genetically, atavistically, narratively. I believed, still do, that we are destroying the planet we inhabit. We have set ourselves apart from nature. We continue to perceive ourselves in a relationship that is about 'Earth' and 'Us'. And because of it, we are endangering all flora and fauna. While we were still struggling to stand upright, walk on two feet not four, plants were learning to convert sunlight into food. They were sophisticating organic chemistry and, through their own processes of survival, learning to work with water and the seasons. I hoped that somewhere within all these pasts lay a path forward.

As I gazed across at those grazed lowlands, at a Constable-like landscape not too dissimilar from the images of my childhood in the Kentish or Irish countrysides, hay and carts, and bovines feeding, many deciduous trees rather than the languorous palms and silver-leafed olives of my new existence, I understood I had shifted my point of seeking. My quest was the source, but it was also the future. I wanted intimacy with the Mediterranean shores, to know its past, to learn from its history, hoping for pointers to a future that I could not yet see.

I turned and stepped into the parking lot, moving towards the caves, light of foot.

Foolishly, I had not understood that the original caves had been permanently closed to the general public. No material I had read in advance had warned me of this.

During the 1960s and 1970s the paintings were becoming damaged by the damp breath, exhalations of carbon dioxide, of the crowds flocking to see the rupestral art. So, in 1977, it was decided to close the caves. In 1982 they were reopened but with very limited access, which explained the exceptionally long waiting list. The replica cave was opened in 2001, at which point the originals were closed entirely, so as to be able to protect and study them. The neo-caves, I was assured, were a faithful reproduction of the original: even the colour pigments for the artwork had been fashioned from the same powders. Every bump and incline, every rockface, nuance and contour had been represented down to its minutest detail. The ticket I had purchased offered me access to the neo-caves as well as the remarkable museum. At first, I was extremely disappointed. I had not travelled such an incredible distance to look at copies. But to walk away would have been ludicrous. The next tour was due to begin shortly, at eleven thirty. It was the one I had booked.

Picasso, who from his earliest years in Paris had been attracted to and challenged by primitive art, visited these caves, the originals, of course. Famously his conclusion was 'Beyond Altamira, all is decadence'.

The drawings, polychromes of red, charcoal and ochre, reduced me to tears. I was not alone. In the laterally spacious, numinous chamber where the height at certain points reached no more than one and a half metres, we marvelled at how the ceiling decorations had been achieved – did these 'primitive' people lie on their backs while drawing? Altamira has frequently been described as 'The Sistine Chapel of Prehistoric Art'. No wonder. I and the others in the party – we were ten ordinary individuals – stood or crouched in awe, most of us dewy-eyed. I noticed tears rolling down the cheeks of a heavily-lined middle-aged Italian; a Korean couple squatted, holding hands, staring at the ceiling, frozen in disbelief. Beholding these depictions of animals: a pregnant bison, herds running freely, using the textures and surfaces within the caves to bring creatures' body parts and movements to life; horses painted over, palimpsests for other horses, red deer, wild boar; all with a breathtaking sense of dynamism, of flight . . .

Might these paintings have been representations by early hunters of what they had witnessed: the thunderous power of a herd on the run or the perfect stillness and grace of a beast grazing, watering, oblivious to man the stalker, watching, tracking? Or might these drawings, many with explicit sexual details, have been achieved by the women while their men were away hunting with spears and fishing hooks? Mothers and children at home base while the men were hunting, gathering . . . I even asked myself whether these interior spaces might not have been the earliest of classrooms. And what fuel did these ancestors use to illuminate these nocturnal, inner chambers? Did they work exclusively by firelight? 'Far inside the darkness, barely lit by an oil lamp made of stone, with lichen for a wick . . .' So was it the fat from game they used to fuel these primitive lamps or might there have been a vegetable oil? A pressed fruit?

Without exaggeration, I was seeing the world anew. Or for the first time, discovering it before Original Sin. And, of course, this was accurate. These works had been completed, sealed away and long buried before the scribes of the Bible had gone to work, before the parables of our Creation had been narrated. Many experts of today claim that these caves were a religious centre, that rites and marriages took place within them. I do not know. I do not want to overlay our theistic theories and belief systems on to the free spirit of the artists of these works whose repositories of stories were right in front of me, on the walls and ceilings. I wanted only to cherish what I was seeing. Purity. It was exactly what I had been hunting for in my search for that first arm that reached up into a tree and picked off a ripe olive from a silvery branch, then tasted it or squeezed it between fingers, rolling it to and fro and crushing it. The pleasure, the amazement, when the realisation dawned that there was a viscosy liquid inside the pulp, a gift from nature that could be utilised.

After the guided tour, I hung about in the museum for another three or more hours.

In the caves, on walls and ceiling, were handprints and the outlines of hands. The hands were rather small, not much bigger than the average modern adolescent's. The outline had been painted by someone pressing his palm, fingers outstretched, against the cave's surface while he or another traced its outline. Or so I had assumed; but not at all. Consider this: the hollow bones of birds, of such fragility, resembling tiny straws, had been loaded with a red pigment and then blown through, aiming the powder at the hand, delicately tracing its shape and staining the cave with the image. It was ingenious. Why hands and not feet, I asked myself? The catacomb was so shallow that the painters could, with almost equal facility, have lain on their backs and pressed their feet against the walls. Was it because hands talked, hands painted, hands cooked, hands made love?

Feet were the source of motion. They ran and tracked, while whole bodies hunted.

Cuts of hunted and slaughtered meat were cooked as steaks on their open fires and seasoned with herbs gathered hereabouts. Early steps towards a Mediterranean cuisine. A choice of tastes: with seasoning or without? A prelude to a more sophisticated kitchen. And then I found a note telling the visitor that the wild olive was in existence in prehistoric times and had grown along the Rift Valley. Yes! Syria, Lebanon, the Beqaa Valley, the sweep of land where I had found the oldest trees and the earliest traces of olive pressing, represented the most northerly point of the extensive Rift. There was no further information on the wild olives, nothing to say that the trees grew here around Altamira, nothing at that point to shift my thinking from the Middle East as the earliest source of olive farming, unless the trees were growing further south, all the way down to Ethiopia or Kenya, but I had no knowledge of this.

When I eventually left, instead of heading back to the town I walked to where the original caves were situated. On my way I bumped into the guide who had escorted us through *la cueva nueva*, the new cave. I asked him whether I could take a peek from the outside.

'*Sí, sí, no problema.*' He pointed in the direction, a matter of fifty metres from the reconstructed complex.

I thanked him, but, as I drew close, a guard appeared from out of a wooden hut and shooed me away, shouting angrily.

'Just a quick look from the outside?' I called.

A small yapping dog appeared at his feet. Iron gates reminiscent of an antiquated prison barred the entrance. He gesticulated agitatedly so I smiled, thanked him, paused briefly to make a swift mental note of the view down across the valley as it might have looked from within the shelter of the caves, and then I strode away in the direction of Santillana del Mar, Picasso's words playing in my mind: 'Beyond Altamira, all is decadence.'

What small creatures kept company with the Stone Age communities, living, nesting in crevices within the cave shelters? Were there brooding bats, birds singing, small mammals to feed? Were there nesting wasps or feral bees? I was fascinated by the hunters' relationship with their surrounding nature. The artwork in the inner sanctum showed no trees, no heavens, no water. It was clear from all that was on display within the museum that these early men were skilled if primitive masters of stone and bone. Extraordinarily refined artwork on the shoulder blade of a large mammal; delicate work on smaller bones. As far as we know, they invented the catapult and fish hooks; they learned to tailor clothing and footwear from the skins of the animals they had slaughtered for meat. The wide vestibule must have been their hearth, where they would have congregated, gazing out at the rain or snow, deciding upon fishing trips or mollusc hunting down at the beach when the weather was clement. Did they swim in the sea? Did they make music? Recount stories, play and act together?

Before agriculturalists, this was an epoch when all land was each man's public common. As far as we know, nothing was staked out by individual tribes. What was their relationship to the plant life, to the vast open spaces and forests? Running beneath canopies of tall trees, the sky masked, feet pounding on earth, what did they make of the undergrowth, its wildernesses and fruits? They had herbs for seasoning. These communities must have expressed interest in trees, in berries ... and their earth was untainted by chemicals.

During my descent, a pair of caged mynah birds was screeching a hell of a racket, dogs barked incessantly, someone was vigorously chopping wood. Variations on original melodies.

From the entrance to the cave, the view had looked out upon a wide plain dotted with homesteads and grazing livestock. Due to the extremity of their climatic conditions, the vegetation the Palaeolithic people lived among would not have been identical to ours, but the pictorial composition from their limestone rock shelter would not have been entirely different. Today, sheep are grazing – sheep had not existed then – and stone and wooden houses are part of the picture. They had looked upon dense forested areas, holm oak forests, a northern variety of the native Mediterranean species, where an assortment of animals ranged, herds of wild beasts roamed at leisure, roaring, bellowing, screeching. Vast areas of those forests have long been cleared. Originally, the wood would have been chopped to build fires. Like the olive, holm oak burns slowly. Later, its hard wood would have been ideal for tools and carts, even wine vats, until eventually much of the forestland was cleared to construct more sophisticated habitations and to lay out fields for crops and the domestication and husbandry of stock.

Our climate today is less harsh, but is it conceivable that a sub-species of wild olive survived this close to the Atlantic? Holm oak and olives frequently coexist round the Mediterranean basin, both are natives to the region, and, because of their similar low pendulous branches, can be mistaken one for the other. The uncultivated olive tree, *Olea sylvestris*, was already known in prehistoric times in the Middle East, but might a distant cousin have grown here alongside evergreen oaks, offering shade, raincover to the tribal peoples of Altamira? The olive fares best in calcareous soils, limestone lowlands and coastal plains. This area offers all the requirements.

Beyond the caves I was on a high. I spent one more night in Santillana del Mar. I strolled about, in and out of the plazas, the narrow lanes of shops decorated with bric-a-brac hanging from walls and edifices and I took photographs. Rather too much religious iconography for my taste; the town had been a religious centre in the Middle Ages. Still, the stonework was attractive as was the medieval architecture and I was particularly taken with a life-sized stone sculpture of a bison in the central square. But I was not sorry to leave. If I could have returned to the caves . . . but I had no reservation.

I set off before dawn the next morning in a taxi chauffeured by a warm, extrovert woman who smoked and talked incessantly. It was five o'clock; how had she the stomach for it? To the bus station in Torrelavega where the early coach to Madrid was delayed. Not the drunken driver from Barcelona? No, it was another; a different company; a new direction altogether.

A gentle, waltzing descent southwards.

Central Spain

We waited in the cold, dark station for over an hour. Once the coach had arrived and we got under way, the scenery was, at times, quite spectacular. Travelling east, doubling back towards Santander before looping inland, the landscape was dotted with lone chalets or hamlets where the church bell towers had curved silhouettes that reminded me of human shadows. Once, there had been vast oak forests in these parts. Long since felled. Large tracts of pine had been planted on the lower hills, forestry land possibly. Again, I had the impression that I was in northern Europe, not Spain, not a country bordering the Mediterranean. I was missing the Med with its evocative scents and colours, glad to be on my way, though the vegetation around me was rich and green. Sightings of a few holm oaks interspersed with eucalypts and deciduous trees. Rolling fields, arable farmland. On the lower hills along the route south of Santander the ground was flecked with pockets of snow. Had there been bees in this vicinity during the two periods of occupation at Altamira? I had not seen any evidence at the museum. Too cold, perhaps, for them to survive. *Apis mellifera* had not been hybridised back then. Set back from the road were many stone farmhouses crumbling into ruins. Passing brooks, streams, fed by snow, burbling fast and troubled. Geese, ducks, turkeys padded about in fenced gardens the size of small allotments. Each with its own well-stocked, neatly amassed log pile. Smoke snaked skywards above the chimney stacks. Settling my bill at dawn, I was watched over by a fat, dozing dog, grumpy at having been disturbed. While waiting for the taxi, the receptionist, who had climbed out of bed across town to see me on my way, mentioned that the inhabitants hereabouts cherished their countryside and mistrusted the influx of overseas occupants, mass construction and commercialism. They feared the *Benidormisation* of the Pyrenees. I realised then that I had not seen a single estate agent's offices in the town. *Benidormisation.*

There grew a darkness, a brooding gloom, about the region that both season and damp might have accounted for. The earth was dense, peaty in colour. Houses of crumbling stone. Horses and bulls haunted the hillsides. Spanish iconography all the way from Altamira to Picasso. The old stone houses and cottages with their red terracotta roofs were pretty, characterful. We were leaving the coastal districts now, beginning our ascent towards Madrid. This topography was so different from the arid plains I had shot through on the journey to Altamira. We were obliged to cross the Cordillera Cantábrica where the peaks and slopes were, by turns, snowcapped or bathed in soft mist. West of the Pyrenees begins this mighty limestone wall that divides Spain and France, the ranges that serve as a natural weather boundary between the climes of northern Europe and, way south, the Sahara. The driver negotiated the swings and verticality with skill, as though we were skaters on top of the world. I grabbed a jacket, feeling the drop in temperature. Ultra-sleek windmills crocodiled the summits. At one point, the coach swung a spectacularly altitudinous curve, exposing lofty precipices plummeting to what I took to be the distant Atlantic, but it could not have been. It must have been a vast, glacier-fed lake, a tarn. A sign to the left: Laguna San Pedro de Romeral. I was not sure, and lacked a comprehensive map.

I could not imagine that much had changed here since the last Ice Age. I read that a variety of Cuckoo flower blossoming in springtime, *Cardamine pratensis*, had been in existence in these eminences since post-glacial times. The intermittent upland streams, *aguacheras*, were coated in ice. Small horses were grazing on plant life that was white, frozen. How did the beasts survive in these gelid conditions? Were they wild? Who might they belong to? No homesteads, no farms; man had barely set a solid print here. Humanity was confined to lower boundaries.

In spite of the delays encountered, I enjoyed these long-distance *coches* with their access to country above the tree line, where no railway tracks had been laid. By turns I read or scribbled, but mostly I gazed out of the window at the timeless landscape. Five golden eagles glided by, right up close; it was thrilling. There were flocks and flocks of raptors in these high Cordilleras. I had never seen such congregations, flying five, six together, swooping to nests, perching with curled claws on cloud-capped outcrops. And then, suddenly, eleven eagles rose up out of the bleached stone, wings flapping hard and slow, a hunting party. We had reached imperishable summits, cresting from one to another, where the rocks were craggy and bearded; ridged, serrated, barren. I was twisting, turning, missing nothing. Spotted a couple of griffon vultures, but I could not be sure. Bears inhabited these perpendicular drops, but I saw none.

Approaching Burgos, a crossroads for a thousand years, a city founded in 884 as a fortification against Moorish invaders beating a path northwards. The surrounding countryside boasted plenty of fortified castles, *castillos*, hence Castile. In the Sierra de Atapuerca, fifteen kilometres from city centre, a prehistoric site has been discovered, revealing evidence of the oldest human settlement on the continent of Europe; bones and teeth belonging to an early man, Homo Antecessor, dated at 80,000 years. There was possibly a former incarnation, too, residing in this area, up to one million years ago. Sabre-toothed tigers had also roamed these high plateaux, millennia back, when the region had enjoyed a milder, more African climate. Beyond Burgos, woods of holm oak but no olives, little farming activity. Were we too high for olives? And back when the sabre-toothed tiger existed here, might the wild olive also have flourished? Passing the turn-off for Segovia, romantic Segovia, 1000 metres above sea level, below the snows, clad in pine forests lacking livestock, and no tigers or olives!

I was sitting at an outdoor café in Madrid's principal square, Plaza Major, a seventeenth-century, old city marvel. Early, sunny February. Tourists everywhere, taking advantage of cheap flights, snatched weekend breaks. Booze flowing, voice levels rising; British, American

accents decibels above the rest. The number of police in this ped-
estrianised cobbled square of frescoed buildings, where coronations
and bullfights had once been the entertainment, was only marginally
less than that of the foreigners. A lone woman at the table beside me
attempted to strike up a conversation. A native of the city, a Madrileña,
but also half Italian – handsome, forties, shoulder-length, immaculately coiffeured brindled hair, clad in beige slacks, twill cotton shirt,
quality sneakers, gold signet ring – she spoke of her husband and
family. I had assumed she was gay. Curious, though, that she was
sitting alone, sipping beer in this square full of strangers on a Saturday.
She warned me off the neighbourhood, particularly at night. Big drug
problem. Gangs patrolled with guns and knives. Their hits were *los
extranjeros*, the tourists.

Approaching was my rendezvous, a Tunisian Doctor of Economics
working in Madrid, a specialist in olive oil trading. I had met him a
couple of years back at an olive symposium. An elegant man in his
late thirties, well turned out in a perfectly pressed suit, tie, with a
black briefcase, he offered his hand. Dr Kili spoke Spanish and French
fluently, with little trace of accent. He had been resident in Spain for
over a decade and loved it. His sons, both born in the capital, spoke
the language better than Arabic. I wanted his opinion on what had
catapulted Spain into first position in the international market after
years of brushing the Italian shadow. He had agreed to a 'brief
meeting'.

His answer was simple. 'We have over three hundred million olive
trees, but go to Andalucía. Eighty per cent of our product grows
there. It is the largest olive-growing expanse on the planet. This
country has turned itself into a highly successful olive-production
machine. We have become the centre of the olive world. Fortunately,
olives and oil are fashionable and Spain is producing considerably
higher quantities than anyone else. We are now the dominant player.'

'Do the Italians challenge these figures, this loss of primary position?' I would find this out for myself when I reached Sicily and
ascended the Italian coast, but I wanted to hear both points of view.

'They cannot argue facts. In terms of fruit and oil tonnage, Spain is
without competitors. The other olive-producing countries, including
Italy, will now be obliged to reconsider the market.'

'And that means?'

'Super-intensive olive orchard production. Quality, but above all quantity. Economically sound investments.'

'How much oil can the market sustain?'

'Leading Spanish producers and governmental organisations are aggressively seeking new territories, creating markets within countries who, traditionally, have never been olive-consuming peoples.'

'Is there a downside, ecologically speaking?'

'I think this is very good for Spain.'

I pushed a step further and asked directly what data his offices might be holding on the use of pesticides on Spanish olive farms.

'I am not in a position to give figures, but all pesticides require phytosanitary registration with our authorities before they can be imported or sold. You can be assured the matter is highly regulated.' Dr Kili glanced at his watch. He had arranged to meet his wife and two sons, he said. 'A shopping expedition.' He rose, offering his hand, his apologies. I thanked him for his time. It had certainly been brief!

A few yards in front, a swarthy individual in trilby, black, shiny trousers, highly polished stacked shoes was singing popular Italian opera gustily while accompanying himself on an accordion. Quite a feat. *Los extranjeros* paid no attention but a lively crowd of clapping Spaniards had gathered. A balding, elderly waiter in burgundy uniform arrived with the food I had ordered. I hadn't eaten well since Barcelona. I craved fresh Mediterranean dishes, but the salad placed before me was the fare served everywhere: tinned tuna, tinned asparagus on limp lettuce, two quarters of tomato and strips of raw onion.

'Olive oil?'

He returned with a thin liquid the colour of sallow skin, advising me to remove my mobile and camera from the table. I placed euros alongside the untouched dish, gathered up my belongings and strolled to the San Miguel food market, musing how best to fill my Saturday afternoon.

As I left the square, a one-legged man, crutches, flat cap, empty trouser leg folded up towards his waist, held with safety pin, upper torso entirely flagged in lottery paraphernalia, waved at me. 'Winning ticket,' he rasped. I shook my head. I had been rather taken aback by the sight of so many disabled throughout the country selling these tickets. At every coach stop, kiosk and coffee bar.

The interior of the renowned food *mercado* was deserted, save for stallholders packing away goods. I enquired whether it would be open the following morning.

'It's Sunday! You think we don't need rest?' was the trader's response.

I wandered the vacant alleys until I reached a poultry stall, festooned with headless birds, where a handful of customers were still shopping. An elderly crone clutching a tartan trolley bag was giving out about something, screeching like an irate peacock. The queuing Madrileños ignored her. I wondered what was making her so furious. The fowl trader, moist, podgy fingers plucking skilfully at a goose, responded to her in monosyllables. Quite suddenly she swung and levelled her anger at me. Her baggy, grimacing face was shocking, flushed from booze and deep-rooted fury. I recoiled, but she yelled until her lungs rattled, until spent of force, then she made for the nearest exit, dragging her wheelie behind her. But she could not negotiate the iron door. I stepped to assist. She shuffled through and at the last moment turned, smiled, *muchas gracias, señora*. Even so, I doubled back and exited by my port of entry.

Outside a bistro in a neighbouring square, where boisterous foreigners were lunching, where it was windier, lacking the suntrap quadrangle of Plaza Major, napkins were flapping against cutlery like expiring fish. From around a corner arrived three armed officers. Two men and a woman, pushing through the higgledy-piggledy arrangement of tables, striding into the bar. I followed. All in black, a female, puffed face, thirties, was sobbing openly. The police encircled her and led her outside. A barman hurried to the door, calling after her, 'all will be fine'. I had assumed she was under arrest. Quite the contrary. She was the victim. Credit cards, passport, cash, bag, all expertly pickpocketed in the grand Plaza. As I retraced my steps I spotted the security cameras on every pillar.

My trajectory to the Museo Nacional Centro de Arte Reina Sofía took me the length of Calle de Atocha with its scruffy shopfronts, its closed-up, wartime feel, its shops with darkened windows or stores offering *articulos religiosos* that bore no relation to religious articles.

This was *barrio* Atocha, an insalubrious quarter littered with sex shops and XXX-rated video outlets. Outside Mundo Fantastico Sex, a steady traffic of assorted men with stale, furtive faces were shuffling in and out, hands deep in pockets. When I eventually reached Atocha Square, it was populated with black Africans trading from cuts of cloth laid out flat on the pavement. At each corner was attached a length of string. The instant a police officer or cruising law car was sighted, the illegal hawkers swiftly drew their contents into the home-made swag bag and fled.

Atocha station, the site of the 11 March 2004 bombings, extending the length of one side of the Plaza del Emperador Carlo V, had been fenced off. I wrongly assumed that the station was out of use, that the purpose of the digs was reparation of bomb damage. Later, I learned that major renovations to one of the metro lines were the cause of the disruption.

Free entry to the museum. I had only to show my passport. I ascended directly by the external glass lift to *la plancha dos*, the second floor, where *Guernica*, along with studies made in 1937 for the painting and photographs of work in progress taken by Picasso's mistress of the moment, Dora Maar, were on permanent display. Standing in front of *Guernica*, immense, black, grey and white, directly after Altamira, was disquieting. Guernica, Gernika in the Basque language, is a small city in the autonomous Basque region west of Bilbao, neighbouring Santander, where I had just travelled from. On 26 April 1937, the Nazi Condor Legion, acting on behalf of General Franco, bombed the city in one of the first carpet-bombing operations to take place. It preceded the destruction of metropolises such as Cologne, Coventry, Dresden and Hiroshima. In Guernica on that spring after-noon it was market day (even though market days had been outlawed by Franco's Nationalists). Everybody was out of doors, at their most vulnerable and quite unprepared for what was to come when the local church bells of Santa Maria sounded the alarm. The Luftwaffe let rain from the skies a hundred thousand tons of bombs that killed or injured sixteen hundred locals, a third of the population. Many were hampered by laden shopping bags. Those who were able ran from the town centre or buried themselves in shelters and watched on helplessly as their city was destroyed, pounded to rubble.

Witnesses spoke of how the fighter planes continued, back and forth, back and forth, for more than three hours, endlessly strafing the fleeing, panicked crowds beneath. The city burned for three days. The flames and smoke could be seen for miles in every direction.

The carnage caused an international outcry. Franco denied all involvement. The German commander claimed that the highly equipped bombers had been targeting a nearby bridge, a target that did not suffer a single hit. After the news of this decimation of innocents, Pablo Picasso set to work on his masterpiece, his response to the barbarism. It was intended for the Paris Exhibition of 1937. The painting was never exhibited in Spain, at Picasso's request, until after the death of Franco when it was taken first to the painter's home town of Málaga and then later installed in its own private *sala* at the museum where I was now viewing it: a heaving, grieving chaos, a tangle of bulls, horses, human limbs and weeping women locked together in a claustrophobic space beneath a naked overhead electric bulb. It was all the more shocking seen directly after the elegance, simplicity and innocence of the rock art. Bison and horses, bulls and horses have remained the imagery on this land mass for at least eighteen thousand years.

Perhaps because I was on an olive quest, roots of a Mediterranean theme, in my mind's eye I compared this story, this artwork, to the Roman annihilation of Carthage. Once the magnificent and powerful Phoenician city had finally been levelled, it burned for days on end. As at Gernika, the flames had roared high, visible for miles in every direction including out at sea.

Beyond Altamira, all is decadence.

I failed to discover in which year Picasso visited Altamira. It had to have been before 1934, but I found a postcard in the museum shop: a photograph by Man Ray of hands painted by Picasso, circa 1935. The left was black with white markings and the right was the reverse. I wondered whether this experiment was a direct result of his visit to the rock chambers. I also came across a Robert Doisneau photograph in which a bald-headed Picasso in matelot T-shirt holds both hands levelled against a window, studying them intently. The hands of creation. I tried to picture those prehistoric artists in the caves of Altamira, their hands, instruments of their art, pressed against the indentures of the rock walls, contemplating them, reproducing them, leaving indelibly their signatures.

Strolling back to my hotel in the vespertine light, clear, crisp, wintery. Interspersed with the relentless roar of autos and motorbikes with sawn-off silencers were the sonorous, forbidding peals of church bells. Saturday evening, the first mass of Sunday. Clustered outside the ornate churches were black-coated *mamas*, in headscarves, mingling with a smattering of elderly gentlemen, hats in hand. If the Muslims had maintained control of the peninsula, I would have been listening to the *muezzin*'s call. There are three major galleries along this wide, tree-lined Paseo del Prado: the Reina Sofía, which I had just left, the world-famous Prado and the Thyssen-Bornemisza. Within the wellhead of this Golden Art Triangle, I sat and watched the weekend *paseo* of the Madrileños. The Neptune Fountain was in view and beyond lay the Museo Thyssen-Bornemisza. On either pavement of this *avenida* grew forty species of magnificent trees including magnolia and acacia though, alas, I found no olive. These alleys of venerables had spent the past five years waiting to be uprooted in a drastic remodelling of the historic boulevard. Until Baroness Carmen Thyssen-Bornemisza, former beauty queen, Miss Spain in 1961, fifth and final wife, now widow, of the late Baron Hans Heinrich von Thyssen-Bornemisza, stepped in, objecting vociferously to such arboreal destruction. The Baron, a Dutch-born Swiss citizen with a Hungarian title, had gained his phenomenal wealth in the steel and armaments industries. His private art collection was judged to be second only to that of Queen Elizabeth II. Carmen, who had married the Baron just a few years before his death, had been instrumental in the transfer of his artworks to her mother country. A coup for Spain and her national reputation. When the plans for the remodelling of the Paseo del Prado were made public, the Baroness threatened to remove their museum from the capital if a single branch of the trees was touched. In stylish suffragette fashion, she chained herself to one of the ancient trunks, promising to climb its canopy and remain there until the plans were redesigned. Baroness Thyssen-Bornemisza had successfully extricated two not inconsiderable fortunes from the sibling inheritors of her past husbands. She was not a woman to lose a battle and eventually her powerful voice, supported by numerous other campaigners, proved too forceful. The Portuguese architect overseeing the redevelopment scheme was forced to return to the drawing board. I smiled silently at the feisty, fabulously wealthy Baroness's triumphant passage from youthful beauty pageants to internationally respected connoisseur and patron of art who, today, was standing up for The Tree with the determination and passion of a virago. It brought to mind a Minoan ring, rediscovered in 1926, exquisitely fashioned out of gold some 2200 years before Christ. Engraved within it was a Goddess of The Tree descending to the island of Crete where two mortals were paying homage to a tree, almost certainly an olive. I rose from my bench. Night had fallen on the Paseo. I felt winter blow and a stab of loneliness, homesickness, as I strolled on past the Ritz, guests dressed up, congregating. I fancied I might contact the Baroness and suggest to her that, within the remodelling plans for this stately avenue, the developers plant a cluster of olive trees, to honour the plant that has brought Spain international recognition and premier leadership.

My contact in Extremadura, a Brit who had settled on an olive farm in the lesser charted wild west of Spain, was in Brussels advising on a 'sensitive project'. An octogenarian couple, also farmers, I was due to visit in Mallorca were leaving for the States and the soil specialist I hoped to hook up with in Córdoba was off on a lecture tour in Turkey. I looked east, west and south and judged that, whichever way I turned, I would probably lose out. So, when I returned to my hotel and found an email from Simon, the Brit in Extremadura, I decided to grab the opportunity. He was back home but for a limited spell.

There was a choice of two Sunday buses travelling towards Portugal from the Estación Sur, one morning and one overnight, arriving Monday morning. Travelling after sunset meant no sights beyond the windows and, because I love setting off on a journey very early in the day, I opted for the morning ticket. A windy winter's daybreak with discarded papers blowing to and fro in the streets, hoardings rattling like chained ghosts as I left the hotel at 6 a.m. by taxi. Along the way, venturing to the south of the city, youths grouped aimlessly about the deserted, shabby streets; little of the stately capital hereabouts.

I was reflecting on my previous evening's conversation with Michel. A list of birds had been declared by the Ministry authorities back home as 'agricultural pests', including starlings. Traps were being used. There had been an outcry by lobbyists at the senseless destruction of wood pigeons caught in them. Man against nature. I was wondering where it would end.

Coach ticket purchased, I was directed to Departures in the basement.

'Which quay?'

'Between one and eighty-six. Check the screens.'

Below, at transport level, teeming chaos, as though the entire city's down-at-heelers had congregated. It dawned on me then that although I knew where I was going, clutching detailed instructions from Simon, I did not have the coach's final destination. Without it, there was little chance I'd track the quay from where my transport was leaving. Groups of new Europeans stood about smoking, drinking coffee from paper mugs. Compared to the mass of Spanish and South American Indian faces, they looked pinched, pale, shifty. None spoke English and none understood my Spanish. I collared a pudgy-faced employee hurrying by. He glanced at my ticket and shrugged. I hurried back up to the ticket booth. It was unmanned. My coach was leaving in twenty minutes. I charged along the line of desks, shouting beyond the queues to sales staff, but the response was always the same. 'Can't help. It's another company.' I hared back to departure level. There must have been fifty coaches at their stands. I targeted those whose drivers were at the wheel. I had ten minutes. Each shook his head or continued to read his newspaper. I was becoming frantic until an inspector latched on to my sleeve and dragged me across the terminus. 'Aquí,' he was shouting, waving his free arm. 'Aquí.'

Four minutes to departure. Hoisting backpack, I climbed aboard. There was barely a soul and no driver. I took my chances.

Madrid is the highest capital in Europe, perched at over 600 metres. The journey westwards towards Portugal remained altitudinous, leading firstly through scruffy, uninspiring, randomly constructed zones. Insignificant towns banked up against one another, an endless spill of concrete. *Benidormisation*. After two hours we were still spiralling, higher and higher into dense mountains. Storks were nesting in bell towers and on rooftops in the upland villages. This midland territory was different again. The route was elevated, cloud-cloaked. I was beginning to doubt whether the *provincia* of Extremadura could be an olive-growing region at all. Or was I to discover a hardier variety that could withstand this ruthless climate?

Simon was employed in an advisory capacity for a slew of organisations striving for a greener environment. He had also written a paper, a copy of which sat on my lap. I was perplexed, taken aback to read that his position on olive farming was that it was a negative business.

As far as Simon was concerned, the olive tree produced highly nutritious foodstuffs, offered medicinal properties, a means to an income in remote impoverished Mediterranean areas as well as an opportunity to keep communities and traditions alive. It was also a visual enhancement to the landscape. In fact, its silver-green foliage, its gnarled and twisted trunks, its low-swinging branches, its stone-walled terraces were as familiar and quintessential to the Med as the tideless sea itself. As well, the groves provided essential habitat for a wide variety of endemic flora and fauna and migrating birds. I was with him on all of this. So what was the problem?

Simon's reasoning seemed to be that too much of a good thing was dangerous. He argued that the subsidies given to farmers by the EU were based upon production and ignored earth maintenance.

I had never really considered olives from this angle.

Due to the giddying altitude – we were penetrating the Cordillera Central – the weather had degenerated dramatically. It was damp, drizzling, cloud-wreathed. Nondescript towns. One after another, passengers disembarked, weighed down by scruffy shopping bags, until only three remained. Beyond the windows a very different Spain, untouched by Europe or tourism; a less privileged population. Avenas de San Pedro was our coffee stop. Bells pealed, while bands of church-goers mounted the hilly streets. Surprisingly, in this remote outpost, the women were not black-clad. After Avenas we twisted up and round hairpin bends, passing a turn-off to the San Pedro Monastery, past high stone walls protecting terraced olive groves. Direction: Candeleda in Sierra de Gredos. The scenery changed dramatically, grew lovely although it was raining and steeled by clouds: alpine forests; stone drinking troughs, crossing the Río Pelayo I spotted wild goats. Storks were nesting on electricity pylons, even the rusted roof of an abandoned lorry. I spotted two females, heads covered in white scarves, riding their mules sidesaddle up the hillside, a Spain fast disappearing. Rivers, boulders, gulleys, chalets, stone cotes barely sufficient to sleep one shepherd. Our altitude remained close to 1500 metres. I was glad of my sweaters and thick socks.

Candeleda, a modest but attractive hill station, generated a vibrant Sunday atmosphere. Olives, drystone terraces, trilby-hatted, ruby-faced farmers in checked shirts with cherry-wood canes and solid boots, orange trees heavy with fruits lined the main street, jollying up the wet noontime. Simon had described the journey as two and a half hours. It was close to one. I had been on the bus since seven thirty. Outside the bars, meshed and puckered faces huddled together. These were flat-capped labourers with rolled umbrellas, tired cig-arettes glued to lips. Back out in the open areas, farmers stared from the doorways of their rural abodes at the downpour keeping them from their fields. Madrigal offered the same picture of weathered faces and caps staring glumly at the rain, drumming fast, tapdancing on the roof of the bus.

In 1932, Luis Buñuel, Spanish film director, shot a documentary, *Tierra Sin Pan – Land Without Bread* – exposing the impoverished living conditions in this region. I felt the bite of that poverty even today.

We were drawing towards Portugal.

I was wrong about Extremadura. It had been an olive-producing region for many centuries. Terraced groves were everywhere; trees as bent as arthritic fingers. My hopes of unearthing a really ancient olive tree here were soaring. In the high fields, rings of old stones. They encircled figs or stood alone. I had no notion what service they might have performed. Their presence was too frequent, I judged, to be wells. I had come across similar circular walled enclosures in other parts of the Mediterranean.

Cuacos de Yuste: journey's end.

I stepped off the bus into afternoon drizzle, and no one to meet me. As I stretched my legs along a high road that overlooked the village, an ageing pick-up pulled up at the bus shelter. Simon, curly mid-brown hair, silvering sideburns, physically fit. No difficulty identifying one another. There was not another soul about.

'You must be in need of coffee,' he smiled, approaching.

We entered a bar up the hill with roaring log fire. I was in the company of an amiable well-educated Englishman, glasses, softly spoken, with a London, possibly East End, accent that had been polished. After, we set off for his holding twenty minutes' drive out of town. As we bumped along the winding dirt tracks through an area that could not, by any standards, be judged over-populated or polluted by tourism, Simon bemoaned the many negative changes to his neighbourhood. Much of what I had seen up to this point led me to believe that these elevated posts west of Madrid were developing at a slower pace than anywhere I had visited until now. What I was witnessing were the ruins of a post-civil war inheritance; decades when hunger and deprivation ruled, decades from which the inhabitants were still in the process of recovery.

'The twenty-first century is a relative stranger here,' Simon explained. 'It's why I like it.'

I saw few expressions of luxury, barely modern comforts. I asked Simon about the Franco years and the effects on this province.

'Better ask Mercedes. She's the one to discuss such subjects. She was born and raised in Cáceres, not far from here. But be warned: her parents were staunch Francoists.'

Three red-brick hangars, equipped with what appeared to be hooks on sliding rails, stood in wide, flat, overgrown fields. Simon tutted and asked me if I knew what they were. I shook my head.

'Tobacco plantations. Those ugly outhouses are for drying the leaves. This particular district of Extremadura is well represented, agriculturally speaking, by its cherries, raspberries, capsicum, *pimiento* or pepper, brought to the region by Columbus, and its olives, of course, but the produce that accrues the highest revenues is tobacco. Did you know,' he asked, 'that tobacco gleans the highest subsidies of all European crops?'

I hadn't known.

'My neighbour receives sixty thousand euros a year in EU support. My olive and fig trees set on five hectares of land earn me the princely sum of twenty-eight euros. He sits in cafés and boasts his good fortune and says he no longer needs to deliver one ounce of tobacco because he can live off his grant.'

I was puzzled. The fields had gone to rack and ruin. 'But if the farmer does not produce tobacco, how can he expect finance from Brussels?' And then I remembered. 'The system's changed.'

Simon, at the wheel, nodded. 'And I was one of those who fought for the changes.'

Back home, whenever we took our olives to the mill, there were forms to be completed. Our fruits were weighed and the weight registered. Gérard, the miller, or his ageing assistant Alain, examined the drupes before shunting them off for washing. On completion, before we were entitled to carry our freshly pressed oil to the car, we climbed narrow stone stairs, dangerously slippery from olive paste, to the shop. There, we received a document that detailed the miller's fees, the kilos of olives delivered, the quality of the drupes (fresh, mouldy, worm-eaten etc.), their colour, level of ripeness, maturity, the quantity of oil pressed from the fruits, measured not only in litres but also in kilos . . . Endless bureaucracy!

Michel filed these records and, at the end of the season, he was obliged to send the originals to the olive authorities in Marseille, who forwarded them to Brussels. Approximately ten months later, paid directly into the farm bank account, we received half a euro for each litre of oil produced. As modest producers of approximately four hundred litres a year, we were honoured with some two hundred euros per annum. Both Michel and I had frequently asked ourselves whether it was worth the hassle, but to maintain our AOC we were obliged to follow every step of the tiresome procedure. That was until a couple of years ago.

'When the system changed it caused chaos in France,' I recalled.

Every *oleiculteur* had been obliged to play noughts and crosses with a furnished aerial map of their estate, marking cadastred olive trees with red crosses, water sources with black circles, dotted lines etc. With this came a forty-six-page file. Forms. I handed ours to Michel who is expert at applying for film subsidies and should have been ideal casting for the task. However, the file proved so complicated and time-consuming that he ended up completing it during a flight to Taipei and, due to its registration deadline, was obliged to FedEx it from Asia.

Due to the size of our holding we were among those who lost modestly on the deal. One hundred and eighty-six euros is our allocated aid. Today, olive farmers are paid by the tree rather than by production. In other words, whether we have a rotten year or bumper crop, our subvention sits at one hundred and eighty-six euros. Should we decide never to harvest another olive, never press another litre of oil, that is our affair. We are paid for the registered trees and we can religiously count on our predetermined stipend.

'So, your neighbour, the tobacco merchant, has stopped working altogether and now simply collects his allocated sixty thousand a year?'

'Precisely.'

I asked Simon why he and others of like mind had battled so determinedly for the system to be overhauled.

His answer was instantaneous. 'The old method invited massive corruptions. The present way,' he conceded, 'is not foolproof but, generally speaking, less is being leaked out of the grant banks.'

I wondered how accurate this was or whether, after so short a time, the balance sheets had not yet been fully accounted.

In France, the reorganisation had met with habitual Provençal resistance. Dead set against any changes, the farmers went mad. Few of them could make head or tail of the forms. I couldn't! So, due to procrastination, late or inaccurate returns, many had forfeited their grants altogether. Matters got so serious that our local branch of the Chambre d'Agriculture Alpes-Maritimes held regular one-day seminars on Accurate Form Completion. At one of these sessions, I learned from the Niçoise chief inspector of olive oil, a handsome young bachelor in his twenties, that several of the *oleiculteurs* had stormed out in fury. One is reported to have risen to his feet, beetroot with rage, screaming 'Names, give me names. I want the names of those who thought up this fandangled system and I will take my hunting rifle to Brussels and personally blast every last one of them to shreds.'

I glanced at Simon, picturing his chances against a furious French farmer with loaded gun. 'The very mention of the name Brussels down our way causes violent apoplexy.'

'It's only for ten years,' Simon assured me, 'and if it proves non-negotiable, the bureaucrats will go back to the drawing board and think again.'

I smiled, imagining the reactions of our agriculturalists to yet another round of bureaucratic innovations.

'So will these tobacco fields eventually be sold off?'

Simon let out a deep sigh. 'The bugger's asking one million euros. He's received an offer, too, from a leisure company which is hoping to construct a golf course. Over my dead body,' he mumbled.

Was his neighbour aware that Simon was professionally involved in eco-farming?

'I don't want anyone to know! Nor that I am in the anti-tobacco lobby. Round here, they'd lynch me. The only thing that keeps that crafty widower sweet is my wife. He's taken a shine to Mercedes.'

Tobacco had become the highest subsidised crop because without such financial support Greece had refused to join the Union; its tobacco farmers would have been landed in a crisis. I had not been aware of the role tobacco played within the Greek economy though I was very aware of the astounding number of cigarettes smoked by the Greeks. It seemed a contradiction when France, following other countries, had banned smoking in public places.

'I was fascinated by your thoughts on olive farming.'

'Let's talk over lunch.'

We had arrived at Simon's rustic idyll where a flat, curving dust track led us to the house. The excessive damp and continuing light rain had given the thick olive trunks a deep rich hue. His trees were young, stubby, well pruned.

'We bought five hectares and a barn,' he explained. 'It lacked all amenities: water, electricity, habitation. I converted the barn into a house myself. We still don't have planning permission,' he laughed.

'What?!'

After he had purchased the property, he had submitted his plans to the local council in Cuacos de Yuste, but had been greeted by bemused expressions. The clerk accepted them and shook his head in disbelief. 'I've never seen these before.'

Simon never heard another word and read the silence as acqui-escence. He went ahead with the conversion and even built a second storey. He dug a well, installed electricity and was now in the process of completing a swimming pool. 'But affairs are getting stricter, linked to national cadastres. I will register the pool at some point. I've been too busy.'

Such an easy-come, easy-go attitude stumped me. I wondered whether Spanish farmers took their agricultural battles so lightly, or as seriously, as the French. Glancing at the Englishman at my side, I doubted it. He did not look as though anything would ruffle him.

Mercedes, Simon's wife, dressed like a widow in black slacks and black woolly zip-up jacket, was on her laptop when we entered the simple, comfortably furnished kitchen. She, by comparison, wore a worried frown, immediately apologising for being so preoccupied.

'I'm a lawyer and spend most of my working life challenging Simon's tax demands.'

It was decided that we would drive to a neighbouring town to eat Sunday lunch. Rico, their handsome ten-year-old, fluent in both Spanish and English, accompanied us, with his Gameboy. En route, we stopped off in Cuacos at Simon's office to drop my bags.

'You can eat *migas* at the restaurant,' said Mercedes as we toured the renovated town house. The ground floor had been converted into offices while the upper levels were rented out to tourists. In this instance, me.

Migas was a traditional Spanish dish of crumbs, leftovers, that varied in its preparation from province to province. Here in the mountains of Extremadura, where the men were regularly away with their flocks, it was a shepherd's breakfast of stale bread, fried in garlic and olive oil, and then jazzed up with spicy *chorizo* or ham. Simple fare. In modern Spanish society, it had become a fashionable appetiser in restaurants.

I had grown tired of *patatas bravas*, potatoes smothered in luke-warm ketchup sauce, so culinary alternatives instantly whetted my appetite.

The light was fading on the wet, remote, late afternoon when we finally arrived in Garganta La Olla.

'The historic town of brothels,' smiled Mercedes. 'Look out for the blue houses.'

The colour had signalled to the soldiers of Charles V that the building housed prostitutes. Mercedes could not say why they had chosen blue. A proportion of the district's population, those with blue eyes and fair skin, were the legacy of all those illicit couplings.

Hurrying in the rain along cobbled streets, across plazas, negotiating mud and streaming water, every restaurant, tavern and *cantina* was closed or full, save one. We settled there. The family proprietors found us a forgotten table at the back where we sat, dripping puddles round the hard wooden chairs. The other diners were locals. Mercedes and Simon exchanged niceties with several while Rico remained engrossed in his Gameboy and two white cats lay dozing on the wooden floor by a crackling chimney.

I called for a bottle of the house red to fortify our damp spirits. Our orders taken – *migas* was not on the menu, but Iberian ham from the acorn-fed, local black pig was. I opted for that while my hosts shared a steaming tureen of lamb stew. Simon told of his first *migas*, in the province of Castilla y León, north-west of the capital.

'I was young, alone in Madrid. For fun, I offered to assist a shepherd with his transhumance. Did you know it's a practice that originated before Christ in Arabia? Benito and I took a week herding the flocks up into the higher reaches of the Sierra de los Ancares, relocated for summer pasturing. I awoke after my first night, stepped out of the tent and was surrounded by two thousand sheep. The altitude, the sun rising warm on the June morning, the vista, boy, it blew me away. A couple of booted eagles were circling overhead, eyeing the livestock. Benito spotted them. I kept an eye while Benito fried up the *migas* over an open fire. I still recall the taste.'

'It's peasant food,' Mercedes topped up her glass. Her third. 'Originally cooked with *manteca de cerdo*, pigs' lard, which is why it's frequently dressed with bacon or ham. *Mantequilla*, butter, was for the aristocrats and was probably brought to the peninsula with Charles V and his royal soldiers.'

'And olive oil?'

'Originally, the Iberians cooked with pigs' lard or goat and sheep fat. Then came olive oil from the east. Olive oil has been used here for two thousand years, but it would not have been available to the shepherds so far from home and at altitudes above the olive line.'

I mentioned Simon's paper, but he did not pick up on it.

I spent three days in Cuacos de Yuste, more time than I had intended, partly because of coach timings and also because I was still awaiting answers from the scientist in Córdoba and the olive farmers in Mallorca. My next port of call depended on who responded first.

On the second day, I managed to corner Simon. We took a walk in his groves.

'Two hundred and fifty thousand hectares of Extremadura are dedicated to olive cultivation. It's the third most productive region of Spain. The olive tree should be a model for drought tolerance in the Mediterranean, but its production is being abused. It could have a vital role to play in our future, but people are greedy and modern man underestimates it.'

'In what way?'

'Over-intensive farming uses water reserves recklessly, damaging the soil, threatening bird and insect life.'

'Why would anyone want to over-irrigate olive trees? They require so little.'

'To use them exclusively as fruit-producing machines. The harder you water the greater the crop yield. It's about making fast money and destroying the land into the bargain.'

Simon's own farm, growing *manzanilla* olives, was a 'hands-off' affair. Both the olives and wide-leafed figs were heavy with rain water while the trunks and branches from roots to upper crowns were coated in a silvery lichen that almost matched the grey-green of the leaves. It created a frozen magical illusion, but was surely sapping the trees of their force? Simon's response was, 'Lichen is extremely sensitive to pollution, therefore an excellent indicator of clean air. I see its role here as that of a meteorologist, a forecaster of a healthy environment. I choose not to perceive it negatively as a parasite.'

'But it will erode the olive wood, surely?'

'Eventually, yes. Do you know how it is formed?'

I did not.

'It's fascinating; it's a combination of an alga and a fungus. When the two grow closely together and intertwine they create an altogether new species, lichen, and, once mated, one might say, the two cannot be separated. They are a new material. The alga photo-synthesizes energy and feeds it to the fungus while the fungus leeches water from the wood and passes it to the alga. It is a remarkable marriage, an example of nature's ability to harmonise.'

'But why risk the trees? With a minimal amount of intervention you could prevent the trees from being sapped and your olives could still be here in a thousand years from now.'

'Are you suggesting I coat them in fungicides?'

'Of course not.'

'I am fond of the olives and figs but I am equally attached to the lichen. Everything dies at some point, including olive trees. I prefer not to interfere. My philosophy is a hands-off approach to farming. When you go south you will see the diametric opposite at play and it might cause you to rethink. I am an olive farmer, but first and fore-most I am an ecologist.'

So, these acres of fruit bearers set among monolithic ancient stones, about which Simon knew nothing, all fended for themselves, and if drupes remained at harvest time then they were picked and pressed or, in the case of the figs, made into jam. If they were eaten by birds or bugs then, as far as Simon was concerned, it was all part of the ecological cycle.

Was this the only alternative to pesticides?

I attempted to engage him on the subject. 'I never use any chem-icals. My concern is the health of the planet.'

'But surely, there are alternatives? A solution provided by nature?'

'Water is the single most pressing issue. Intensive farming is the danger.'

Was I missing the point?

Even if Simon was reticent, non-communicative, Mercedes and Rico seemed eager to talk, grateful for the diversion of a stranger in town, who, in slate-black winter, was willing to listen. While Simon pottered about in his garage, Rico and Mercedes fought for my attention and I asked myself whether he had invited me all this way so that his family would be, if not entertained, then at least occupied. The rain rarely let up and, when it did, the wind howled like a banshee, reverberating against the mountainous granite slopes. It was a curious sojourn locked away in the middle of nowhere with this family. I slept alone in town and spent my days with them.

When Rico found me wandering in the rain, juggling camera and brolly, he invited me to his *palacio*.

'You can take a picture of me in it.'

It was an ingenious construction of which he was very proud. Not a tree house, more a Daliesque installation, created out of a gallimaufry, much of it filched from his father's workshop, strung together between several olive trees. Here, weather permitting, he spent his days. Wooden bridges aided access from one area, one branch, one tree to the next. Chicken wire protected his olive seedlings in boxes on the ground. A bicycle hung from a branch, as did flowerpots. Lanterns to illuminate; a blue bucket collected rainwater; coloured plastic crates, upturned bottle containers, functioned as steps; a tarpaulin had been transformed into a sail flapping between branches; a woven basket contained sopping, inedible sweets. Its imaginative resilience was splendid. When I asked the boy what had inspired him to create his 'palace', his frank, straightforward reply took me aback: 'To sail away from Dad'.

Mercedes taught Spanish to two black African monks who were the sole remaining occupants at the Yuste monastery where Charles V lived out his last days. She invited me along to see the grounds. I was in search of ancient olive trees, I told her in the car, hoping she might know of a hidden grove of knobblies and suggest a detour. She shook her head.

'The olive tree suffered during the civil war when thousands were felled for firewood to keep the refugees from freezing to death, not only in Extremadura but all over Spain. Many mills closed or were destroyed. Farmers, millers lost their livelihoods. For the marginally more fortunate, bread and oil became the staple diet. There was little else. Oil gained a reputation as "war food".' Later, Spaniards turned their backs on their precious commodity. They were ashamed of the poverty it represented. They needed to distance themselves from all reminders of hostilities. During the years of dictatorship, the olive industry fell into decline. 'You will be very fortunate if you find ancient trees in Spain,' she concluded.

I recalled that Simon had described Mercedes' parents as Francoists. I broached the subject gingerly, but she was open to discussion. She was nine when Franco died. She recalled how she and a girlfriend had giggled at the news. His body was laid in state in Madrid. Images were transmitted endlessly on a television screen in their local café. Her mother had been angered by Mercedes' sacrilegious attitude: laughing at death, laughing at the loss of their leader. For a long time after, her parents had moaned that life without Franco was terrible, was worse, but lately they said nothing. They knew in their hearts it was getting better.

'But nobody forgot the past,' Mercedes muttered. Whenever news came of the demise of one general or another, there was a palpable reverberation of emotions. 'What those emotions were depended on whose side you had fought on. Every village, every family,' she said, 'harboured secrets, did not whisper the past. In remote country areas such as this where farmers, olive producers, survived to be centenarians there were many who carried memories of the massacres, of the cruelties dealt between one brother and another.'

Bells were pealing. Every quarter of an hour they were ringing somewhere. It was a constant reminder of Spain's Christian supremacy, of the victorious hard-won history of its Catholic Church. It occurred to me that since arriving in Spain I had not once heard the *muezzin* calling his faithful to prayer. Spain's Catholicism was sovereign.

Mother and boy told me that in winter cranes crowded the skies, flying in from Eastern Europe, while spring was the finest time to visit. Then, the cherry trees blossomed into snowy canopies up and over the passes and valleys and buttercups in full flower gladdened the olive groves. In that season the crumbling, cramped stone walls and the slate-black hillsides grew beautiful. Towards autumn came the chestnut season, the gathering of the fruits for roasting, promenades in the chestnut forests and then the olive harvest . . .

'The Extremaduran people,' boasted Mercedes, 'are proud of their cuisine. Legend has it that when the convents and monasteries were sacked by Napoleon, their recipe books were stolen by French soldiers and it was from those handwritten pages that the finest French cooking was born.'

Before I said my farewells to this family, I walked miles through dripping olive groves, hunting for just one ancient example. Mercedes was with me, her skin pale as candle wax. I was wondering how, if so many thousands of groves had been destroyed during and after the civil war, Spain had reached its present position of production leader, but my companion had no answer.

'Why don't you return for Easter?' she offered, heavy brows furrowed. 'I promise to ask friends, neighbours about ancient trees, long-forgotten olive stories.'

I explained that I had planned to be in Cádiz for Mardi Gras and, from there, the boat to Morocco. I sensed her disappointment and profound loneliness. She confided that there had been times when she had wanted to die; she had miscarried a little girl, their second child. I felt my stomach clench. This was a subject I knew a little about.

Mercedes had spent a week in intensive care before her womb 'exploded'. She knew then that she was dying and she longed to. Loss had overtaken her. Her life was saved by an Egyptian doctor who had visited her every morning. 'You must look for reasons to live,' he had counselled. 'Only you can find them.'

I turned to study her. Mercedes' beauty was ordinary, earthy, unrefined. Broad of jaw, slender, yet with a restrained force. She seemed to be the very essence of *la peña*, grief, sorrow, regret.

'And then I remembered Rico. He was my reason to live.'

I wondered about Simon, with whom I had spent so little time, who had answered so few of my questions, who seemed so absent. Mercedes told me he loved it here, out in the middle of nowhere, surrounded by his slowly dying olive trees, but both she and Rico longed for Madrid, dreamed of London, craved the beat and pulse of city life.

I recalled my own loss and its ensuing crisis, and how nature and the creation of our new groves had given me my reasons, my impetus for this future.

I returned to Cuacos de Yuste for my last evening. My bus back to Madrid with an immediate connection to Córdoba was departing early the following morning, the Feast of the Purification of the Virgin. There were no cafés or bars where I could find a meal so I settled for sliced sausage, bread rolls and half a bottle of Rioja purchased at one of the two grocery stores still trading at 7 p.m., where tomatoes whiskery with mould lay rotting in wooden crates. The rain had stopped and the sun had come out, but the wind had picked up. Still, it was a relief. As evening descended, I walked the village. Storks were nesting on the principal church tower. A local paused, watched me photographing the birds.

'The tower was restored two years ago,' he told me. 'Split clean down the centre during the 1755 earthquake in Lisbon, it was. Most of the townspeople would have preferred that the riven original had stayed.'

Lisbon. All Saints Day, 1755. Three earthquakes in quick succession. They all but destroyed the city and killed over 15,000 people. The shock and the tsunami waves were felt and experienced as far away as England and the West Indies.

'Why keep the damaged original?'

'A reminder of the power of God, the force of His anger.'

Large farming women waddled across the squares in fur-trimmed slippers, carrying buckets of water, geese trailing at their feet. Dressed in black with headscarves, they reminded me of Muslim women and, like their Islamic sisters, they refused to let me take their pictures. The men, though, open-mouthed old codgers with not a handful of teeth between them, idling away retirement on stone benches, leaning on canes, hanging on to their flat caps, pressed against stone-walled façades, paying no attention to the wind rolling flotsam up and down the lanes, were perfectly delighted to pose for the camera.

I returned to my little house with its hazy but pleasant view over the sodden olive groves and wintry hillsides. Simon arrived. I had not been expecting him. He had come to request another night's rent. I had left it on the table and offered him a glass of wine, which he refused.

'I thought you might like to see the cellar,' he announced.

After the civil war the country was starving. Food shortages every-where. To retain one's own produce, particularly olive oil, was made illegal. Here in Simon's house was an underground storeroom, a cave.

We descended to the small rectangular space. Knocking through the foundations into the adjoining building, the proprietor from whom Simon had purchased his property had stockpiled tall urns of olive oil, lined up in rows against the lime-plastered stone walls of his neighbour's home. Unfortunately, the man next door discovered the stash in the illicit cellar, *his* cellar by rights, and informed the Civil Guard. The oil was confiscated, the farmer was imprisoned and from that day to this the two families had not exchanged a word. Enmities ran deep. Grudges were harboured here.

'For two or more decades after the war years, olive oil was the staple diet for millions of Spaniards, but once Franco had gone and the country seized its new beginning, many dug up their groves, either to plant crops with faster, less back-breaking returns, such as tobacco, or they sold the land off. They bulldozed the trees to make way for tobacco farms. Tobacco had already become a heavily subsidised commodity even before Greece negotiated with Europe. In the sixties and seventies, the virtues of the Mediterranean diet had not been discovered and the international market had minimum interest in olives. Its tree was of little worth; its oil sold for next to nothing. Tobacco was set to be the future. But when you go south you will see that the Spanish are reinstating their olive history with a vengeance, but without thought. It's a fiasco. Go to Andalucía, and you'll understand my deep concern.'

We shook hands. I thanked him for this unexpected tour, and he confided with a note of desperation that Mercedes had expressed her desire to leave.

'She wants to take Rico to live in England. England is full of those who haven't left, who haven't managed to get out. I don't know what to do.'

I felt deeply sorry for him but I did not know what to tell him. That his extremism was alienating, that perhaps Mercedes' reasons to live did not lie in the olive groves . . .

Early the following morning, set to go, I drank my *café* at a bar in the square. The bearded patron, wiping his espresso machine with a cloth, never uttered a word. His lips were drawn, tight as an extended elastic band. Perched on high was a television, sound up, announcing the weather and news. No one was paying it any attention; I was the sole customer. From behind a door, an old woman in black appeared. She must have been ninety, with a clawed face. Tiny as a sparrow, unsteady as a skittle, she began to holler. I could not understand her screeching. The barman paid her no attention, kept polishing his shiny coffee machine. She screamed again, gripping the door frame with luminously white-fleshed talons, while emitting an unsettling high-pitched hum. Eventually, the man slapped his cloth against his immaculately clean counter and went in search of whatever she wanted. Returning, he handed her a pen and without a word, lips pursed, continued his housework. Mother and son? I wondered about his broken dreams, about their story, his father doubtless long since departed. I wished him good day as I settled two coins in a plastic saucer on the counter, but he only scowled at me.

A caravan of rose-coloured clouds, now that the rain had let up, appeared from behind the stone and wood houses in the plaza. In the distance, iron-walled mountains, austere, forbidding, snow-capped. I stood a moment, looking, reflecting . . .

The woman from the grocer's across the square eyeballed me, then disappeared inside to her rotting foodstuffs. Climbing the cobbled lanes on my way to the bus shelter, from where I had disembarked a few days earlier, I passed a school where a black-clad woman was dragging a fat snivelling boy armed with satchel to the gates. The bus arrived; the same driver; one passenger. I boarded and took a seat, pausing an instant to bid farewell to a harsh, cruel earth.

Andalucía

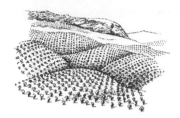

Andalucía, Spain's southernmost territory. It is where the Spain of our imaginations springs to life: flamenco, bullfighting, gypsy women in brightly coloured, frilled frocks beating their feet against the ground, Baroque churches, Moorish palaces and fortresses, sherry barons in Cordobes hats cantering on horseback across their estates, fiestas, *ferias*, music, soulful and passionate, the sweet scent of orange blossom and hectare after hectare of olive orchards . . .

I was crossing the southern limit of my earlier experiences. From here on until I reached mainland Italy – Andalucía, Morocco, Algeria and Sicily – were uncharted territories: an exciting prospect. I was on my way to Córdoba, once Corduba, the Roman capital of Baetica and, later, capital of the western Islamic Empire, to meet up with a research scientist, a soil specialist, whose contact details I had found through a friend working at UNESCO. From Madrid, along the dull E5 motorway through Castilla-La Mancha, I journeyed across flat brown land. A man on the bus claimed that *tapas* originated in this central province of Castilla-La Mancha during the sixteenth century when it was discovered that mature cheeses disguised the taste of sour wines. Thus began the habit of serving a lump of smelly cheese with a glass of second-rate plonk.

The Despeñaperros Pass, a natural, dramatic breach through the Sierra Morena, gateway to Andalucía, straddling the border between the two provinces. Here, kites hung heavily overhead while articulated lorries and coaches climbed in funereal procession due to a massive rock slide that had blocked off much of the defile. Either side of us were pine-verdant, craggy mountains shooting towards a thunderous sky. In spring, these mountainsides were golden with blossoming broom. In former times, bandits had lain in wait for the muleteers and journeymen moving north from the fertile lands of Andalucía, travelling this bullion route to Madrid, from the metal-rich estuaries and the ports of Cádiz and Sevilla, transporting mineral and agricultural wealth including famed Andalucían olive oils. At that stage, the pass was the only passage through and it grew in notoriety and danger because of it. There had been a staging post, a transportation stopover offering sustenance and a bed to the itinerant and weary. Don Quijote and his sidekick, Sancho Panza, from Cervantes' immortal novel, had stayed at the inn. Alas, long since gone. This Despeñaperros Pass, or Pass of the Overthrown Dogs, gained its name after a battle between the Christians and Moors in 1212 during the long and drawn-out years of *La Reconquista*, the repossession of Spain by the Christians. From here, after a humiliating defeat, the Moors fled with their tails between their legs.

Our fifteen-minute coffee stop, first steps on Andalucían soil, was at a considerably less romantic location, a cafeteria set back from the roadside somewhere past Guarromán. The day was growing noticeably warmer. In its predominantly concrete garden cacti, palms and succulents sprouted as well as a few desultory, dusty olive trees laid out in a central weed-cluttered patch, each dripping with large black fruits. Their harvesters were sparrows. I helped myself to a couple of drupes and bit into them. They were not as sweet as the Romans I had tasted in Malta but neither were they overly bitter. Their deep burgundy flesh ink-stained my fingers.

Back on the road, young olive groves planted in military rows in tilled red earth where not a weed or blade of grass sundered the regimented scene. I fancied that the earth, with its startling rustiness, its deep oxide-red, had been dyed with blood. After generations of violence and fighting, it was as though the corpses had fallen like forgotten fruit and steeped the landscape.

Andújar, the largest producer of bottled sunflower oil in the world; a surprising fact, but out of sunflower season the only plant life was the *olea*. Andújar had once been an elegant Roman civil city, but I saw no trace of it as we passed through its ugly suburbs though splendid displays of flowering, feathery mimosas redeemed it to this passing stranger. In the Iglesia de Santa Maria hung El Greco's *Christ's Oration in the Garden of Olives*.

The larger, elegant farmhouses set in the rolling plains were known in the south as *cortijos*. Gerald Brenan, who had resided in a village in Las Alpujarras up until the civil war, wrote in *South from Granada*: 'The great *cortijo* or farm of the Andalusian plains is a direct descendant of the Roman villa. It has the same offices and rooms, excepting the hot baths, laid out round a spacious court. The ground floor contains the old mills, wine vats, and store rooms, and sometimes the stables, while the upper floor is divided between apartments for the owner and living-rooms for the bailiff. Over the monumental entrance-gate there is a niche for a sacred image, and above the house there is a *mirador* or lookout tower.'

After the Catholics had reconquered Spain, the Moors, as well as all Jews who had not fled, were forced to take on the Christian faith. These 'converts' became known as Moriscos. But in spite of all promises to the contrary, the Christian monarchs eventually exiled them and divided up their properties between ranking clergy, military and aristocracy. Many of these had no knowledge or interest in the land and it was left to the less fortunate to labour for them. This system, known as Latifundia (meaning in Latin 'spacious farms'), had been perfected by the Romans. Its legacy was hardship and poverty for all those who had no estates of their own, who toiled the soil for a pittance and were kept firmly in line by manager or overseers. Alternatively, the farm workers paid rents, collected by live-in bailiffs. Andalucía still suffers from such a hierarchy. Many of the *cortijos* remain in the possession of estate barons living elsewhere.

I was gazing upon a sea of olives, no other crop. Olive oil opulence. There are an estimated 179 million olive trees in Andalucía. Beyond the early cultivation of the olive, the Romans, as elsewhere, generated a level of oil production that grew into a thriving empire-wide business. Later, the Moors contributed improved agricultural and irrigation techniques and alternative medicinal and culinary practices. For a while after the Moors and Jews had been driven out of Catholic

Spain, olive oil was looked down upon as an inferior product, an eastern legacy. The Catholics preferred lard and, later, butter.

From the window, much activity in the grounds of the magnificent *cortijos*, labourers hard at work, pruning the trees. I spotted a tractor with trailer transporting branches still studded with drupes. I wondered if these were to be left to wither or if they would be separated and pressed at a later stage. Instead of one central torso shooting up from the root base, the trees possessed a trio of slender, slanting trunks, each hung with but a few branches. Low, severely pruned, tailor-made for easy harvesting. And the ground . . . I had never looked upon such weedless fields, as though they had been vacuum cleaned. Most of the groves were planted on inclines, without terracing. In the Jaén province of Andalucía, close to 150 million olive trees are farmed. Were the fields and plains kept so pristine, so denuded, by massive doses of weedkiller? Was this the olive fiasco Simon had spoken of?

Running fast, parallel to the roadside, I sighted the mighty Río Guadalquivir. Its source, headwaters, north-west of Jaén, flowed from the Sierra de la Cazorla. It was slushy and mushroom-toned; polluted, not attractive. The 660-kilometre Guadalquivir was the backbone of the region. At its mouth, where I was heading later, access to the peninsula had been perpetrated by the earliest of traders and colonisers arriving from the east in long-oared galleys. They had crossed the Mediterranean greedy for the famed silver and iron that was mined along its banks . . .

But for the time being there was nothing but olive trees. I wondered whether the river's pollution was caused by olive farming. I had not discussed with eco-warrior Simon what impact the mountains of olive waste and the vegetable water were having on the countryside. Where to store it? What to do with it? Andalucía was harvesting and transforming the fruits of close to five million metric tons of olives into oil every year. Aside from the used water, this created three and a half million tons of dried waste. One of the great bonuses of olives is that everything, every last part of the drupe, is usable. What remains after the fruit has been pressed for extra virgin oil is a pomace that can be pressed again several times over until the final drop of oil has been wrung from it. This ultimate extraction produces an oil destined to be made into soap. When that last vestige of juice has been removed all that remains is a desiccated brown paste, the waste, the crushed residue of skin, stones and pulp. In Middle Eastern countries, the Arabs still feed this dried waste to their camels, believing it offers valuable nutrients. Some farmers return it as mulch to the trees. Spanish farmers used to press it into dried briquettes, similar to Irish peat blocks, to burn in their fireplaces. At home, at our local mill, as elsewhere in southern France and other countries, the waste feeds the fire that heats the water used during the oil extraction. But Spain's residue was phenomenal. It would be impossible to burn such quantities at the mills. To utilise a small portion of these millions of tons of paste, two local electricity plants had been constructed, one in Córdoba and the other in Jaén, and there were others in the pipeline. A German organisation had made a bid for the contract, but I knew no more. But as for the vegetable water, a greasy residue – *margine* we call it in France – I had no idea what was happening to it. I was hoping that I would learn more when I met the scientist in Córdoba.

I arrived in Córdoba late evening. The taxi from the bus depot sped through narrow, high-walled streets until, passing through a gated entrance, it deposited me in a splendidly romantic courtyard. I had fallen upon somewhere exquisite. The very reasonable room rate must have been due to the season. My unkempt windswept hair, hiking boots and cargo pants caused the porter to question my reservation. However, at reception I was greeted warmly and offered fruit-juice punch while I filled out the registration form.

'Welcome, Señora Bridgewater. We sincerely hope you will enjoy your stay with us.'

'Drinkwater, thank you.'

A swift glance into the formal dining room decided me against staying in and I went ambling off down historic lanes until I came upon a cobblestoned plaza where I found an inviting *taberna*. It was well after ten o'clock. Not late for the Madrileños, but I was not acquainted with the habits here. At the bar, I requested a table and a glass of red wine. Within moments, a rather dapper gentleman was at my side.

'Join us, why don't you?' Normally, I would have refused this Englishman, but I was tired, fancied some company and he seemed kind. I followed him to the upturned oak barrel where he and his wife were enjoying generous glasses of *fino*, tawny sherry.

'We were talking about you earlier today,' said the woman before I had settled my glass. I was taken aback. They were from Norfolk. 'We spotted what we think was an exceedingly old olive tree standing alone in a field at a crossroads. We thought its age must have been the reason the farmers had kept it.'

I was hooked.

They had driven up that afternoon, along the N331, from Málaga where they were holidaying. 'Somewhere close to Antequera,' said the woman.

There had been Roman settlements in the vicinity of Antequera. Might this be a Roman tree? Delighted by the encounter and that my olive quest excited others, I scribbled directions hastily on a napkin and confirmed that I would seek out their discovery.

St Valentine's Day in Córdoba. Heavy drizzle, but mild enough. My mobile had not been charged since Madrid and all telephone and Internet connections were down at the hotel, a designer's extravaganza, fabulously palatial, built over Roman ruins, visible through the glass floor in the main salon. However its elegance was out of sync with its Fawlty Towers management. I was in possession of a room key that locked me out, hot water taps that produced no water and was addressed as Señora Bridgewater.

I took a walk to the river, falling under the spell of the city instantly. Córdoba, capital of Andalucía, had, along with Baghdad, been the greatest city of the Western world. Descending cobbled streets lined with fruiting orange trees, I inhaled the damp air perfumed with citrus fruits. Wooden boxes of misshapen, green-tinged oranges were positioned on the steps of many of the doorways along with scribbled notes, *Sírvase*, 'Help yourself'. Cocks crowed, chickens clucked in the city. Down at the water, disappointingly the Roman bridge that crossed the coursing, mouse-brown Río Guadalquivir was inaccessible, scaffolded for renovations. Workmen were everywhere, shouting to one another, their cries lost in the forceful downstream flow.

I strolled the bankside down along the Paseo de la Ribera in the rain, photographing the impressive wooden water wheels. One of the greatest, most practical legacies of the Moors to Andalucía was their irrigation systems. The Romans knew a thing or two about irrigation. Pliny wrote in his *Natural History*: 'There is no doubt that gardens should be attached to a villa and that they should be kept irrigated, watered if possible from a flowing stream, but otherwise from a well with a wheel, valve pumps, or by drawing with shadufs.' But the Moors surpassed the Romans and, what is more, they had a lovely term for the business of irrigation, 'the invention of summer'. These wheels down at the riverside were added by the Moors to original Roman mills. Today, they were abandoned, decaying, occupied by birds, plants and occasional rats. Like the sludged, contaminated river flowing fast at their bases, this seemed a sad relic of a once glorious past.

The taxi dropped me outside the main building of the Institute of Sustainable Agriculture. It was housed in a *finca*, a farmhouse that for centuries had been the summer residence of the local bishop and was still known as the *Alameda del Obispo*, or Birch Tree of the Bishop. Directly after the civil war, Franco's party had requisitioned it with its one hundred hectares and had converted it into civic offices. Today it was a research institute.

The interior was a maze of locked doors along corridors reeking of school dinners. Nobody recognised the name of the doctor I was meeting. Across the country lane and a field carpeted with oranges, I tried the laboratory blocks. Here, I was greeted by antiseptic hospital smells and Dr Mendoza, who had kindly accepted my request even though he was leaving for Izmir the following afternoon. He cut a dashing figure in black sweater, jeans and spectacles; mid-thirties and seriously attractive. I had been expecting a gentleman of a certain age. His office was a box spilling over with files, books both in Spanish and English and a computer. His expertise was soil and, given that olive trees were the dominant Andalucían crop, his research was the effects of intensive olive farming on soil.

'And the results?'

'Not good news. Our water situation is acute,' he began.

I had read in an English newspaper and, indeed, had been invited to discuss the problem on a BBC Radio 4 programme, that Spain's olive crops were shrivelling due to drought. 'Is it due to climate change?'

The doctor shook his head. 'Certainly, we have suffered one or two droughts but I believe there is also marketing hype in these press releases. True, the level of water in the reservoirs is falling and is not being replenished, but the trend towards lower rainfall levels, signalling global warming, is not the nub of the issue. Drought is not Andalucía's primary concern. Our bigger problems lie elsewhere.'

I begged him to spell it out.

'In a few simple sentences,' he began, 'we are using our water faster than it is being replenished. This is caused by expanding agricultural needs and growing urbanisation.'

'Where does the olive tree stand within all this?'

'The olive plantations are being greatly extended. More importantly, they are descending from their traditional growth places in the mountains and stony hillsides into areas of arable farming.'

'The olive tree is a Mediterranean treasure. How could it become the cause of such deep concern?'

'It is not the olive tree itself but our farming methods that are causing the damage. Excessive irrigation in orchards that lack traditional drystone walling to shore up the earth, is causing the topsoil, the richest soil, to be washed away. Andalucía boasts 1.5 million hectares of olive plantations. These trees are being sprayed with a number of insecticides while the ground around their root base is being drenched in weedkillers. The earth is being over-irrigated to push up fruit production. Such an excess of water is causing the soil, packed with chemicals, to run off. The contaminated water is ending up in rivers, reservoirs, dams; all contain a high percentage of pesticides.'

I was silenced.

'In short, we are poisoning our wells and springs, our water sources, poisoning our people and bleeding the land of nutrients and water for future generations.'

'But the olive tree does not require heavy irrigation. It thrives happily in arid conditions. It does not suffer during a normal hot, dry Mediterranean summer?'

'More than that. It has a remarkable facility to aid in the regeneration of subsoil water levels. Not dissimilar to the Moroccan iron-wood.'

I had never heard of the ironwood tree and I was taken aback by the depth of the problem.

'The more the farmers irrigate, the greater the crop yield and the less the olive works for itself. The arithmetic is simple. A heavier crop load produces more olive oil.'

'And greater financial rewards?'

'Exactly. Unfortunately, there's more. We are facing serious infringements of water rights. Illegal boring. And the Basin Author-ities seem to be losing control.'

'Do farmers have limited rights?'

In Jaén, Dr Mendoza told me, 200,000 hectares carried certified Basin Authority entitlement whereas, in reality, 320,000 hectares were being irrigated. The difference was illegal. The olive producers were digging their own wells, boring deeper and deeper to subterranean levels that had never previously been touched. Without licences to do so.

'They are stealing, we could say, the earth's groundwater. And it is not being replenished. Slowly, day by day, year by year, we are destroying our soil. We are creating an unproductive earth. Here in the Andalucían groves, the losses are the most acute. This is desertification.'

'Soil turned to desert?'

'Yes. So, there you have the problems that lie before us. Polluted water, soil loss, desertification. All brought about by unsustainable farming.'

'The lack of weeds and growth in the denuded orchards, what is that about?'

'Less growth around the feet of the trees, the fewer predators to steal the water. Starve the land of all plant competition and only the olive tree is fed.'

To maintain such barren fields, phenomenal tons of weedkillers, herbicides, were being packed into the soil. This, too, was causing erosion and pollution.

'Until the late twentieth century, it was believed that earth acted as a proctective filter that stopped pesticides seeping into underground waters. Our studies have shown that this is not the case. Pesticides are reaching subterranean beds yielding groundwater. They are also denying migrating birds, as well as endemic species, insects, too, in fact all varieties of flora and fauna, of their natural habitats and nutrition.' The doctor drummed his fingers against an empty coffee mug. 'So there you have it. The impoverishment of our terrestrial ecosystems at the hands of man.'

'And the situation is . . .?'

'Potentially devastating. We have to stop the degradation before it becomes irreversible.'

We sat for a moment in silence. I was attempting to take this in. I was out of my depth.

'What hope remains, if any?'

He smiled. Here was where the science of soil erosion came into its own. Much study was being undertaken by his team on how most effectively to reintroduce the olive waste and its pruned branches back on to the land, to use the trees' by-products as soil amendment.

'Compost out of the dead branches, for example.'

Unfortunately, for the time being it was only cost effective on the great estates which owned their own *almazaras*, mills, from where the waste materials did not have to be transported. There was also a big push to encourage organic farming—

'No more pesticides?'

He nodded. 'And to teach farmers about soil management, how to preserve and care for their earth.'

'What about Dacus, the olive fly?'

'Specialists are seeking alternative methods to combat the fly.'

'Nothing yet?'

'Alas not.'

I asked him about the market for such phenomenal quantities of olive oil. 'Surely, such a glut will drive prices down?'

He shook his head. 'Much of the oil is sold to Italy. This has been the pattern as far back as the Romans. Monte Testaccio on the banks of the Tiber River in Italy, close to the port of Ostia, was found by nineteenth-century archaeologists to be, not a hill but a tel, a mountainous collection of millions of shards of terracotta jars all originating from Spain, all fired during the Roman occupation of

Spain, 212 BC to AD 422. It was calculated that they would have contained in total some two thousand million litres of olive oil, which certainly outstrips most modern harvests!'

'But today Spain is no longer under Italian domination.'

'We have our own operators who control the oil businesses. Olive oil is fashionable. Its health and medicinal properties are endlessly lauded, and the positive aspects of the Mediterranean diet cannot be denied, but there is a limit even to that market. The goal now is to create awareness in the countries that traditionally had never considered our products. China, Japan and Russia are the obvious future customers.'

Dr Mendoza rose and I realised that I had taken up too much of his time. I thanked him for his generosity. He offered to drive me back to the city. Negotiating the traffic in a decrepit Fiat, two bucket seats for small children in the rear, I asked how he had fallen into the soil business.

His maternal grandparents had picked olives. They had been hired hands up in the north of the province, which was one of the districts where he was testing the earth. To reach the farms where they gathered, they had walked ten to twelve kilometres and returned the same distance at night. His grandfather had also been a shepherd. They scratched a meagre existence, and when the war came along he was drafted into the *Nacional* military, fighting on Franco's side. This had been a source of shame for Dr Mendoza until his grandfather had explained that you fought on the side of those who were controlling the district you lived in. It was as simple as that. It wasn't about conscience or political allegiance; it was about survival. The land where his family had resided remained beautiful and relatively unspoiled. Dr Mendoza had enjoyed hiking there as a student. By working for its protection, he felt he was giving something back.

We had arived at a busy intersection just north of the Alcázar de los Reyes Cristianos. The traffic was dense and I hurried to gather up my belongings.

'Thank you,' I said, pushing open the door. 'Enjoy Turkey.'

'If you are interested in the future, go to Morocco, visit the Algerian Sahara. Desert returned to soil; now there's an exciting challenge.'

*

I spent the rest of my last day mooching about beautiful Córdoba, which had certainly fared better than Baghdad, walking, people-watching, reflecting. Simon had advised, 'It's important not to be overly romantic. You must be realistic about the olive tree. You do us a disservice otherwise.' I think I was in shock.

At every corner I was nagged at by gypsy women with penetrating eyes and hair swept untidily back into ponytails, attempting to palm me off with rosemary. 'Señora, take one for your amigo,' they pleaded, offering up aromatic sprigs clutched between blackened fingernails.

The people, los Andaluzes, had another look here and their manners were more extravagant. Aftershave wafted in the air as the men strolled by. In the bars, the bodegas, resembling saloons in a western, women lounged against the counters, drinking beer, gossiping with the staff. They were dressed in thigh-hugging jeans ripped at the knees and stack-heeled boots. Their skin was dusky with flatter, splayed Spanish-Amerindian features.

In the taberna where I ate lunch only one other table was occupied, by a young French couple, hands locked, engrossed in each other. Beams of dark wood criss-crossed whitewashed walls jollied up with brightly designed ceramic tiles. The broad black head and frozen fearful eyes of a bull adorned a space close to where I was seated. There were dozens of photographs, Hemingway moments in the ring. Trickles of blood, ribboned lances, matadores: repeats of the same man in a black embroidered montera hat striking a series of heroic poses. While I was leaning in close to study them my phone rang. It was Michel. I hadn't been expecting him. Our daily calls usually took place in the evenings.

The wild boars had paid a visit and ripped up sections of the recently laid water pipes up at the top of the land.

'I don't believe it,' I sighed, glancing back at the photos on display. I am dead set against bullfighting. I am also dead set against boar-hunting, but if I could have got my hands on our offenders I would have stuck them in the ring with the matadors.

An old girl shuffled in, a midget with scratched voice, shrieking like a parrot, hawking lottery tickets. My waiter and his colleague both hurried to the counter, digging into their pockets for cash. A football match kicked off on the overhead TV set and I received no further attention. In fact, had I been so inclined I might with perfect ease have walked off without settling my bill. The streets were deserted and the shutters on the shops had been clunked closed. Siesta time. Nothing would happen now till early evening. I meandered back to my hotel, peering down crooked lanes, at secluded, flower-decked patios, still fuming about the boars and our thousands of euros' investment they had run over, deciding that a hire car was my next step. I had enjoyed my excursions by coach but I had destinations off the beaten track to visit, people I hoped to meet up with, and I wanted to pass along the byroads of *la Ruta del Aceite*, the Oil Route. I had not heard back from Mallorca, but I could not linger for it was still my intention to reach Cádiz for Mardi Gras. Unfortunately, Lent fell inconveniently early this year and time was pressing. I took a day to track the tree suggested to me by the Norfolk couple – Roman, I was still hoping – but I was unsuccessful. I must have misunderstood their directions. I drove in circles for several hours, up and down the same stretches of road, but I never found it. I was out of luck.

The route, initially south-east from Córdoba, was flanked with razor-headed hills covered in endless rows of *oliviers* growing up out of bare, parched earth. Jaén province produces almost as much olive oil as mainland Italy. Beneath each tree was a shadow, like shreds of black silk, which I could not make out until I pulled over. Was it the netting used to catch falling fruit? No, it was the ruby-black fruits themselves. I was puzzled. To gather such a number of olives from the ground would be labour-intensive, financially unviable. The conundrum was explained further along the road when I saw half a dozen men on a hillside, stuffing fruits and branches into large buckets. The small hummocks of fruit were rolling down the inclines, powered by the wind force of two vacuum leaf collectors. Once at the foot, they were raked into piles, then thrown by hand into the plastic containers and finally wrapped up into a large cut of white cloth. I pulled over, grabbed my camera and began to photograph the unusual scene, but when the men spotted me they broke into shouts, yelling, cigarettes between lips, swearing obscenities. They dropped the containers and hid themselves behind the foliage as though they were Muslim women. Were they immigrants, were they stealing the olives? I called out, attempting to engage them in conversation, to discover whether they worked for a private *cortijo* or a larger, more industrial producer. Eventually, one fellow, in stained white T-shirt, with a hooked caliph's nose, came out from behind his tree.

'What you want?' he yelled.

These were casual or day labourers, known as *los braceros*, and probably had no involvement with olives throughout the rest of the year. They did not understand my Spanish, or chose not to, so I was unable to establish whether such brutal treatment of the drupes was usual practice hereabouts. Were these fruits intended for an international market? Were they flying a Spanish label, or were they to be shipped off to Italy and sold from there as an Italian product? He waved me away and turned his back.

I cut off the Baena road and climbed north-east towards Martos, then swung off the beaten track following directions into parched hilly countryside south of Jaén. Awaiting me, alongside two matrons, was Perico, a bachelor in his early thirties with thick horn-rimmed spectacles, a well-established chef's paunch, double chins with a bud of a beard and clipped punky hair slicked to a single point. This young chef, running the kitchens in the hotel where I had stayed in Córdoba, had inherited his grandfather's seven hundred olive trees. The old man had planted up his *finca* on an all-but-forgotten bluff east of Baena, a town that could lay claim to the throne of the olive kingdom. Originally, Perico's smallholding had boasted twice as many plants, a third of which had been more than a century old.

His grandfather had been a Republican and had gone into hiding to escape death or prison. He had spent his 'underground' years as a captain and as a baker feeding comrades. Sometimes the men had hidden themselves in ancient groves where the silver-leafed canopies offered protection against aerial attacks. On occasions, they had secreted themselves within the concave trunks of centuries-old trees, used them as temporary bases during the civil war when they were on the run from the *Nacionales*. Meanwhile, Franco's military had swept down upon Perico's family farm, when his grandmother was home alone, and chopped down half their investment. It had been a punishment, payback for her husband's politics. Afterwards, the government had seized the best sections of land. Eventually, when the grandfather was at liberty to return, he wept at the sorry condition of his farm and spent the following two decades rebuilding it. Beyond the war, olive oil was a major source of nutrition. It was a staple in an impoverished diet, during the 'hungry years' when entire families were starving.

The grandfather was ninety-five now and in retirement, but he had continued to farm and harvest well into his late eighties. Perico earned his living as a chef because the smallholding was not sufficiently lucrative to meet the family's needs. They were up against the majors or 'more ruthless' estates and big industrial producers. In order to hold his own in the marketplace he had joined forces with a neighbour who also ran an organic holding. Perico worked his groves in the mornings before heading off to the hotel in Córdoba and on Sundays. A chef, in Perico's words, was a natural extension to living off the land: 'From the soil to the kitchen.' He always cooked with olive oil, but not necessarily his own. He searched out oils from around the globe, taking delight in discovering their diverse flavours. Was I aware that, today, there are over 2000 varieties of olive trees (I was not!) and that in Mexico there is an olive that grows to the size of a peach?

His parents had expressed no interest in the farm. He had three sisters, no brothers – he was the youngest – and his father, also a chef, had died of a heart attack at fifty-eight and so the farm and its responsibilities had fallen to him; but he would never sell it.

'Not even if I become a famous chef and go to Paris!'

Both his grandparents and his mother lived on the land as well as two of his sisters.

'A household of women,' he grinned. He introduced me to both matriarchs, 'the true chefs' of the household. We all trooped through to the kitchen, sparse and whitewashed.

His grandmother, Immaculada, was in her late eighties; her white hair slicked back into a tight bun, hooped gold earrings that softened the severity, a checked wrapover frock and dark bedroom slippers. Her hands were mottled with liver spots. She had a flared nose, strong, rustic features and chestnut eyes that rested unwaveringly upon me. Her daughter, Perico's mother, Rosa, was a darker-haired version of her parent. Both women spoke of the *posguerra*, the post-civil war days, when people all around were dying of hunger. Their memories were unhappy ones, a bleak period in Andalucían history. The family had been so poor that at nine Rosa had been obliged to go into service at one of the local *cortijos*. They would have starved without the extra cash. Later, she picked cotton on an estate close to Córdoba and at weekends walked home to help with the farm. Back then there was no electricity. They walked everywhere. They washed their clothes in the stream and they were paid for doing others' laundry, too. With domestic work and olive oil, they eked out an existence.

Perico's reflections were more upbeat. When he was tiny, his grandfather had carried him side-saddle on his *mula*. During the ascent to the mountainous orchards the old man had sung and hummed to beast and boy and, when they reached the groves, he'd called out 'Come! Come, Perico, the trees are growing goodies.' And they were.

'My grandfather had hidden sweets in every branch for me to harvest. I had grown up believing that the olive was a magical bonbon tree. Even without sweets, there is nothing quite so beautiful as a strong, well-cared-for olive tree. The groves of this region have sustained the people for centuries. We depend upon them.'

Before I left, he handed me a bottle of his oil, lovingly cradled between hands with severely chewed nails.

Winding my way back down rambling tracks, flanked by trees groaning with purply fruits, penetrating the Sierra Subbética Cordobesa, I was held up behind a tractor pulling an enormous trailer laden with unsorted olives and leaf debris. There was nothing to do but follow it. In fact, it turned off for Baena, *Ciudad del Olivar y el Aceite*, the City of the Olive Tree and Oil, and I decided to follow it. I had no appointments in Baena. I had been hoping to meet up with two brothers from there who were, if the market was to be believed, possibly the organic olive-farming stars of southern Spain, oilmen for generations. They claimed their family had been producing the finest cold-pressed, organic olive oil 'since George Washington became President of the United States'. Unlike most other Spanish companies, these brothers had cracked the American market. What intrigued me most was one of their products, Flower of the Oil, *Flor del Aceite*, which, according to their advertising, was the *grand cru* of all olive oils.

I had never encountered this product before. The fruits were gathered from the trees by hand and crushed the same day by granite stone mills. Normally, the crushed paste, or *arujo*, would be pressed and from that pressing would come the first extraction of extra virgin oil. But with their system this rare and exclusive product, the pomace, was left for several days to drip its golden liquid at its leisure. Normally, a pressing yields somewhere in the region of one litre of oil for every five kilos of olives. This process needed eleven kilos of fruit to produce one litre and this very exclusive oil was on sale in the United States in numbered bottles, at a price. I was both fascinated and sceptical.

The brothers' promotional material claimed that the reason their oil was so exceptional was that they still handpicked from every tree – 'a skilled gatherer can clean a tree in twenty minutes' – and because they were still pressing the old-fashioned way at a mill their family had purchased from a local duke in 1795. Their premises were situated behind an arched gateway within the town of Baena. Unfortunately, every time I telephoned I had fallen upon their manager. The brothers were away.

Where could they both be in this crucial season of pressing and pruning? In Russia, I eventually learned, touring, lecturing on olive oil. Vanguards for the future Spanish markets.

The tractor and trailer led me, as I had guessed it might, directly through the open gates of an olive mill, an *almazara*. The sign announced the *Cooperativa Olivarera de Baena*, the local olive farmers' cooperative. I was right at the pulse, the heart of this liquid kingdom. I pulled over alongside a row of smart four-wheelers and tired old vans decked out with nets, tools, strimming utensils, every requirement any oilman could possibly dream of, grabbed my camera and took a stroll round the back where I heard powerful rumblings of heavy-duty machinery.

This was a mammoth plant, both an impressive and a disturbing sight: at least a dozen chutes, sorting arms, iron steps, ladders, wheels, shunting belts and queues of farmers waiting in line to dispose of their leafy pickings. Some negotiating brimming-with-fruit trailers the size of small bungalows. Men in overalls and peaked caps yelled above the thunderous roar of machines, directing the process. There were weathered old codgers, young bored-looking blokes smoking, iron bridges that led from one section of the plant to the next. Gleaming stainless steel containers in rows, each containing probably five thousand litres of freshly pressed oil . . . it was endless, while all around us in the warm mid-February winter sunlight were stark hillsides clad in olive trees.

I attempted to strike up a conversation with one or two of the men waiting in line but they were not interested. So, after a few snaps, I went inside the mill itself. I expected to be sent packing – that or at least an enquiry as to my identity and purpose – but I continued pointing a camera wherever I felt like it. The scent of the oleaginous paste being churned and crushed hit me instantly. It was so powerfully pongy and tangy, I felt I had been steeped in it. A couple of the blue-overalled employees paused, leaning over their shunting trolleys, but when I smiled and nodded they did the same and continued with their contribution to this ancient ritual. A tiled, low-temperature room set apart contained two long rows of lofty, polished stainless steel drums. I calculated that there in front of me was sealed a minimum of 120,000 litres of oil. In the olden days, or even back home in France when we first got involved in the oil business, this would have been the darkened corner where maybe half a dozen twenty-litre demi-johns filled with newly pressed juice had been stored to settle.

It was dazzlingly industrialised, as though I was on an immense oil rig somewhere. There was not a woman in sight. This was male territory. I decided to leave them to it. I felt troubled. The organic brothers were still not back from their travels; I had missed their shop and tour-of-mill opening hours and the surrounding, weedlessly regimented hillsides only added to my concern. Before quitting Baena, I made one final stop in the centre of the hilly town where a few broad-trunked trees grew and a quartet of life-sized bronze figures were harvesting olives on a strip of grass as though in a field. What was remarkable was that I had seen not an inch of grass anywhere, not a rogue blade, aside from this one green patch turfed up as a memorial to a method of farming that was fast dying. Here, at the centre of the world's twenty-first-century olive kingdom, a still life, frozen images, recalled the olive story. Fleeting moments of an ancient tradition, but nothing of its poetry.

*

My first sighting of the Sierra Nevada with its snowcapped peaks that never melted left me longing to share this exquisite moment with Michel. Granada was an indulgence, a present to myself. I was not going to pass through Andalucía without spending at least one day at the Alhambra. A *granada* is a pomegranate and the fruit is the symbol of the city. I suspect that this tree with its startling carmine-red flowers was a Moorish legacy.

My entry through Granada's rush-hour suburbs was unimpressive and I made a last-minute decision not to stay downtown but to go immediately to the hilltop where the Alhambra palace and gardens stood. Alhambra is Al Qal 'a al-Hamra or, rather mundanely in translation, Red Fort, which does not begin to describe its magnificence. I checked into the Alhambra Palace Hotel, too big and too expensive even with a knockdown room rate, but the receptionists were friendly and it was within easy walking distance of the fort, which, as soon as the car was parked and bag dropped, I set out for. I needed no ticket. Entry was not possible at this late hour – booth closed – but I could wander freely about the grounds. I hurried through the Puerta del Vino, which in the sixteenth century (after the expulsion of the Moors) was the entrance to a wine cellar and from there, crossing the Plaza de los Aljibes, I found myself before the walls of the old fortress, the Alcazaba. From its summit, a spectacular view. One of those worth-the-whole-trip moments. I watched the sun go down, the evening's veil falling lightly upon the white city at my feet, lanterns lighting up, dogs howling, women screaming at bawling children, an occasional bottle smashing, down in the extended valley, the *vega*, Granada's vast and fertile plain, much of which has been eaten into now by city sprawl. Views in every direction. In the distance, the snowy caps of the sierras. Their snowmelts fed the three rivers that surrounded Granada, and they watered the groves and the city. A mighty bell on the Torre de la Vela close to where I was leaning had, until recently, been rung at specific hours of the day, sounding far and wide across the outstretched plains. But it had not been calling the faithful to prayer. It bade the labourers begin the watering of the parched red earth. *Al-Hamra* also described the colour of the soil, from which they baked their red bricks.

During the Middle Ages, heavy seasonal rains and the melted snows washed layers of silt on to these plains and it was with this earth that the Moors, renowned for their horticultural and irrigational skills, created fertile valley lands. During the years of struggle between Christians and Muslims, when the Catholic monarchs were fighting to regain Spain, they laid waste to these well-planted plains in an attempt to starve the Arab farmers off their land and deny food supplies to the city of Granada. Many fled; the fields were left untended. It was the beginning of the end for the *vega*. It never regained the same levels of productivity.

Turning my eyes towards the dipping sun, westwards across the *vega*, somewhere lay Fuente Vaqueros, the village where Federico García Lorca, Spain's greatest twentieth-century poet and dramatist, was born to wealthy landowners in 1898. The family had moved to Granada when he was barely a teenager, but his writing was forever imbued with rurality, the earth, the olive trees, the farms of his childhood. Riding with his brother in a mule cart, they had paid visits to Granada, his 'city of dreams'.

I strolled through the open spaces of the fort, views in every direction. Couples passed by, families, too, taking in the evening air, marking the *paseo*. The sky was velvet-grey; it was warm for February. I could hear water running from several directions and, eyes closed, I might have believed that I was in the Levant. I felt enveloped by beauty. The perfumed nights of the Orient. Spain smelled sweet, like every black-haired girl with a fragrant flower nuzzling at her ear. From the day I had arrived over a month earlier, I had been seduced by the country's perfumes, and it was not yet spring. Up here were box bushes and tall spreading bay trees. I walked alone, without fear, relishing the quietude and I felt an immense sense of belonging, of completion. On the other hand, reflecting, I felt helpless at the potential erosion of this earth.

From Lorca's *The Gypsy and the Wind*:

> The sea darkens and roars,
> While the olive trees turn pale.
> The flutes of darkness sound.

★

Returning to the hotel by a shadowed pebble pathway, three adolescent boys approached. I skipped aside to let them pass. One danced
a two-step, veered my way, begged a cigarette. 'I don't smoke.'

His fluffed-skinned face broke into a grin and he bowed a good
evening, '*buenas tardes, señora*'. He must have been ten or eleven.

I had read of the hotel's theatre, designed in neo-Moorish decor,
and was keen to see it. The receptionist, when I made the request,
was more than happy to accompany me to the basement. It was
unoccupied, silent, and she left me to wander without constraint.
The auditorium was intimate, perfect for café theatre. It seated one
hundred and sixty and these days was used for conventions. I stood
on the modest stage with its swept-back, red velvet curtains, its oval
proscenium arch, enjoying the fact that on 7 June 1922, the twenty-
four-year-old Federico García Lorca, not long out of university, who
loved music, particularly gypsy music, as much as poetry and drama,
had participated in an evening of words and song right here. Lorca
had long been a particular favourite of mine. I had first come across
his work, his plays, when I was at drama school in London and we,
as students, had performed (crucified!) *Blood Wedding*. I had known
nothing of olives then or the world of the Mediterranean and I had
absolutely no idea that my future would lie in this direction, but his
words, images, those plays, had embedded themselves deep within
me.

The legendary Spanish guitarist Andrés Segovia, perhaps the father
of modern classical guitar, also an Andalucían, from Linares in Jaén,
had been on the bill that night, too. So successful was the soirée, that
it launched Lorca's career. When the receptionist returned, I asked
her whether she knew anything about that June performance.

'I've never heard of those men,' she answered, 'but loads of famous
people've performed here.'

'Really?'

'We had Engelbert Humperdinck once, and, another time, the
King of Spain.'

Beneath a starlit sky I wound down the hillside from the Anteque
ruella Baja, descending in semi-circles, lost among pretty *ruellas* until,
almost by chance, I found myself at my intended destination, the
Plaza Nueva. Granada, jewel in the Moorish crown and their impene-

trable stronghold, was the last city in Spain to be reconquered by the Catholics when, after a relentless siege throughout the winter of 1491, the Nasrid king, Boabdil – the Nasrids were the last Muslim dynasty to rule southern Spain – accepted defeat and surrendered the keys of the city to the offending armies. Spain's *Reconquista* had, after centuries, finally been accomplished. This square, Plaza Nueva, was built as a memorial to that victory and in order to underline the power of the new Christian rule, a monumental bonfire was lit in the plaza, fed by the entire library of 80,000 books that had lined the walls of the Granada Muslim University.

From the plaza, after a glass of wine, where I was plied with more complimentary *tapas* dishes than I could manage but the waiters could not offer me an explanation for the origin of *tapa*, I strolled aimlessly, surprised by the many English voices in the bars. I ate alone in a *taberna*, strolled some more and eventually got lost again, this time in an insalubrious *barrio* where smashed bottles lay about the cobbles and graffiti and blood smeared the walls. I felt a little afraid, even more so when I picked up pace at the sound of raucous, drunken callings somewhere behind me and found myself running into a cul-de-sac that reeked of stale beer and urine and where weeds the size of healthy shrubs were growing in hillocks of composting debris.

The following day, sunny and warm, this first-time visitor was at the ticket booth before opening. The Alhambra: a bewitchment that I resolved hereon to experience regularly. I was seduced, but so much to take in. I focused on plants, fountains, the cloudless blue sky visible above the *Patio de los Arrayanes*, the call of doves, a neatly clipped balustrade of myrtle bushes, enticing views through arched windows to the cubed white houses of the Albaicín quarter, the original city, and the sublime *Palacios Nazaríes*. I took a break at the Courtyard of the Lion, *el Patio de los Leones*, the heart of the harem's daily life. Disappointingly, the renowned club-faced cats had been removed for restoration, the fountains were dry and the courtyard was no longer planted up with aromatic shrubs and herbs. The American writer and diplomat, Washington Irving, who wrote *Tales of the Alhambra* and was rather a legend in this part of Spain, eulogised this complex. He fantasised about the delicate arm of a hidden princess, beckoning with dark, soulful eyes from behind latticed shutters. Which is all very well, but those women were forcefully cloistered. Nonetheless, the architecture was dazzling. A spot in which to linger out of the heat of high summer, fingers rippling through cool fountain waters. Here, the harem's occupants had idled away their fruitless days, or walked the gallery above, gossiping together, awaiting the call to the boss's bedroom.

Onwards, hiking to the Generalife, an Italianate summer palace with gardens, conceived above terraced orchards on a high platform of land. It was a maze of patios, stairways, balconies, artificial pools, secreted belvederes and blossoming flowers. The concept of 'garden' was a Muslim one. They aspired to create 'gardens', a partnership of plants and water, as a representation of Paradise on earth. Lusty-leafed bushes, delicate, sweetly scented flowers, running streams beneath canopies of tall trees that shaded them from the blistering heat. And this must have seemed like paradise to peoples whose history, whose genes, were born in arid desert lands.

I was still thinking about the picture Dr Mendoza had painted of a world without water, an unproductive earth. It seemed all the more shocking here, amidst such lushness.

Standing atop the *Escalera del Agua*, a curving staircase with water burbling down its stone balustrades, I felt the sun beating on my back. In the distance, snow glistened on the Nevada caps. Out across the *vega* hung a pollution haze the colour of unripened olives. Do the rivers of Granada still flow through the orange and olive groves? How different, if at all, would Andalucía be today, with its critical irrigation issues, if the Moors had not fled? Are we losing vital knowledge, I asked myself.

The city's mongrels were silent, sleeping in the noonday sun. In the background, a melody of languages from other visitors. All about me, water was tinkling, falling, running, swirling. Shafts of soft sunlight fell across the burnished, pre-spring foliage. The scent of juniper wafted heavenwards while feral cats were crouching at the poolsides where large carp swam blithely to and fro, frogs plopped into ponds at the first footstep. The 'gardens' of an enchanted palace.

In the Patio of the Sultan's Wife, *Patio de la Sultana*, I stood beneath a seven-hundred-year-old cypress tree. It bore a plaque, witness to a royal adultery. Adultery, or a harmless flirtation? Beneath the silent branches of this cypress, a junior back then, Zoraya, the sultana, met with her lover, Hamet, until the lovers' trysts became known to the sultan. Entering this walled garden, dedicated to his beloved queen, the sultan discovered his favourite wife in the arms of another. Out was dragged the cuckolding rogue. There and then, Hamet and sixteen princes of his clan were condemned to death. Legend has it that the fountain in the *Sala de los Abencerrajes*, where the men were slain, has been eternally stained with their blood. Or perhaps it was rust. I descended to the Christian palace of Carlos V, watched my second Granadian sunset and bid *adios* to the heights of the Alhambra.

Down among Moorish houses and mansions, the pretty narrow streets of the Albaicín district, the historic Arab quarter where the city of Granada was born, today a UNESCO World Heritage Site, I learned an interesting detail from Gian-Carlo, a striking, black-haired Sicilian gardener I struck up conversation with in a bar. A *'carmen'* was originally a vine or vineyard. In traditional Andalucían houses, it became the enclosed, vine-bowered courtyard. The *carmens* were spring, autumn, late evening retreats. There, nightingales sang, perfumes reeked, vines were fecund with fruit. And when the sun declined, taking with it the blistering temperatures, and one by one the stars appeared, the neighbouring locals took up their guitars. All around the streets of the old city quarter, music played and folk in their *carmens* tuned in to the gypsies. I had hoped to hear the flamencos echoing round the alleys but on this evening they were silent. The roar of motorbikes, yes, but no guitars, no nightingales, only sparrows.

Víznar was but a short drive from Granada, ten kilometres to the north-east. I asked directions of the rubicund porter. Up to that point he had been friendly, but I had the distinct impression that the very mention of Víznar caused a shift in his mood.

In 1928, Federico García Lorca had written a series of poems, today fabulously set to music, *El Romancero de Gitano*, his anthology of gypsy ballads. These had brought him international renown and a trip to New York. Returning in 1931, he set up his own travelling theatre company, Teatro Barraca, and began to write his greatest theatrical material. Masterpieces, plays that rung with gypsy folklore and, most poignantly, the plight of women in rural societies, repressed sexually and emotionally, constrained by Church and family. Those early years of the thirties were a rich and fertile period for Spain: the advent of the republic. Attitudes were changing fast, almost daily. The monarchy was down and it looked as though, after centuries, the stranglehold of the Church and the heavy conservatism that had for so long been associated with this country, including the feudalism of absentee landlords and dynastic farming families, were finally to be cast aside.

That was until July 1936, when, in Lorca's own words, the 'flutes of darkness' sounded.

Federico slipped home to spend the summer with friends and family in Granada. Tragically, it coincided with Franco's arrival on 16 July from the Canary Islands via Spanish Morocco. Franco's military uprising against the democratically elected left-wing government, the Popular Front, was under way. The future dictator with his army of Berbers landed in the south and moved north, taking the country as they progressed. It was no time at all before Granada, one of the first cities to fall, was besieged and the Falangists, Franco's fascist party, took control. Executions were under way. Gangs, thugs, death squads, *las escuadras negras*, sought out their enemies and gunned them down in cold blood. Lorca was a public figure, a charismatic young man in his late thirties. He was an outspoken Republican sympathiser and he was a practising homosexual who spent his life performing with his theatre for the peasantry who loved his works, frequenting ports and hanging out with gypsies. In short, a radical leftist homosexual and enemy of the conservative state.

'Homosexuals will be killed like dogs,' General Quiepo de Llano, one of the voices of the Falangists, had promised. He was true to his word.

Granada, August 1936; Lorca was dragged from the home of the poet, Luis Rosales, where he had gone into hiding (the house is now the Hotel Reina Cristina). The precise details of all that happened over the next couple of days, before his execution, are obscure. Some accounts say that he was thrown into the back of a lorry where he was handcuffed to another political prisoner and carted away to jail. Others say that he was driven off in the car of a local Falangist sympathiser. Wherever he was detained, two days later, at dawn on the morning of 19 August, he was taken to the outskirts of Víznar, at the foot of a ravine – so evocative of his own poetry – where a lone olive tree stood. He was in the company of three others, all declared enemies of the fascist regime. The executions were carried out by a Falangist death squad. One of the assassins later boasted that he had shot Lorca, as he clung to that olive tree, 'twice in the arse for being a poof'.

Lorca died beneath that olive tree. What became of his body has been the subject of speculation for generations. Some argue that he was tossed into a mass grave at Barranco de Víznar. Others suspect that his family, who refuse to give consent for the exhumation of that grave, dug up their hero and buried him privately on their estate. At the end of the civil war in 1939 Spain was littered with unmarked graves. The Falangists never admitted to Lorca's murder. A news item stated that his body had been discovered on the road between Víznar and Alfacar and that he had died of 'war wounds'. Franco banned Lorca's work. Wherever his bones lie today, Lorca's murder remains an inglorious stain on modern Spanish history.

A fellow poet and friend of Lorca's, Jorge Guillen, wrote that when Lorca was close, the weather was neither hot nor cold; rather, it was 'Federico weather'.

I felt those rays. It was mid-February yet an inviting, blessed day. I found Víznar without difficulty, set high within olive groves and natural sierra parkland. Víznar, originally a small village, a *pueblo blanco*, where a sprawl of rather bland, uniformed white habitations had recently been constructed. No sign led a visitor to the Parque Federico García Lorca. Within the town, I drove hilly streets looking for a bar or a passing individual, a shop, a mechanic or labourer at work, but the entire village was closed up. I checked my watch. It was not a weekend and not yet midday, so, puzzling. I circled streets twice, passed through a central square with the principal church in one corner, but still not a soul. It was as though the villagers had sealed themselves away. Were the inhabitants bored with Lorca pilgrims? Was this a score in Víznar history that they were tired of being associated with? After making the circuit once more, passing through horseshoe arches, descending streets that were more suitable for mules, I returned to the central plaza and stepped out of the car. A post office ahead, closed, but no bar, no meeting point other than the church whose doors were locked. The air was clear, sharp, cooler at this altitude. I wandered until eventually a solitary figure in brown trousers, check shirt, cap, approached, climbing from the direction I had first covered. Under his arm, two sticks of bread. I crossed and asked the route to the Memorial Park. No flicker of warmth enlivened his expression, as though he resented my question, my presence here.

'It's not here,' he replied.

'But this is Víznar?'

'It's not close to the village,' he muttered.

For a moment, I felt sympathy. I was about to ask if he knew anyone who had been alive in 1936, who remembered that day, that dawn, over seventy years ago, but he had already continued on his way.

I proceeded out of town along the narrow, winding descents, ascents of the white-walled *ruellas*. I drew up beside a woman carrying baskets. She confirmed that I was on the right road. 'But,' she warned, 'there are many bends, curves, *mas* climbing. It will not be easy.' She had spoken the word *mas*, much, in English.

Beyond the village, I pulled over, taking photographs of the hilltop settlement beneath which terraced groves of olives and blossoming almonds sloped down the mountainside. I climbed up and down dried gulleys where dead leaves lay rustling, ravines that were fed by the snows of the Sierra Nevada, looking for solitary olive trees, hoping for a clue. I had a photocopied print in my wallet that I had found on the Internet of a spiralling olive that was captioned 'Close to this tree lie the remains of Lorca'. Judging from the photograph, it hardly looked old enough to have borne witness to that bloody sunrise. In any case, I found no olive that resembled it.

Spiralling ever higher, I peered out for a signpost, but the road remained unmarked. Eventually, the park. I pulled over. In front of me was a flank of several three- and four-storey blocks of flats and another under construction. After a completely empty road with not a ruin or shepherd's cote to dot the horizon, these constructions had been thrown up directly in front of the Federico García Lorca Memorial Park. I wondered at the permit that had allowed it. The grounds themselves were massively disappointing: a concrete, melancholy affair, lacking flowers, where the overriding impression was one of neglect. At its centre was a fountain, bleak, silent, without water. The dry channels that were fed from its base were blocked with poplar leaves, rotting, forgotten since months. A granite stone marked the spot that is purported to be where Lorca's assassination took place. There were no olive trees, solitary or otherwise. It stood above the olive groves, curtained by pines climbing the high altitude hillsides. Beyond Lorca territory.

Seventy years and six months after his murder, I walked alone in this place, pacing from one memorial plaque to the next, reading the words of the man who perhaps captured the hearts and confusions of the olive-farming southerners of Spain better than anyone before or since. But this park was not Lorca's; it was honouring all those who had lost their lives during the civil war. And Lorca would have wanted it so. He was a brother, a son of Spain.

I drew out a scruffy page I had printed off. Dark hair, lightly slicked, parted to the side, Lorca in evening dress resembled a young Dirk Bogarde in Hollywood. Then, from the same wallet, words I read aloud to the stark hills with the wind gusting against the broom and the leafless poplar trees. These lines were written by Lorca himself, the last stanza of a poem entitled *Lament for Ignacio Sanchez Mejias*. With them, Federico might have been writing his own eulogy. I wanted him and the soft silvery light through the distant olive trees which, from where I was standing were partially blocked out, to have the last word on his death because the reassuring fact is that Lorca's voice lives on. No bullet or censor could have silenced him.

> *It will be a long time, if ever, before there is born*
> *An Andalucian so true, so rich in adventure.*
> *I sing of his elegance with words that groan,*
> *And I remember a sad breeze through the olive trees.*

★

I felt a need for open spaces. The route to Almería cut through a vast, arid, bouldered landscape. I stopped the car on several occasions to take in the rocky scenery, to breathe. My destination was the Mediterranean coast. It had been a while since I had seen the sea. Although today Almería was not renowned for its olives, it was a chunk of land that had been tramped over by almost every trader, coloniser and pirate. Cartagena had originally been the Phoenician Qart Hadast. Yet to look at the landscape, you could believe that no man had ever made it to this part of Spain. Here was spaghetti western territory, dry desert lands with not a habitation to break the isolation.

I made a brief sandwich stop in Guadix, east of Granada, fretted with caves and coated in a film of red dust. Harsh central plains, opulent mining districts. Guadix is believed to have seen ancient settlements as far back as Palaeolithic (Stone Age) times. Thousands of years later, in 45 BC, Julius Caesar set up camp, calling it Julia Gemella Acci, to mine the silver in the surrounding hillsides. Later, the Moors settled and built a town that almost rivalled Granada. It was they who renamed it Guadh-Haix, or River of Life. I took a brief walk by the river where they had planted lines of mulberry trees from which grew up a vibrant silk industry. I was surprised to find the caves still inhabited. Many had been transformed into stalls selling pottery and brightly coloured ceramics to tourists. Others ranged from hovels to curious little whitewashed houses. Even today, these homes changed hands by verbal contracts only, nothing in writing; its community stood witness to all verbal agreements. The town had suffered greatly during the civil war and both Republicans and Nationalists had left reminders of their grisly work.

Gently descending in a south-easterly direction, I drove through irrigated desert zones; undulating expanses of green, of vineyards farmed along lower reaches of the Sierra Nevada. The almonds were in full blossom, in fields shared by silvery olives. Exquisite against the rich red sandstone of the snow-capped Nevadas.

By the time I was skirting Almería, night had fallen. I took the exit for the country town of Pechina. A Peruvian barman back in Córdoba had recommended a converted monastery somewhere nearby. I asked directions of a man in his garden. The request amused him.

'Cross the motorway, follow the corkscrew road. Be warned it's steep and there are no street lights.'

Blasted into the mountainside, the ascent proved nerve-racking. I almost turned back, but it was late. I was tired, hungry. The end of the road, quite literally, delivered a village with unrivalled views to the distant Mediterranean. I saw little of the surroundings that evening. The monastery, or bishop's palace, had been converted into a spa, a *balneario*. I found myself at the reception of an eighteenth-century, two-storey building, constructed on the ruins of a Moorish and, prior to that, Roman bathhouse. The original marble baths in the basement were still in use. I secured the last room, a refurbished monk's cell in a medieval setting. The cells abutted the upper gallery. Beneath was a central courtyard with furniture of sorts and a caged, yellow-crested bird. At an altitude of 461 metres it was cold, wintry, but the room had heating and hot water. It was basic but, apart from the screeching cockatoo, tranquil.

The dining room, a converted chapel of pseudo-Moorish design with tiles to shoulder height and cream arabesque patterns above, was dedicated to house guests. The woman who had welcomed me at reception, broad of beam and world-weary, had donned an apron and was now the waitress, or chef, or both. At the table opposite, an elderly Englishman in the company of a small boy and a young woman who was asleep on his shoulder. His Oxbridge accent reverberated round the high vaulted spaces and dominated the room.

'Holidays in France,' the old man opined, 'were always so much better.'

'Why was that, Gramps?'

'The food, dear boy, the food.'

Three other tables were occupied by *Andaluzes*, staying for the weekend to take the waters. After dinner I took a stroll round the village, which consisted of a cluster of houses and one bar. I dropped in for a glass, out of curiosity rather than thirst, and found the family at table: beshawled grandmother, husband, wife, teenage boy who suffered from some physical affliction, eating dinner in front of a blaring TV perched high behind the drinks counter. Apart from myself, there were no other customers and my entry was greeted with bewilderment.

'Are you open?'

All adults nodded and the father, purple nose as big as a courgette, wearing a brown trilby, rose. I ordered a glass of wine and took a swig, wishing them *buen apetito*. They watched me, calibrating, scouring my features as though I had come from another planet. Specks of sand-grit freckled the counter. The wine was bitter, corked. Out of politeness I drank what I could, left a few euros and bade them goodnight. Outside, a handful of stick-legged boys were kicking a football about beneath a street lamp. Dogs barked, a cat was ripping black rubbish bags to shreds, spreading orange skins and empty fish tins across the street. Behind the hotel was a sprawling, half-constructed oriental-styled building, abandoned. In front, a few palm trees and a line of camping cars and caravans with predominantly German number plates. That was it.

The hot springs of Sierra Alhamilla, thermal and curative, were discovered by the Phoenicians, or possibly considerably earlier, and then later by the Romans who constructed the underground marble baths. In 711 came the Moors who irrigated the Valley of Andarax that lay at the feet of the village, southwards to the sea. Here, they planted up oases of palm trees, the vestiges of which I found when walking later. I also found cave dwellings. A few had been fixed up with doors. They did not appear to be inhabited now. No one could tell me who had occupied them. In *South from Granada*, Gerald Brenan asked himself whether Odysseus might not have sheltered in certain of the Andalucían caves during his long and weary travels. Who knows? This corner of Spain had been inhabited for millennia. Personally, I had a hunch that the Minoans, those mythical bull- and olive-worshipping, peace-loving people from Crete, brought the olive tree here, but there is no proof of that. Or the Mycenaeans (neighbours of Odysseus), who took the lovely island between mainland Greece and Africa from the Minoans: might they have sailed with silvery saplings this far west? Might Odysseus have returned home and talked of this unique place?

During weekends, Andalucíans flocked here to refuel, fill plastic bottles and containers from the springs that flowed at a consistent 58 degrees Celsius and at the rate of 603 litres per minute. The few residents hereabouts also used it for washing their laundry. The Germans and other travellers seemed to be taking advantage of it for everything: tea, laundry, washing, open-air showers ... When the queue at the village well, *fuente*, had lessened, I put my hand to the volcanic waters rushing forth and found that they were indeed boiling hot. The morning was fine with a light wind and barely a cloud hanging over the sea. The location, fifteen kilometres outside the city of Almería, marked the entrance to a vast and natural, protected mountain range, the Sierra de Alhamilla Park: 8500 hectares of sparsely populated, high-peak slopelands. Really magnificent, dramatic and undiscovered. The couple at the hotel told me later that only fifty permanent residents, including themselves, lived within the park environs.

I was hunting for botanical footprints, Roman ruins or, even better, Phoenician, and found many skeletons of buildings, tumbledown terraces, drystone like ours, that would originally have been for olive and almond orchards. Sad-looking, wrung-out palms were clinging to life in among the *garrigue*, and a few stunted wild olives, *acebuche* to the Spanish, barely bigger than gooseberry bushes. Cacti survived alongside flowering thyme, clumps of other aromatic herbs and rubble. Evidently, there had been high-level agricultural activity here at stages throughout history. I wondered about the mountainside's magic waters. Had this always been desert territory? Or was this an example of soil erosion? I pictured a future world in which we travelled for miles with plastic containers to queue for water.

Intermittent blasts throughout the morning were accompanied by columns of black smoke rising from beyond the wrinkled folds of hills. It was an army base east of Almería at Viator. I stepped off the winding tarmacked path and began to hike up a mule track where, after a kilometre or two, I came upon a chain with swinging sign attached to two green pillars. It read: *FINCA PARTICULAR, PRO-HIBIDO EL PASO*. PRIVATE FARM NO ENTRY. In smaller lettering in Spanish: *Boundary patrolled by rural guards. Private lands. Authorised vehicles only.* Nothing prevented access either side of the pillars so I kept going, continuing on a few metres until I was barred by a locked iron gate. I hesitated, looked about into dusty emptiness, and then climbed over it. Ascending mountain curves, I found myself within the grounds of a secreted olive farm. I proceeded slowly up a winding sand track, fully aware that I was trespassing. 'If someone encroached like this at our place . . .' I was thinking, but as unexpected discoveries go this was too good to ignore. The olive trees were irrigated with ground pipes fed from crudely fenced-in water sources. They were in extremely good health and possibly several decades old. The earth at the feet of the trees was dry and crumbly, off-white like limestone. There was no one about so I continued on up to the first house, the original property. It was a decaying white cube, a typical southern Mediterranean home with a painted green door, surrounded by cacti and agave plants and a leafless fig tree. To one side was a terrace with an overhanging wooden trellis where a vine must have grown. It was abandoned but attractive, a romantic idyll of rural Spain. Fifty yards higher, past crumbling stone outhouses, was the present home, a modern incarnation of the original. I turned to look back down the mountainside and was stunned by the view. It swept right across the Valley of Andarax to the sea. On either side rose the rust-brown, grey and purple folds of the hills, southern sierras, falling away to the Mediterranean. And what silence in this Almerían olive grove. I was curious as to why the property was so heavily guarded. There seemed to be nothing of immense value here, unless ... yes, the water.

Over a quick bite at the hotel I learned from an impoverished looking waiter that water was the source of more acrimony hereabouts than anything else and that not far from this village a man had killed his own brother because the fellow had rerouted, or cut off, the natural direction of a spring. I set off again, descending a steep gradient into the valley, following the flow of the springs, the path alongside which the Moors had created their irrigation channels, their *acequias* (*as-saquiya* in Arabic, water carrier), and installed their palm groves, many of which were still in existence, if rather scrappily. Olive groves had been planted, far more recently, across a canyon-like shelf of land with an oriental Saharan-scape. Originally, the water had traced a gulley south to the flat plains, the *vega* inland of the sea. But there had been so much strife between families and neighbours over the rights that, today, a municipal body managed the flows. Each household or holding was entitled to water for a designated number of days per month, anything from one to two or perhaps even five. The monastery, now spa resort, had negotiated thirteen days. Their triumph had caused fury within the village and its environs.

I met a farmer in the valley who told me '*muchos, mas historias,* many stories. But families won't breathe a word. People are secretive. Yes, two brothers fought. A shot rang out, one killed the other.'

'Why?'

'This is the driest spot in Europe. Who can survive without water? Water's worth more than gold here. Without it, no livelihood.'

I scanned the horizon. Everywhere was dusty, grey-soiled, volcanic. Holdings with their own source-fed water displayed signs, NO TRESPASSING, in bold lettering. Where water reached, vigorous olive plantations sprouted. They were frequently at the heart of the ancient palm groves and were dwarfed by the lofty date trees. Olives require less irrigation than most crops so their cultivation made sense. But I had yet to discover the additional benefits of olives as the plantation of choice. That was still to come.

Another fellow, walking a golden retriever, crossed our path and joined in the conversation. He had worked most of his life as a 'chief mining technician' for a French company in Nouvelle-Calédonie, New Caledonia, in the Pacific. Originally from a fishing village along the coast not fifty kilometres west of here, Roquetas de Mar, he had settled here after retirement because his birthplace was *'pourri'*, rotten.

He spoke excellent French. I asked him about the water wars.

'I don't know details about the murder, but the conflicts between villagers were *"mucho profondo"*.' They ran deep.

The farmer, now seated on a sawn-off palm trunk, recounted how several families had requested permission to run their water pipes beneath the hotel but the proprietors, the Don and Doña, who had renovated the monastery, had refused. 'Those were unhappy times. Bad days.'

But all had been resolved.

'Do you work for a newspaper?' he asked suddenly.

I assured him that I did not.

The retiree was bemoaning the destruction of his seaside home-land. Tourism and forced vegetable production. He confessed that he would never have returned to Spain at all had it not been for the earnest requests of his wife. I am not of the *tierra*, he said, not a man of the soil. I am here for my family, living in this 'remote dog's kennel'. While he was talking I was making a silent guess at his age and decided early seventies. He would have been a boy when the civil war took place. Almería had been almost the last city to fall to Franco. It was staunchly Communist. The shipyard workers down in the port had fought hard, held out to the bitter end. Many committed suicide when the region finally fell. They had preferred to die than face the consequences of dictatorship. The city had been shelled by the German navy, too. The damage had been less extensive than the air raids on Gernika, but it had left its scars. I was curious about this man with his dog, a quartet of warts round one eye and a long, baggy face, about his past. What age had he been when he had quit Spain? He had spent years working in North Africa, employed by a French company mining nickel. Had he fled from the hands of the Falangists?

'No one tells you anything; everyone will feed you a different story. The past weighs too heavily on their shoes. All you'll hear is that it has been sorted,' he said.

I took a trip to Almería. Looking seawards from my distant hotel, I had thought that I had seen pools of water, reservoirs glistening in the valley sunlight. In fact, this was my introduction to *plasticultura*. What I had been gazing upon were *invernaderos*, elongated plastic greenhouses. The extensive forced farming of fruits and vegetables, exported widely across Europe, had changed the fortunes of this region after the deprivations of the war.

The port city of Almería had been christened Portus Magnus by the Romans, but later the Moors had given it a far more poetic designation, Al-meriya or Al-mariyat, Mirror of the Sea. The city sits at the water's edge dominated from on high by the *Alcazaba*, fortress, built by the Moors in the tenth century. It was during the Omeya dynasty that this harbour saw its greatest days, both as a military base and as an outlet for its silk products. During those medieval centuries there were, incredibly, over 10,000 textile mills within the city. Fed by the area's mulberry farms, they were manufacturing silk, damask, velvet and brocade. The city fell to the Catholics in 1489. Later, when the Catholics had taken control of all Spain and the Moriscos had fled, the farms fell into decline and this coast became a hunting ground for Berber pirates who infested these waters (as well as other western shores of the Med), pilfering, smuggling, raiding, causing dread within the inhabitants' hearts. Not until the late nineteenth century, when a new harbour and a railway were constructed and the area's long-renowned mineral wealth was once again mined, did opportunities revive. Both the British and the Belgians invested considerable sums and the city found itself back on the trading map.

I descended from my outlying retreat into the city by the Avenida Federico García Lorca directly to the docks where ships awaited departure to Morocco and Algeria. Six hours to Melilla. I walked up and down the waterfront. It was a windy afternoon. The portside palms were agitated, fronds clacking like castanets. The air reeked of brine and diesel and greasy hamburgers from a nearby takeaway. A few scruffy Arabs in lamb's wool hats, creased jackets with too-short arms, carrying cardboard cases exited the lonely shipyards. Others were hanging about smoking, awaiting the next embarkation. I could have crossed to Africa from here, but I was not ready to leave. I wanted to travel west, follow the Mediterranean and onwards to the Atlantic Ocean, passing by the more northerly of the two Pillars of Hercules (Gibraltar) until I reached Cádiz and neighbouring it, the mouth of the Guadalquivir River, in search of the long-lost city of silver. I was not done with Spain just yet.

Praise of Almería is not frequently sung nor is the city so regularly visited, but I loved it: the starkness, the dusty, remote situation, its rose-tinted sierras reflecting the setting sun. Perched at the western end of the Mediterranean, it was a country with its own self-contained personality. I spent two days tramping portside streets, peering into *bodegas*, staring into faces of men, old as Christendom, holding up counters, trying to divine their pasts. I chanced upon a small hotel where, they claimed, Clint Eastwood had stayed whilst shooting *The Good, the Bad and the Ugly*. On the walls in the bar were snaps, stills, of Eli Wallach and Charles Bronson. I ate lunch at a corner restaurant, no bigger than a dog's mat, in the old town. Aside from mine, there were three tables. One occupied by a family of ten attacking a Sunday meal. Another contained four old codgers seated beneath the television, volume high, watching a football match. Among the players, the Englishman David Beckham for Real Madrid. The four-course set menu was nine euros; change from six pounds. During the meal there was a power cut. It troubled no one. The door was pulled ajar, to let a little light in, but it slapped back and forth in the wind, so was closed again. Darkness was preferable. No candles were delivered, but more wine was poured. People cried, shouted, laughed and banged the tables as though it was Christmas or bingo night. Only the youngsters were glumly silent. Pedro, the proprietor, a brawny fellow with a worryingly ledge-like paunch and limp, intimate friends with everyone except me, sat with each party and drank a glass, smoked a cigarette while his robust, perspiring wife, when not bill accounting, poured drinks or fought with the dead coffee machine and yelled orders into the kitchen. From one table to the next gossip was exchanged, news transmitted. They all appeared to know one another. Several of the aubergine or blood-vesselled faces were as ancient and creased as the surrounding mountains. I wondered what they had fought through together. Their camaraderie seemed tight-knit, but who could tell? I was an outsider. Mostly, I enjoyed the independence and anonymity this role provided but here I would have welcomed a ferryman to guide me to the memory banks of recollection, secrets, history. The door opened and a man in stained overcoat and bedroom slippers entered. Round the tables he paraded, shook hands with several but took no seat. From the far corner, a woman began to sneeze. Loudly, non-stop, until a man called for candles, *por favor*, to calm the woman's noise. The slippered fellow flounced out as though in a huff, leaving the door to slap in the wind. Candles were delivered. The woman fell silent.

My entrée was a substantial plate of paella. It was a meal in itself and obliged me to refuse the next dish. The diners took this in. Eyebrows were raised in my direction, mouths fell open. The notion that I would eat no more became a general concern.

'Is there a problem with the food, *señora*?'

I shook my head. Embarrassed, I swiftly reconsidered my order and ploughed on through fish, lamb and crème caramel coated with piped artificial cream.

'Nothing of Spain remains along this southern coast,' the retired miner had bemoaned. Sitting in this *rincon taberna*, I would have disagreed. Here was the Spain of people, noisy, ebullient, in each other's lives, and fierce in their convictions.

Although the city was enjoying Sunday siesta hour and the streets were deserted, I decided to walk northwards from the southern end of Avenida Federico García Lorca, the city's widest and most prestigious thoroughfare, originally a *ramla*. Lorca had spent time here as a child, had become a local hero to the workers and dockers and had frequented the bars down by the port. His 1932 play *Bodas de Sangre* – *Blood Wedding* – had been inspired by a real-life incident, a rural tale of buried passions, a tragedy of elopement, jealousy and murder that had taken place in Nijar, one of the inland towns of the Sierra de Alhamilla. Lorca had read of the events in a local newspaper and had followed their outcome assiduously.

Along my way I noticed a few teenage girls huddled round a statue, pawing it with a kind of awe and posing alongside it, taking one another's photographs, giggling skittishly. As I approached, they disappeared, abandoning the seated bronze figure of a young bespectacled man with one leg tucked beneath the other. Resting on his thigh was his guitar. It was clearly not Lorca or a gypsy guitarist though flamenco was popular hereabouts and had been sung in the local mines. Nor could it have been Laurie Lee, the English writer who fought for the Republicans during the civil war. The image, in army fatigues and boots, was too modern and in any case Lee played fiddle not guitar. While I was puzzling over its identity, with its serious, contemplative expression, other girls, a nubile pair, stopped and stroked his head. 'Who is this?' I asked, but they just grinned and ran off. The next passer-by, a student, also paused to admire the work. I enquired again.

'John Lennon, Los Beatles.'

I stared at the artwork. Yes, it was Lennon though I would not have guessed it. In 1966, he spent six weeks filming in the desert outside Almería, and had lived in a small apartment on the El Zapillo beach at *El Delfín Verde*, the Green Dolphin. Later, he had moved to a villa in town where he celebrated his twenty-sixth birthday. Ringo had flown over for the festivities. Lennon's first wife, Cynthia, had accompanied him throughout the shoot. Their Rolls had broken down and they had been obliged to travel to the set by taxi. He was photographed on several occasions sucking a Spanish lollipop (the Spanish claim to have invented the lollipop) ... So much delicious local trivia. But the greatest tidbit of all was that John had begun writing 'Strawberry Fields Forever' here, possibly my all-time favourite Los Beatles song. I thanked the young chap for the information and continued on my way.

I was growing attached to this corner of Spain, its off-the-map, abraded sand plains. Despite brother kills brother, bride elopes causing bloodshed on wedding day, I felt a united resistance here, a gut ambiance I had not felt since Catalonia.

Still, it was difficult to understand why a barren and agriculturally unproductive region at the far reaches of the Mediterranean should have been of interest to the eastern travellers of prehistory. The action in BC Med was elsewhere, until it was discovered that there were minerals in these hills. But I was still puzzling as to why the riches of this southern coast were allowed to leave. When the Phoenicians anchored their long-oared galleys to found the city of Cartagena, north of here, and Almería became a port and trading post, a necessary stopover on their way to Cádiz, before their forays out into the Atlantic Ocean, turning right for Portugal and left or south to Essaouira, what was it that they offered the Iberian peoples in return for those precious metals? They brought their own glassware from the Middle East, peacock feathers from Libya, but such goods were surely not the hook? The quantities of precious metals lifted from this coast, from Almería to Cádiz, were so substantial that the financial gains must have assisted greatly in the construction of Carthage. Unlike the Romans who came after them, the Phoenicians did not conquer, they did business. The indigenous peoples interacted with them. So what was the exchange? I did not have answers but was hoping that Cádiz or its neighbouring, long-lost silver city of Tartessus might furnish me with clues.

Towards the Pillars of Hercules

Leaving the spa, searching for petrol, I took the motorway turn-off in the wrong direction and found myself somewhere near Tabernas, mini-Hollywood. Here, with its stark red deserts, was where those classic spaghetti westerns of Sergio Leone were shot, *Lawrence of Arabia*, too, and *Patton*. Not forgetting Dick Lester's *How I Won the War* starring local hero John Lennon. What was surprising to me was that they were all filmed during the Franco years.

As I sped back down towards the seafront west of Almería, I spied gullies overgrown with blossoming almonds, thick-skinned succulents, prickly and sappy cacti. They were almost the last living plants I saw for a stretch. Travelling the coast road, something I had avoided since arriving in Spain, I found myself enmeshed within the worlds of *plasticultura*, industry and tourism. I understood the comment made by the man walking his retriever up near the spa: 'rotten'. It was hard to describe the ghastliness, the neutering of the landscape, the damage. South of Sierra Nevada was Sierra de Gádor, backdrop to this ugliness. Lovely, purple mountains at the feet of which climbed the plastic greenhouses, rising like a plague of shiny, inflated slugs. This small coastal plain was the Campo de Dalias. Once upon a time, it had been sand dunes and salt flats, but no longer. Today, it was 20,000 hectares of plastic longhouses within which were growing 'early season' flowers and vegetables. From these lower ranges, the greenhouses swept down to the water's edge, thus destroying beaches and shorelines, obliterating earth and ground. A few coastal lagoons supposedly still existed, but I could not find them.

Tempranera agricultura (out-of-season agriculture) was bringing in an income of close to 1.5 billion euros and its effect on the local economy had been phenomenal. Today, there were *plasticultura* millionaires with their own yachts moored off a coastline that was no longer visible. In an area that had been gravely depressed during the civil war the locals' success should be applauded, but the problem was water and it was acute. The annual rainfall here was about 200 millimetres: next to nothing. To irrigate such a vast expanse of unseasonable growth, the farmers were drip-feeding the crops with water sourced from artesian wells (man-made springs from which water flows by its own natural pressure, without pumping). Unfortunately, the demand had grown to such a degree that the agriculturalists were sinking deeper beneath the soil to underground resources, but these, too, were being sucked dry; nothing left in reserve, nothing restored. Scientists' warnings had been heeded by the government and they had made attempts to divert water from the northern Río Ebro, but this had met with such outcries that the plan had been shelved. It seemed that hope now lay in a massive desalination plant that had been purchased by local fruit and vegetable producing enterprises. I recalled once more the haunting words of Dr Mendoza.

Such an eyesore was the coastline that I decided to make a detour, to cut off the road just east of Adra and choose an inland route. I slipped *Spanish Night*, conducted by Plácido Domingo, into the CD deck and tracked up into the lower regions of the Alpujarras, zigzagging back and forth, but I wasn't much more excited by this landscape either. I drove through one village where the main street was walled on either side by the endless plastic sheds and it felt as though I had entered a perpetual tunnel. Yet, beyond, in the sunlit hillsides where few greenhouses had been installed, where the settlements were barely bigger than hamlets, or lone farms, where traditional methods were alive and kicking, the countryside was lovely and tinged pink with flowering almonds.

I realised that my romanticism was at odds with the short-term financial advantages *plasticultura* or super-intensive olive farming had given back to post-dictatorship Spanish communities. Still, a larger, more global picture was emerging. I was beginning to glimpse it and to understand that my battle back at the olive farm to run our insignificant holding without pesticides had far deeper implications than I had really envisaged. What happens when the waters run dry or when pesticides have poisoned the rivers and groundwaters?

Not an apocalyptic scenario likely to come to pass during my lifetime perhaps, but even if I don't have children of my own to inherit this earth, Michel has and those girls, Vanessa and Clarisse, also have offspring. Future generations. The children of our children.

Still aiming to reach Cádiz before nightfall, I was losing time and decided to return to the sea, but I had looped backwards and forwards to such a degree that when I hit the coast I found myself back at Adra, an uninspiring industrialised port, shot with smoking columns, grey docks and tar-black cargo ships. I drove directly through, acknowledging, though, that it had a fascinating ancient history. The Phoenicians had left their mark here, having founded a major fish-salting business and a factory for garum. For both, they would have required gallons of olive oil. Before too long I was passing Albuñol, known for its almonds and wine-farming. The Phoenicians here, too, it would have been who introduced vines to this coast. Palestinian wine was lauded in the centuries before Christ. I recalled the waitress from Empúries and her mention of the *arbequina* olive, imported from the Holy Land during the eighteenth century. A story about which I had failed to find any trace.

I got snarled up behind transport lorries and my progress was laborious. I cut inland again when the coast road grew too depressing, but lost my way hopelessly on secondary routes. I had hoped to make at least a brief stop in Málaga – it boasts an eminent olive-oil past and much of its produce today is deemed fine, a guest at the spa had informed me – but my schedule was tight now. Mardi Gras was only a day away. If I was intending to stick to my goal I needed to keep moving. Torremolinos was stupefying; I had never encountered such construction. A Hellopolis! Much of these major tourist spots, built by or for holidaymakers from the north, stand on olive and almond orchards, dating back to Roman if not Phoenician times. As the 'hungry years' drew to a close, local farmers and fishermen were grateful to sell their holdings at any price, to any bidder, foreigner or otherwise. And for those who had olive farms close to the sea, a new door was opening: tourism. At that time, olive oil was not fashionable, not remunerative. Spain's future, the quick peseta, the opportunity to interact with easy-living foreigners after years of oppression, lay in massive deforestation, in construction, *Benidormisation*.

After Marbella, once through the high-life resorts the mountains grew green again. Nature! It was a relief to spot herds of grazing goats on the hillsides. After the Costa del Golf, another Costa of Construction, my first sighting of Gibraltar looming large and, from such a distance, resembling a camel's saddle. Above it, floating like a displaced flag, was a narrow plume of smoke.

I stopped for coffee and a sandwich at a roadside shack east of Algeciras and overheard a plumpish woman, rouged cheeks, with Liverpudlian accent talking to a pensioner, her father perhaps, and a small boy as they tucked into chips, prawn salads and beer: 'When I git me own house, I'm gonna buy a bottle of olive oil and put it in it.'

Tarifa: the southernmost point of Spain and continental Europe. Tarifa: the first port in history to levy charges against boat owners for the use of the docks, and possibly the origin of the word 'tariff'. West of the city, I stepped out of the car to inhale the fresh, briny air coming in from across the Gibraltar Strait, aqueous gateway to Morocco, where I was heading in just a few days' time. There were a few wet-suited bodies on boards bobbing in the rollers; gulls were circling in the warm sunlight, gannets scavenging. I had reached the Atlantic once more. From Altamira with its prehistoric artists, weeks ago now, to Tarifa on the Costa de la Luz, the Coast of Light, this wilder expanse of sea, on my way to unearth secrets of a fabled silver city.

Hereon after the coast was less constructed, the resorts, bungalow homes, seasonal rents were inhabited by surfers and a hardier, saltier tourist. The wind was blowing in off the water, swirling the sand into whorls, bending and twisting the untamed vegetation with its force. This was the Levanter. It had transported the galleys of 3000 years ago, perhaps even earlier, from the eastern shores of the Mediterranean through the two Pillars of Hercules (Gibraltar and Ceuta in Morocco) to an Iberian river people rich in untold mineral wealth. It had considerable influence, often blowing hard for days along this Cádiz shoreline, creating an almost persistent cloud over the Rock of Gibraltar. For a brief spell in the 1680s the diarist Samuel Pepys had been Commissioner of Tangier. He described the Levanter as being so forceful that it bored holes in the stones of the fortress walls. It was known to be a twister.

Cádiz, where the inhabitants call themselves *gaditanos*, claims to be the oldest continually inhabited city in Europe. It was founded by early sea-going Phoenicians from Tyre, a port city in southern Lebanon, in 1100 BC. Hungry for the local metals, they founded their settlement on a small island that is separated from the mainland by an intermediate island, Isla de León, and they named it Gadir, 'fortress' or 'walled stronghold'. Interestingly, I learned later in Morocco that *agadir* means 'wall' in Berber languages. Agadir, Morocco.

Located at the mouth of the Guadalete River, near the entrance to the mighty Guadalquivir River valley and the ancient city of Tartessus, they chose their base with expertise. Gadir served as their principal port in the vicinity and it was from here that they loaded and despatched their long-oared galleys (better adapted to these seas than sailing ships) with precious silver and iron. The local Iberians possessed these resources in abundance: alluvial tin panned from their rivers since early times, a little gold but, above all, they had silver running through the confluences of waters, the 'unlimited, silver-rooted springs of the river 'Tartessus', according to the Greek geographer Strabo. The iron was obtained from Tartessian mines situated further inland at the mouth of the Río Tinto, the Red River, so named because it flows a deep, almost blood red. The scale of the operations was enormous, sufficient to justify journeys that involved crossing the entire width of the Mediterranean. A galley's round trip, from Tyre and back home again, was calculated to take three years. From Cádiz, the boats possibly travelled onwards to trade. They did not stay: the Phoenicians were not colonists. They were merchants, pioneers, seafarers, who brought with them new skills and the experiences of an advanced civilisation.

A blustery early evening greeted my arrival into Cádiz, penetrating the suburbs and new town first where the streets had been decked out with paper lanterns and an assortment of party frippery, all flagging '¡*Esto es Carnaval!*' Continuing on, I crossed from the mainland by a narrow channel to the Isla de León and then to the island where the original city was born. Old Cádiz sits at the tip of a peninsula that on a map resembles a slightly crooked finger. Between mainland and peninsula, the curved, enclosed bay is a natural harbour. It would have been an ideal placement for the Phoenicians' galleys: a protection against fierce Atlantic winds and marauding pirates.

I was fairly exhausted after a full day's driving but sightings of the old city walls and ocean rollers lifted my spirits. I had been looking forward to Cádiz for a very long time. First, practicalities. I had made no booking and a room during carnival proved impossible so I was obliged to settle for the state-owned, higher-end-of-the-range Parador Atlántico. It was situated at the tip of the island finger, on a westerly nub of southern Europe, braving the Levanters, alongside a tropical park, so I was not too unhappy.

At reception, a notice apologised for the noise and the music: 'Sorry for all, but this is *carnaval*!'

Along with my key I was handed a map marking the locations and approximate times of the evening's festivities.

'Of course, with *carnaval*, you must expect anything or nothing,' the weary receptionist warned me. 'Frankly, I'll be glad when it's all over. The racket is enough to drive you *loco*.'

Spain is renowned for its noise and I had been exposed to almost deafening decibel levels on a regular basis throughout the past weeks, but carnival in Cádiz left me feeling as though an express train had run through the centre of my head.

Once settled in a room with view of sea and lighthouse, I set off, party map in pocket, striding by the city ramparts, listening to the crashing waves, towards the *barrios* of the old city, the *casco antiguo*, a maze of wafer-thin lanes and stone-walled alleyways, decorated with flowerpots, fanning out on to neat plazas where much of the action was due to take place. In spite of the fact that our farm is only half an hour's drive from Nice, we had never participated in its carnival, which boasts a colourful parade. I had visited Brazil on several occasions but not during its pre-Lent fiestas. So, this was my first carnival. I had chosen it because Cádiz is judged by most to be Spain's liveliest and most anarchic city and I hoped it might include some ancient history of the place. What had surprised me when I saw the schedule was that it was not due to end on Ash Wednesday. Whether for reasons of tourism or other, I did not know, but it continued a full ten days into the fasting forty. An act of anarchy in itself, perhaps?

I wandered the lanes, hunting the fun, and my first thought was that the passages were so narrow in the *casco antiguo* that no parade of any substance could pass through. Stalls rigged up in front of grocery shops or *bodegas* were offering beer, Andalucían-style fast foods and boxes of confetti, but everywhere seemed pretty dead. Until I turned a corner into a small high-walled plaza and came face to face with a dozen musicians, plastered in make-up. Several sported impressive textile phalluses (each more than a foot in length) while others, butch blokes, were in high heels and skirts, all with insane wigs. This group was a *chirigota*, a musical comedy act full of word-plays, satire and risqué badinage.

After a little tuning up and general faffing about, they broke into raucous song accompanied by plastic and metal kazoos, bass drums, whistles, guitars, basically any hardware that would create a racket. They intoned, recited and sang in what I think was a local dialect ditties that were hard for me to comprehend, but were evidently bawdy or controversial judging by the gathering crowds, appearing now from every nook and cranny, which roared, laughed, retorted and whistled. Soon, I was surrounded, hemmed in. Everyone was screaming, many in costumes, clutching open bottles, falling about. The mood struck me as similar to student rag week, an inebriated gaiety, and I extricated myself, pushing and shoving until, after turning circles in the old town, where children peered down incredu-lously upon the events from first-floor balcony windows, I found that every corner offered another version of the same thing. Perhaps I was tired, perhaps carnival was not to be experienced alone, perhaps the following day, Mardi Gras, was to be the big event. A little after eleven, I made my way back to the water and strolled sedately along the seafront. After close to two months in Spain I had become accus-tomed to its aromatic, seductive scents, but Cádiz stank, an unpleas-ant concoction of feral cats, urine, vomit and stale alcohol. Groups of youngsters living in trucks or caravans were seated at the kerb's edge smoking dope, swigging booze from bottles, singing and strumming their guitars. The lighthouse in the distance was blinking.

The Greeks, who arrived here after the Phoenicians, invented the lighthouse when they built a tall tower on the island of Pharos in the Alexandrian harbour in approximately 290 BC. So mighty was the tower, standing at approximately 135 metres (one of the tallest structures on earth), that it was nominated the last of the Seven Wonders of the Ancient World. After cracks, weather damage and losses to its height from various natural disasters, it was finally destroyed by an earthquake in the fourteenth century AD. After 1500 years of guiding mariners safely in and out of that antique harbour, nature laid it to rest. Recently sections of it have been recovered from the Alexandrian seabed, but still little is known of its light source. At its pinnacle, in the beacon chamber, it was thought that a mirror reflected sunlight during the day while a fire oriented the approaching ships by night. The light was visible from a hundred nautical miles out to sea. For a long while that fire was believed to have been fed with logs, delivered by pack animals clambering three lofty tiers. Later, this interpretation was judged unrealistic. It would have been a fire risk and spectacularly labour intensive to transport so much timber. Timber that, due to Egypt's dearth of forests, would have been imported, possibly from nearby Lebanon. How about that it was fuelled by oil, certainly in its earlier years? Why not? Olive oil fuelled the lights of the cities of both ancient Alexandria and Rome, so why not the Egyptian lighthouse? It was a Greek architect, Sosatros', vision and by that stage, the third century BC, the Greeks were master olive farmers.

I was curious about this windy Cádiz peninsula, about how the galleys and sailing ships negotiated the exposed, frequently tempestuous sweep into the bay, to drop anchor here. Rudimentary forms of beacon lighting had been in use prior to the Pharos of Alexandria, but might the Phoenicians have taught the local people, the Iberians, to create light from oil? Before Alexander the Great had conquered coastal Egypt and founded the city of Alexandria in 331 BC, the Egyptians had lit their lamps with a wick made of linen dampened in castor, sesame or safflower oil. Although there have been claims that olive cultivation began around the Nile, it is far more probable that the Greeks, certainly the Phoenicians and, before them, the original Canaanites, introduced the Egyptians to olive oil.

But what could the Phoenicians offer in exchange for those ship-loads of silver they so coveted? Was it their rich knowledge of civil-isation, their alphabet? They were skilled shipbuilders, too. Right into the twentieth century, fishermen around the Cádiz area used to carve a horse's head on the bows of their boats, a direct throwback to early Phoenician designs.

Back at the hotel, too early for bed, I strolled to the coffee shop, careful to avoid the bar where a handful of pensioners were tippling sherry and listening to a pianist in a long straggly wig and party hat, his contribution to carnival, playing 'Sealed With a Kiss'. The coffee shop was hardly livelier. I ordered mineral water and pulled out Simon's paper on olive cultivation. Moments later, a man in dark glasses, figure-hugging white shirt and silk scarf wound tightly round his neck strode up to the counter, ordered a Martini, plonked himself at my table and smiled obsequiously. 'Mind if I join you?' He spoke in English but with an accent I could not place.

'I'm working,' I told him plainly.

'Well, I'll just drink this and one more and then I'll be on my way.' He called to the waitress and ordered another for himself and a white wine for me. 'And put whatever else she's had on my bill, too.'

I thanked him politely and rose. He must have noticed my papers because he told me quickly as I turned that, although he was an interior designer by profession, his hobby was working as an olive-taster.

He had caught my interest. 'Where?'

'Puglia, southern Italy.'

I found him unpleasant but the coincidence was extraordinary given that I had that very evening, before going out, arranged a meeting with an olive-disease expert from Puglia. I sat down again, still refusing the drink.

'I hate Mardi Gras with its unmistakable stench of urine,' he announced. He was Scottish-Italian. 'Puglia is the olive centre of the world.'

'Spain produces more fruit,' I countered.

'Their farms lack soul, they lack the vital ingredient that makes for the finest oil: passion. Go to Puglia, see the trees, how they are pruned with love, with creativity. Nowhere understands the art of olive farming the way the pugliesi do. Here they are boring so deep and so frequently for water that it is not being replaced. In certain areas, it is sea water that is replenishing subterraneanly. Salt water. Mass production in agriculture is one of the gravest dangers of our time. Consider mad cow disease. Sleep with me.'

I bade him goodnight and left.

'It's a good offer,' he called after me. 'Consider your age.'

Within my room, after a long phone conversation with Michel, the incessant blinking of the lighthouse, a reminder of the city's maritime roots, left me awake. I had to agree with the obnoxious stranger that Spain's factory approach to olive farming was troubling me, dampening my enthusiasm. Intensive farming leached tradition, destroyed rural ways of life, traded short-term gain against a tomorrow that was marching inexorably towards a hot, barren earth.

But what could I do?

The following morning, Tuesday, Mardi Gras, the city was so silent it might have died or its inhabitants fled from the plague. The rank odours of partying and raw fish hung in the salted Atlantic wind. I had been dreaming of visiting this city of crumbling grandeur for many a year and I was now saddened that I had chosen carnival time. The wind coming in off the ocean was blowing vigorously, a challenge to the hangovers. It had rained in the night and washed the streets but it had not rid the heart of the old city, with its labyrinthine lanes, of rancidity. Soggy streamers, confetti and smashed oranges lay in between the cobbles; every step was treacherous. I went in search of the archaeological museum, housed in the grounds of what had been a vegetable garden in an earlier incarnation, but closed until the afternoon. It was midday, *mezio*. Shutters began slowly to unroll. The cold metallic clunk matched the chilled noon. Traders appeared, approaching this day of Mardi Gras with lethargy, heavy heads, disinterest. Men in hats with paunches sat in silence reading newspapers, tiny cups of black Arabic coffee on the small round tables in front of them. The high-level noises and bustle of Spain had conked out. I mooched about admiring the architecture with its faded elegance, then hugged the seawall, breathing the heaving swell of water slapping the ramparts, its fine spray showering me, and chanced upon the immense, tangle-rooted *Ficus gigante* trees brought to the city by

Christopher Columbus on a return trip from the Americas. Six hundred years old but almost as impressive, as gorgon-like and expansive as the Bechealeh olives.

In 1492, the same year as the heartbroken Moor Boadbil lost his treasured Granada to the Catholic monarchs, Isabella and Ferdinand, Christopher Columbus set sail from Cádiz for the Americas. Through his discoveries in the colonies of Latin America, Spain found new wealth, new power. The might of Catholic Spain turned its attention across the blustery Atlantic Ocean intent on gold and imperialism. Coincidentally, Christopher Columbus, who came from a family of Italian weavers, had a favourite uncle who was a lighthouse keeper. It was he who had inspired the navigator's seafaring dreams.

In a small park at the waterside, beneath another of the magnificent *ficus* trees, I came upon a bust of José Marti. I found it surprising that he should be here, he who liberated Cuba from the Spanish and who is revered by all Cubans as a national hero. It was a reminder to me that Cádiz had long been respected for its liberalism and tolerance, which was quite possibly evident in the anarchic carnival songs, sketches and agitprop that I, because of insufficient language skills, was unable to appreciate. The city had been a fierce opponent of Franco though it swiftly fell to his army after he had landed on this southern coast.

After my visit to the archaeological museum, with its pair of magnificent Phoenician sarcophagi, I returned to my hotel by way of the park, Parque Genovés, passing a colony of whistling, garrulous parrots in the treetops at the waterside. An army of keepers and attendants were sweeping up, clearing the previous night's debris in preparation for the next onslaught of jovialities. There were smashed bottles, shards of glass everywhere and the air smelt of burned sugar. Feeling ill at ease, not quite sure how to respond to the roisterous enthusiasm beneath the coloured wigs, fancy dresses and drunken painted faces, I had decided to move on. Carnival is not for the lone voyager, I decided, or perhaps not for me at all. I paused to take a final photograph and spotted twin cats, black as glinting coal, hunkered beneath one of the tropical trees. Their green marmoreal eyes were fixed hard upon me; dark hearts of Spain.

*

Although it had rained in the night, dewy whorls flying round the lighthouse, the break of day had brought calm. The sea was a rich blue with madder-brown rocks breaking its surface, slick and shiny as pods of basking sea lions. Morning found me crossing back over the Bahía of Cádiz, glancing westwards towards the windswept shoreline and the town of Huelva, towards the Coto Doñana National Park. I had to pull over to fully appreciate a bleached watercolour of a rainbow, tantalising and nebulous. At the end of the rainbow lay a lost city, a city of fabled treasures, Tartessus. I was off to find it. One day I would return to Cádiz, I promised myself, but not during carnival. One pleasing tidbit I had picked up in a bar over a glass of wine the evening before was that the tradition of *tapas* had originated in Cádiz on the occasion of King Alfonso XIII's visit to the city. It had been an inclement day with a brisk wind and the royal entourage had stopped at a *taberna* for refreshment. The king ordered a *copa* of wine. The waiter, nervous of sand flying into His Majesty's drink, covered it with a slice of locally cured ham. When the king enquired as to the purpose of the ham, the waiter explained. His royal highness, tickled by such ingenuity, tucked into the meat and instantly commanded a second glass with the same *tapa*, cover.

Sanlúcar de Barrameda is one-third of the sherry triangle. It is also a town perched on a scraggly river beach at what feels like the end of the Western world. A last outpost before the waters, the marshes, before the penetration into wild nature, to where the river delta has gradually been blocked off by a huge sandbar that stretches from the mouth of the Río Tinto, near Palos de la Frontera, to the riverbank opposite Sanlúcar de Barrameda. This entire area had been designated as national park, Parque Nacional de Doñana; it represents Europe's largest wildlife sanctuary and was the inspiration for the foundation of the World Wildlife Fund.

I parked the car at what, until recently, had been the hitching rails for horses, a setting-down post for the customers of the sherry *bodegas*. Two old geezers, both possessing the mottled, bruised complexions of lifelong sherry drinkers, were waving, indicating a designated space, which I obligingly pulled into. One growled into my window with fiery breath and squeezebox voice, 'two euros fifty'. I handed it over and he hobbled away gratefully as the other approached, flapping a book of tickets.

'Two euros fifty,' he requested.

'I have just paid your colleague.'

The old timer shook his head. 'I'm the attendant. He was just trying it on.'

Off the Cádiz peninsula it was noticeably warmer. Small parties of Spanish tourists or inhabitants from neighbouring Jerez were sitting at one or other of the open beach cafés down along the Bajo de Guia, the riverfront, sipping sherry, smoking fat cigars, imbibing the heat of the sun and alcohol after a very decent lunch. The seafood in Sanlúcar de Barrameda is highly praised and hailed among Spain's finest.

I took a brief stroll to and fro in search of a booth for ferry tickets but saw none. The architecture was not of the solid, imposing central Spanish styles. It was delightfully Art Deco and mostly freshly painted in white or earthy colours, as though the place was waking up to the new century, and its Fabrica de Hielo, the Ice Factory, was particularly stylish. While photographing it, I discovered that it contained a visitor's centre. Here was where I would find my boat ticket.

The Parque Nacional de Doñana is the most extensive, roadless area in Western Europe. To reach it by car is impossible and forbidden unless escorted by a ranger in one of the park's own jeeps. Another method is to track the route of the earliest colonisers and pioneers and penetrate the wetlands by boat. This was what I was hoping to do.

'Sorry, there's only one boat in service. It sails upriver once a day, departing at ten every morning.'

'Tomorrow morning, then?'

'Sorry, it's fully booked until next week.'

I had not anticipated difficulties.

'How about a seat on one of the ranger's excursions?'

A telephone call was made. 'Sorry, they're also full. In any case, the jeeps don't leave from here.'

To join a landroving trip, I would have been obliged to drive inland to Sevilla, two hours away, and skirt the exterior rim of the parkland, another two hours.

'There's no road through. We can fit you on the boat trip the week after next, if you want to make a reservation.' The young woman at the desk shrugged her apologies.

I thanked her kindly and disappeared to browse awhile at the displays, to read about the park's ecosystems, its flora and fauna, biding my time, wondering what course of action I might take from here when, serendipitously, the receptionist appeared at my side.

'Two places have been cancelled on tomorrow's water excursion.'

Mañana!

Down at the beach, along the riverfront where I was walking, were several upturned, poorly maintained *tarafes*, the small fishing boats, variations of which are to be found everywhere around the Med. These were in a sad state of repair. A man in high waders was calf-deep in the spume, fishing. Scruffy and unpretentious. I felt an instant rapport with this place, where the sea met the land. Vineyards and fish, an easy-going combination of farmers and fishermen. What was I hoping for here? One 3000-year-old tree dating from the arrival of the Phoenicians. One clue, forgotten, overlooked, that confirmed what I fancied of their exchanges with the local Iberians. Yes, I liked this place. A cohesion of essential Med elements. It only lacked the sierras. And a place to sleep. There were a couple of small choices but I did not fancy them so I was weighing up my options. After my riverside promenade, I returned to one of the waterfront restos where lunch was still drifting on, even though it was after four. I ordered a cup of coffee, pulled out my map, then scrutinised the crowd. A fair number were Spanish businessmen, tanned, paunched but not excessively so, thickish wedding rings though few were in the company of women, and slicked hair. I took them for sherry barons with their expensive leather shoes, corduroy trousers, leather jackets, small neck scarves and substantial cigars. From behind me a sustained wailing broke out. I turned to see a trim busker with shoulder-length grey hair and whiskers. Arms raised above his head, he began to clap and sing. The music and rhythms were extraordinary, atonal. The entertainer beat the palms of his hands together, *tocando palmas*, and pounded his feet, stamping, kicking up clouds of dust, shuffling between one table and the next. His variation on flamenco was unfamiliar to me and was certainly not appreciated by the present audience. Diners at several different tables were hissing. As the singer drew closer I saw that he had no teeth, the bags beneath his eyes were almost carmine, his long, wavy grey locks were in fact a wig, his neck was turkey flesh and beneath a three-quarter-length dress coat he was wearing an embroidered waistcoat with white rosary beads as a necklace. I gave him a few cents as did a large crowd of merrily drunken Brits from the north of England who were knocking back the sherry and having a whale of a time. Suddenly, I had a picture of what this scruffy, mouth-of-estuary resort must be like in summer invaded by coach parties. The Spaniards, disdainful *Andaluzes*, ignored the gypsy's requests while the waiters imitated and mocked him, but he soldiered on, braving their unkindnesses until someone, I did not see who, went too far and he grew angry. He began to shout with the high-pitched squeals of a pubescent chorus boy. His delivery was strident, attenuated. He spat words at the pace of galloping horses, and then burst directly into song again, whipping his arms in the air and pointing in an accusatory fashion. Still his audience baited and jeered him. I threw coins on the table; time to be on my way. My destination for the night had been decided.

Jerez, Xerxes to the Moors. Jerez, within the sherry triangle, heartland of sherry production, is possibly the last bastion of authentic, traditional flamenco. Even so, I had not programmed a stop. This was a detour from my olive route, but I needed a bed and, like many, I am romantically attracted to the gypsy myth and their heart-rending music. I can even lay claim, proudly, to a dram of gypsy blood in my veins. My father's grandparents on his mother's side were 'travellers', 'tinkers', itinerants in caravans, rounding the wild coasts of southern Ireland. Or so my Irish mother always claims.

At the reception desk of my dull, travelling salesman's hotel (everywhere else had been full) in Jerez' town centre, set within a fabulous palm-fringed square, I requested directions to a club situated within the *barrio gitano*, the gypsy quarter. In Córdoba, I had been given the address of this particular *peña*, club, 'where there is sure to be first-rate music', should I ever fetch up in this corner of the sherry kingdom.

'I don't recommend it. There are better nightclubs in town,' the desk clerk answered. His face had the grey lifelessness of a pumice stone. I explained that I was not looking for the touristy *tablaos*, the flamenco shows.

Eyebrows pressed tightly together, he sighed, clearly bored by tourists in search of authenticity. 'That *barrio* is dangerous. I refuse to give you directions. I wouldn't give them to a man. We're responsible for our guests. In any case, such events are spontaneous or known only to those involved in their circles. You might find yourself alone there and nothing happens, or you might end up in difficulties. A brawl, a knife fight. I strongly advise against it.'

But I was here now, in Jerez, and I was determined to hear flamenco. I would not be fobbed off with a tourist show. In any case, I suspected that the danger level was, as is usually the case, pumped up.

'Better to send you to the red-light district than the neighbourhood you're seeking.' He pulled from beneath the counter a fancy brochure with garishly printed photographs, a flyer for a flamenco cabaret show. 'This has suited all our clients.'

We were getting nowhere.

To travel in Andalucia you need three francs a day and a gun.

Words pronounced by an unidentified Frenchman who had toured southern Spain in the company of the writer Alexandre Dumas during the nineteenth century. It would seem that little had changed during two centuries, if I was to believe these dark warnings. I thanked the clerk and took the lift to my room. At 9 p.m. I returned downstairs and requested my car keys. I had expected that a night porter would be on duty. Unfortunately, it was the same fellow.

The club I had been recommended lay at the heart of a medieval *arrabale*, a district that had once been marginal, pressed up against the city boundaries, but later had been granted the status of *barrio*, Barrio de Santiago. I was not convinced that the risk I was about to take was so extreme. However, to appease this earnest young gent who was all but refusing me access to my car, I removed my jewellery and, along with my camera, slid the pieces across the desktop to be locked in the safe. In exchange, my keys.

The *barrio gitano* was poorly lit and surprisingly deserted. I cruised up and down shabby, echoing lanes that reeked of drains, trying to get my bearings, looking for a parking spot. Would the car be stolen? It was a hired vehicle, it was insured. I wasn't going to fuss. I pulled over, checked there was nothing on the seats, locked it and walked back towards a church I had spotted in a *plazuela*, small square. A quartet of young gypsy men were standing outside it, in the street, talking, smoking. I dug in my pocket for the scribbled address and crossed paving stones. Their conversation died away as I approached.

'*Hola.*'

One acknowledged my greeting. The others glared mistrustfully. In their twenties, poorly attired, dark, tired eyes with black moons beneath, two wore kerchiefs round their necks, all were in jeans. Aside from these *barrio* youths there was no one about, but I was not worth the robbing. My mobile had been left on the dresser and I had secreted in my skirt pocket a handful of euros, sufficient cash only for a couple of drinks and an entry fee should it be demanded. One took my scrap of paper and they all leaned in, studying it sullenly. It was handed back without a word.

The fellow who had nodded moved his head, indicating the *peña*. 'Right across the street, behind you. Two hundred metres.'

The club, with a small light above its door, halfway down a semi-concealed alley leading off the square, was nothing more than a plain old barn, a shabby space converted for the purpose of performance. Fewer than a dozen others were seated at tables, dining. These were the paying audience and they were predominantly *payos*, non-gypsies, foreigners, which was a little disappointing. I did not wish to eat and was shown to a table set to the side of a shallow, planked rostrum rigged up as a stage. Faded photographs in dark frames had been nailed to the whitewashed walls as decoration. The room smelled of hay, reminiscent of its original purpose, stables, I supposed. The tablecloth was an uninviting shade of mustard and rather stained, but the host was very welcoming, offering a choice of sherries but recommending the Manzanilla, 'a briny tipple'. His fluent French was delivered with a strong Andalucían accent. As he poured the honey liquid into my *copita*, he nodded to a quartet of folk eating at a table by the stage.

'They're French,' he smiled. 'You can always spot them.'

Two bespectacled men with sharply dressed, small-bosomed

women. The men looked as though they might be scientists or archaeologists.

Carlos, the waiter, was also a gypsy but, unlike his compatriots who were arriving in dribs and drabs, congregating together round one table near the bar, his hair was cropped short. The others, both sexes, wore theirs tied back in ponytails. Two of the men had woven cloth bags slung diagonally across their torsos like satchels.

Carlos went off to chat with his *gitano* pals who I supposed were also here to enjoy flamenco. Hanging from the walls were wood and leather harnesses. On the stage, six green chairs, wood with rush-matted seats, had been set in an untidy line. Two held guitars. A naked bulb hung above them.

The beamed ceiling was very high, which explained why the room was so chilly. Gusts of warmth were supplied by one overhead gas heater, the type used in street cafés in the boulevards of Paris. Because I had removed my watch, I had no idea what the time was or how long I had been there, but I was on my second glass of sherry. No other spectators had arrived but for those round the gypsy table, which was now crowded. Among the gathering there was one child, a plump, squat girl of about eleven, wearing a sleeveless icing pink-and-white dress. I wondered whether she was to be in the show: her outfit seemed so inappropriate for both the season and the time of day. Two women were among the group, both big boned, Amazonian, with frizzy, unconditioned black manes. One, the larger, older, was wearing cowboy boots. She reminded me of an ancient fertility goddess and I suddenly wondered whether the roots of these people might be Hittite or Assyrian. What relationship does the gypsy have to the olive tree, I was asking myself. Originally nomads, they were not agriculturalists, but many had been forced to settle. If their children were to be educated, if they hoped to benefit from health care, then, to a certain degree, they were bound to the ways of the state, be it France or Spain, but the journeys their ancestors made across deep centuries touched upon the olive routes. In Syria and Lebanon I came across caravans of travelling, down-at-heel fruit pickers who followed the crops, the seasons, and were described with a spit of disgust as 'gypsies'. Occasionally, in my ignorance, I had referred to them as 'bedouins', but was swiftly corrected. Rather like the olive, gypsy roots have disappeared, lost with time. Might they, in earlier centuries, as they migrated from the Middle East to Europe, have earned their bread harvesting olive crops? Might they have been marginally instrumental in the transmission of knowledge of olive farming along the way? It is possible that 'flamenco' comes from an Arabic word, *felagmengu*, meaning 'wandering peasant'.

During these musings I had failed to notice that the table of gypsies had emptied, save for the little girl and an old man with droopy moustache and cowboy hat, and a septet was trooping in single file across the vast room, up on to the stage. They had changed their clothes, predominantly into black, not the vibrant flamenco costumes I associated with this music. The group consisted of the two big-boned women and five men, one of whom was pale-skinned, wore sneakers and hair piled in a bun high on his head, Sikh-like. The other men were in Cuban-heeled boots and sported embroidered scarves. As they mounted the low stairs, they paid the audience no heed. Two of the males were guitarists; the lighter skinned youngster was a singer while the scarved pair were dancers.

The younger of the two seated women opened the performance by lowering her head slowly between her knees, arching her back like a cat and then emitting a drawn-out ululation, beckoning the gods to bestow the muse. '*Olé*,' 'bravo!' was repeated over and over by one or another, triggering encouragement, revelation, in what seemed spontaneous play, lacking theatre, as though I was a silent witness at an improvised gathering. This was possibly inaccurate, but there was a sense of invocation, of riding the waves of inspiration when they arose. When one took the stage, those who were not playing guitar clapped their cupped hands, *tocando palmas*. The heavy woman was pawing, stroking the floor with the sole of her boot like an agitated bull biding its time in the ring. During these moments of stillness, moments of anticipation, the gypsies were speaking aloud, calling *olé*, petitioning. Their language might have been Andalucían or *caló*, Spanish Romani, or the original, gradually disappearing, universal tongue of gypsies. It was not Spanish. They performed singly or in pairs. The songs were *cante jondo*, 'deep song', I think; hoarse, wailing, blues music. I regretted that I knew so little, that I was unable to identify the different forms, black and haunted. When the big woman stood up, stepped centre stage, bent her heavy body forward, beat her fist against her breast, stood up straight and held her arms out-stretched as though pleading with an invisible force or even us, the onlookers, her naked voice was stripped back, full of pain, suffering, incomprehension. This was as far removed from the popular Gypsy Kings' tunes of *flamenqillo* as to be another genre altogether. I had read of an old-style flamenco, *tonas*, that originated in prisons and with the *gitano* blacksmiths. Was it *tonas* I was listening to? I learned later that these evenings take place in several bars of this *barrio* and take many forms. The music is always different, sometimes giving preference to the guitar, which on this evening was merely back-ground to the mesmerising singing and dancing. The description, *duende*, sprang to mind when two dancers, one in particular, seemed to commune with an altogether different universe. And then a surge of activity as the trio, including the large woman, galloped themselves into a frenzy, up and down the cramped stage, causing the onlookers to yell and shout. They leapt, they spun their scarves, matador cloaks in a bullring, sweat spilling off them like dancing beads, feet mur-dering the wooden boards in a fast, upbeat crescendo. At moments, I was reminded of Balinese dancers, at other times those curious high-pitched desert calls I had heard in the East, and then chords of Camarguais music. Yet it was a show like nothing else. Still, there were ghosts, split-second hauntings of other cultures, a melting pot. Byzantine chants, Gregorian plainsong, too.

Afterwards, the troupe returned to street garb and, hanging about near their table, my insignificant bill settled, I walked across to con-gratulate the gypsies, as I would actors after any show. Close up, they were very different. Save for the sheen of perspiration on their unshowered skins, the shine, the magic had departed. What remained was seedy, sad, flabby, several middle aged, and I guessed, as they nodded their indifferent acknowledgement to my praise, that they were headed home to backstreets or rundown tower blocks on the city's outskirts. One, the lighter-skinned Indian-looking fellow, was pacing about. All the stillness and centre of concentration dispelled. He was twitchy, lacking quietude, and I asked myself whether he was anxious to get going, to score drugs. Another resembled a lonely old homosexual with mascara bleeding beneath his eyes.

I went back outside and walked the deserted lanes, footsteps echoing, slowly to the car, neither stolen nor damaged, of course. I settled into the driving seat and closed the safety belt over me, but did not immediately start the engine. I was experiencing a mixture of emotions – elation at having witnessed such charged performances with raw, authentic energies and a sadness for what it must mean to be a gypsy, an outsider, in twenty-first-century Spain.

I awoke to driving rain, hardly the most propitious start to a boat trip up the Guadalquivir River. As I left Jerez, the vineyards on the rolling hills with their special chalky soil known as *albariza*, that partially contributes to the unique flavour of sherry, were hidden behind a blanket of fog. This was the weather named by the ancient dwellers of the Mediterranean – *imbribus atris*, dark rains, torrential downpours with low clouds that cut off the sun and screened the views. It was very disappointing. How different it must look during summer and the autumn season of grape-picking, *vendimia*, when the scorching weather has waned and the fields are filled with fruit and harvesters.

The Phoenicians brought the vine to this region. Once the Romans had gained control of the peninsula, they shipped tall jugs of the brew to all corners of their empire, including Rome itself. The boat journey between Gades, the Romanisation of Gadir, now Cádiz, to Ostia, along the shores of Rome, took nine days. The Moors, being Muslim, were not imbibers and the wine industry might have fallen into ruin when Islam gained control had it not been for British merchants who arrived in the fourteenth century and, seduced by the wines of Xerez (pronounced 'sherrish' by the Arabs), launched the 'sherrish' grape in England and sherry was born. Even today, the British, followed by the Dutch, are the greatest drinkers of these particular sacks.

The weather delayed me. A route which the evening before had been straightforward was complicated now, confusing. While I was thinking about soil or peering out into the darkness at inviting *cortijos* on rolling plains and long, soft slopes peppered with rows of winter vines, I took a wrong turn on the outskirts of Sanlúcar and ended up in its harbour of Bonanza. A huddle of fishermen tried to signal that I needed the *porto pesqueria*, three miles downstream, not this larger port where fleets of small trawlers were docked. Both Columbus and

Magellan set forth from here on major voyages, I remembered, but I could not delay. Eventually, after getting lost down backstreets several more times, I drove into sleepy Sanlúcar where not one beach bar was open and tracked down a much-needed cup of coffee behind the esplanade at a dingy little counter where two men were serving while another pair sat sullenly on high stools drinking *café con leche* and watching television. Both were eating breakfast, toasted bread dripping with olive oil. I ordered the same. The men looked at me in amazement. The oil was sharp, of poor quality.

While we waited on the grubby, white-sand beach for our boat, the *Real Ferdinand*, to be readied, the rain began to ease, the sky to clear. Gruff-faced fellows with umbrellas and bulldogs on sturdy chains strode by, a Japanese woman bore down upon an unsuspecting sparrow, chasing it to and fro in attempts to photograph the terrified creature, while retired, hollow-faced fishermen in caps sat about smoking: the morning traffic along the strand. As we were pulling anchor, a large party of Spaniards arrived, loud and excitable. Our number comprised the newly boarded group, two lesbians from Brittany and myself. The Spaniards were hollering, unable to concentrate as the vessel heeled and began to nose sedately upstream. Here, where our boat was chugging, was the broad mouth of this mighty river, the port of entry for some of the greatest maritime civilisations in Western history. It was an impressive ingress, not as monumental as the Amazon perhaps, but substantial just the same. The Moors called it Wadi-Al-Kabir, the big river. Originally, there had been two arms surging powerfully into the ocean. Today, there was just the one, heavily polluted.

We floated by Bonanza. Two forestry rangers were accompanying us. Sabrina spoke English, the other Spanish. Sabrina, from Sevilla, early twenties, enthusiastic, clad in wet-weather gear, confirmed that both Columbus and Magellan had embarked on grand voyages from here. She pointed out the lighthouse and a large shed used for fish auctioning. In this end-of-February season, before the long dry months, the exposed mud and sandbanks were ideal feeding grounds for flocks of breeding birds, both migratory and endemic, and she promised us sightings of many. The Spaniards were feeding crisps to gulls, and photographing them as they swooped and skidded alongside us, snatching greedily at the goodies before beating a hasty retreat. Fortunately, a few drops of rain again sent the entire Spanish troupe scuttling and fleeing to the lower deck, to a television lounge where they enjoyed our entire four-hour transit in front of a pre-recorded video. This left me alone with the French women and Sabrina, whose knowledge of the local wildlife was formidable. We talked of olives and the history of the area.

'There's a post within the park, an alternative entrance, with tourist office, known as Acebuche,' she informed me.

'Acebuche?' Wild olive. 'How did the post acquire its name?'

She did not know, but guessed it had been inspired by a particular tree still growing there.

'Is it wild? How old is it?' I was pulling out my map of Doñana, scrabbling to locate Acebuche. Was this to be my Phoenician treasure? My Western relative of the Lebanese mighties? 'Are we going there?'

She shook her head. 'No, it's not that old. Several centuries,' was all she could tell me. 'I think it's cultivated.' She had no other information.

During one of two forays we made into the drenched parklands, wild boar and fallow deer were grazing. Although we were bordering the Atlantic, the landscape was Mediterranean. I learned that seashells from the Atlantic had, over millennia, been washed inland. Silt and sand from the riverbanks had also clogged up the waterways. I thought of the Phoenicians and their murex molluscs used for their famous purple dye, prized by the Romans. I felt convinced that beneath the earth on which we were standing lay layers of shells, of river silt, subterranean pellicules of history. We found cork beehives. They dated to the Middle Ages, but the method of fashioning them and the use of the cork oak were far older.

'This region contains many habitats: lagoons, salinas, scrubland, salt marshes, *dehesas*.'

I asked Sabrina about the *dehesas*.

'Forests of evergreen holm oak, *encina*. It's a prehistoric tree and along with the olive, carob and cork oak defines the Mediterranean topography.'

'And where the holm and cork oaks grew was to be found the wild olive.' If there were *dehesa* forests then I felt sure that at some point these coastal regions were swathed in wild olives. I was trying to picture those early exchanges between Tartessian Iberians and the merchant sailors from the east. Had the sailors known that the wild olive grew in abundance here? Had its discovery proved a bonus, its cultivation an added skill to trade?

'All are essential trees for enriching the soils found in these lower arid regions of Spain,' explained Sabrina. 'Similar to the wild olive, the holm will regrow from a stump, important after forest fires in this waterless climate. Its longevity is not as renowned as the olive; still, there are surviving holm oaks that date back seven hundred years. Many consider these forests, cork, holm and olive, to be the original primeval Mediterranean forests.'

In prehistory, when the cave peoples of Altamira were around, much of Spain was covered in holm, but as time went on and man evolved, thousands of acres of these trees were felled for firewood, charcoal, logging, building homes and, later, agricultural purposes. 'Unfortunately, because the trees frequently survived in poor, arid soils the agricultural crops planted in their place didn't do well and, eventually, the land was abandoned. Instead of the trees, scrub plants grew up, which is what we know today as the *maquis* and *garrigue*. However, elsewhere the holms were only thinned out and within the spaces grew cork oak, which gives its acorns in winter, thus offering food supply year round to sheep and cattle but, most importantly in Spain, to the delicious Iberian black pigs which graze within the *dehesas* and feed exclusively on acorns.'

'And what of the *"monte negro"*, those low, humid areas within the national park, which in olden days were forested by luxuriant spreads of cork and wild olive trees. What happened to those forests?'

Sabrina could not tell me. She was not a historian. 'Ask the captain later,' she said.

The outlying life consisted of wild white horses, tall juniper bushes, umbrella pines: Mediterranean. A black stork, I saw, and gorgeous purple herons perched on wooden landing posts on the riverbanks. The list of birds within the parklands was rich, exhaustive. While we talked, I was leaning over the side, looking back towards the single mouth of the Guadalquivir spilling its mighty, now polluted, gallons into the ocean. I was photographing cormorants and keeping my eyes peeled for the Spanish imperial eagle, rare, with less than a dozen breeding pairs still in existence.

By the time we tied up alongside an area of swamplands, *marismas*, the rain was heavy, curtaining off the views from the boat. These *marismas* were originally lakelands, known to the Romans as *Ligustinus*. Apart from myself and the girls from Brittany, no one fancied getting drenched. Here were flamingos, not a rarity for me as a frequenter of the Camargue. We crouched among tall reeds, hiding out of sight from the birds but eventually, thanks to the appalling weather and the discomfort, the excursion was abandoned and the boat returned to Sanlúcar where the Spaniards disembarked hastily in search of sustenance. I stayed aboard with the two women and the captain who served us hot coffee from his flask while the wind whipped at the tarpaulin cover and I was reminded of the howling banshees back in Ireland. It was then that we spotted four ospreys.

'So what of Tartessus?' I asked the florid-faced captain. 'I'm fascinated by those earliest encounters. The arrival of the shallow-keeled galleys, oak-oared, transporting men from the east. The reaction of the Iberians standing on the shores. This river flowing silver, and why they allowed the strangers to load up their boats.'

'The kingdom of Tartessus was said to be rich beyond all dreams. It was a fabulous land, a land of the imagination. Its rivers and estuaries, according to the stories, flowed silver. Even its king bore the title, Arganthonios, "The Silver One". Classical and biblical writers had eulogised its wealth. It was Tarshish in the Bible. But few believed in it. Until navigators, treasure hunters, who sailed here, beyond the Pillars of Hercules, and returned to the east with fantastic tales of a river running with silver and gold, of rich and pleasant men, of fine bulls and fertile plains . . .'

I glanced outside at the rain, the lack of fertile plains, wondering about these fine bulls and the bulls of the Minoans. 'So do you believe that Tartessus lies here?' I asked.

'Buried beneath these forever shifting wetlands, yes. Maybe right here where the *Real Ferdinand* is rocking in the wind.'

'Might it have been their alphabet that the Phoenicians traded for silver?'

Our skipper, pouring shots of brandy now, shrugged, waved his head. 'The Tartessians were famed for their literature. They spoke a language that is extinct. Few traces remain.'

I had not known this. The Phoenicians gave their alphabet to the Greeks who passed it on to the Romans and so on until it became the root of our modern alphabet, but these people could read, write.

'They had music, too. Their primitive dances were also renowned.'

I had heard this. Surely seeds of the music from this silver city evolved into flamenco? The Romans were always keen for the women from this region to dance for them. The girls from Cádiz, who even then used castanets, were frequently hauled off to Rome to entertain in the Imperial City.

'Do you believe it was the Phoenicians who discovered the city?'

'Yes, and there might have been an earlier encounter.'

'Minoans?'

The captain was not sure.

'I have a suggestion and wonder what you think . . .'

I proposed that whether in those far-off biblical days it was the Phoenicians or the Minoans, well over a thousand years earlier, who had sailed up this mighty river with herons along its fecund banks, the art of olive cultivation, of grafting, was surely a skill delivered here, and with it came the possibility of reaping liquid gold. From the river flowed rich deposits of silver and from the grafted wild trees sprung the makings of a delicate, edible gold. The strangers from the east disembarked on to these sands, bringing in tall clay pots a golden oil, one that was consumable, could be used for cooking, for preserving food, for medicinal purposes, perfumes, too, also for light. Then the sailors discovered – or perhaps they already knew – that the silvery-leafed tree, the wild olive, the *acebuche*, was growing here.

'We will teach you to work your silver trees, to create your own liquid gold,' they promised, 'and we will transport the oil and sell it for you. In return, we will take your silver from the water . . .' Silver for liquid gold: that might have seemed a fair exchange.

The mysterious disappearance of Tartessus, this wealthy, mythical kingdom, somewhere around the sixth century BC has never been explained. Some claim the Carthaginian-Phoenicians were angry with the Tartessians for trading with the Greeks and expressed their displeasure by razing the metropolis to the ground.

The captain shook his head. 'I don't think so.'

Others suggest that Tartessus fell victim to conflicts between Greeks, Carthaginians and Celts, all greedy for the silver and tin mines. Whatever the true story, today not a single trace of this shining city remains and, like the Minoan civilisation in Crete, no conclusive explanation has be found for its disappearance. Both are candidates for the lost city of Atlantis.

The rain was chucking it down now, waves slapping hard against the boat's hull. The captain, the two ladies from Brittany and myself had hunkered down for the afternoon, drinking but not excessively, kicking around ideas on history to make historians turn in their graves.

The captain raised his glass. 'To Atlantis,' he winked.

Morocco

At Algeciras I bought a one-way ticket and joined the straggly crowd, predominantly Arabs, awaiting the ferry to Tangier. In front of me, an old, wizened pensioner in green woollen hat and rose-pink slippers patterned with blue hearts. Behind me, a Moroccan living in Essex, forties, stocky, balding, talking English to the back of my head. I was too tired to engage. He spotted my passport.

'Irish. Are you a Catholic?'

Twenty of his friends, he claimed, had married Irish Catholics, each of whom 'without the slightest prompting' had converted to Islam and covered themselves, which he judged 'terrific'. Disrobing a woman of her veil, headgear and long skirts before sex was an arousal that beat all experiences, he was confiding to my hair. The queue shuffled forward while we waited for the boat to be prepared. This was not a conversation I wished to engage in and I tried to lose him but he stuck limpet-like to my shoulder, and I grew suspicious.

'I am a liberal Muslim, but I love women in *hijab*. It gets me so excited.'

I pulled a book from my pocket. Although he lived in Essex, he was an optician in Rabat and returned twice a month to keep 'an eye on his concerns'. Was this a feeble joke? His expression was deadly serious. In his district there was a great deal of drug-trafficking. This morning he had delivered a car to a 'relative' in Gibraltar. Yak-yak, non-stop, as though on speed or exceptionally nervous. I noticed then that he was travelling without luggage and I became convinced that secreted somewhere about his person were illicit substances, contraband of one sort or another, and he was latching on to me, a mature Caucasian female, to offset any customs suspicion. I crossed to get my passport stamped and then headed to the loo where I stayed till boarding was announced.

A kerfuffle on the quay. A ferry had just docked from Africa, passengers were disembarking. Uniformed immigration officers greeted them, inspecting their papers before they set foot on Spanish soil. Several were pulled out of line, pushed aside. Shouting began. These men were *indocumentados*, illegal immigrants, to be returned to Africa. A pathetic party of strays they were: wrinkled and soiled as trodden leaves, sour-faced yet vulnerable.

I made my way to the upper deck, passing by a small, cloistered cubicle encircled with unpolished shoes. Within, a handful of Arabs prostrate at prayer. On the deck, I watched Algeciras disappear into the hazy distance; the sea opening out southwards. North to the right, the Rock. Who would ever have imagined that the strategic position of this limestone protuberance would achieve such significance? Suddenly from behind me, his voice.

'Gibraltar's name in Arabic, Jabal Tariq, means Mount Tariq. Islam is woven deep into the Spanish culture, which is why they hate us.'

I sighed. It was a fact that Gibraltar's title had been chosen to honour Tariq ibn Ziyad, Moorish, Muslim conqueror of the Spanish peninsula in AD 711, but I had no desire to engage in history or any conversation with this particular passenger. Ignoring him, I returned to the fuggy interior lounge observing as I went that Mr Morocco-from-Essex was now in possession of a Vuitton briefcase.

I spotted one harassed American couple feeding three snivelling baby blond boys. Otherwise Arabs, most of whom were asleep: flat out in the prayer room or leaning over themselves on chairs, hugged, folded as though cramped or sick. Arabs in skullcaps, Arabs in socks, slippers, looking worn out, hands over eyes, fingers up noses, travelling with immense quantities of luggage stuffed into plastic tartan bags. I had been told that the prejudice against them in Spain was untenable. Judging by their demeanours, I could believe it. I found a seat close to the salt-sprayed window. Moments later, he was hovering close by me.

'Morocco is on red alert,' he warned. 'There have been bombings in Algiers, military targets. You shouldn't be travelling alone, you're not safe.'

He must have read my disbelief.

'I have friends high up,' he insisted. 'Friends in the police, security. Where are you staying tonight?'

I threw on my backpack, gave him a withering look and paid some insignificant sum to climb stairs to the 'Business Lounge', empty save for one solitary passenger, Daphne, a sad-eyed English divorcee who reminded me of an unkempt bloodhound. Living in Andalucía for thirty years, she had bought and was renovating a tumbledown riad – a traditional North African townhouse with interior courtyard – in Tangier. I asked if she had heard news of bombings. She nodded. A boy had been killed near the kasbah. It was very surprising, shocking.

'The country is on red alert.'

'But I thought the bombings were in Algiers?'

She knew nothing about Algeria. A small Arab boy had been blown up the day before with his bicycle. She was acquainted with his family and intended to pay them a visit.

'Are you afraid?' I asked her.

She shrugged. 'What's the point? Life goes on. Why are you travelling alone?'

From Daphne I heard again of the ironwood tree, popularly known as the argan, growing uniquely in central Morocco.

She offered another possible explanation for the origin of *tapas*, one that nobody had proposed in Spain, but after two months in the country and encounters with so many varying cultures did not seem too far-fetched. In Sanskrit, she said, *tapas* meant heat or austerity. She suggested that those rationed portions, described as *raciones* or *demi-raciones* on Spanish menus, might have grown up out of the philosophy of lack of excess, eating with due measure, particularly during the climatically hot months. Indian, Sanskrit. Hinduism. While watching the gypsies dancing in Jerez, I was distinctly aware of influences from India, Asia, gestures that at moments were reminiscent of places as distant as Indonesia. The melting pot, the tapestry of the Mediterranean.

While Daphne and I were tossing back and forth a potpourri of ideas, thoughts on Indian music, cultures, past travel experiences, she turned her wrinkled face towards the sea.

'Look,' she remarked without a flicker of emotion. 'Dolphins.'

It was a calm, end-of-afternoon crossing. Lights were dancing on the water. As we left Gibraltar behind us, a pod of dolphins was swimming alongside the boat, fooling around in the slipstream, deep in the Strait.

The Pillars of Hercules are the pair of rocks that form the gateway to the twenty-kilometre-wide Strait of Gibraltar, *Estrecho de Gibraltar*. The more northerly pillar is Gibraltar itself while the second lies to the south on a tip of Africa that has been retained by Spain, Mount Hacho in Spanish Ceuta. According to mythology, Hercules was commanded to perform twelve labours. Labour number ten involved crossing the Atlas Mountains in North Africa to reach an outlying island beyond the Mediterranean, where he was to steal a herd of red cattle from a triple-bodied monster, Geryon, nephew of the Gorgon Medusa. Our hero, Hercules, son of mighty Zeus, wielding his club of olive wood, decided that instead of hiking over he would simply rip the mountain apart. Smashing with his olive club, tossing rocks here and there, he split apart the range that had barricaded the Mediterranean Sea from the Atlantic Ocean, thus creating a passage through, the Strait of Gibraltar. On either side of this newly opened access stood a towering mass. This became known as the twin Pillars of Hercules.

'Dolphins, see them?'

I nodded. The Phoenicians, as far as we know, were the first Mediterranean sailors to pass through the Pillars out into the Atlantic Ocean, the 'further beyond'. They hunted these mammals and called them 'sea-horses'.

'I killed a *nahiru*, which these people call "sea-horse", in the midst of the sea.' So wrote one of the Assyrian kings in 1100 BC when he was on a mission to Phoenicia to collect cedar wood and pay a visit to the city-peoples living along the coastal shores of Byblos and Sidon. It was they who took the king out on that fishing trip.

1100 BC, the foundation of Cádiz.

A felicitous sighting, I was thinking.

Pink clouds hung above the mountains as we approached the African shoreline. Morocco, named by the Arabs, Al-Maghreb al-Aqsa, 'The Farthest Land of the Setting Sun'.

Morocco sits at the extremity of the world of Islam and at the western edge of the southern Mediterranean. In spite of the news of exploding bombs, I felt excited to be returning to the Maghreb, to the splendours of the desert, cubed white houses, mountains and oases but, as a woman alone, I was bound to face the prejudices of Islam.

I made a swift exit from the boat, haring along the jetty, dreading the arrival of the Essex-Moroccan and was almost on African soil when a young man came hurtling after me, 'Madame! Madame!' I did not spare him a glance, taking him to be a hustler until he drew up by my side, panting, waving two fifty-euro notes.

'You dropped these,' he said with a smile, 'when you pulled out your passport.'

Everywhere had posted warnings against Tangier rip-offs. I accepted the cash gratefully, pleasantly surprised.

Out into the portside evening with its stench of diesel, gutted fish and congealing blood and the chaos of North Africa, birds cawing, flapping from flat rooftop to rooftop. Filthy lorries huffing pollution, screeching brakes, queuing to board for Spain. As far as I could recall this was the first time I had ever crossed continents by foot. Taxi touts begging business, but I had no idea where I was going. Nothing booked. Tomorrow Casablanca, towards the argan forests, so a simple overnight hostel. Gaggles of small pubescent boys, black unkempt hair, eyes dark as mine shafts, were hurrying after me. I was their Pied Piper. They wanted dirhams, cigarettes and in return were offering sex or to carry my backpack.

'Hotel, Madame?'

'Cigarette?'

'One dirham, please!'

'Buy boy?'

'I have nothing. Rien du tout,' I shrugged and they grinned, mimicking my shrug.

I felt no fear. I strode to the first square. As I crossed, an arm settled on my shoulder and I almost jumped out of my skin. I swung about and the stranger veered off in another direction. I *did* feel fear. I had left Europe behind. Spanish, French, languages I could converse in; gone was the imposing face of Catholicism, which I was not comfortable with but I had been educated in so I understood its thinking. Now I was in North Africa where Islam was the dominant mindset. Frequently, too, poverty, decay and corruption were to be found. I sat outside a bar, requested a glass of mineral water and looked about me. The street was dusty and disorganised, a few weeds growing up through broken, displaced paving stones. A policeman was blowing a whistle and directing traffic. No one was paying him any heed. Behind him was his harnessed horse with blond mane, grazing on a bit of scrub alongside a rubbish tip and a man beneath a tree, torn trousers round his knees, defecating. Samuel Pepys described Tangier as the 'excrescence of the earth'.

I hiked up towards the kasbah to find myself a place to sleep, to the medina, the old walled town, glimpsing the esteemed Hotel Continental, still remarkably intact. It had opened in 1888. Alfred, one of Queen Victoria's sons, was its first guest. Hustle and shove. Shops crammed with second-rate items I could not imagine anyone desiring, Arabic music wailing from numerous nearby cafés, dirty-faced boys offering themselves as guides to the Sultan's Palace. The women were in *hijab*. Kids were selling stuff off the streets and at the scent of police thrust everything into ragged Berber blankets and skedaddled. The inability to stroll about after dark as a woman alone. In-your-face salesmanship. Eventually, I found a room for a price that I could afford in the *nouvelle ville*, the new town; a faded Art Deco signature of a once glorious past. I enquired, while checking in, about the bombings.

'There have been no bombings. Elsewhere, yes, not here,' the receptionist lied while staring into the face of a computer.

Tangier, straddling the tip of Africa between sea and mountains, built on low hills, and capped by the bluest of skies. Every great seafaring nation of the Mediterranean had dropped anchor here, and it became one of the most cosmopolitan and renowned port cities of the twentieth century. Administered by both Spain and France, Tangier was designated an International Zone in 1923. In her 1920 travel book *In Morocco*, the New York heiress and Pulitzer Prize-winning author Edith Wharton described Tangier as a 'pale-blue town piled up with brown walls' where the signs above the shops were displayed in English, French and Spanish and cab-stands were to be found in every square. It gained a legendary, not to say romanticised, James Bond-type reputation as a haven for spies, crooks and traders of one sort or another, bank traders and free money market traders. It attracted the high players in all manner of lowlife activities. Even today a tax-free status is offered to foreign companies which base their businesses here, I learned from Daphne. During the forties and fifties it had become *la Ville de Plaisir*, the City of Pleasure. Somerset Maugham, Cecil Beaton, William Burroughs, Truman Capote and a host of literati were regulars to these crooked Arab streets. Even the comic-strip heroine Modesty Blaise kept a house on a hill overlooking the city! Jack Kerouac hung out here. Paul Bowles, the American writer, one of the city's most renowned internationals and the longest literary resident of them all, used to pass Errol Flynn as he sat drinking coffee in the Petit Socco, while attempting to hide behind the pages of a newspaper from the staring eyes of girls. It was a city of contraband, of international espionage, of millionairesses and homosexuality – sex between males was legal in Tangier back then and it became known as one of the most glamorous and openly gay resorts in the world.

But that was the twentieth century. What I was passing through now was a city in tatters, gasping for breath, staving off the death rattle. I had a bite in the hotel's dreary dining room and fell on to the bed exhausted, too tired to venture back out into the chaotic streets. There I lay, mobile phone in hand, staring at circles of damp and mould on the ceiling, highlighted by the flashing neon colours of night in the marketplaces and back alleys, beyond my fifth-floor windows. How *triste* this tangerine city of sated desires, and I was wondering who, if anybody, would take responsibility for the bombings. During my late-night call to Michel, he suggested that I might consider returning home.

I lifted the shutter and let the pastel brilliance of a new day flood in. A disc of sun rising mandarin, suffusing primrose-yellow wings across the water beyond Tangier's crescent bay. Who would have guessed from that distance at the stench and hustle ashore? Beyond satellite dishes and washing hung across the flat roofs, the dawn promised harmony and tranquillity, a flamingo in flight. I was up and out of the hotel a little after seven, determined to continue. Reception agreed to store my pack for a few hours and I drifted at leisure through early morning streets being cleaned, much as the streets of Paris are washed each morning. Here the process was achieved by moustached men with raggy towels on their heads working with straw brooms and metal buckets. Down the plunging lanes of the *ville nouvelle* where several of the façades had been whitewashed, like the Spanish *pueblos blancos*, rendered attractive for foreigners. At least they had not been pulled down and replaced by concrete. I stopped at a *pâtisserie* that might have been designed for a musical so extravagant was its marble decor, so charming the girls who weighed and served the sticky delights, while in the background beneath an ornate chandelier a swathed Muslim woman on hands and knees scrubbed the pristine floor.

In 1912 Matisse visited Tangier and again the following winter. He called the city 'a painter's paradise'. I walked to St Andrew's Anglican Church, perhaps his most famous Tangier canvas, and tried to find other images reflecting his work, but the sights had changed. Paul Bowles, who moved here in 1947 at the suggestion of Gertrude Stein (neatly described by Paul Theroux as a big lesbian directing artistic traffic), and lived here until his death aged eighty-eight in 1999, wrote at the end of the fities:

'There must be few places in the world which have altered to such an extent in the past quarter of a century.' He had arrived as a young man, artistically uncertain, and had found his life and voice as a writer within this French North African community.

Tangier came into being in the fifth century BC as a port for the Carthaginians (why not the Phoenicians earlier, when they founded Cádiz?). They called it Tingis. The ground on which they built their trading post was surely named after the Berber goddess Tinjis. Even today, the port remains a sacred site for Berbers. Morocco during those pre-Christian eras had been densely forested and inhabited by elephants, tigers, lions. After the fall of Carthage, the Roman galleons arrived and Tingis was taken and served as a far-flung Roman colony and entrepôt.

Morocco has changed hands many times over the centuries but proudly claims to be the only country in North Africa not to have suffered Turkish domination, keeping its own native rulers until the nineteenth century. This fact has had a particular effect on the country. Although it extends further west than anywhere in mainland Europe and its coastline is more Atlantic than Mediterranean, the character of Morocco is infused with orientalism, an exoticism rare in the modern Islamic world. Its last dominating influences were the French and Spanish whose colonisation lasted a mere forty-four years, the shortest in North Africa. The country gained its independence in 1956 and today is ruled by King Mohammed VI who is both the military leader and religious despot.

'In Tangier the past is a physical reality as perceptible as the sunlight.'

This might have been true when Paul Bowles wrote these words in 1958 but it was less apparent today. Because I had time to spare I returned to the port, the city's *raison d'être*. I wanted to see it in daylight. I walked the esplanade where washing lines had been erected on the grubby beach and hung with damp, sandy clothes. Scooters and lorries were parked there, too. Families were living rough, gaping craters on the beaches promised construction that might or might not happen, men swept the streets with brushes and, as they swept, the dust and sand blew in. Serious-faced gents in fezzes and brown *djellabahs* watched the world from the sidewalks. The backdrop: layers of crumbling colonialism, inhabited high-rises with many broken windows not fit to be condemned, street-side cafés with up-to-the-minute aluminium Italian chairs where men with dark glasses, iron-grey hair and moustaches sipped soft drinks, mint tea or endless tiny cups of coffee and smoked pack after pack of cigarettes. Nobody seemed to have a purpose, endlessly wheeling barrows and hand carts to and fro for no particular reason – hawking for customers to fill them, perhaps? Others, wheeling fruit boxes. Ragged limestone rocks on which stood Art Deco buildings in a state of decay, as though the entire city was about to tumble from the hillsides into the sea. Dozens of idle cranes pierced the skyline, all construction at a standstill. A city of myriad levels, hills, heart-stopping views of sea and mountains ('You don't look at the city, you look out from it,' Bowles wrote), vertical keyboards of stairways leading to passages, hidden doorways, illicit mysteries, to dead ends. Down near the port a man in a beige woolly Noddy cap was on his knees planting geranium shoots at a non-existent roundabout – and that seemed to sum up modern-day Tangier for me; a place where the inhabitants were gracious and gentle, but with nothing to do, no longer cosmopolitan but comatose, as though the sap had been sucked out of them. Everybody had passed through, traded, pimped, spied, buggered, bartered, sung its praises and sailed off.

'When are you leaving?' Paul Bowles had enquired of Theroux as they sat together, two strangers, smoking joints.

'Tomorrow.'

'Everyone is always leaving tomorrow,' Bowles, who died in the city, had responded.

And now the Tangerines wandered about like neurotic wraiths, back and forth at this nib's extreme of the Mediterranean, as though their innards had been removed, and there was nothing for it but to wait in cracked shoes or bare feet for the next boat into dock, to beg, and hope, *inshallah*, God willing, for the city's next golden age.

As moved as I was by its broken spirit and as much as I would have welcomed a longer stay, I had destinations to reach. I wanted to take a journey back in time. My plan was to hug the Atlantic coast all the way to Essaouira. Essaouira, because it was the farthest outpost of the Phoenician trade route, and, from there, inland penetrating the Atlas Mountains where a unique and special tree grew wild. There, and nowhere else. The ironwood, or argan tree, from what I had discovered was the twin soul of the olive. Still farmed today, its fruits are pressed for their oil in much the same way as olives were pressed back before the Greeks or Romans.

Afterwards, Roman Volubilis and from there, by train, across the border into Algeria.

Four coaches a day departed from Tangier for Casablanca. I took the first. It was due to set off at eleven but was delayed and surprisingly packed. This was not the tourist season yet all the seats were occupied by Arabs and their copious luggage. Before boarding, I gave my last tuppence' worth of dirhams to an old lady with whiskers on her chin who had not been actively begging but sitting alone on a step, eyes shut, mumbling. When I pressed the coins into her upturned palm, she lifted two fingers to her lips, arms as thin as nails, and blew me a kiss.

Au revoir Tangier. Poverty and sunlight.

I was in Casablanca by evening. Stepping from the diesel-reeking bus, I set my first foot on the soil of Morocco's largest city. Its population of over three million was growing by the day as desert folk moved north, seeking their fortunes (which invariably did not materialise) and the majority ended up in one of the numerous shantytowns that ring the suburbs. Although Casablanca claims to have the feel of a Mediterranean 'jewel by the sea' – albeit a decaying one – it sits on the Atlantic coast. Its cinema heritage, though every frame of the 1942 film *Casablanca* was shot in Hollywood, created expectation, a romanticism that proved, for me, at least, unfounded.

Anfa was the original seaside settlement. It was rechristened Casablanca by the Portuguese in 1468 when they attacked their southern neighbour and took control. Up to that point it had been a base for Berber pirates who had found themselves a strategically perfect niche from which to harass all shipping passing from the Atlantic through to the Mediterranean. Casablanca blossomed under the Portuguese who ruled until the city was turned to dust by the Great Lisbon Earthquake of 1755. There, at the surf-beaten water's edge, it lay in ruins until the end of the eighteenth century when the Moroccan leader Sidi Mohammed III decided to reconstruct it and changed the city's name to Dar-el-Beida, which also translates as White House. No one I met throughout my journeys in Morocco referred to it as Dar-el-Beida, however. It was affectionately nicknamed Casa, as though it were a friend or an intimate address.

Walking beneath palms and minarets down squalid streets, listening to the *muezzin*, I searched for a cheap hotel. The French influence was everywhere. With its Mauresque architecture, much of it cluttered around Place Mohammed V, at the heart of Casablanca's *ville nouvelle*, with the main post office, *la grande poste*, as a fine example, it did not feel so very Arabicised. First impressions introduced me to yet another city falling apart at the seams. I searched for a bed and a newspaper, found *Le Monde* but no mention of the Tangier bombing – it must have been reported, if at all, a day earlier. Next an Internet café, a cramped, dark room at the far end of an alley where the men were courteous – no women, of course – but the computers were dinosaurs. Along the streets, women, voluminous as sacks, slumped against walls, begging. In the Pharmacie de Paris, a bijou of the *ville nouvelle*'s French colonial decades, the assistant cautioned me against wearing jewellery.

'Gold will be ripped off you.'

I was seldom so careless and thanked her for her consideration. Returning to my *pension*, I held the paper bag of purchases close to my breast to protect a gold chain I had forgotten to remove and was thrown off guard when a girl with a small child under her arm approached, begging. I shook my head. She pressed closer while calling to an older woman who appeared from beneath the shadows of a cluster of palms. The girl tossed the infant to the other and grabbed for the chain. I veered in an arc and stepped on fast. She followed for a few steps but then left me be. My own fault, but it shook me up.

The honking of horns. Puddles of soiled, soapy water bubbled in the damaged gutters. Crossing the wide boulevards was a life-and-death experience. The traffic was demented, but the view across to the ocean from the flat roof of my boarding house almost redeemed the tired, bedraggled state of this business capital. The central place of worship, Hassan II Mosque, was imposing, impressive, its pro-portions formidable. Only Mecca is larger, but this one boasts the tallest minaret in the world. Its glass floor reveals the crashing ocean waves beneath it, but I was not impelled to visit. I had grown tired of churches, mosques, symbols of religion. Religion and the Medi-terranean: now there's a subject.

The world famous piano bar owned by 'Rick', Humphrey Bogart in *Casablanca*, was a figment, but a café bearing that name, situated in a restored mansion house built within the walls of the medina close to the Place du Jardin Public, had been opened, but neither Bogey nor Miss Bergman ever set foot in this gin joint. It was a recent addition to the city; an enterprise belonging to an American who had worked in the US Embassy in Morocco and after 9/11 retired herself out of politics, deciding instead to kick-start a little tourism and interest into this washed-up, surf-sad town. I tried to find it, toyed with the idea of an aperitif in the piano bar, limbering fingers on keys before a few chords of 'As Time Goes By', but when I learned the pianist was Issam (pronounced I-Sam), I suspected it might be a disappointment. Instead, I passed my one evening in Casa within the medina, surprisingly deserted, before accidentally landing up down at the eerily dark dockside. A sickle moon cast little light. Aside from the echoes of distant hammering, the busiest port in Morocco had shut up shop.

My bus the following morning was due to depart at 6.45. At the rather smart coach station I was informed that no seats were available to Essaouira for three days.

'Tomorrow begins the holidays', I learned.

I had to think back. I could barely remember what month I was in. March. I could not afford to wait around for three days. I was advised to take the train to Marrakesh, which departed at seven, and from there continue by bus. This involved leaving the coast, which was disappointing. Still, I hurried outside and grabbed a 'petit taxi', a small red car, and begged the Casa Voyageurs train station. Give him his due, the driver, wheels skidding round every corner at breakneck speed, made it. To my astonishment, the station was bedlam. Not queues, but cattle stalls. Arabs were pushing, shoving, waving their arms, smoking, shouting. The customary phlegmatism was out the window. I glanced at the black hands on the station clock. Eleven minutes to. I had no hope of reaching a booth before seven, let alone the quay. I shuffled within the crush of bodies while wiry men in black leather jackets passed cash from outstretched arm to outstretched arm, begging another for the purchase of his tickets. Every locale in Morocco was being called, in Arabic and French. Four minutes to go and I had given up when someone leaned forward and asked me my destination. The tall, hooded gentleman took my cash, cried out 'Marrakesh!' over the heads of scarved, fierce women, and handed it to a clerk. Like the parting of the seas, folk moved aside and I stepped forward.

'Take this, pay the difference on the train' I was advised. I thanked everybody heartily, all were smiling, nodding and then straight back to their scrum.

The train was in. It was thirty seconds after seven. Someone yelled, directed me to a carriage. A matchstick octogenarian hauled up my pack and settled me into a first-class compartment where a composed and very chic Arab woman in jeans and European clothes, without headgear, sat with her coltish and equally pretty daughter watching a film on a laptop.

'Bonjour,' she said as I threw myself, puffing, into a window seat. This was my first introduction to the pleasures of travelling in Morocco by train – the French built most of the roads and laid the railway lines. For a dollar or two extra I could always upgrade and I had some of the most enlivening conversations, met interesting travellers, without exception all Moroccans. Pulling out of Casa, we passed one of the infamous shantytowns, home to rural migrants, a *bidonville* of the most miserable sort with corrugated roofs, lacking facilities including fixed electricity and plumbing but where most habitations displayed a satellite dish.

'Tomorrow is the Prophet's birthday and there will be celebrations everywhere,' the elegant woman smiled as though to explain the discomforts I had just experienced. 'It is like your Christmas. Every-one is on the move, visiting loved ones. It coincides with the finish of the school term and a week of holidays.'

A second mother entered, thickset, with daughter in tow. She wore full Islamic apparel, save for the face veil. Her daughter, though, wore Western clothes but was less elegant than her counterpart. The second mother was reading an Arabicised *Hello!* magazine. We females fell into conversation, nattering convivially. I fielded the usual questions about my purpose of journeying alone, but this time we were all unaccompanied women. They expressed no disapproval and I noted that I was the only one wearing a wedding ring. Were they both divorced? I did not ask. As to the bombing in Tangier? The women exchanged glances.

'These events are all too frequent, alas.'

It had been reported, but no one as far as they were aware had claimed responsibility. They were fascinated to learn of my olive quest and both confirmed that the regions near Meknès and Fès produced excellent olives, as did Sraghna, near Marrakesh.

'And the argan?'

'Ah, the Moroccan olive tree! But their forests are disappearing.'

The vegetation was changing as we moved away from the coast towards the centre of the country. A heat haze rose from the earth. It was still early, of course, though I had been up for hours. I sighted the first olive groves on the outskirts of Settat. Beyond, we rode through parched towns with blank red sand where shallow hills were punctuated with groves. I felt the approach of the desert. Curious, when I had been preparing for the ocean.

On an official Moroccan website I had read 'the olive's history in Morocco can be traced to Greeks who colonized Sicily'. It suggested that these Greeks had also delivered the olive to mainland Italy, and eventually, as trade routes opened up, had brought the tree west. After came the Romans who were responsible for planting huge groves in North Africa. 'By the tenth century, cultivated oleasters covered the islands of the Mediterranean and ringed the shores of southern Europe and northern Africa. The olive is one of Morocco's most fabled crops and has recently re-emerged as one of its most important.'

Again, so many differing hypotheses. Mine was that the Phoenicians were here first, followed by their descendants, the Carthaginians, the Greeks later, and, after the destruction of Carthage, the Romans who, as ever, made major business out of the oil, but I had still to discover where the Phoenicians had left their mark. If the Phoenicians had known of the argan tree would argan oil have become a staple of the Mediterranean diet? Would the argan be the plant encircling the basin? Or had the Phoenicians attempted to cultivate it and found that it was limited, that it would not root elsewhere? After the sterility of the Spanish olive business, I was excited at the prospect of discovering the earliest traditions of argan farming.

I was gazing upon an old earth with a complexion that shifted, sagged, dried up and sometimes flooded. An earth in constant change, wearing its experiences of time. Beyond the window I was looking at ridged land with soft stones, men in robes on bicycles, on donkeys. Shepherds, boys in torn-off trousers or old men in the hooded *djel-labahs*. Sheep, a few, red sand and occasional eucalypts. I had not expected to hit Berber Africa quite so soon. Dry land and then a river with greenery, rushes and small groves of olives and palms. The ladies explained that these views from the window, these desert-like scenes, were unnatural and had been caused by lack of rain.

'When there is rain, this is a wheat-farming district, but today, *très peu*, precious little, for farmers to live off.'

I was amazed. I saw no signs of farming. It was desert.

And as for the beasts, their grazing had almost entirely disappeared. It was developing into a serious crisis.

'When were the last rains?'

The women frowned, calculating. 'Three years ago.'

Such excitement expressed by the more conventional of the two Muslim women as we approached the outskirts of the immortal city and passed by palm groves, *les palmerais*.

'So green!' she cried with joy, like a child seeing snow for the first time.

Men with liquid-black expressions, rags over their heads, several with crutches upright at their sides, leaned or squatted against mud-baked walls.

Pressing my nose against the glass, I regretted that I was only passing through Marrakesh.

Another almighty scrum awaited me to secure a place on the bus to Essaouira, but in Marrakesh I was introduced to the system of the *grand taxi*. The inner cities were serviced by the small cars, *les petits taxis*, but the big taxis, usually sturdy old Mercs, were the intercity alternatives to coach or train. I would have continued on to the coast by train but the route had no railway and, yet again, the coaches were full. It was a question of grouping up with five other passengers and sharing the price of an intercity ride. A quartet of backpackers hassled me to join up with them, but I hung out for the bus. I had a hunch that I could swing a cancellation, which I did. The last seat. It placed me on the aisle alongside Douglas, a downbeat, unemployed bachelor from the outskirts of Manchester who returned to England at regular intervals to collect his dole cheque and then 'pissed off again', usually to southern Spain, where his 'auntie had a condo' on the Costa del Somewhere, to live as 'cheap as chips' until the next cheque arrived. He moaned from start to finish and I was obliged to pull out my notebook and bury myself in scribbling. Even so, he leaned over my pages, mumbling, 'I wanted to be a writer once. You're not saying summet about me, are yer?'

I hoped he would sleep so that I could stare across him out of the window. The agriculture directly out of Marrakesh appeared bountiful with olives both young and more mature. Some were thriving while others were drought-burned and desiccated. We travelled through a swathe of Sahel; a duned wasteland with occasional trees. Mud-baked walls enclosed the occasional properties or tiny settlements, *nourwals*, where goats fed off clumps of scrub. We were held up by a troupe of donkeys on the road, but arrived more or less on schedule. I gently extricated myself from lonely Douglas who was keen for company and suggested a night at the youth hostel together. I wished him well and set off merrily along the windy street, whorls of rising sand pricking at my skin, in search of a bed. I loved Essaouira from the moment I stepped off the bus into its blustery blue-and-white heart. Its romanticism, its utter remoteness. Its white minarets, its red-brown fortress, on the ramparts of which in 1948 Orson Welles had strode in windswept robes, shooting the opening sequence of his award-winning film *Othello*. From Francis Drake to Jimi Hendrix, the visitor lists had been eclectic.

For those earliest of incomers, the Phoenicians, Essaouira, or Migdal as they knew it, provided their farthest outpost. It was the margin, the extreme limit for those long-distance merchants who were interacting, staking claims, transporting knowledge everywhere round the Mediterranean. This was foreign. Here, where the Atlantic rollers beat at the rocks and the wind ripped the guts out of their boats. Archaeological research shows that Essaouira was occupied as far back as prehistoric times. So who greeted those easterners when they dropped anchor? The bay in front of the harbour is almost closed off from the open sea by the large island of Mogador, making it a relatively protected zone against those fierce Atlantic gales and a natural choice for those sailors who landed first on that island before setting up a mainland base during the seventh century BC. What must it have looked like? What must it have felt like to reach this distance, this 'far beyond'? But what did they trade here? Examples of Phoenician red pottery dating from the seventh century BC have been unearthed but no painted ostrich eggs, oil lamps or jars used for the transportation of wine and olive oil. All of these commodities have been found at their other North African sites. Might they have attempted to engage these natives in olive cultivation, the purchase of its oil, and were refused because the locals had their argan trees?

It was a long way to come to go shell-seeking even given that the dye from the murex brought them fabulous returns. Migdal was visited again in the fifth century BC by their descendants, fleets of Carthaginians led by their navigational hero, Hanno. A trading centre was established and, later, a purple-dye factory to process the murex and purura shells found in the rocks along this coastline. The dye was shipped to Rome for the imperial togas.

I found myself a bed in a two-storey house on the seafront over-looking the waves, five minutes from the old city. An Arabic proverb: he who travels much learns more than he who lives long. I felt in the running for such knowledge! It was early evening. I had been on the road since before dawn. Such a circuitous route here from Casa, but I was happy. How must this windy outlet have seemed to those first voyagers so far from their eastern shores? Did they find nothing but rocks, islands and surf? I dropped my bags in my room with view and small table by the window, and set off. The beachfront was a generous golden arc of sand with gulls flying low in the evening light. The wind was still up. There were monkey puzzle trees lining the esplanade, and, in that respect, it reminded me, with its surfers and vegetation, of Manly Beach, Sydney, Australia. The Moroccan equivalent of the Spanish *paseo* seemed to be under way for the seafront was crowded. Mothers, accompanied by young daughters in scarves and long dresses, strolled arm in arm. The tourists – and there were more here than I had encountered anywhere so far on this voyage – bore the surfer's look: faces forged by the sea's salt and by excess. Also drop-outs, ex-hippies and druggies.

Within the lovely walled medina, a poem of white façades and shuttered blues, none of the restaurants served alcohol. Mint tea was the beverage. I moseyed about for a while taking photos and then, at the very edge of the old city, found a fish bar overlooking the ramparts where I ate alone, reading, and drank a glass of high-priced wine with my grilled herring.

I was up and out of my digs by six thirty the following morning, eager to take a small boat across to the island of Mogador – this appellation was given by the Portuguese in 1506 – but the wind was high, it was Mohammed's birthday and no one seemed willing to make the short crossing. The catch was in, though. The fishermen had worked overnight. It was a glorious, if breezy, morning with fleets of blue fishing boats slapping in the dieselled, greasy water. I stood with the strays, dogs and cats, as hundreds of slithery silver sprats and sardines flapped for their lives in the salt water puddled within the base of the skiffs, damned in their efforts, for they were destined to be served as *fritures*. The fishermen, barefoot, trousers rolled to their knees, were wading among their catch, somehow avoiding to squash them, and pouring buckets of water, drawn from the polluted portside, on to the expiring creatures while scooping them into baskets and tossing them to the first of a chain of men each of whom passed the basket on to the next in line until, eventually, the fidgeting mounds of silver stripes had landed on the quay and were emptied into plastic crates piled high. This same activity was taking place all around this inner anchorage while gulls screeched, hopped and gobbled greedily at the few escaped offerings. I was the only woman, the only onlooker. It was early: the holidaymakers were sleeping or at their breakfasts.

This fishing port had a laid back, timeless feel to it, but Islam governed. The activities I had been observing were repeated all around the Med, yet this was the Atlantic, though its history was Mediterranean. From Phoenicians to Portuguese to the French. Religion was laid on later. It was not part of the tradition, not part of man's knowledge or survival skills on land or sea. If I had been observing this scene in Portugal, Spain or France, it would have been identical, save for a church spire or two, instead of minarets breaking the skyscape.

Afterwards, I wandered aimlessly, observing the festivities. Musicians with unfamiliar stringed instruments and exquisitely embroidered, coloured pillbox hats, lunch stalls displaying freshly caught red mullet, bream, slabs of bigger fellows I couldn't recognise, all decorated with cuts of lemon and seaweed, alongside crustaceans. I followed the curves of the port past *les douanes*, customs, to the fish market and a sheltered corner where a band of Arab fishermen were crouched in hoods and turbans, mending their deep-red nets in the sunshine. A boy seated on a wooden box was selling cigarettes. A man in dark-red *djellabah* who resembled Father Christmas bought himself a single smoke. Blue fishing boats everywhere; a sailor's haven for over 2500 years. Salt and fish whiffs on the wind. Near the port police I discovered a scrawny marmalade cat skulking in the shadows, its face a mass of congealed blood from where it had been ripped and clawed in a fight. Nearby, a flea-bitten dog chained behind a wooden fence protecting a littered patch of scrub.

Back through one of the medina's terracotta gateways where women in white *haicks* sat cross-legged on the ground, begging. I bought goat-skin slippers for Michel and learned from the vendor that this vigorous local wind was called the *alizee*. Herbalists everywhere, displaying argan soaps, oils and 'anti-wrinkle creams' dubbed the 'new olive oil, only better'. Over a glass of mint tea, I spotted *amlou* on the menu, a dish of ground almonds, honey and argan oil. It was too late for breakfast so I ordered a salad dressed in the endemic oil. It tasted nutty, slightly bitter. I fell into conversation with a lanky retired Englishman reading the *Daily Telegraph*, wearing faded red Moorish slippers. I was surprised to learn he'd been a resident for over a decade.

'Saouira,' he corrected, 'Arab name, it means picture. Brits have been here since the nineteenth century when this entire coastline was Mogador. We're a mixed bunch, not just hippies and dropouts. A remote station such as this suits our island mentality. Back then, this place was a thriving port and the British shipping lines conveyed Indian cotton and tea from China and India. There were British clubs and a British Consul. Substantial Jewish community, too. Cricket was played beneath the palm trees. It was splendid, all told, until the bloody Berbers rode in with rifles at the beginning of the twentieth century. Well, that was the end of the fun and games for our boys. The French took control in 1912. Bloody shame.'

I was fascinated. So many galleys, vessels and warships had sunk off these storm-tossed shores, brought down by cannons and gale-beaten rocks. How much blood had been shed in the endless battles for supremacy?

'There's an actress here, too, ex-*Dynasty* star, Stephanie Beacham. She owns a riad somewhere within these walls. She's rarely in residence though.'

He could not tell me her address, which was a pity. Stephanie and I had known each other since our twenties. She had visited us at our olive farm.

Later, I found an account by a nineteenth-century English resident of Mogador describing a sea bombardment by the French in 1844. Many of the inhabitants had fled while the British, including the Consul and his wife, bravely hung on. A strong north-easterly had interfered with hostilities, which seemed to end in chaos when 'wild tribes' (Berbers) pillaged the city and put to the sword many of the Brits and Jews. The author described the situation as 'a pandemonium of discord and licentiousness'. Mogador was 'left in a heap of ruins, scarcely one house standing'. Evidently, the port was reconstructed because it continued as a trading post and centre of commercial exchange. I also discovered that the cotton imported by the British was not from East India but Manchester and was delivered by camel train to interior cities, some as far afield as the salt-trading centre of 'Timbuctoo'. Essaouira exported the finest of all Moroccan produce and this included substantial tons of olive oil. In 1855, it was recorded that 'trade last year was greatly increased by the unusually large demand for olive-oil from all parts, and there is no doubt that, under a more liberal Government, the commerce might be developed to a vast extent'.

Olive oil *from all parts*. I wondered what had been intended by 'all parts'. I was equally interested to note that, at that stage, Moroccan ironwood oil, argan, was not listed at all as an export from these shores. I walked the beach, negotiating rocks, searching for an idle fisherman who would row me over to the uninhabited Ile de Mogador, actually two small islands and a cluster of islets. It was the beginning of the Eleonora's Falcon breeding season out on those purple islands. These rare birds of prey, named after a fourteenth-century Sardinian princess who introduced laws to protect them, flew from Madagascar to breed here and I decided that perhaps protection of these extraordinary long-distance migrants was the reason I could not find a ferryman. Continuing on towards the lighthouse, I perched on a clump of rocks, attempting to glimpse one of the falcons, but was out of luck.

At the bus station I found that no buses, whatever configuration I gave the trip, went where I was headed. Immouzer was sixty-two kilometres inland from Agadir by bus or *grand taxi*, and further from Essaouira. I first needed to take a bus to Agadir and from Agadir another bus or taxi inland on roads that wound through a gorge known as Paradise Valley. Once in Immouzer, I would be obliged to find another mode of transport, for there were no buses, to take me onwards into the High Atlas Mountains. The fact was that where I was intended was off all beaten tracks. I drifted among a chaos of taxis, buses, hawkers and tourists trying to nail down a solution that would make the journey feasible. I had not come this far to turn back. The chauffeurs of the *grands taxis* had agents who ran round shouting destinations. When a potential passenger cried 'Yes', he led them to a vehicle where they waited until another five had been secured. The taxis rarely departed without a full complement of six.

One such agent advised that I skip the journey to Agadir altogether, hire a *grand taxi* in Essaouira and go directly to my destination. He warned, though, that not in a month of Fridays would I find five others travelling my way. I bowed to this and we found a driver who, in this week of festivities, said he preferred not to work and that I was requesting a distant trek that would keep him from his family. Negotiations! Eventually, between the three of us we struck a deal. The price quoted was one hundred euros, one way. In European terms this was not a fortune, but in heartland Morocco it was a tidy sum and a chunk out of my budget. If I required the driver to wait for me, it would be double the price plus the cost of his overnight in a hotel. It was too far to drive there and back in one day. We shook hands, until the following morning, on our one-way arrangement.

That evening I climbed the Portuguese ramparts and looked out to sea, watching the sun set beyond the islands. Below, the outlines of a Phoenician dye factory. The Greeks had named them *Phoenikas*, 'men with purple faces'. When they transported the purple product, the sea sprays mixed with it, covering the sailors, turning their skins purple. Dye factories, fish salting, olive oil. Surely the Phoenicians delivered all these skills here? The Romans came after, greedy to take control of the precious factories for themselves. Did they fail in attempts to persuade the locals to forget the argan and take the olive?

Sand, sea and sunken history beneath the modest fleets of twenty-first-century sardine boats bobbing in the harbour.

The village where we had broken down was strict Muslim. There were no women to be seen anywhere although we had driven by a Women's Cooperative for Argan Pressing. I walked back to it, but it was closed for the holidays. Mohammed, my driver, was now insisting I remain in the car. While I waited in the windy but stifling midday heat, not twenty kilometres outside Essaouira, for the repair of the punctured rear tyre – the spare was worse – I passed the time reading faxed pages from Michel, information he had found somewhere for me. I was pleased to receive it and to know that he was still enthusiastic about my travels.

The argan tree, *Argania spinosa*, also known as Moroccan iron-wood, is a shrub-like, thorny evergreen with an almond-sized fruit and kernel which, when pressed, gives an oil that is 'as highly prized and ten times more expensive than olive oil'. Similar to olive oil, it has low fat content, is high in unsaturated fatty acids, reduces cholesterol and prevents arteriosclerosis. The Moroccan Berbers use the oil for cooking, skin care and medicinal needs. It serves the same purposes as olive oil, but the methods of gathering are different. These fruits are prized by wild goats that climb the argan trees to eat them. After digesting them, the stone is excreted within their dung. The Berber women collect these hard-shelled seeds and press them.

Like the olive, the argan tree is hardy: it can tolerate excessive heat, poor soil conditions and extreme drought. But unlike the olive, if drought hits, the argan goes into a dormant state and only refoliates when the rains return. The tree can survive for up to two hundred years, so it lacks the eternal staying power of the olive. Its flowers are small, pale yellow. The olive's are white though the wilder shrubbier oleasters can produce flowers with a creamy yellowish tint. The fruit of the argan takes over a year to ripen and reaches maturity in June/July the following summer. The olive's maturation is briefer, but for those who prefer very black drupes the process can take as long as ten months. The argan is endemic to the calcareous semi-desert conditions in the Sousse Valley in south-western Morocco, and to nowhere else in the world. Here, the *arganerie* forests cover some 828,000 hectares, but the area has shrunk to half its size in a century. Due to human intervention – felling for timber, firewood, charcoal, land clearance for agricultural purposes and climate changes – the forests are under threat and UNESCO has designated them a Biosphere Reserve. In earlier epochs these self-seeded forests covered a far more extensive region and it has become harder for them to propagate naturally. Major programmes are in place to reforest with nursery-raised trees in order to combat desertification and to protect the tree itself.

I stared out of the window at three men engaged in the repair of a simple puncture.

Originally, the argan forests had extended across this vast plain, a semi-Mediterranean steppeland, to the open sea coasts. I wondered whether their produce had been bartered with the foreigners who traded here. Had the Phoenicians or earlier traders taught the Berbers how to press these unique fruits?

'On either side of us stretched away to the horizon what looked like orchards of old buttressed apricot or plum trees laden with ripening fruit. I could scarcely believe that I was in a natural forest and that the trees, centuries old, had not been planted by man.' From David Fairchild, *Exploring for Plants*, written in 1931.

It was late afternoon by the time we were back on the road. The tyre-patching had taken close to six hours! I had suggested I return to lovely Essaouira for the night and we start afresh at dawn but at this Mohammed had grown sullen. He had been booked for today, he said. Hardly my fault, I gently pointed out, but as he spoke no French, my Arabic was less than basic and his Berber dialect was another universe to me entirely, conversation and argument were all but impossible. We slogged on. My concern was that once through the Sousse Valley we would be climbing into the Atlases after dark and I would see nothing. He assured me this would not be the case, though I had no certainty he had understood me. On we went. Every time we came to even one single argan, its branches laden with feeding goats – it is a most bizarre and comical sight; a pyramid of shaggy-haired, horned creatures scaling, one on top of another, a stunted tree – he pulled over for photographs and was puzzled when I insisted we keep moving. Frequently, a single goat, legs akimbo, was munching happily at the apex of one of the stubbies.

Rural hinterland: ochre plains; basic living conditions; donkeys ridden side-saddle by boys geeing them with sticks; blankets in the sun airing over prickly scrub and wadis as dry as dust. The soil was variations on beige. Donkeys, when not journeying and transporting, rested in the shade of the argans. The original wild olive would have resembled this tree. The men in their long brown *djellabahs*, hoods lifted when the wind blew, walking in file, friezed against the skyline put me in mind of a caravan of camels, single-humped hereabouts. Sub-arid vegetation; a tortoise walking in the road. Occasionally, I attempted conversation or shot a question, but without luck. Eventually, Mohammed put on a cassette and we sank into our separate silences; the low whining music and the views beyond the window our sole points of contact. Three hours in, the *jebels* were becoming more frequent, the land undulating, less flat. We had reached the lower ranges of the Atlases. The earth grew salmon-pink dotted with argans and olives. Living quarters so primitive they might have been Stone Age. Occasionally, a lone vendor sat at the roadside. What trade passed? Small yellow flowers on the argans. A fully formed argan, after rains when it was in leaf, from the middle distance was not dissimilar to an olive, but by comparison the *olea* was sweeter looking than its desert cousin. It possessed grace, an elegance, with lovely leaves of silver and dusky-green to give it a class that the thorny, twisted, sparse-leaved argan lacked.

Hairpin bends, ascending, steepening. Gazing out on magnificent scenery, not a dwelling, not even a stone bothy in any direction. The colours were Monet-soft, ochre, sand- and straw-hued, delicate, pleasing to the eye. A rusted van appeared from nowhere. In its rear cab sat a camel, gazing back at us, chewing with loose, dribbly lips. Nothing existed here but vast nature. Donkeys grazed, goats, too, on the treetops gorging on argan fruits. The rivers, the streams, the wadis, every one bone-dry. But even here, four hours' drive from any settlement, where clothes dried on mud walls, where mud-brick blocks had four walls and little else, displays of satellite dishes. Islam was in communication with these Berbers.

Mohammed grew upset, cursing under his breath.

'What's up?'

'*Barrage, barrage*,' he repeated over and over. 'Lose time.'

A road had been closed off. *The* road. He reversed agitatedly, swung off on to a descending piste. Bone-shaking, rutted; his mood grew worse. Eventually we linked with another path. This pleased him. Before I knew it we were upon a cast-iron bridge traversing a *barrage-reservoir*, an extensive dam. Its proportions were spectacular and possibly supplied most of these Atlas communities. Once across, Mohammed drew to a halt. I took some photos: lake set against mountains in the middle distance. Goats grazed at the waterside. Two soldiers came running, boots thudding against the echoing bridge. The first buttonholed my camera, but I refused to let go. A tug of war ensued. I was in hot, incomprehensible debate and called for Mohammed's assistance but he was barefoot on all fours, praying, lost in his spiritual world while I was fighting to keep a grip on my material one. Eventually, I calmed the young soldiers who were informing me that the king's brother was responsible for this magnificent piece of engineering. I duly admired it, they lessened their hold and I retrieved my camera. Everyone shook hands, but Mohammed was still praying. I was keen to be on the move before any change of heart. When he was done, my driver rose to his feet, donned shoes, brushed the gravel from his forehead and we continued.

From now on, a spiralling ascent. Evening was falling. The radiator grew temperamental. Regular roadside stops to feed it. The day was closing in around us. We still had distances to go. Mountain life, Atlas life. Convoys descending on donkeys laden with burlap sacks bursting with – what? Argan? Camels ascending laboriously, worn down by their loads. Pale pink houses and a pale pink mosque. Stone-terraced walls. Barefoot children. Rural Berbers living simply, in a fashion as old as time. How far in a few short days from the mass industrialisation of Spanish olives! Everywhere, miniature posts of stone. Cairns, demarcating property boundaries. Stones as basins for earth, stones to hold water, stones for the foundations of their modest abodes. Not the mud-brick quarters I had seen in the Sahel. These homes, with rectangular walled gardens, were constructed from locally quarried limestone, and the masonry work was skilled.

Girls, no more than six years old, slippered feet, faces hidden behind scarves, floral ankle-length dresses, herded their goats, driving them homewards, shooing them up mountainsides. Fresh-faced children charging after their beasts. Easy-limbed within the open unconstructed spaces. Yet even the most undeveloped girl-child was attired for Islam.

Where patches of mountain had been tamed, cultivated, I found olives. Not wild growth; these had been chosen. At each radiator stop I strolled the narrow road, squinting towards the summits or down into the valleys. I might have been in Turkey, the Taurus ranges. A remarkable similarity. It brought home yet again that these mountains were born, all from the same sea, seabed deposits that erupted so many millions of years ago, almost at the birth of the planet, heaving up limestone, clay, sand and mighty primitive submerged rocks to create an enclosed ring of mountains round the water's rim. These ranges are the bones of the Mediterranean. They have been instrumental in the geological formation of the Mediterranean's terrain, its flora and fauna, a topography that remains more or less the same, save for the African deserts, the entire journey round.

A few wild olives in the gulleys and almonds, too, pockets of trees. Their petals had fallen and they were in light-green leaf. Imagine if I had been here three weeks earlier when the pastel blossoms had been flowering. Mohammed was pouring yet another bottle of water into the greedy, drunken radiator. The evening was absolutely lovely: softly golden, benign, silent. The cradle of an ancient way of life. I spotted groups of scarved women huddled together on the ground, shoulder brushing shoulder, narrating secrets beneath the almond trees, laughing, smiling, serious faced. This was their world. This was how it was, how it remained for them, and observing it, it seemed for a split second to be the perfect otherwhere.

I stepped freezing, socked feet on to the balcony from a dormitory room that had been damp, cold and really not too comfortable. Due to the altitude, 1200 metres above sea level, it warranted heating but the hoteliers had not been expecting an extra guest and I had arrived at close to nine, the depths of night hereabouts. The residence was a curious place. It conjured up ghosts of a post-World War I sanatorium in Switzerland. I half expected to bump into Freud at breakfast. The facilities were basic. The atmosphere was hushed. People whispered. I was an unexpected stone rolling in late, after the service of dinner had begun at tables embracing a central open fire. The hook-nosed, black-haired Berbers in burgundy sweaters were gracious and accommodating. They were Muslims but they served, expensively, a Moroccan Cabernet to the handful of guests, all of whom were French except for one morose German couple who consumed copiously and exchanged barely a word between them. Why were these people in this middle-of-nowhere spot, this austere retreat? Were they, like me, eager to learn the magic water arts of the argan? No, they were hikers, enjoying the mountains. From my balcony, the exhilarating view swept across ridges and valleys and sparse forests to distant crests folding into ulterior shadowy eminences. This region was renowned for its cascades where ancient olive trees plunged from on high to a narrow plateau where, at the foot of the waterfall, swirled a bubbling natural basin. A two-hour trek through the groves to the baths was a well-trodden path, but, alas, there was no water, no cascade, no pool, nor had there been for three years. Untimely droughts are not uncommon in the Mediterranean, but this was different, unexpected. Climate change?

Lahrcen, the night porter, registered me. When I explained the purpose of my visit, he agreed to assist in whatever way he could. At first he suggested that I enquire at the Hotel Cascade, nestling at the foot of the barren falls. There lived a family who farmed argan trees, 'but not here,' he explained. 'We are too high here. Argans cannot survive at this altitude.'

'Somewhere more remote,' I had begged, off the tourist track.

'Leave it with me.'

I was alone in the dining room enjoying the last mouthfuls of a rudimentary breakfast – bread, coffee and a wide selection of home-made jams – missing my daily conversations with Michel who was in China, when moustachioed Lahrcen, bleary eyed after a night's tour, tiptoed in. 'I've found you a family,' he announced without emotion.

'Where?'

'From my own village. A taxi'll take us. It's ten kilometres from here but a difficult *piste*,' he warned. 'The driver'll be here when he's finished what he's doing.'

'Can't we go in your car?'

'I walk to and from home. I'll take you to meet women who press the argan nut in the traditional way. In one hour, be ready.' He crept from the dining room.

Another table was now occupied. A Muslim family. The mother was young, plump, pink and full-cheeked like a hamster, swathed from head to foot in robes and scarves. The father, a little older, hair tinged grey above his sideburns, was also in a long robe and slippers, *babouches*. They had a small son. Conversation was in Arabic, between father and offspring. They were Arabs, not Berbers. The mother said not a word, only stared dolefully into her breakfast.

I waited for the driver at a round table on a pebbled terrace along-side a dried-up fountain in the brisk morning air. Birdsong resounded, mellifluous, crystal-clear in this early spring, highland weather. Eventually, Themen pulled up in a Peugeot not fit for the knacker's yard. I was warned again that the transit would be uncomfortable. Hardly surprising. The vehicle lacked springs altogether and was without seat belts. Although Lahrcen spoke passable French, Themen's was minimal and much of the conversation was translated. Both men were Berbers.

'It would be rare to find Arabs in the Atlases.'

They spoke of 'Moroccans' as though they were a race apart. These Berbers clung to their ethnic identity and it overrode nationalism. They were Berbers first, Moroccans second. Themen lived with his wife and children in the clifftop village where the hotel was situated, but Lahrcen's home nestled within the valleys.

'Where I'm taking you, no tourist has ever been,' he grinned.

I thanked him for the honour. I did not take his words seriously.

Our way led us along the tarmacked road I had arrived by. The water crisis in the region was acute, I learned. Wells were empty; concern was mounting; no rain for three years. The same cry every-where. Some families were quitting, leaving for cities, for jobs, an easier existence, families with no experience of urban living. The majority ended up in the shantytowns.

We swung off the tarmac and descended a winding bridle path. No gutters, no pavements, just pebbled passage. The tones were pastel yellow, salmon and beige. They lacked nuance, the earth was too dry. Overtaking a pensioner in a turban riding a donkey, buckets flapping against the beast's haunches, he waved. He was on his way to collect water. Sometimes it was necessary to travel distances.

'That's my village across the valley.' Lahrcen was pointing to a settlement some kilometres ahead. The Peugeot continued down the mule track, powder rising up around us, hazing the view.

'You walk this every day?'

He nodded. 'Crops are poor. Families can't survive by farming. I'm fortunate. Few have jobs. I'm chief night porter.'

I smiled. There were no other night staff.

His village was composed of a population of one thousand. It was bigger than it looked from this five-kilometre range. As we snaked a descent, we passed small files of women in coloured but faded clothes, or solitary females, all weighed down, bent by provisions stuffed into plastic sacks on their backs. They had come from Agadir by bus and tramped the remainder on foot. I thought back over the climb Mohammed and I had made in the car. The nearest bus station, which was not a daily service, was over twenty kilometres away. This shopping expedition took the women four days. There was just the one taxi in the vicinity and we were in it, but in any case these highlanders never travelled by car. They walked or rode camels and donkeys. There were no vehicles at all in Talmste, Lahrcen pointed out.

Frequently at the track's perimeters stood neatly piled stacks of stones, waiting to be taken for house construction when someone required them.

To reach the inner heart of the settlement, we were obliged to negotiate an upwards maze of tiny lanes and impasses. The car made various false starts, over-revving, leapfrogging towards rocks. On several occasions, we rolled back while the gearbox screeched in agony. People waved and smiled at our approach. They paid no attention to the car's high jinks. Both men were known here.

Eventually, Themen switched off the engine and we piled out, abandoning the Peugeot.

Lahrcen's house was an uphill trek. Its structure comprised a jumble of buildings, each a single room leading through to the next hut. I was introduced to his wife, rotund and vibrant, waiting with her coat on, cradling a number of bags as though ready to leave. Alongside her, standing to attention, a line of three children of diminishing height. The tallest, a girl, was clutching the left ear of a white goat with a plump brown chicken perched on its crown. The second girl, the youngest, had a purple birthmark that covered one side of her face.

Outside, there was an oven, a blackened hole in the wall, with flat iron pans to bake their flat breads. The doors had all been painted in blues and greens, not dissimilar to our farm, and it gave a sense of serenity and harmony to the whitewashed home. There was no furniture, not in any of the rooms I was shown into. A few rugs on the floor, but that was about it. Lahrcen proudly showed me the new kitchen, more a walk-in cupboard or ancient scullery with two bottle-fed gas rings, a boiling kettle and an early-generation Frigidaire. Outside, plants, lacking water, were surviving in big square tins, rather like in the white villages of Greece. The traffic was the echoing clop of donkeys or the slip-slop of children's slippered feet. On the flat roof was the washing and the satellite. Four hundred stations could be received, Lahrcen bragged. It struck me as unlikely. He enjoyed watching the Agadir football team. Here, there was no football because there was no level ground to play on.

'Shall we go?'

I nodded, snapping shots of the homes, collapsing biscuit tins hugging the hewn rock slopes.

'Do you have enough film?' Lahrcen asked. 'If not, we've a shop in the village.'

'Thank you, the camera is digital.'

'Digital?'

'Numérique,' I repeated. 'It needs no film.' I showed him the last couple of shots. He seemed amazed.

'Do you want me to fetch my camera, just in case?'

I smiled. 'There's no need, but thank you for the thought.'

'Well, let's go. They'll be waiting for us.'

Worried, wiry Lahrcen with robust wife at his side patted their offspring, chivvying them back into the house and we returned to the car.

'My wife's coming with us.'

That was fine by me. 'Will the children be safe alone?' My question amused both parents and I learned that no door was ever locked here, neighbours looked out for one another and there had not been a crime within living memory committed in the village.

As we walked, I noticed that all the doors of these flat-roofed stone and mud houses were decorated with bold designs in brilliant colours. It seemed to create an atmosphere of extravagant happiness. There was also a mosque, just the one, but none where we were headed. There was a school, too, with black numerals painted all over the exterior walls. My presence was a curiosity to those who passed us on foot or donkey. All were scaling the hillsides fetching, transporting, heaving canisters of water. Most were dusty women whose faces were deeply wrinkled, but whose skin was scrubbed, glowing. A rectangular water basin, fed from high-altitude snowmelts, had been constructed down in the palm of the valley. It was the only one in the vicinity that had not dried up. A small group of the scarved women were seated on the muddied and tiled surface at its side, with children splashing and horsing about close by. As is so often the case in remote communities, the fountain was a meeting place, a focal point for gossip, laundry and interaction.

We piled into the Peugeot – men in the front, women in the rear – and began a treacherous trajectory along a sandy corridor. A wall of limestone to the right and a deep precipice to the left. I forced myself not to consider the possibility that the taxi, with its treadless tyres, would skid and plummet. Brakes, wheels, gearbox, no part of this machine was mechanically primed for the outing we were embarking upon. On several occasions, we were obliged to stop, return to first gear and proceed again. Once or twice Lahrcen and wife got out to push. I was not allowed to! We were going to Lahrcen's in-laws who they had not seen in six months. It was perfect timing; this was the holiday season, Mohammed's birthday, when families made the social rounds. For a fleeting moment, I thought I might have been duped, that the night porter had set this up to obtain a free ride, but I quickly saw this for its pettiness.

The mountain slopes were tiered with drystone terraces to conserve the precious rainfalls, protect the flimsy topsoil. Olives and almonds grew.

'Many of the families hereabouts are olive farmers.' Lahrcen seemed delighted by this fact. But the argan could not survive at this altitude.

I leaned out of the window, shutting out the yawning abyss alongside us, clicking right and left. A sense of privilege washed over me, an immeasurable gratitude to these people. An hour later, still frogging along, I began to believe Lahrcen; no tourist had penetrated this mountain's interior. The sight of me caused children, playing outside lone bungalows alongside tethered black or white kids, to roar with laughter, to jump up and down with glee. When we eventually ditched the car, continuing on foot, they followed behind us, heckling excitedly.

'I hope you're not offended,' whispered Lahrcen. 'They're being cheeky.'

'Not in the least. What are they saying?' I swung back to take a shot of a trio of unscrubbed, snotty-nosed urchins. As I did, one launched a stone that struck me in the shin. Lahrcen was after them in seconds but they fled, crouching behind the rubbled wall of an abandoned property. Slowly, heads popped up uncertainly, then grinning. I walked back and showed them the photograph. Their eyes grew bright and big as though witnessing magic. Not for the first time did I wish that my camera printed off instant images, like the defunct Polaroid.

Two women were waiting outside the house as we approached. Lahrcen's wife plodded on ahead to greet her mother, handing the plastic bags of gifts to the elfin-sized woman. I was welcomed with respect; bowing of heads and shy gestures to come inside. The house of stone and earth had been carved into the hillside. It was substantial, three storeys including stables on the lower level. This family was land-wealthy and, far more crucial, water-rich. Across the narrow strip of caked lane in front of their home, the cliff plunged deeply. Perhaps thirty metres down the precipice was a verdant, irrigated ledge with olives and palm grove. Water arrived by an open conduit that had been fashioned out of baked mud. It was fed by a source back along the valley and resembled the ancient Roman channels, but the Romans had probably taken the principle from the Middle Eastern qanat system. The canal supplied this family and two other properties further back. Its simple principle had to be almost as old as agriculture itself.

The road went nowhere. It stopped a few yards further along. Here was journey's end. No Berber settlements had penetrated beyond. We were situated at the higher level of an inner cavity, a massive breach in the mountain. Now I understood Lahrcen's remark. No one came here. Perhaps a sturdy 4x4 could make it but otherwise the only access in and out was by foot or on a beast. If the water dried up on this mountainside, this family and the others we had passed would be done for. Their sole means of survival was the rewards of their land. They farmed the olive trees clinging to the lower levels as well as the modest palm groves. Here and there, lower down, grew a rogue, hunchbacked argan and elsewhere the in-laws owned an argan forest. Its oil they sold. It fetched them better prices than olive oil. They were also entitled to harvest certain of the wild crops. The rights to collect the fruits – a yield of about eight kilos per tree – were strictly governed by Berber village traditions and everyone adhered to the unwritten rules. In this way, each family who so wished was entitled to profit from the wild forests. It reminded me of the British medieval system for commoners' rights, which guaranteed peasants access to trees growing on commons and open parkland.

By local standards, this family was comfortably off but their live-lihoods were entirely dependent upon nature. There was no form of employment here, no community in a sense that we would under-stand it: no post office, church, mosque, school, hospital, medical care, veterinary surgeon, telephone, not even one shop, and barely a handful of neighbours. They cared for their own animals. Children lacked formal education or they were obliged to return back to the mouth of the pass. There had been one other tiny school soon after leaving Lahrcen's village. If they fell sick, they healed themselves with plants or they found a way to get out. It was one of the most isolated hamlets I had ever come across. But they had satellite and with it they followed the football and they received the news. The channels here, as elsewhere in the Mahgreb, favoured Islam.

'When the Arabs moved north from the Arabian desert, waging wars along the way, spreading the message of Mohammed, the Berbers of North Africa embraced Islam and took the Arabic language, though many of our tribes have maintained their own tongues,' explained Lahrcen.

'From where do Berbers originate?' I asked my male hosts.

'Right here in the Atlases,' said one. 'The Yemen,' replied the other. To my knowledge, there were no definitive facts on the origins of Berbers. I had hoped these men might share a folktale or two that would have given me clues.

Lahrcen's had been an arranged marriage. His wife had been fifteen and he twenty. Living within his in-laws' house was a dynasty. His wife's parents, the mother-in-law's parents as well as a brother-in-law, wife, their two children and one other younger, unmarried sister. The toothless grandmother was skeletal. Dressed in a pink floral gown that resembled a floor-length nightie, chunky jewellery and a bright orange headscarf, she was a tiny bird with vibrant plumage. All the women wore brightly coloured robes and scarves and all had the palms of their hands and their fingers hennaed with intricate designs. The grandfather looked as old as the mountains in his faded green *djellabah*, beige slippers, a towel for a turban and a chin stippled with the dregs of a grey beard. The brother-in-law was remarkably handsome. I found most of the Berber men striking, with hooked noses and blazing black eyes. Semitic faces, oriental, regal.

I was ushered into a ground floor, open-air living area. Awaiting my arrival was an ancient, one-person-sized pressing stone on a very low blue table. To work at it involved sitting cross-legged on the floor. The entire family was gathered round it. I took two photos of the table before the ladies set to work and then the camera's battery went dead. Lahrcen berated me.

'I knew I should have brought mine,' he cried.

What I noticed was how physical these people were with one another, how Lahrcen's mother-in-law stroked and patted him, cradling his head in the crook of her arm, how she kissed him on his forehead and how frequently they laughed. A debate was in progress as to who would demonstrate the pressing of the fruit. Lahrcen volunteered, because he could talk me through the process as he did so. This decision resulted in eruptions of hysterical laughter. Since time immemorial, argan pressing had been a woman's task. When Lahrcen settled on the floor, the women pulled their scarves across their faces to hide their giggles, tears running down their faces. I reversed to try another shot, hoping the battery might flicker back to life, and as I did so I nearly fell through the floor. Because the family had been gathered round the pressing stone, I had not noticed that, in the centre of this roofless room, the floor was missing. It was intended that way. Beneath us was a menagerie of goats, chickens, spring lambs, ducks, rabbits. One rabbit was sitting on a goat's back. Only the donkeys and dog were absent. The two donkeys had a stable alongside the property's entrance while the dog was chained by the front door. If he was let loose below, he would eat or frighten the poultry. The animals were fed from where I stood, vittels tossed into their underground pen. A kitchen, where they ended up, no bigger than the one I had seen at Lahrcen's, abutted the room we were standing in. There was no furniture at all besides the low, round table for the pressing stone. Upstairs, reached by a hand-made wooden ladder, was where they slept, lay about on cushions and watched television.

Lahrcen was cross-legged, ready to begin the demonstration. The four stages of pressing lay in a quartet of blue bowls: kernels still in hard shells, kernels after the nut had been broken open, roasted kernels and finally the oil, pressed before our arrival for the display.

'Unlike the olive, we only press the kernels. The most difficult part of the process is the removal of the pulp and cracking the nut. The removed heart is then roasted. Now, here we go.'

I was struggling to follow his commentary because the infectious squealings never abated.

Our demonstrator placed several roasted kernels on to the stone press, which was worn and shiny and looked as though it had been carved from beaten bronze. A sprinkling of water, and he began to grind hard with a thick stone pestle until the seeds started to dis-integrate into paste. His face was turning red and he was now giggling himself.

'From these crushed roasted nuts will slowly trickle drops of thick amber juice, but it takes about twenty hours.'

As with the olive, this was labour-intensive and it took large quantities of fruit for one litre of oil. The women were laughing so much that Lahrcen said he could not continue, which amused them all the more. He encouraged me to taste a mouthful from the pre-pressed offering.

'We pour a few drops into our pans of couscous. It has a distinctive nutty flavour, don't you agree?' Lahrcen's wife was saying.

I nodded.

The pestle brought to mind early twentieth-century photos from Greece where the women also sat with crushing stones and mashed the olives until they bled oil. This was no different. And in Malta, here was what I had written when I visited the BC stone temples on that island: 'At one of the temples, I found coralline limestone slabs into which rounded and semi-smoothed central, circular dips, indentations, like the cup setting in saucers, had been carved . . . a quern. I have since learned that no fewer than eleven querns have been found at these sites. Querns that experts believe were used for pulverizing olives and have been dated as Copper Age, 3000 B.C.'

What I was witnessing now was only one stage more developed than those prehistoric temple pressers. In other words, these Berber communities were still working a traditional, primitive method, a fundamental system that has been used around the Mediterranean for eons before recorded history.

During the return journey, Lahrcen explained that the argan forests were keeping the desert at bay, maintaining the ground. If the forests are lost, the Sahara will move north.

As we arrived back into his village, the sun was beginning to disappear behind the high-range mountains. Evening fell early here.

'It's a pity about your camera,' my friend said. 'Hopeless, really, those newfangled contraptions.' With that, Lahrcen bade his wife go and fetch his while he accompanied me to purchase a roll of film.

'It's not necessary. I'll charge the battery at the hotel.' I was assuming our outing had reached its conclusion.

The village store was a tarpaulined stall with a kerosene light, plenty of insects flapping and a gang of youths in jeans and *djellabahs* smoking, killing time, directionless. My arrival silenced everyone. When Lahrcen introduced me, they nodded and stared cautiously as though I might explode.

I requested a few dirhams' worth of rock-hard, brightly coloured sweets for the children. When I drew out my purse, the young men crowded round, watching hungrily as I pressed the requested seventeen dirhams on to the counter. Two for the sweets served in paper, and fifteen for the out-of-date film stock.

'There's something I'm keen for you to see.' Lahrcen was accompanying me down an inclined lane. His wife came plodding, puffing, holding up his plastic camera, less robust than a throwaway. After much fumbling and clumsiness, I managed to feed the useless film into it.

He seemed rather excited. 'You can get it processed in Casa or back in Europe.' From his pocket was pulled a monumental key. He beckoned me to follow. I sniffed the pungent aroma of ground olives even before we had turned the corner where, outside a flat-roofed stone shed, was a great mound of dried, discarded paste.

'My father was the village miller,' Lahrcen announced proudly. 'He's ninety-one, retired last season, and now the mill is to be mine.' He turned the pantomime key in the solid lock and we stepped into total blackness. Even with the door fully open, due to lack of windows and apertures, it was hard to see anything, but there was no doubting its purpose. My guide lit a match and eventually my eyes adjusted.

'This press is more than three hundred years old,' he announced. 'Take pictures, please.'

I pointed and clicked with his rudimentary plastic apparatus and its flashes fleetingly illuminated the silhouette of a stupendous stone press. Originally, it had been turned by camels, but today by donkey. I pushed at the stone crusher with all my force but it did not budge a centimetre. It was as solid as the mountain upon which we stood.

'I knew it would please you,' he grinned, 'which is why I left it till last.'

I wished that he had not waited. Even more, I kicked myself for forgetting to charge my Zeiss-lensed marvel, but that's life.

'Do you spray crops, use pesticides?' I asked.

He shook his head. 'Against what? Lack of water is our problem.'

After we had locked up, he handed me the roll, which I never processed because it was exposed at the outset. I promised to return one day to introduce Michel to this future miller and his family. He begged nothing. I had agreed a fair fee with Themen who had accompanied us, even without the Peugeot, throughout the day, but I dug into my pockets now and handed over some notes. Lahrcen shook his head. I insisted.

'That's kind. Village life gets harder. I knew you'd like my olive press. You won't find an older example in Morocco, maybe not in North Africa. What a pity you haven't a decent camera. Buy one like mine. They're not expensive.'

On our way back to the hotel we passed a man and boy sitting beneath an argan tree with a large stuffed sack. I assumed they had been collecting the fruits. They waved. I urged Themen to pull over, offer them a ride. This pleased everyone. They had not been harvesting but visiting family some distance away, walking since dawn. I asked what the sack contained. Almonds and bread, the remnants of lunch. I was starving, Themen, too. We had spent almost an entire day, walked a dusty distance, but had not been offered refreshment at either home, not even a glass of water. Both families had been warm in their welcomes so why this should have been, I could not tell, but we fished greedily into the bag and, like a pair of gannets, gobbled down the strangers' provisions.

Few options for transit between these Atlases and Volubilis. A *grand taxi* from my mountain-station hotel to Marrakesh (very expensive) and onwards by train to Meknès or a return taxi to Essaouira, coach to Marrekesh and train to Meknès. I chose the latter. It gave me an extra night at the seaside port and I fortuitously fell upon one of the sixty days in the year when the wind was not blowing. The port I returned to was a Mediterranean idyll: white gulls, blue skies, calm seas. Mohammed's birthday had been celebrated; the Muslim tourists had disappeared. It was a tranquil parenthesis.

My afternoon bus to Marrakesh was empty aside from one silent, bearded European and the occasional farmer. I nabbed a window seat. I was back within the flat littered expanses of the Sahel where barely a weed grew yet numerous herds of goats were feeding. How different must it have been half a decade back when there was rain.

My silent contemplation: water, the source of life, is the most precious commodity on the planet. What if the rains do not return?

Black plastic bags, wind-trapped in tree branches, flapped like alarmed crows. Flat, square olive mills, flat, square houses with startlingly scarlet bougainvillea snaking their red-earthed walls. Many of the small groves were enclosed behind mud-baked enclosures. The walled homes seemed to be sealed off from the outside world. Protection against Saharan winds or invaders, I could not tell. So many men in pointed hoods and pointed slippers perched on the scorched earth at road's edge. A beige, timeless universe where the light was by turns soft, dusty or burned out. These desert peoples were Berbers, not Arabs. After *Homo erectus*, the Berbers were the first humans to migrate north from Central Africa. Their presence here in the Sahels reaches back eons.

At the coffee stop I sat with the European, Jakob, a geologist and palaeontologist from Berlin, working down in the south-east. His skin was burned by all weathers and he wore a heavy black diver's watch. He seemed reluctant to discuss the project he was here to research.

'Worm fossils,' he shrugged.

I asked him about the argan forests.

'A Tertiary plant.'

'Which means?'

'It's been around for about 1.5 million years. The natural forests have acted as a buffer against the march of the Sahara, against desertification for a long time, but they're disappearing fast. Programmes have been launched to educate locals to the tree's role and there's overseas spend on marketing schemes to push its oil internationally. It's a race against time.'

Once more Marrakesh with its pink-ochre walls. Such a contrast, such a cosmopolitan circus, and the avarice! This was not a city to be introduced to in a day; it was rich, varied, raucous, corrupt, crowded with slickly practised hustlers, horse-drawn carriages, orange juice vendors, snake charmers who harangued me, 'This is work! We want money!' as well as every other tourists' whore.

I hurried off to find the olive souk. On display, piled high in jars, in bowls, glass cases, pyramids of them in tubs were succulently fat olives, pointy olives, mini ones, drupes of every shade, spiced with every herb known to man, all sold by bristly moustachioed men in white sheets and crocheted skullcaps. Marrakesh should have been much more than a stopover, and I would dearly have loved to hang out for days and engage, scratch a little beneath its meretricious veneer, spend more than one evening lost within the crowds and crazy-hatted vendors in smoky Djemaa el-Fna Square, but my Algerian visa was a limited feast. I had been given a tourist stamp that entitled me to thirty days within a pre-selected ninety. I had marginally miscalculated my chosen dates because I had not bargained on spending so many weeks in Spain. The consequence was that I needed to reach Algiers within the next six days or I would overrun. Aside from this constraint there was another difficulty: the borders between Morocco and Algeria were closed. There was no way into the adjoining state from here, except by air from Casablanca. Either that, or return to Spain and take a boat from Almería. Given the restrictions, I opted for the plane from Casa to Algiers.

Before leaving the country, I still intended to visit the Roman city of Volubilis, lying to the north of Meknès. Meknès, like neighbouring Fès, was situated at an axis, a mighty crossroads. East of Morocco lay Algeria, Tunisia, Libya, while to the west were the cities of the Atlantic littoral. Descending from north to south, the passage led from the Mediterranean towards the Higher Atlas Mountains, from where I had just arrived. Had the border between Morocco and Algeria been open, I could have continued on to Fès, marginally north-east of Meknès, and from there turned east, through the historically important pass of Taza and onwards by train or bus to the Moroccan–Algerian border town of Oujda. It would have allowed me to trace an ancient, authentic olive route, a transit road that had been travelled regularly by the Romans and possibly many caravan peoples before them. But that option was not available to me.

When I returned to my hotel, I learned that a transport strike had been announced, commencing immediately. The trains were only partially affected. Mine to Meknès, the following morning, was still scheduled to run. However, the station, situated towards the city's outskirts, was not within walking distance. The concierge organised a private car for my departure.

'And the price?'

'Who can say, *Madame*?'

'I have a plane ticket, just purchased, from Casa to Algiers to fly in two days' time.'

The concierge shrugged. 'Who can say, *Madame*, how long a transport strike will last, but it is nationwide. All problems in Marrakesh will be problems in Casa and Meknès. Perhaps worse. You might as well stay here. We have a room, a higher rate, but . . .'

No car showed up the following morning. A different concierge, another receptionist: both washed their hands of the matter.

'No one should have promised you transport. There are a few buses running, but not directly from here to the station, or you can hire a horse and carriage. But why not stay? We have one room left.'

I grabbed my bags and shot across the square to the bank of carriages. The queue was endless. I confirmed with one of the drivers that a horse-drawn taxi would be willing to clop the distance to the station, and the fare would be six euros. I joined the queue. By the time I reached the head of the line, twenty minutes later, only one horse and cab remained and the driver was demanding two hundred euros. I began to haggle. Meanwhile, another demented passenger appeared, jumped aboard and off they went. I hiked to the nearest bus station. It was pandemonium but after several false attempts I eventually boarded a bus that delivered me more or less within walking distance of the railway station. Beyond the windows, harassed, perplexed, angry folk were running about the streets as though a fire had gripped the city.

I was warned that the train would be packed and that my best option was to jump aboard, stand as far as Casa and then pray for a seat, *inshallah*. This was a nine-hour journey. I hoped for better luck. In fact, the first class was relatively empty and I found myself in a carriage travelling with one other, Brigitte, a petite red-haired French woman, a photo-journalist living in Rabat. She had also come from Essaouira where she had been covering a story on the nation's evolving tourist industry. From her, I learned that Tangier's harbour was to be moved marginally east so that the port city could be marketed

as Mediterranean. Had this ever been in any doubt, was the question
I raised. She recounted depressing episodes of riads in Marrakesh
rented out with minors, boys as part of the package. Paedophilia, she
said, was rife.

'The city has been rechristened Arnakesh.'

Arnaqueur, French for swindler. 'The City of Swindlers?'

She nodded. 'Such perversions serve no one, only justify the
extremist's determination to stem all liberties.'

She had been a Moroccan resident for seventeen years but now she
was '*ras-le-bol*', fed up to the teeth with the country. Islamic extremism
was 'twisting' the mentality of the people. Morocco had been
renowned for its progressiveness, for being the most open of all the
Maghreb countries. Sadly, that was no longer the case. Women's
rights were diminishing not expanding.

I quizzed her about the Women's Cooperatives, about the work
the Berber women were doing to preserve the argan forests. 'I heard
the cooperatives are giving jobs to women, offering them the opportunity to step outside their homes; opportunities for those who are
unemployed or living below the breadline.'

Brigitte said she had little faith that this was anything more than a
marketing ploy, an opportunity to commercialise the products.

'But if it stimulates rural prosperity, guards tradition and protects
the forests?'

She dismissed this with a wave of the hand. 'The country is closing
down, growing more restrictive.' Female Arab journalist friends, colleagues of hers, were getting out before it was too late. 'It's time to
leave,' she said, shaking my hand as the train pulled into Rabat.

In her place came a young Moroccan woman, unveiled, in Western
clothes. She nodded and we sank into our individual worlds. Moments
later, the train ground to yet another standstill. We had been on go-
slow since departure and were now over an hour behind schedule. I
calculated that Michel, who had left Beijing about the same time as
I had left Marrakesh, would, at this rate, be back in Paris before I
reached Meknès. Frustrated by the delays, my travelling companion
went off for coffee and returned with two cups. It broke the ice. She,
a Moroccan teacher from *les banlieus*, the suburbs of Paris, with big,
perplexed eyes, was on holiday, visiting cousins. She reiterated the

French journalist's point of view. Extremism was taking hold. She hated coming back and only did so because staying away would be perceived by family as an insult. She cohabited with a boyfriend outside Paris. It was over a year since they had moved in together but her parents, who lived fifteen minutes from them, knew nothing about him. He was not a Muslim and premarital sex was officially frowned upon by her religion. She feared her choices would kill her mother. She had two younger sisters, both of whom wore the veil.

'I thought they would follow in my footsteps and break away, but quite the reverse. They live at home. They watch Arabic television. They never go out without full dress code.'

When I told her I was travelling to Meknès she said, 'Me, too. Meknassa-ez-zitoun.'

'Meknès of the olive trees,' I confirmed.

'Yes, that's its original Berber name. They built their villages around the olive forests there. You will see. It is a very fertile part of Morocco with a rich olive history.'

'Any idea how or when it began?'

She could not say, but for sure it was a Berber story.

Upon arrival at Meknassa-ez-zitoun, I hurried out of the station to face yet another scrum for a taxi. The journalist, Brigitte, had recommended a colonial establishment on one of the hills close to the town. While I was queuing, my attention was drawn to a policeman hanging about outside the station, shaking everyone's hand. Folk were slapping him on the back, kissing him on the cheek. His behaviour struck me as bizarre. He had a rather comical appearance with a pencil-thin moustache and a shiny peaked hat that made him look as though he had popped out of a Jacques Tati film. A lean fox-like fellow sidled up and the two men stood side by side pressed up against a glass door talking, but always facing straight ahead. I was behind them. Slowly, the non-uniformed of the pair drew a black plastic bag from underneath the back of his jacket and passed it surreptitiously to his neighbour who secreted it between his upper thighs. As soon as the act had been completed, the deliverer walked off. The policeman turned, now facing my direction, and shoved the bag inside his jacket, which bulged and looked ridiculous. At that point he caught my eye. 'What are you doing, what do you want?' he barked.

'A taxi,' I sighed.

'No problem.' And with that he was marching authoritatively on the street, whistling, hailing passing cabs. He pulled one over. There was a passenger aboard. The poor bemused fellow was hauled out and instructed to get in the queue with everyone else, while I was installed. I offered objections, but the officer, shoving me into the rear, insisted. As we pulled away, I glanced back; package like a pigeon's breast beneath his chin, the lawman was saluting me on my way.

The hotel was a shadow of its former self, its glorious Art Deco days, colonial France, but they had a room available and a restaurant where dinner and local wines were being served. This promised a pleasurable completion to a long journey until the desk clerk warned me that the strike would continue into the next and the days beyond. The trains were also to be affected though it was a drivers' strike, an anti-governmental display for changing regulations to permits. I explained that I wished to visit Volubilis. The clerk promised to find someone.

I had encountered hustlers of one sort or another at various points throughout Morocco but this place struck me as being in a class of its own. On my way to the restaurant, a broad-breasted, dusky-skinned doorman, the height of an American basketball player (more a bouncer than a doorman), came bounding up the stairs after me.

'You know, you look great, showered and in a skirt, *très belle*. When you checked in you looked like a lorry driver. I am the trainer. Massage is my speciality. Why not book me for later in your room?'

Over dinner, my waiter, a decent doddery old bloke, a Muslim, praised my choice of wine and sat down at my table and poured himself a glass! After my meal, too hyped up to sleep, I strolled in the gardens round the disused swimming pool and then wandered into the bar. There was a very tangible sense of local Mafia operating in there. Men in shiny suits smoking fat cigars, drinking spirits, surrounded by girls, molls, in high heels, short skirts or skin-tight jeans, leather jackets, chunky jewellery. I could almost breathe the corruption. When this party's bill was delivered, the chief among them, handsome, oil-haired, slick-suit in his mid-thirties, pulled out a solid roll of notes from a back pocket (thus exposing to me, seated at a table behind him, a gun wedged in his belt). His greedy-eyed guests went silent, so green were they for his fortune.

Meknès is a wealthy town due to its agricultural resources, particularly olives and wine. The district boasts more wine cellars and olive mills than anywhere else in Morocco. Were these olive barons or prohibition crooks? I had already seen in Libya how lucrative was the black market alcohol business.

Thirty-one kilometres north of Meknès was Roman Volubilis. A taxi picked me up as arranged. Olive groves climbed the sloping, folding hillsides; olive groves speckled with flowering poppies. We passed a man lying on his side in a pasture watching over three cows grazing. Alleys of towering olives bordered the roadsides, as plane trees do in Provence. They were leafy and elegant but lacked water. Assan, my driver, confirmed that it had not rained in a year; parched were even these fertile plateaux. Still, it was lovely to behold. Sweeping fields, gently sloping inclines carpeted with yellow flowers. Goats in the groves fed on the wild herbs girdling the trees. Donkeys and men with hoes ploughing fields. Barbary figs as hedges, demarcating the boundaries. And time seemed expansive here. It breathed gently, exhaled slowly. No rush amidst the majestic, proud orchards.

'See in the distance,' said Assan, 'Volubilis.'

The Roman pillars and arches rose up out of the red hillsides; the city itself situated in the midst of the wide, generous plain of Jebel Zerhoun. As we approached its entrance, a farmer with two donkeys was tilling a patch of sunflowers and sapling olives.

First, it was a Neolithic site; after, a Berber region, then Punic-Carthaginian writings were dug up here. Excavations indicate that the location was settled by Phoenician traders in the third century BC. Eventually, inevitably, in marched the Romans. Their mighty city, built upon the ruins of the Carthaginian one, dates largely from the second and third centuries AD. Volubilis was one of the most remote outposts of their empire. Originally annexed in about AD 40, under their auspices it grew exceedingly rich, living off the oil of the land.

A long line of stones, broken treasures, flanked the pathway as I entered the archaeological site. The first to the right was an olive press, a stone as substantial as and just a little older than the one I had (barely) seen in Lahrcen's mill. Not much in the design had changed since this Roman example.

The city proved to be a liquid goldmine. I had never encountered so many olive presses and I began to get some insight into the extent of the business that had operated out of this graceful yet remote western outpost of the empire. One house in four owned their own olive press. Originally, the site was Oulili, a corruption of Oaulili, oleander. Berber or Phoenician, I did not discover. Here, the inhabitants, around 20,000, developed thriving trades in olive oil and game. As well as olives, lions, panthers, elephants were their business. Lions from the wild forests surrounding Oulili were shipped to Rome for their gladiatorial arenas.

Roaming the site, flowering marigolds everywhere, the scale of its achievements could not be ignored. Its position on this magnificent plain, its main streets and villas where it was still possible to glimpse its past living within the remains of the coloured mosaics decorating floors and walls. They offered a hint at the riches that had been accrued here.

From this lucrative agricultural region, the Romans built their administrative capital, linking all North Africa. Here, they were in touch with their holdings in the northern belts of what today are Algeria and Tunisia, all the way to Libya and onwards, no doubt, to military posts as far east as Palmyra, once the glorious oasis city in the sands of Syria.

With such a wealth of land and groves in North Africa, the transport routes and bureaucratic systems Rome had set up all along the coast from the Moroccan Atlantic to Libya gave her an unsurpassed advantage and the Roman Empire became the unforgiving mistress of the Mediterranean, of the Western world.

Here lay the demarcation point of yet another Olive Route, a landbased way. But the olive's had never been a single route; the olive's history, its transportation, was a web, a tapestry of exchanges woven by many civilisations, back and forth across the Mediterranean or trekking its circumferences. Caravans of camels set out from here, but they were never intended to complete the treks to Syria, Antioch or beyond, quite possibly linking up with the Silk and Tea Routes coming from China. There were staging posts. An exchange of manpower, beasts and commodities. From Volubilis to Algeria. From there, continued the next convoy. Or to harbours further east, entrepôts, where the oil would have been loaded on to galleys and from there set sail for further, more exotic or more northerly destinations. It was an endless and intricate relay of exchange and barter.

Unlike so many other Roman sites throughout the Mediterranean, Volubilis was not abandoned when the Romans eventually departed. The city survived and was occupied for centuries by the Berbers who had never greatly cared for their masters and had only accepted them to the degree that it had suited them. Still, the Latin tongue was spoken here until the Arabs arrived, bringing Islam with them; another language, another faith. But what did not change was the agricultural stability. The power of the olive and its produce has lived on here.

Yet more car problems! Assan's was neither a puncture nor the radiator. This time it was the hub cabs and it was me who alerted him to the noise.

'It's nothing,' he said until the clatter of a hub rolling along the road convinced him. Moments later, the vehicle tilted to the left. Assan panicked, lost confidence, doubted the taxi would deliver us back to the hotel. He needed assistance. I was considering trains, my dawn flight the following day from Casa to Algiers, a non-refundable ticket. Eventually, a small lorry approached and the driver offered to tow us to Moulay Idriss where the nearest garage was to be found.

On a hilltop stood the mausoleum of Moulay Idriss, a murdered great-grandson of the prophet Mohammed and one of the most revered of all Muslim saints. The small town, named after him, receives more pilgrims than anywhere else in the Islamic world, save for Mecca. While Assan tended to his wheels, I walked this strangest of pilgrimage locations. A white-walled maze of dwellings and stores decorated in green mosiacs. Green, the sacred colour of Islam. Non-Muslims were not permitted beyond the gates of the massive mausoleum wherein the tomb of Idriss was encased. I was taking snaps from an exterior passage when a young man approached and offered to escort me. My polite refusal was countered by nastiness, by a bizarre rebuke. 'You French, you're all the same. I'd never buy a car from one of you lot!'

I stepped away to kill time within the labyrinthine inclines. A young student approached. He wanted to apologise for his fellow citizen's bad manners. I shrugged it off but the teenager stuck with me, walking at my side, pointing out this and that. We passed a middle-aged man giving a piggyback to a blind, crippled veteran. The ascent was steep, to a holy shrine in the skies, hiking towards heaven to pray. Outside the ladies' hammam, logs were stacked in the cobbled lane. Donkeys with shopping; wimpled women with heavy bags. Beasts or foot were the sole access to the upper reaches of the village. There were no cinemas. All forms of entertainment were forbidden. There was no hotel. This religious centre hosted an annual festival that lasted several days. Many thousands of Muslims converged to worship, offering prayers and votives to the saint buried within the sepulchre.

'Where does everyone stay?' I asked.

'They pitch tents in the olive groves. A few inhabitants rent out their houses. This village is the poor man's Mecca.'

It was starting to rain. My driver had achieved whatever temporary repairs were possible. I gave the boy a few dirhams and climbed back into the taxi as Assan warned that it would be a slow return. He was not exaggerating. It was late afternoon when he delivered me back at the hotel. One train to Casa was still scheduled to run, but I had no transport. Assan's taxi was done for and reception failed to find another.

I set off with my luggage, walking in torrential rain, and soon got lost. At a highway junction, I took a wrong turn and ended up at the gate of Bab el-Mansour. I was way off course. There was no time to appreciate the splendours of this major Meknès tourist attraction, which in any case was almost obliterated by the rain. Its main entrance had been turned into a rather tacky art gallery. Sodden as a river rat I wandered in, to see if someone could help me, could ring for a cab (or ring for my husband, safely arrived home in France, to come and get me! At that moment I wanted nothing more than to be sitting on our terrace, enjoying the company of friends). They shook their heads and pointed to a solitary *calèche* sheltering against the city wall.

The driver agreed to take me to the station. If I could find a train, all well and good. If not, I intended to hire a car. We splashed through potholes brimming with water, clopping by streets banked up with small blue cars, the local *petits taxis*. (Every town's *petit taxi* was a different colour.) At the station I was informed that the only train scheduled to run to Casablanca, because all others had been cancelled, had just been withdrawn without notice.

'Maybe it's just late?'

The stationmaster shook his head. I begged an address of a car-hire firm or a travel agent and the grim news was that these, too, were on strike, out in solidarity. I was left with no way back to Casablanca, to the airport, to my plane for Algeria due to take off at seven thirty the following morning. I thanked the official and returned out into the thunderous weather.

Looking skywards, I smiled. Finally, rain. The farmers, the agri-culturalists would be delighted. I had eaten nothing since breakfast. I was soaked to the skin, fed up, shivering with cold, hungry and worried. Everywhere was closed. Eventually, I found a 'pizzeria' and entered a darkened saloon where a trio of morose Arabs were slou-ched against the bar drinking whisky. The barman came to greet me, that or block my entrance. I recalled the bar in Barcelona!

'What do you want?'

'Some food, please.'

'We have nothing.'

'But this is a pizzeria.'

'Only in the evenings.'

'Coffee?'

'No coffee. Whisky or beer.'

I settled for beer and sat alone at a counter facing a wall, luggage on the stool at my side. I could not bear the expressions of the men, staring as though I were a sinner or harlot. It was one of the only times when I wanted to shout, 'Stop judging me because I am a woman. Christians are not forbidden alcohol. You are the guys break-ing the rules, not me.' Of course, I said nothing, downed my beer meekly and ambled back to the station to find out about nearby hotels.

'Sorry to trouble you again, I'm looking for . . .'

'Weren't you enquiring about a train to Casa?'

I nodded.

'It'll be here in fourteen minutes.'

I could not believe my good fortune.

The train was packed to the gills. The first class equally crowded. I was so embarrassed by my trekking boots, wringing wet trousers, blackened-by-rain leather coat that I actually made an announcement, explaining my predicament. And what a response! Tissues to dry my face were whisked from a handbag. Plans to help me reach the airport were afoot. (It was now I discovered that Casa Voyageurs, the central station in Casablanca, was not the one that serviced the airport.) How to get from one to the other? One man commenced calling friends in the city, requesting a lift on my behalf. Another, a voluptuous mother figure, a teacher, handed me a bar of chocolate. Alongside her, tucked into the far corner, was a lecturer at the university in Lisbon who spoke every language on earth, it seemed. Apropos of nothing, he told us of his ability to read Catalan. The Portuguese found it closer to their mother tongue than Spanish was his explanation. In what way might he assist? Conversations flowed, jumping from French to Arabic and back for my benefit. Such courteous people. A hellish afternoon had been transformed into lively discussion, ranging from the bombings in Tangier, the changing face of Morocco, the appalling mess caused by strikes, the unhealthy hold Muslim parents had over their children and, with grave expressions, Islamic Fundamentalism. Throughout all, the fellow opposite continued to make enquiries on his phone. As we pulled into Casa at 10 p.m., a room had been booked for me at the adjoining hotel and it had been established that one train, only the one, ran at dawn from this principal station to the airport.

It was as though our team had won the lottery.

I spent my final Moroccan night at the station hotel, dining there, too, because downtown was beyond walking distance, and rose at dawn to a filthy, wet morning all set for my flight to Algiers. Even the porter, while I drank a cup of coffee, ran to pre-purchase my train ticket.

I was to finally reach Algeria. All that was left for me to overcome now was the bone-deep fear I felt about visiting such an unknown land alone.

Algeria

After my Meknès soaking and the stresses of the Moroccan transport strike, my plane took off on its short trajectory east, high above the Roman olive belt, flying safely over the closed frontier between Morocco and its Maghrebian neighbour, and landed into the Algerian capital, all without incident. Until I reached passport control where I was refused entry.

'Why?!'

My papers were not in order.

The immigration officer was barely a girl, lacking scarf and veil, slight of build, short-cropped chestnut hair, in a mid-blue, trouser-suit uniform. She grinned, hand over mouth, stifling a giggle. 'It'll be fine,' she reassured, while repeating that my paperwork was not in order and I could not continue to baggage claim. After my numerous attempts to gain a visa I was exasperated, which seemed to amuse her all the more. I was fascinated by her appearance. There were others like her, young women in neighbouring cubicles also without the *hijab*. I had expected the strict face of Islam to greet me.

'Where's the confirmation docket for your hotel?'

'I cancelled the booking. I'm staying with an acquaintance.'

After Christmas, during a lunch party at the farm to celebrate our new season's oil, our French beekeeper's wife, Algerian-born Marie-Gabrielle, offered to contact friends, also apiarists, who lived out-side Algiers. I was already travelling when Hocine, her beekeeping colleague, caught up with me on my mobile in Spain. It was he who suggested I stay with him and his family during my few days in the capital.

'But you have declared a hotel.'

Attempting to placate the insistent young officer, I handed over the few details I possessed: Hocine's mobile number and full name. I was ushered into an empty corner. She disappeared with my passport, returning a short while later with a burly, moustachioed senior in putty-coloured uniform and sturdy boots. He rang Hocine but the line was dead. I also tried to telephone, but I was not picking up an Algerian signal.

'I am sorry we cannot let you in' was the decision. 'You must collect your luggage and return to Casablanca.'

'Wait, please!' I pleaded, playing for time, repeatedly punching out Hocine's number, but the network refused all connection. Eventually, after consultations with other staff members, other burly men with black moustaches, and various internal calls, because, inexplicably, no one had a phone signal, the immigration clerk stamped my passport and welcomed me to her country with a broad smile. What made the difference, I could not say. I did not stop to enquire. I scooted to the carousel where one piece of luggage was still turning: mine.

Outside the terminal, pressing, shoving crowds. Impossible to scan all faces, but no one awaiting me. How would this beekeeper find me? If he had remembered my arrival at all – it was over a month since we had been in touch. My mobile remained signalless. My immediate future loomed formlessly. But I was here, in Algiers, in Arabic El-Jazair, 'the islands', a tribute to four islets that had lain beyond the bay and are today integrated into the city's port. I ambled up and down, a tight grip on my backpack, chewing over choices. The rain with its louring sky was as unremitting as it had been in Morocco. Thin, yellow-eyed hustlers; harassed, bedraggled unemployeds; wizened elders with cigarettes hanging between limp fingers; all touting taxis to town. I declined. First impressions: a wall of faces; impenetrable, lined, strained faces, bad-skin faces, expectant strangers. And police officers. As I weaved my way through the throng searching for someone I would not recognise, who would not recognise me, I was all at once aware of the high level of police and military presence patrolling the exterior of the terminal.

Then, through this crush of madness, my name. Hocine, the history professor-turned-beekeeper, worried expression, suede jacket, work-soiled khakis, host for the early duration of my stay, pressed through bodies to reach me.

'*Salaam, salaam.* Apologies. I'm never late,' he begged. 'I set off with three-quarters of an hour to spare. Something has happened. There are police everywhere.'

Settled in his pick-up, we slid into a solid bank of traffic halted every hundred metres by roadblocks, police, security. Bonnets, boots; every vehicle transiting the aerodrome was inspected. Ours, also. Naively, I assumed these were everyday measures.

Hocine frowned. 'This is not normal.'

My phone sprang to life. It was Michel, anxious for my whereabouts, my safety. Bombs had exploded in both Casa and Algiers. Seventeen dead in Algiers. 'Where are you?'

'Exploded where?' I replied weakly.

'The details have not been released in Europe. Where are you?'

'Algiers airport.'

I read the concern in his silence. 'For God's sake, be careful. I love you.'

I loved him for not ordering, begging me home, but I feared, after everything, I would be forced to leave, to strike Algeria off my Mediterranean itinerary.

I repeated the news to Hocine. His expression closed down. Swiftly, he began searching for an exit, a slipway to cut out of the chaos. The rain was pelleting against the windscreen. I wound down the window and sniffed like a tracker dog at the wet midday, searching scents, fire, singeing, burning, but either the bombs had exploded far from our present position or the inclement weather had obliterated their lingering plumes of destruction. We were creeping forward at a snail's pace, seemingly getting nowhere.

Moments later, Hocine's wife was ringing. Suicide bombers had detonated explosives close to the Prime Minister's headquarters and the national library. Buildings had collapsed. The numbers reported dead were confusing, but the latest count was seventeen. Hundreds injured. Hocine hit his phone pad and began shouting in Arabic. I observed then, as I had frequently before, that Arabs shout when on the telephone.

'Change of plan,' he muttered.

We skipped the capital altogether and drove for about an hour to the district, the *walida*, of Blida. Passing through flat plains, once orange groves and today a muddled mix of flowering fruit trees and pockets of ugly, ill-organised buildings, we swung off the road, squelching through mud, into a yard, with armed guard at the entrance, where a line of rectangular one-storey outhouses awaited us: the headquarters of Blida's Beekeepers' Cooperative. Here to welcome us was Algeria's President of Apiarists, Mohammed, nicknamed Hamzoui, to avoid the continual confusion caused by half the male Islamic population bearing the *prénom* Mohammed. Hamzoui, pronounced Hamshwee, I discovered during the ensuing weeks, was a remarkable human being with a network of contacts that would have made any businessman green with envy. He shook my hand warmly and led us through to his office; the least prepossessing director's space I had ever encountered: four peeling walls, two fold-away chairs, a desk scattered with a collection of files, an outmoded computer and a large woman, Hamzoui's assistant, who rose to greet us as we entered.

A brief tour of the cooperative, where a handful of reed-thin, tobacco-eaten, black-fingered labourers were employed in the construction of hives from organic materials. They spoke no French and were possibly illiterate. Back in the desultory quadrangle, standing in the rain. Above our heads on the flat roofs, legs planted akimbo, sodden young guards in combat gear, wielding rifles. Private security. Hamzoui pointed to a distant building within the cooperative compound.

'I used to live in that house. We loved the countryside. I miss it. Town life is not for me.'

During the 'Decade of Terrorism', the nineties, Hamzoui had been attacked twice. On both occasions, his wife had returned home and found him bleeding on the floor. Beyond the cooperative enclosure were forests where the terrorists had secreted themselves in camps. Moving to an urban environment became an imperative.

'A pity,' he smiled. 'Nature suits me.'

We set off on an extended tour into the mountains. The conversation – though the men spoke together in Arabic, I deciphered the obvious words – was of the bombings. The numbers murdered were higher than originally estimated.

'You're not to worry or feel concerned,' reassured Hamzoui. 'You are in the cradle of beekeepers and I have set up a *réseau*, a network, which will guide you across Algeria. You'll want for nothing; you'll be safe.'

Relieved, grateful, that they were not advising me back on a plane, I peered beyond the window, silently anxious for my immediate future. In better weather, our winding scenic ascent would have revealed the alpestrine forests flanking us. Under different circumstances, it would have been attractive, but walled by clouds, a curtain of misty grey rain and my sodden spirits, it left much to the imagination. At the foot of a glistening elevation, a gathering of Muslims photographing a trio of beige monkeys. Hocine pulled over, assuming I would want the same. Close up, the primates were bedraggled, uncared for. I snapped away, observing domestic litter jettisoned everywhere, and returned to the car.

Sentry points high above us, positioned within the rocky crags. Military; patrol of the long-distance traffic, particularly after dark. Black African illegals, highway robbers. This was Route One. It bisected central Algeria, descending some 3000 kilometres to Niger.

Algeria is immense: second only on the continent of Africa to Sudan; four times bigger than France; ten times the size of Britain. Its population of under thirty-four million resides predominantly along its Mediterranean coastline, known as the Tell, with pockets in the mountains and, beyond, yawning desertlands. An Islamic republic with 99 per cent Sunni Muslims and the other 1 per cent Jews and Christians, there is no Shi'ite representation in this closed land. Independence, after a century and a half of French colonial rule and decades of bloodshed, was achieved in 1962. Beyond independence, the country suffered brutal civil unrest climaxing during the 1990s in a decade of bombings, terrorism, kidnappings and murder. These years became known as the 'Decade of Terrorism' or 'Black Decade'. Due to its inflamed history, there had been precious little tourism.

Visitors to the archaeological sites, to a stretch of Mediterranean that I had been promised was bluer than anywhere else, and to the isolated Saharan locations were predominantly Algerians themselves or Muslims from neighbouring Islamic countries. Western tourism had not been encouraged. Unrest remained a reality though my new acquaintances swiftly reassured me that the nineties were behind them; Algeria was building a new and better future.

'Without tourism, how does the country survive?' I asked.

'We have a buoyant economy, rich in crude oil, second only to Libya. Unlike Morocco and Tunisia, we have no financial need for tourism, but . . .' Hamzoui fell silent.

'The downside is Islamic Fundamentalism seeking control?' I suggested.

Hocine nodded. 'One of the extremist cells, linked to Al-Qaeda, was probably responsible for this morning's atrocities.' He drew up outside an alpine restaurant. It was three in the afternoon. We were directed to the mezzanine level, empty of other diners. This was the 'family salon', where women were tolerated. We ate brochettes, salad and olives, drank water and talked through the 'programme' they had prepared. I tried to explain that, hugely appreciative as I was for the trouble they had gone to (and I was deeply touched by their consideration), I intended to travel by bus or public taxis, following a flexible itinerary. I pulled out my notebook.

They shook their heads. 'No matter what you have declared on your visa papers as your profession, you are at risk,' warned Hamzoui with characteristic calm. He reiterated facts. Scores of journalists and writers had been killed or imprisoned by groups with extreme religious and political ideologies, the majority with links to Al-Qaeda. Between 1993 and 1997 more than one hundred figures working within the Algerian media had been murdered.

'That was the nineties, Hamzoui, when violence was blighting your daily lives. You have just told me that Algeria is building a brighter future . . .'

'No one expected this morning's events,' he continued gravely. 'At any given time, somewhere in the region of three thousand young Algerians are in Afghanistan or Pakistan receiving a religious, ideological/military training. There, at *madrasas* [Islamic religious schools], they are educated by mullahs. A chosen few are sent to London, occasionally to Paris or Brussels. These boys are trained in warfare, in the honour of suicide sacrifice to the Holy War. More than 50 per cent of them will be re-infiltrated into Algeria to fight as soldiers of that Holy War, the Jihad. Boys without *risha*, roots, the disenchanted young whose families have nothing, are the prime choices. From the shantytowns, *bidonvilles*, where dissatisfaction is inbred, the terrorist pods are seeking their bait.'

'Are you suggesting I leave?'

Both men shook their heads.

'We hope you will stay,' said Hocine.

'We need your voice,' added Hamzoui. 'Consequently, beekeepers, associates of mine, all across the country, have accepted to welcome you. Without them, you will be obliged to register with the local police wherever you stay and hand over your passport. Hocine and I know your business, but I have not told my colleagues. You are fascinated by the olive, its future and by our Mediterranean history: that is sufficient. Better to be prudent. At every moment we will have someone accompanying you.'

I listened silently to these two men closing down my itinerary.

'In the light of this morning's grim events, after Blida, you will be delivered into the safe hands of other beekeepers who have been instructed to do the same. Right across the country. Beekeeping families will house and escort you. I trust all the people I have proposed. The Association of Beekeepers will not let you down or out of our sight.'

I suddenly pictured myself as a human parcel. Panic rose, but not for fear of the perils I might be exposing myself to. So determined was I to investigate this desert land that I had not considered the pitfalls. It was the entrapment. Still, I made the wise decision to respect the concerns of these considerate strangers; within forty-eight hours, I felt certain, I would be at liberty to roam freely.

That first night was spent with Hocine and his family close to the centre of Blida. Built on a Roman military site, Blida was refounded by Andalucíans in 1535. They developed irrigation works and orange farms. Blida: 'A Bouquet of Roses', the 'First Rose'. Such poetic allusions I saw nothing of, no sweetly scented town. Looming tenements, endless rows of faceless barracks constructed for the military. The neighbouring agricultural lands had also been requisitioned for army personnel. Barbed wire, high walls, rifles at the ready. They returned me to Israel, except this was scruffier, sodden and somehow more hopeless. Here, no massive US investments to sustain the position. Home-drilled oil had financed all this. What the capabilities of this high-profile military were, its expertise, if push came to shove, I had no idea.

Boys were kicking a football in the mud-soaked, octagonal yard in between eight decaying high-rises. We climbed flights of echoing cement stairwells. His wife, with three shy children clinging to her pink and burgundy housecoat, waited, door open, to greet me warmly. Hocine made his excuses and disappeared to pray. I was handed slippers to replace wet boots, and a dressing gown. Apologies were made for the lack of water. Tapped water was available only two hours out of twenty-four, but those two hours varied. During the remainder, they used the litres they had conserved in plastic pails. The evening passed slowly. The television played mutely. Al-Qaeda claimed responsibility for the day's massacres. The death toll was now thirty, countless injured. Over and over, repeated footage: a veiled woman in tight close-up, terrified eyes, screaming voicelessly, smoke billowing from levelled rubble behind her.

'To kill a fellow Muslim is a mortal sin,' Hocine said.

'Surely, to kill anyone, Muslim or not, to take another's life . . .'

'Yes, yes, but to murder a practising Muslim . . .'

The dining corner was off the living room. While a sumptuous couscous was being prepared, Hocine and I sat on a sofa, later my bed, perusing a foolscap illustrated book, lacking jacket, of black and white drawings, copies of the prehistoric cave engravings from Tassili N'Ajjer in the southern Sahara, close to the Libyan border. He must have dug it out knowing that Tassili, with its immense spread of Neolithic artwork, had been intended as my final Algerian destination. When Stone Age tribes had inhabited those ranges, six thousand years before Christ, their lands had been savannahs, not deserts. Tassili N'Ajjer, Berber for Plateau of Rivers. I had been hoping their artwork might depict their vegetation, offering examples of prehistoric wild olives.

Regretfully, I had cancelled Tassili, not due to this day's events but because the temperatures in April were already reaching highs that would be unbearable. In that moment, though, I longed to be down in the south and bemoaned the fact that I had not flown there directly, safely out of danger's grasp.

Drifting in and out of sleep, I listened to the weather slap against the rusty, ill-fitting shutters, howling through the cracked, membraned windows. I listened to cats scrapping, hissing malevolently, to some poor devil attempting without success to kick-start a diesel engine. Restless, I half heard Hocine rise before four for the pre-dawn prayer, the *fajr*, first of the day's five sets. He would collect water, too, if the taps were delivering. Half asleep, I was picturing a future without water. The *muezzin*'s call roused me, but I stayed awhile curled upon my sheep's hair mattress. My prayers were that this leg of my journey would pass without incident. Perhaps, when adversity kicked in, life and death stuff, I would run home. When had a lone European woman last tramped this troubled earth? Doubts drummed with the rain.

Due to the intemperate weather Hocine's bees were unable to leave their hives to gather nectar. Raindrops damage bees' wings, and they are unhappy in the cold. Unfortunately, it was the orange blossom season; the flower's nectar fed the region's most lucrative honey crop. Hocine was worried. It had been raining for almost a week; the blossoms were being driven from the trees, their riches scattered. But *inshallah*, God willing, all would turn out for the best. Still, it was clear that my host's financial future, his investments, were at risk. As the day broke, the rain's force became a deluge, a barrage of water. I was going to Tipasa, a Phoenician then Roman port city. Hocine, unable to work, accompanied me with his eldest daughter, Z'hor (Rose).

Remnants, traces of a century and a half of French colonialism were everywhere. Elegant, historic buildings abraded. Grim, Soviet era-like apartment blocks, hastily knocked up after independence, seams coming apart, sinking like another layer of history back into the once-fertile French vineyards and olive groves. Semi-completed constructions with reinforcement-rodded antennae abandoned in fallow fields.

Traversing a vast plain where vendors were selling potatoes: fifteen years back Hocine had kept his hives in these pastures until they were burned by terrorists. Explosives had been planted in the earth around the hives. When the beekeepers arrived to tend the colonies and collect honey, their footsteps detonated them. His two brothers had suffered shock but had not been physically injured. His cousin had lost a leg. No explanations for these acts of violence against ordinary non-partisan citizens. Back then, in the nineties, this area had lacked a military presence. Lawlessness ruled. Today, the military, the security forces were the law. It was essential.

I silently recalled Palestine, the groves that had been illegally uprooted by Israeli 'settlers' who believed that all Palestine was theirs to take by whatever means. The senseless destruction of rural livelihoods, of campestral futures, by extremists of whatever persuasion for the sake of a cause.

Turning northwards to the coast, the roadsides were fringed with eucalypts. Shade cover, I assumed incorrectly. Their original purpose had been to aid drainage. The extended roots of the eucalyptus are known to be aggressive. Because they absorb great quantities of water, absorb excess humidity, they are excellent in waterlogged soils. The French planted them in the nineteenth century when this area was more humid, but today the region was bordering on arid and they were leaching what essential water remained.

'This is our first rainfall in three years.'

In northern Morocco I had seen rows of towering eucalypts lying at roadsides, dug up not felled, exposed roots withering, and I had silently questioned the purpose of destroying decades-old trees.

'Today, they are a predator,' explained Hocine. 'We desperately need the groundwater.' A positive factor was the pollen. Eucalyptus honey, excellent, curative.

Plane trees, also a French legacy, lined village streets, surrounded by unattractive mounds of rubble and litter. Roads fanning from central squares had grown unstructured, lacking organisation, dirty. I pictured postcard-pretty villages at home in Provence. No doubt these Algerian duplicates had reminded the colonials of their homeland. But what had such northern planning meant to the Arabs and Berbers?

Groups of labourers in fields on their knees digging the rich earth with bare hands, planting tomatoes in the rain. The earth was red and lush. It reminded me of eastern Libya. Olive trees had replaced the rows of cypresses as windbreaks. They served the same purpose but also yielded fruit. Burned-out carcasses of French wine *caves* dotted the countryside. These fields had been vineyards. After the departure of the French in 1962, the grapes were still pressed and wines still shipped to France, but at some point the ex-colonists refused to buy the cargos. Of no interest to the Muslims, the *vignobles* were ripped out.

Once beyond the agricultural and fruiting hillsides, approaching the coast, police were evident at every bank, corner, crossroads, cradling rifles, halting vehicles, rummaging through boots and engines.

Hocine sighed. 'We thought all this was over,' he mumbled. 'Thought we had turned the page.'

I had yet to fully comprehend the impact of the previous day's bombings on the psyche of these people; not until close to the end of my stay did it become clearer.

Until 1962, when the French quit, Algeria had never known independence. Hocine, who had been a professor of history before he had turned to bees, briefly outlined the story.

'We are a country in transition,' he began. 'While the French ruled, education was not readily available to Algerians. We did not own our land. We were treated with disrespect, sometimes cruelly, by our colonists. Such indignities fed the War for Independence. And once the struggle was ignited, rage and hatred, on both sides, engendered bloody crimes. One and a half million Algerians lost their lives.

'Beyond independence, the country formed a one-party system, ruled by the FLN, the National Liberation Front. These were the underground resistance fighters, socialists and nationalist groups who had won us our liberty. However, freedom of speech was censored and the media came under government control. Then, between 1990 and 1991, the Islamic Front began to gain power at municipal and legislative elections. To arrest this swing, in 1992, the electoral process was annulled. Revolts broke out. The more extreme branches of Islam were calling for religious clampdown, which many opposed and the country degenerated into violent confusion once more. This was our Decade of Terrorism. This was when Algeria fought against itself, struggling for its identity, living in fear, resisting fanatics who desired extreme changes. Now we are finding our feet but we still have to understand ourselves, discover who we are. We are a peace-loving nation; Islam is not about murder. The world has a thwarted perception of us, but yesterday's bombings are a setback.'

A first glimpse of the maplessness that was unfolding before me.

Nearing Tipasa, vast allotments had been given over to *plasti-cultura*. Just as in southern Spain, greenhouses dominated the littoral. But as we drew close to the ancient city, the landscape emptied; grew bare, vast, red-earthed, void of construction. The sea was grey, wild, angry. As we drove through the modern town that abutted the ancient ruins a farmers' market was in progress. Men served, men shopped.

Tipasa, founded by the Phoenicians. Algerian-born writer Albert Camus was fond of this location. We took a brief walk round its port where hillocks of stones and sand awaited a reconstruction programme already under way. Passing through a sodden lane of trinket stalls and restaurants, empty of tourists, to the 2500-year-old city. After the fall of Carthage, Rome transformed this trading port into a military base.

Great excitement shoving sinewy weeds and wild branches aside, uncovering damaged but original stone presses and dozens of stone jars used for stockage and transport of olive oil.

'*Azemour*,' Hocine told me, 'is Berber for olive.'

Oil was *aceite*, the same as in Spanish. The Berbers, Moors, it must have been who contributed this word to modern-day Spanish.

Beyond the eastern hill of Tipasa broke the humped shoulder of the Chenoua mountain. At its foot were visible traces of the original port. Perched at the booming water's edge, the first grains of Africa, it was an inviting spot, ideal for anchorage. I roamed for hours, hair flattened against my face, while Z'hor picked wild flowers, running to recite their Arabic names to me. Flocks of olive trees within the walls of the ancient city, worn down, bent like beasts, frazzled, flat-tened, swept by centuries of storms roaring in off the water. A curious picture, like shock-haired birds in flight.

Down within a crescent bay a couple were striding the windblown beach, losing balance. Hocine recounted a pleasing story. The delights of being in the company of a historian! I listened while the surf lashed furiously against ancient stones, gulls strained to negotiate the insistent wind and spindrift fogged the horizon.

When Phoenician merchants first called on these shores occupied for epochs by Berbers, sailing from their coastal cities of Tyre and Sidon in modern Lebanon possibly as early as 1200 BC, they had no means of verbal communication with the natives. (The language barrier had puzzled me everywhere.) An added complication came when the Berbers hid themselves, refusing to show their faces to the purple-skinned sailors from the east. The Phoenicians opened negotiations by depositing items on the beach and then, withdrawing to their galleys, lit smoking fires, signalling to the natives. When they returned certain of their goods remained while others had been swapped. Nothing stolen, always swapped. In this way, they grew to understand what appealed to the Berbers. Next, they wrote messages and left these on the beaches. The Berbers had no alphabet, no written language. They could not read or write. Theirs was an oral tradition but eventually they entered into the mysteries of the letters and found their own scribbled means of response.

A phone call from Hamzoui broke into our wet promenade. He had tracked down a seventeenth-century olive mill. Ottoman! This news set us on an excited trail back along the coast to a rendezvous with Dgeloul, a very European Algerian, an engineer who had heard of this mill operating somewhere in the hills behind Hadjout. We stopped briefly for mint tea at Dgeloul's home, hiked inland of the shore along a lane with sheep and rich damp scents to his olive groves in blossom, and beehives. It had stopped raining; the bees were venturing out.

Our hinterland excursion, following Dgeloul's car, was circuitous and I lost all sense of direction. As did Hocine, while Z'hor lay curled up asleep; a hibernating squirrel, cradling wilting wild flowers, fallen petals at her elbows. In the one-street villages where the women were swathed in black chador and the men wore white crocheted skullcaps, small beards and baggy trousers fastened above the ankles, the homes were the skeletons of colonial cottages. Above one such property a faded sign in green Art Deco lettering, *Boulangerie*. I remarked upon the rubbish lying at the roadsides in decomposing heaps while the deep-throated mechanical growl of the late afternoon prayer call reminded me whose land this was.

'Our people have not learned to care for their country, to structure a social state, to respect their environment.'

The mill, when we eventually found it, was indeed a rare Ottoman jewel (the Ottomans took control in 1518). Out of season, no olives to press, its miller maintained it like polished shoes. Its exterior seemed more recent, reminding me of a country stationmaster's home deep in rural France. Within were two white-tiled rooms with cracked walls. Generations of olive paste had veneered the interior fabric of the building. The place surely had served an earlier purpose for there was a window, now boarded up. It lacked all lighting, creating a cold, dark atmosphere. The press was solid steel fed from granite-crushing stones. I had expected an Ottoman press but on its head was engraved *Lachère et ses fils* and beneath *Hussein-De—— A———*. These final words, names, were impossible to decipher due to encrusted paste.

'Who were these people? Is this machine a replacement?'

The miller shrugged. He was wearing a parka and tartan carpet slippers.

'Do you know anything about its origins?'

He shook his big silver-haired head.

In the adjoining room were two iron *cuvettes*, tanks, capable of holding 2800 litres apiece. Rare and magnificent.

Outside in the damp yard, speckled guinea fowl were feeding off hillocks of discarded paste. It was raining again. A neighbouring building, abandoned, had been storage for wine vats. The miller had managed the establishment since independence. It was part of a worker-controlled farm of 250 hectares. Fifty produced olives and the rest were vineyards for table grapes. Under French rule, its proprietor was French-Swiss, Madame Schwit. According to the miller, Madame had loved an Algerian, married, joined the resistance and fought with them. Arms were found on her property. She was imprisoned by the French. While serving time, comrades advised the sale of her holding. Upon release in 1959, she sold to colonials who lost the farm when the War of Independence was won and lands were confiscated. Madame remained in Algeria, returning to Europe only after the death of her husband. The district was known by locals as Schwit's Commune; a tribute to her loyalty and courage.

In 1994, during the Black Decade, terrorists had robbed the mill at gun point and walked off with 1200 litres of oil, leaving the local cultivators penniless.

We stopped in the village of Merad. There, peeling colonial properties wore the identical cream walls and burgundy shutters of our farm when we first purchased it.

I asked a passing gent how the region was called.

'Schwit's Commune,' he smiled.

A day plagued by rain. Squatting bodies in the soaked fields worked on, planting and hoeing in the abandoned vineyards. The ghosts of colonialism, the scars of the past. A sign read Clos St Jean. Carcasses of rusted Renaults, Citroën vans, lorries subsiding into the unploughed earth. Along the banks, muddied sheep grazed on fists of weeds.

'As I said, we are in transition. It will require generations,' mumbled Hocine.

A profound sea change indeed.

My second night was with Hamzoui, his wife, six pretty daughters and a plain-faced cousin, also a beekeeper with forty hives of her own, one of the first female apiarists in Algeria. The couple's only son had been killed in a motorcycle accident. His framed photograph alongside the Koran and vase with plastic flowers adorned a corner table. The girls were teenagers or in their early twenties. It was they who ran the house and looked after 'Papa'. I smiled, considering Hamzoui toiling all day with queen bees and hives of working girls, and returning of an evening to this domestic arrangement. This household enjoyed running water and – luxury! – a computer with Internet connection. An external Webcam clipped above the screen allowed the family, thanks to Skype, to wave *incessantly* at relatives in Paris. The flat was spacious, ornately decorated. Much excitement erupted when I gratefully accepted the offer of a bath. Four girls, talking all at once, explained the taps, 'hot first, then cold, or you can run them together'. The tapped water was fed through a short hosepipe into a pail. I squatted in the bath and washed from the bucket. Regular knockings on the door. 'How are you getting on?'

'Are you fine?' Behind a plastic shower curtain decorated with coloured fish, my Algerian baptism!

Hamzoui and we nine women sat to dinner. Couscous was, again, the principal dish, accompanied by Day-Glo-red-and-orange fizzy drinks. Talk was of the bombings. At the mention of Bin Laden several of the girls erupted into hysterical giggles. Why? The room consigned to me included a bedside copy of the Koran. The two girls whose bed I had been allocated were camping across the hallway. Five sleeping together; a dormitory of delighted whisperings and secrets.

Hamzoui and I were up at the first call to prayer while the women slept on. We drank bitter coffee in the kitchen while he talked me through arrangements for the upcoming days. I was travelling east. It was a longish distance and entailed changing public taxis at various points along the way. Waiting, at my final destination for this leg, would be the next beekeeper, Achour. Hamzoui was anxious on my behalf. I had purchased a local phone card (not an easy exercise) because he insisted I stay in constant touch.

We drove in incessant rain as dawn was breaking to the Blida bus station. Rubble and more rubbish everywhere. Hamzoui feared for me alone. I assured him that I had travelled with the *grands taxis* in Morocco and that I was not afraid (I was). He hung around for an hour. The taxi was still only half full. Eventually, I offered to pay for two extra seats, a total outlay including my own place, of seven euros fifty. My destination was Tizi-Ouzou, the capital of the mountainous district of Greater Kabylia. East of Algiers, Kabylia was renowned for its olive oil. My fellow passengers were two young men and a bent leprechaun with white beard, cane and swirling rust cloak. It was Friday, sabbath; the roads were snarled with traffic, with open-backed vans carrying hillocks of runner beans, chickens, bicycle wheels, flotsam. A van disgorged its load of tomatoes. They rolled and spilled across the wet, glistening tarmac, striping the lanes with blood-like rivulets. There were controls, road blocks, police every kilometre. The country remained on high alert. Police riding green and white motorcycles, men in bullet-proof vests with rifles, waving us on or pulling us over to inspect the carcass, the engine. The green and white of their flag, of security; the colours of Islam. The countryside was lush, sodden. Swallows flew low. An overturned lorry, like a beast flayed, caused ever more traffic jams, pile-ups, fire engines. Virgin coastline – at one time, the greater part of the Mediterranean had been like this. Storks nesting everywhere. It seemed a while ago that I had seen the same image in Spain.

Tizi-Ouzou, Hill of Gentians, capital of the Kabylia Mountains, located inland of the Mediterranean at the foot of the Atlas ranges. This was Berber territory. In earlier eras, the Berbers had fled to higher ground to protect themselves against all invaders; slowly driven inland from their coastal settlements. I waited in the rain at the taxi station for my contact who was running late. I could hardly make out the passing cars due to the streaming rain. Achour, when he arrived, was an older man, an olive farmer who had inherited a farm and mill. It had been in his family for three centuries. He was also the director of this region's beekeeping community. A man whose small head seemed to be plonked on a pair of broad shoulders and paunched, well-fed body. He was well travelled and spoke impeccable French with barely a trace of accent. He proposed a tour of Greater Kabylia, where there were groves that dated back to the eighth century and leagues of wild olive trees yet to be cultivated. Climbing the winding mountain road out of town, I pressed my face against the foggy glass, hoping for a view. The car reeked of stale nicotine. Achour was saying that the acid level in this area's olive oil was 4 per cent. In Europe, they would not be allowed to sell or consume such a product. It would only be good for soap! Why so high?

A brief stop at a *huilerie* somewhere in the foothills. An Alsatian sat placidly in the pouring rain while a handsome man leaned against the frame of an open door, staring through the bleak weather across the deserted street to steep olive-groved mountainsides. The pressing season was over. He had nothing to do. We were invited in. It was a chaotic, filthy place.

'Tell me about your life as a miller,' I requested in French, translated into Kabylie-Berber by Achour.

He earned the equivalent of four euros for every hundred kilos of fruit he pressed. In time-honoured Mediterranean tradition, it was the women who harvested, climbing the mountainsides with baskets, descending at sunset loaded with olives. Back-breaking work. There was a waiting list of up to two months for farmers to press their fruit.

'TWO months! At home,' I explained, 'if we do not press our gathered fruits within four days, we are not entitled to retain our AOC.'

Once off the branch, every hour an olive is not pressed, its acid level rises. No wonder, then, that the oil here carried a toll of 4 per cent. In Europe, any oil over 0.8 cannot be labelled 'extra virgin'. Here, the crops lay in baskets growing mouldy.

Back in the car, I asked Achour what the problem was.

'There are insufficient mills.'

I was puzzled. The oil from this region was renowned, the finest in the land. It did not bode well for the rest.

Achour pulled over on a bridge.

'Senseless to drive through forests of wild olives in this curtain of rain,' he said.

Two barefoot adolescents appeared selling freshly cut asparagus. Achour gave the boys coins. They shoved their streaming faces through the open window, looking me over, laughing insanely.

'I'll take you to meet Berber women instead, the olive-gatherers.'

Our first stop was Louisa, a big-boned, bovine female in full Berber regalia and heavy pewter jewellery with solid bracelets that resembled handcuffs. Aquiline Louisa owned fifty olive trees. She beat the fruits off the branches with sticks and then gathered from the earth. She never netted the ground. Louisa's had been an enforced marriage. At sixteen her father wed her to a twenty-year-old. She had not been happy. Her first child was born a year later. She had missed her parents and her village. Her husband had been a drinker and beat her and she had suffered at the cruel hand of a controlling mother-in-law, now dead. Still, she had borne ten children.

'I am lucky,' she said. 'My farm lies on even ground, easy to maintain.' Neighbouring women in her hamlet were obliged to scale cloud-capped summits to gather. Louisa offered us a *galet*, which translates as cobble or paving stone, but is a small, flat cake baked with olive oil and flavoured with prickly pear fruits. We ate with our fingers, at a bare wooden table.

Onwards to what evolved into a party at the household of Tassadit, where a chorus of Berber women introduced me to their folk music.

'This mountain is famous for its olive songs,' explained an earnest young girl, trainee of Achour's, in Western clothes, dull in comparison to the trio of locals with their fringed headscarves of many colours, their hooped gold earrings. Reds, black, yellow were their flowing voluminous, beaded skirts. One, with hennaed nose and eyebrows resembled a whiskery brown rodent. They shouted and yelled in their Kabylia dialect, reciting snippets of poetry, then grew quiet, shy. Villagers were appearing, descending from all about. Our number had reached sixteen. The crones recounted their gathering tales. I listened to their stories.

'I was eight years old when I first harvested with my mother. They were better days, no stress.'

'My mother sang me lullabies of her days in the groves.'

Then, bingo. The village's star, the leading *chanteuse*, was wheeled in. Eighty-four, with several silver teeth and one leg. The other had been wasted by diabetes. She lifted her bright skirts and slapped her hand against a long scarlet sock. 'Here is my stump,' she screamed. Alone, she had carried her fruits from raggedy, high ground to mill in a basket on her back, but had made her income singing at circumcisions and weddings. Her reputation had grown from her improvised olive ditties.

She broke into song, belting out the words, and all fell silent. Her voice was taut as wire. The tunes were unexpectedly political, anti-French. She had lost her father when she was five. Female neighbours had brought in the crop for her mourning mother.

'Leave me to cry,' she ululated. Her lyrics were of birds with broken wings found in the groves, of healing them, rearing them before they flew off, abandoning her. The bird image represented the young man who never stayed. Or the sons who went off to war and never returned. The women in the olive fields sang out their grief as they toiled. Always women, *solidaire*, female solidarity. In another, 'a Frenchman came, snatched away the bird I had reared'. French soldiers or colonists killing or imprisoning the young men.

When she was not singing, she talked loudly, still performing, wallowing in the attention.

Achour whispered to me, 'she speaks in rhyme, improvising, using symbols, as she goes'.

She had spoken in verse for so many years it was second nature to her. The others confirmed that she never used plain speech.

'One daughter and one leg left, wheelchair-bound,' she yodelled as though drunk. Everyone was conversing at once, attempting to sing, to translate or they watched on in reverential silence as the beak-nosed songstress elegised her broken-hearted life with music. Her repertoire was entirely her own, never regional folksongs.

'Are you recording this?' one young man hissed in my ear.

'I have no tape-recorder.'

'Quick, pass me your phone.'

Played back later, the recording was tinny; grizzled, plangent melodies from a dying world. I was most grateful to the student for his initiative.

A landslide delayed our return to Tizi-Ouzou, boulders ejected from the upper mountain by rain force had crushed a travelling car. A grizzly scene of injured man submerged beneath its mangled carapace. Obliged to pull over, we found ourselves among the population of a village. All were attempting to dig, wrench the fellow out. Men were yelling on phones while the women in their coloured costumes were drenched, sweating, mud-spattered, wielding spades and sticks, heaving at metal while rivers of silt, broken glass, blood eddied at their feet. There was little hope that any medical assistance could reach the spot. It was dark when we turned the car about. The victim had died.

The old woman's lamentations were still moaning in my head.

'I could use a drink. Fancy a swift whisky before I deliver you to your host for the night?'

I had assumed I would stay at Achour's farm and I had taken it for granted that as a Muslim alcohol was forbidden. Achour lived two mountains away. Impossible for an overnight stop. He had arranged a bed with one of his researchers.

One hotel in Tizi served booze. After the deliciousness of washing my freezing hands in warm water, I entered the bar of the white Art Deco hotel. Achour ordered his whisky and I a Stella Artois. Wine was only available with meals. Before putting the world to rights, after a day plagued by rain and louring clouds, we toured the lobby where Kabylia crafts and jewellery were on display.

The women of the tribes, without kilns or wheels, fashioned and baked the pottery. First, they climbed the mountains to collect the clay, carried it home on their backs in baskets, cleaned it, taking out the impurities and lumpy bits, and then they added water to soften and mould it to the form they desired. All this was achieved out of doors on the ground, squatting on haunches in their brightly striped long dresses and bare feet. Once the pot or jar had been painted it was heated, fired, also out of doors, on open flames. This process took anything from three to six hours. After the pot had set, they glazed each article with a resin to seal in the patterns and to make the pottery shiny. They never signed their craftwork because, until recently, these pieces had never been intended for use beyond the family circle. Achour explained that it was possible to tell the provenance of the different objects – pots, pitchers for transporting and storing water or olive oil, others for the milk of goats and ewes, couscous bowls, oil lamps – by the designs and the colours of the dyes used to decorate them. The larger pots were water-carriers. Placed on their backs, strapped to their waists, the women clutched the handles, while climbing or descending the tracks from wells or streams to their stone homes.

Cereal was the foundation of their diet, prepared with olive oil or sheep's fat. Eating meat was a luxury reserved for weddings and special occasions. Special jugs and dishes were kept aside for those celebratory events. *Ideqqi* was the name given to these Berber women's art. Clay shaped by hand, fired in the open air, their objects closely resembled findings from archaeological sites all across the Mediterranean. Unfortunately, the pieces were so fragile that it was almost impossible to find examples that had been baked more than thirty or forty years earlier. One or two, perhaps a century old, like those encased behind glass at the hotel. As with the folksongs, the symbols on the pottery narrated stories of the women's lives, bearing witness to their experiences.

Back in the bar, Achour talked of his childhood. Like the asparagus boys we had encountered, he, too, had gone barefoot and slept on rugs in front of an open fire, but he had been educated and he was the exception. After the long walk from school, he was obliged to work with his family, gathering olives and tending sheep.

'Shepherds, barefoot or semi-clad, were nicknamed "potato feet",' he laughed.

Compared to many, his parents were wealthy yet they always helped their neighbours. It was the tribal tradition. Recently, he had structured a government-aid scheme that created opportunities for the underprivileged, training them in beekeeping, offering them an opportunity to earn an income while also learning the values of nature. A similar arrangement existed for the cultivation of olive trees. To encourage the farming of olives, a state-subsidised pro- gramme had been put in place. In northern Algeria, there existed millions of hectares of wild olives. Individuals willing to learn to graft them with hardy cultivars were recompensed.

'You know deforestation is at crisis level here, and we already have so little arable land. Soil is losing its water and does not replenish even in weather as wet as this. The olive tree has a root system that attracts humidity back to the earth. Land regeneration, olive cultivation, these are means of creating a future. The people here are heartbreakingly poor,' he sighed. 'You will see as you travel on eastwards.'

Achour ordered another drink and then recalled olive dishes that had been lost over the centuries but have long been known in the Kabylia Mountains: smoked and perfumed olives, *zaitun mubakhkar*. Recipes, he thought, that had originated in Baghdad. Olives from the oasis city of Palmyra were considered a great delicacy in the Middle Ages. In the Tunisian adaptation of *A Thousand and One Nights*, they talked of salted and limed olives.

Outside, Tizi, in a foothills settlement that had taken us a while to find due to the inclement weather, we stood together, getting drenched, and shook hands. I thanked him for the wealth of the day, for his broadmindedness, 'the illicit drink—'

'Our secret.'

And his company.

'*Tanmiert*. Thank you, in our Kabylia-Berber language. A parting thought: if you tend an olive tree kindly, harvesting with con- sideration, four angels will look down from on high into the four corners of your home, but if you maltreat a tree the four angels of melancholy will creep into your dreams and weep. I hope you do not think that we have gone too far, talking of the world, drinking together. Next time we meet, may it be in Paris.'

Achour's research assistant, Assia, awaited me, a neat-faced woman in her early thirties who stooped as though slowly subsiding. Housed at her mother-in-law's who occupied the downstairs floor, Assia, husband and two children were as poor as church mice and I wondered silently what strains she suffered. In the kitchen, with dirty pots and pans piled high because no water flowed from the taps, we ate couscous (again!), but this was the plainest I had been offered, and we drank water. The children screamed and fretted noisily at the table.

'It's rather late for them and the food is spoiled. We were expecting you a while ago,' Assia apologised, or covertly accused.

I felt guilty, reflecting my conversations and secret imbibing with Achour downtown.

While we spooned the cold food, the mother-in-law in rich burgundy, ankle-length dress swanned in.

'I love your outfit,' I smiled.

'From the market in Tizi, second-hand from Syria.'

She talked of her olives. Hers were for family only and she harvested alone. The fruits were pressed after a month in storage. I expressed shock.

'It has always been the custom here,' she explained. Her husband spent his life in France. He had sailed off when she was twenty-two. Now she was sixty. He sent money regularly and popped back occasionally.

'It's difficult; neither widow nor wife.'

My thoughts turned to Quashia. All his life he'd worked in France, returning to Algeria two or three times a year to holiday with his family.

Unexpectedly mother and son both rose. 'Goodnight and safe onwards journey,' bade the mother with son nodding behind her. With that, they were gone. Assia packed the children off to bed and returned to the kitchen. I was a little confused until my hostess explained that her husband was sleeping at his mother's, vacating his share of the marital bed.

I protested vociferously. 'I'll find a taxi, return to town.'

But Assia would have none of it and hurried off to fetch water from the flat below.

I washed from a bucket of cold water in the lavatory – the sanitation was a sorry story – and was utterly humiliated when I discovered that the few litres I had used and then flushed down the loo had been intended for everyone. I protested again. 'This is a terrible inconvenience, please . . .'

Assia looked as though she might burst into tears. 'I promised Achour that I would look after you.'

For her sake, I desisted, until in the bedroom I grew uncomfortable again. I am in the habit of sleeping naked.

She handed me a traditional Berber robe with beads, glitter, heavy materials. It weighed a ton. I donned it and lumbered into bed. My hostess joined me moments later, snuggling towards me. I switched out my bedside light and rolled on to my side, at the farthest extreme of the mattress, curled up like a creature in hibernation. Assia left her light on, 'in case the children come', and inched nearer.

I lay on my side listening to the rain.

She wanted to be close and, I suspected, intimate.

'We are used to this,' she said softly. 'Sleeping all together, many of us, sisters, cousins, in one bed.'

'Yes, but I am not your sister or cousin . . .' My response was unnecessarily abrupt.

'You are my sister in womanhood.'

True.

I wondered about the depth of intimacy between Assia and her husband and in what manner these women supported one another's emotional needs, but I did not ask. I did not want to open myself up to inadequacy, an inability to deliver. Still, I swung my body towards her so that I was lying on my back staring ceilingwards, signalling that if she needed to talk I was ready to listen. She did.

'I look forward to Fridays, our sabbath, but I spend it in housework. I never go out. That's why I signed up for Achour's beekeeping programme. With hives of my own to tend, I had an excuse to disappear to the country, to get away. But guess what? I have developed an allergy and the doctor has warned me my life is in danger. I must keep away from forests and my bees. But still I go; I prefer the risk.'

Was this a male doctor, I wondered silently. 'Does your husband help out when you are not here, when you are with your bees? Does he prepare meals?'

Occasionally, he laid the table and he enjoyed playing with his children, particularly his son, but they had no dishwasher, no kitchen at all to speak of and no bathroom so it was more practical to leave the chores to his wife. Sometimes her mother-in-law had hot water so, with buckets, Assia could clean the house.

'It's the same for all women.'

Eventually, I must have dozed off because I was woken by my phone's alarm at 6 a.m. Assia was directly out of bed to make coffee.

'No, please, don't worry.' But she was already in the kitchen. I had no means of cleaning my teeth.

Achour sent his chauffeur for me. Out into the relentless downpour, followed by Assia who lugged my backpack, refusing to hand it over, splashing behind me in the mud, lacking her obligatory headcovering. She took me in her arms and hugged me so intensely we might have been lovers. 'Please stay in touch, email me, thank you, thank you for your company.'

'I'll get your email from Achour.'

'I don't have one.'

I was bound for Bejaia, bumping the curving hillsides in a beekeeper's van; its driver also an initiate of the apiarist programme. Mud, spring mud. Scents of sodden spring. Streets, fields, orchards; waterlogged. My thoughts were on the crippling water deficits these people endured, the lack of quality of life. I remembered a line by the French historian Fernand Braudel I had scribbled months back in a notebook: In Kabylia, when the 'gates of the year', equinoxes and solstices, opened, the Berbers said the season signalled new fortunes: 'barley bread or famine'. We had passed this year's spring equinox by several weeks and I wondered how the harvests were faring at the hands of such a deluge. I wondered at these people's ability to survive at all.

Speeding through squelchy inclining villages. Market day in the altitudinous limestone outposts. A sign outside a café offering 'Sand wishes'. Mile after mile of dense, wooded slopes, sub-arid Mediterranean oak forests. Astounding to consider that Algeria's forests cover only 2 per cent of its vast terrain and that, due to logging by the French and mismanagement by the Algerians, they were disappearing at an alarming rate year after year.

How precious the tree is, I was thinking. How essential. I recalled Achour's remark: 'The olive tree has a root system that attracts humidity back to the earth.' This was new to me. I wanted to know more.

Disappointing the views, veiled by clouds. I recognised all too well the value of rain. Still, I found myself selfishly willing it to let up. The days were blurred, filmy, but then Algeria itself was barely visible, cloaked in a fog of fears and confusions.

And then, miraculously, as though a muslin curtain had been swept aside, the sun burst through and I was gazing upon a distant harbour. From there on, my approach was serene, illuminated, flanked by tumbling groves of twisted centurial-trunked olive trees. I wound down my window. Damp scents of morning gatecrashed the boneshaker that was our transport. Flowering asphodel, images of Spain flooded back. It seemed like a million years ago and as many kilometres. Yet it was merely weeks and but a hop across the turquoise sea glistening as I approached.

Bejaia was a port town of narrow streets, uninviting beaches, brushstrokes of French watercolours yet, ironically, the French never really settled here. So many on the streets were swathed in rags. Several of the shabby hotels we drove by were offering 'water 24/24'. I needed to clean my teeth. I was tired. My skin was crying out for hot water, soap. Achour's chauffeur deposited me at the bustling bus station where I was collected by two beekeepers whose task it was to escort me out of town to the ITAF, the Olive Institute.

I called Hamzoui in Blida.

'How are you getting on?' he shouted.

I begged him to cancel whatever arrangement had been conceived for this upcoming night's accommodation. He was alarmed.

'Please, Hamzoui, just for one night, I'd prefer a hotel.' I did not add that I needed a bath and quiet time to reflect on all that I was seeing, speeding through.

'You are due in Sétif tonight. I have good friends there. They will take care of you. Has somebody insulted you?'

I tried to reassure him, feeling culpable now for this plea of independence. What I had not yet learned, but both Hamzoui and Hocine had, was that the US State Department had issued a travel warning, declaring Algeria a danger zone. Three suicide-bombers had been responsible for the recent murders, death toll now at thirty, and, as a consequence, US citizens had been advised against entering the country. The statement warned of personal safety issues, false road blocks, detonating vehicle-borne explosives and more: 'The US Department of State recommends that foreign visitors avoid overland travel in the mountainous northern part of the country, and particularly in the area stretching from Algiers east to the Tunisian border.'

I was sitting in that territory. Every destination I had planned from hereon was 'overland' and located within that relatively confined section of the Algerian map. What I also did not know was that Al-Qaeda had strategically placed pods, suicide-bombers, along many of the desert settlements I was soon to visit. Aside from the invaluable assistance I was receiving from Hamzoui's network of beekeepers, I was on my own. My travel insurance was now invalid: no one would be rushing to airlift me out, should it become necessary. But I was unaware of all this and pigheadedly continued to insist that I needed a night alone. Without further argument, Hamzoui agreed to notify the Sétif apiarists of my request.

The Director of the Olive Institute, when we finally managed to talk our way past reception, greeted us with the air of a pompous cavalry officer, a bureaucrat with attitude. I was fascinated to learn his lineage. His face struck me as more Turkish than Berber. He, so dapper in navy-blue, double-breasted blazer and suede shoes. More French than the French.

'You have no appointment,' he announced when we arrived at his door. We did not. It had been a beekeeping oversight. He looked me up and down with disdain, as though I'd slept in my clothes.

'Where are your invitation papers?' he quizzed.

I had none. Still, I must have eventually appeased or flattered him because, after glancing at his watch and sighing theatrically, he agreed to a tour.

'What do you want to know?'

'Your institute produces a white olive,' I began tentatively. 'I learned of this variety in Malta.'

He nodded impatiently, confirming that white olives were being cultivated in his groves. Originally from Italy, it was the French who had introduced them to Algeria in 1950. They were described as 'white' because they ripened only to deep yellow.

'But, surely,' he cried dismissively, 'this is not why you are here?'

I took a breath. 'I am interested in the potential role of the olive tree in the battle against global warming, soil erosion, pesticides ... to know whether you and your team of scientists know anything about its remarkable root system ...'

'Ah-ha! You want to know about the work we are carrying out in the south, in the desert?'

I nodded. I knew nothing of it. This was all new material to me and I was excited.

'Six hundred thousand square kilometres of subterranean water exist in the Sahara, a substantial aquifer.'

I was astounded to hear this information. 'Can this be used?'

'We are sowing many young plantations and the saplings are thriving. Their presence will prove a vital asset in the regeneration of the desert. It is an experiment in arid-region production but one that I believe will reap fine results. If you have no time to go south, then you must, at least, visit El-Oued. There, they have planted over thirty-five thousand olive trees and are creating green belts. Their aim is to have over a million seeded by 2010. It is extremely heartening.'

His theme was thrilling even if he spoke as though he were lecturing me. *Chemlal* was the dominant variety in the fertile north. Now it was being transported south. He accompanied us into a laboratory with peeling walls and dearth of equipment. It struck me as sad, underfunded, understaffed, given the crucial nature of its work.

'Picture Texas, multiply it by three. Almost 90 per cent of Algeria's land mass lies south of the Atlas Mountains. Today, desert zones. That is the expanse we have to play with. Imagine if we can transform it to productivity. The areas of El-Oued, Biskra and Khenchelea have clearly demonstrated that the olive tree can adapt comfortably to life in zones that have not been traditionally considered theirs. Well, not since the Sahara was savannah land.' The director picked up a small jar of large green olives and proudly presented it to me. 'These were grown in the desert,' he smiled.

'Are you suggesting that potentially this could stanch the advancement of desert, could transform the Sahara back to the savannahs that once existed?'

'If we succeed, yes. Of course, this cannot happen overnight, but the olive has the wherewithal to help us. Most trees can stimulate a certain level of humidity but the olive goes further. Its roots are an excellent water pump and they create channels for rainfall to reach into the ground and replenish reserves.'

We followed him outside. Adjoining the institute were hectares of groves crowded with a multitude of olive varieties.

'Impressive, eh? I like to believe that what we have here is a substantial olive library,' grinned my host. 'Worldwide mother stocks,' he explained, 'are fast disappearing but at this institute we hold examples of almost every variety known to man. For example, the Italians have been having problems with their *Lecchino*,' he said. 'They came to me. I supplied cuttings from originals.'

'And with the cuttings?'

'They can propagate new trees.'

Thin black piping was suspended like telephone wires between the canopies. Drip-fed irrigation is in use all across the northern Mediterranean, *goutte à goutte*, drop by drop, but I had never seen it suspended like washing lines.

The director must have caught my puzzled expression.

'Regulating the water fed to plantations rather than glutting them is one of the great advantages of drip irrigation. Feeding trees moderately creates a balanced soil. Drowning them with excessive water in order to reap bigger yields is shortsighted and dangerous for the future of the planet.'

'But why are the pipes threaded through the branches?' I asked.

'It leaves the earth round the roots free for maintenance and it stops predators from chewing the cables. Wild boars are a nuisance in these matters,' he said.

'Yes,' I laughed. 'We know all about wild boars.'

Still, I found the hanging pipes unsightly.

When we reached the greenhouses, Monsieur directed me to a six-month seedling. Amazingly, it was in flower. They were aiming to propagate grafted trees that no longer required fifteen years of growth before fruit production. They also aimed to create an olive variety that produced a third more oil than our *cailletier* back at the farm. I was keen to discover the process, but an assistant was calling Monsieur le Directeur to the telephone. Disappointed not to learn more about grafting, I took heart from the fact that soon I would be in Italy where such skills had been honed since millennia. The director bade me a hasty *au revoir*, advised a visit to Tébessa, where I would find the oldest olive mill in North Africa, as well as to Ferkan, a village where the women pressed olives by foot. With that he disappeared. Tébessa was on my list, but El-Oued and Ferkan were new to me.

Entombed in the city of Sétif lay the body of Scipio Africanus, one of the outstanding military commanders of ancient history. It was Scipio who finally defeated Hannibal of Carthage and brought to an end a millennium of Phoenician domination of the Mediterranean Sea. But it is not for Scipio's great exploits that Sétif is remembered today. On 8 May 1945, as the Germans surrendered World War II, a parade by Algerians to celebrate victory (their soldiers had fought with the French) was launched in the city. Some used the occasion as a demonstration against more than a century of French rule, but matters got out of hand and the day ended with clashes between marchers and the *gendarmerie*. More than a hundred Europeans were killed, others wounded, and several, it was reported, mutilated or raped. Order was eventually restored by the French police but reprisals were ugly. During the ensuing days over a thousand Algerians lost their lives and several remote Muslim villages were flattened by French aircraft. What the French did to suppress the pro-independence voices was not France's finest hour and the cruel massacres had a significant impact on the country's determination to unshackle itself from French dominance. My reason for Sétif was neither Scipio, though his military 'achievements' undoubtedly had an impact on Roman and North African olive history, nor was it to ponder the damage caused by the French. My reason was Timgad.

Sétif. A taxi deposited me back in the Atlas Mountains at yet another sprawling, seemingly chaotic bus station, milling with Berbers in brown-hooded *djellabahs*, protection against sand and grit. There was no one to meet me. To reach the centre of town involved yet another taxi ride. This I was negotiating when two men, an Arab and a Berber, pulled up alongside me: Basil, a bear of a man, and Mahyouz, slight and concerned, the Laurel and Hardy of the bee-keeping world.

'We hear there's been a change of plan ...'

'a change of plan ...'

'you want a hotel ...'

'... a hotel.'

'Not so easy ...'

'... not easy.'

We checked me into the 'best' hotel in town, in the central square alongside the principal mosque, but now I was obliged to register at the police station. Security had escalated to high red alert. My insistence on a hotel had changed my status. We stood around for some time while a group of police officers in mirrored sunglasses smoked and chewed the cud with this person and the next. A photocopy of my passport was taken and I was requested to list my destinations from here on. A formality, nothing untoward, but should anywhere 'blow up' a record of my whereabouts was held. Basil and Mahyouz expressed their disappointment that I would not be dining with one or other of their families.

'A fine couscous has been prepared ...'

'... in your honour ...'

'Fine couscous in your honour.'

After a coffee at the best *pâtisserie* in eastern Algeria on rue 8 Mai 1945 where we guzzled almond cakes, talked through my itinerary and then discussed God, I was to be left to my own devices for the evening. However, first, to pay my hotel bill because no credit cards were accepted, I needed to change money. At every previous destination the beekeepers had made the exchange themselves because they welcomed the illicit euros, but here I was directed to the black market economy.

'Thank you, I'd prefer the bank.'

'No, we'll go to *la bourse*, Wall Street, right now.'

'Wall Street?'

The double act led me a block from my hotel, along a French colonial arcaded avenue of lacy verandahs. Once the market district, today a free-for-all falling apart at the seams. There, a host of shifty-lookers lined the pavement's edge waving wads of bills at every passer-by. There were police officers patrolling, milling in and out of the throng, and I grew nervous, but broad-faced Basil, who seemed expert in these dealings, reassured me, while Mahyouz beetled off.

'My colleague lacks bottle. Not switched on, a rural type,' my lumbering guide explained.

A moustachioed merchant in long navy overcoat was chosen. He and Basil disappeared inside an open doorway where a great deal of whispering took place. I, hovering in the gutter, was beckoned over. An exchange rate was proposed.

'But that's the bank rate,' I pointed out.

'The black market has fallen due to the bombings' was Navy-Blue Coat's argument. Basil urged me to accept it, to hand over my not inconsiderable sum of euros. Diffidently, I obeyed whereupon the rogue disappeared, leaving me with nothing.

Basil calmed me. 'It's routine. He's an intermediary, not the dealer. He'll sniff out cash, do the business and be back.'

Having negotiated a more profitable rate for himself, I was thinking, but remained silent.

Basil and I hung out endlessly behind the solid, imposing door in a high-ceilinged hallway where cracked *tommette* floor tiles led to a broad, curving staircase. Aside from the general disrepair and naked bulb, we might have been in Paris. Some time later, another fellow materialised, dawdling suspiciously in the busy street. Sallow-skinned, left eye squinting, burning cigarette between amber-stained fingers, stooped and coughing. A great deal of sideways glancing and furtive bobbings went on. Basil popped his head out, peering this way and that as though expecting a raid. I had never seen anything so openly fishy or plain daft. A wink brought the man to our sides. He pulled creased bills with trembling fingers from an inside pocket of his worn leather jacket. These were counted one by one into my palm. Everybody shook hands. The moneychanger slipped away, swallowed within a crush of shuffling *djellabahs* and peasant bodies while we held back for yet another five minutes.

My time alone was less amusing. My chosen hotel was rigidly Muslim. A diagram with arrows pinned to the wardrobe pointed towards Mecca, offering guests the direction to kneel for prayers. The deep drawl of the *muezzin* called like a sickening cow from the imposing neighbouring mosque. I asked at reception for the opening hours of the restaurant and whether it served wine to non-Muslims and I was practically asked to leave. The lobby was peopled with bearded mullahs, clerics in flimsy beige cotton gowns, sandals and socks, seated on the sofas cradling umbrellas and briefcases.

I took a dusk stroll about the once-Roman city, where all females bar me were behind closed doors, and I was hit on by every male between the ages of fourteen and ninety. At boarded kiosks, I read the headlines on French-printed newspapers, 'L'Alerte Rouge', 'Kamikaze Bombes'. I was hoping to chance upon a welcoming bistro but was definitely out of luck. The hustlers were driving me to distraction so I retreated to the hotel.

The clerk, a miserable specimen with rodenty teeth the colour of sandpaper, beckoned me over and gave a formal warning that alcohol was not served in his establishment and any guest caught sneaking one drop to their room would be asked to leave. I nodded and made my way to the lift. The entire town was dry so he had wasted his breath.

Algeria drove out their French colonisers, but while they were not paying attention the extremists had penetrated deep into the foundations of their territory, I was thinking. Only as I reached the fourth floor did I remember that I was in possession of a quarter bottle of red wine. It had been offered to me in the guest lounge at Casablanca airport. Too early in the day to imbibe, I had vaguely thought I might be grateful for it in Algeria and had popped it into my rucksack where it had lain, forgotten. 'This is its moment,' I smiled. I ran myself a hot bath and sank into it, luxuriating in suds while sipping my wine, which went straight to my head. I was deliciously happy, getting thoroughly clean and, just a tad, illicitly intoxicated.

The next morning before setting off I had the wherewithal to take my empty bottle with me, but what to do with it? It was early. Breakfast over, as drab an affair as dinner had been the previous evening, I took a stroll in the rain with my guilty evidence in my shoulder bag. I was intending to deposit it in a bin. However, this being Algeria, I could not find one. Eventually, round the back of the hotel, opposite the mullah's guarded entrance to the mosque, was a monumental pile of rotting garbage. I withdrew the bottle, slipped it within the detritus and strode on along the lane.

'*Arrêtez, s'il vous plaît!*' The ringing cry of authority.

I froze and turned. Two soldiers, boys, with guns trained upon me, had exited from behind the mosque's dark green iron gates and high-walled courtyard. I clocked the sentry box for the first time. A man with beard and black suit appeared.

'What were you doing?' he yelled.

I shook my head inanely, unable to speak.

'You have just disposed of something. What was it?'

'Nothing,' I mumbled.

'Approach! Hands up!'

Several retraced steps, hands above my head, found me back alongside the shoulder-high mounds of rubbish.

'You threw an object there. What was it?'

I was trembling, staring at the deposits, scanning bags, desperate to see if the blasted bottle was visible. I, a lone foreign female, had sinned against Allah (and, what's more, had revelled in the act). To admit the truth would be folly. Then it dawned upon me. Given the nation's security concerns, these soldiers probably suspected a hand grenade or bomb, set to destroy the religious heart of this city.

'What did you dispose of?' Another soldier had joined the group.

I focused half blindly upon the mound, dreading arrest, incarceration, and noticed a heap of dirty tissues and paper napkins.

'My used handkerchief,' I lied, uncomfortably.

The soldier on the right lowered his rifle, approached cautiously, leaned forward like a stork, and scrutinised the waste. He called in Arabic to his brothers-in-arms. With a wave of a gun nozzle, I was dismissed. I hurried off, praying they would not shoot me in the back. So traumatised was I by the incident that I returned to my room, tore open my luggage and changed my clothes, fearing a warning posted across the country: *Alert! Dangerous Western woman at large, last seen wearing a rose-pink cardigan.*

And so to Timgad, a World Heritage Site: a Roman city in the north-east of the country, fringing, according to the US State Department, the most dangerous area in Algeria. Timgad lay on the northern slopes of the Aurès Mountains and was created *ex nihilo*, out of nothing, by the Emperor Trajan in AD 100. From Sétif to Batna, Batna to Timgad, my route crossed high plateaux, vast in their emptiness, where sheep grazed placidly on tufts of shrubs in the drizzle. In the distance, a hazy outline of soft copper-mauve mountains. I was alone in a taxi with a driver I had hired for the day: round trip forty euros. We were at an altitude of 1300 metres, penetrating Chaouia territory. The Chaouias were another Berber tribe, shepherd peoples who had fought the Romans fiercely to maintain a hold of their lands. And not so long after the Romans had departed, the fiery certain-minded Arabs had invaded, intoxicated by the words of their Prophet, spreading their message, imposing their language. They had conquered, they had Muslimised.

'Arabic is the language in the schools, with French at secondary level. Never taught are our Berber tongues. The Arabisation of Berbers through Islam. They are attempting to erase our identity.' So spoke Assia whose bed I had shared.

'Algeria's problem is a question of identity. Sort that out and the other difficulties will evaporate.' Achour's contribution.

The deeper I penetrated, the more clearly I saw the simplicity yet time immemorialness of Berber history. Their pottery, their ancient argan and olive cultures. Since man had risen up on to two legs and had begun his journeyings north from Central Africa, the Berbers had inhabited these long-distance Atlas ranges and, behind the mountains, they had settled the mighty ocean of sand that today is the Sahara Desert and was, back then, during primeval cultures, lush, fertile plains (possibly with olive trees).

Staring out at the passing world I wondered again, as I had on so many occasions throughout these journeys round the Mediterranean, *what has religion to do with this?* What had the long reach of Islam to do with these Berber farmers, with their remote, prehistoric existences? And, has the Berber mentality always been that of the clan, the tribe rather than the nation?

Their homes were rectangular tents of skins or mud-baked. Old tyres were laid out on sheets of black plastic to secure them against the bleak, unrelenting winds. How was it when the snows fell? Men in dun-coloured, heavy, hooded robes trudged the flat plains. Two Berbers in their brown cloaks, hoods up, sat in the open boot of a car, goat between them, smoking. In the middle of the cloudy, muddied mountain a woman in the full *hijab* squatted by a white wall. Above her head in large red letters, *COIFFEUR. HAIRDRESSER.*

Batna. A dusty, wind-battered semi-constructed industrial nowhere, a metropolis creeping skywards from out of the mountain's groin. At its approach, wild olives and the ubiquitous military blockades. Shops with gaudy lampshades, men loafing in cafés, spitting in the streets, boys kissing boys, playing dominoes, troops of turbaned males on worksites squatting, smoking. Almost every building was a carcass save for the mosques. Again: what had they to do with this sand-ridden, sandblasted nothingness? An insignificant eatery read, L'Espoir. Hope! Aside from that café, nothing was in French, only Arabic. But it was the French who set solid foundations here in the nineteenth century, as a permanently guarded access point to the Sahara.

The rain was easing, but the sky remained overcast, possibly due to the clouds of cement rising like air balloons. I wound down the window and felt the grit scratch my features, irritate my nostrils. To the right, a stone settlement clinging to an incline with Berber shepherds in brown. To the left, a blockade of uniformed police officers standing about with motorbikes. Everywhere, the faces of military, of religion. Looming before us alongside a red Roman fort was a vast grey prison. On the outskirts of town, dark-skinned boys roamed with sizeable goat herds. I remembered Hamzoui's words: *the disenchanted young whose families have nothing . . .* chosen to train to fight the Holy War.

Batna, quite without character, but a strategic nugget and (though I didn't know it then) an Al-Qaeda stronghold.

My head was throbbing. It might have been the altitude or the lack of springs in this rattling husk with its stench of diesel or the newly constructed breezeblocks, squat, grey uglinesses dotted about the sandscape.

Timgad, well preserved, buried for centuries beneath sand and now protected by its altitude and dry winds, had been a military colony, a desert-port station for Roman troops, strategically positioned for dominance over these Berber hill tribes, and observation of traffic in and out of the desert.

Timgad, I read, 'with its square enclosure and orthogonal design based on the *cardo* and *decumanus*, the two perpendicular routes running through the city, was an excellent example of Roman town planning'. The place was completely deserted and I tried to picture its meticulously gridded streets inhabited. Had they been adorned with trees, blossoms falling in springtime? Today, swallows were plentiful and swooping low; storks nested on the Capitol's columns; wild rocket and chamomile perfumed the monuments' sockets; olive presses lay broken, jigsaw pieces of a forgotten fecundity ... Ghosts rose up before me, a few wild olive shrubs shooting up within the ruins, a cypress here and there, imprints of chariot wheels indented the slabs beneath my feet. A grove of olive saplings backdropped the amphitheatre. I imagined columns of marching men, feet beating against the slabbed paving stones. The roofless rising pillars, disciplined skeletons, recalled a regimental exercise. I pictured chariots galloping at full speed through the gates of the imposing Arc de Triomphe. I heard the snorts of sweating beasts, messengers arriving with news from the coast; spreading excitement as an expedition returned victorious from the interior. Fountains flowing, vegetation. But I could not fathom the fish images carved into the steles and on the stone surfaces at the Roman market. Fishes seemed an unlikely inspiration here in the middle of nowhere, so far from the sea, ringed by parched desert lands.

Two thousand years ago, a forty-kilometre lake had irrigated this city. These hilly circumferences were bosky with Mediterranean oaks. Those evergreen woods and the abundance of fresh water had been deciding factors in the choice of Timgad for the Roman soldiers' metropolis. Twenty-first-century Timgad claimed neither a copse nor pond. The Romans felled the bulk of the trees; they denuded the ancient forests to heat the gallons of water required for their public baths. (The Roman latrines were in better shape than most of the modern offerings I had encountered in Algeria.) Eventually, the lake had dried up, curled in on itself as the desert crept further north.

Waterless was the ruined city I stood in; a desolate, windy outcrop of regulated stones yet, bizarrely, a shimmering play of light on one of the distant mountain descents reincarnated the lake and, for a fleeting moment, the mirage was there: Timgad in all its glory.

I paused on a jagged stone stairway, polished by two millennia of footsteps, and leaned against an altar. A Muslim couple were wrapped in one another within the shadows of abandoned stone, snatching illicit desire, perhaps love. In the distance was the bluish outline of Djebbel Chelia. At 2328 metres, Chelia was the highest summit in northern Algeria.

A man beside a pillar was watching me.

At the tail end of the morning, I perched in weed-infested thermal baths, listening to birds, to a plastic bag flapping in branches of a self-seeded fig while munching on a boiled egg.

The man approached, pop-eyed and earnest. 'Drinkwater?'

I was taken aback.

He pulled out a scruffy plasticised card. One word written on it: POLICE.

'Are you French?'

I shook my head, puzzled.

'An archaeologist?'

Again, a negative.

'I have been instructed to keep an eye on you. Tourist control,' he added when he saw my concern. 'What are you looking for?'

'Olive stories, clues.'

He nodded and backed off, 'bonne chance'.

Stirring myself, moving on, I caught sight of the bug-eyed lawman waving, approaching again, this time in the company of another, all in black. 'Le Directeur' of the site.

The toothless, rustic-faced director shuffled forward. 'Anything we can do, Madame . . .' His thought ran out of steam.

The museum had been closed since the troubled nineties. Might he allow me entry? I decided not to request it. He ruled over a forgotten, unexploited backwater. I doubted he even had the key. I bought my driver lunch at the café close by the ticket booth. We ate chicken and ice cream and drank non-alcoholic beer. He offered to pay. When I refused, he insisted on buying me a trinket at the tourist stall alongside the site. I picked a carved wooden camel. We must have been their only customer in weeks. His Berber generosity was touching.

My next overnight was to be Annaba. It involved returning through Sétif, and then an easterly descent towards the coast. En route, Djémila. Basil and Mahyouz, my beekeeping team, linked up with me. Neither had visited the black-earthed city before. A retirement complex built by Rome for its military personnel, fabled for its rich, fertile soil. Two thousand years ago, a river had skirted it, fed from the summits of the overhanging mountains. Twenty-first-century Djémila was a tranquil backwater with no more than half a dozen Berber farms nestling in a verdant valley, each homestead looking back across time towards the skeletons of their ruthless enemy, the Romans.

The construction of the city included four gates, offering access to each compass point. The Gate of Jifel led south to the coast, to a port that had once been a maritime doorway to Rome. Today, Jifel is a gently paced seaside enclave but during the heydays of the Roman Empire with its bustling, lucrative activity, a splendid lighthouse illuminated the passage of cargo ships and travellers in and out of its harbour. Ideally situated within easy reach of the Mediterranean, Djémila, with its clean climate, attracted citizens, retirees, from as far afield as Carthage, some 170 kilometres to the east. I found vestiges of olive presses and oil activity but not an inspiring volume and I concluded that this city might have been an axis point. Volubilis lay to the west, Carthage to the east: both operated massive olive businesses. The caravans of laden camels crossed the Sahel west to east, east to west, tranporting the precious oil. The traders, no doubt, exchanged with the Djémilian agriculturalists other produce grown in the black, irrigated earth, while hordes of stevedores waited at the ports to load and unload the goods, taking care that the amphorae heavy with oil were carefully stored and kept out of the light. Shifting the produce was as vital to the Romans as farming it.

*

Woods of olive trees encircled the foothilled outskirts of Constantine where the women were in the full black *hijab*. Constantine, originally Cirta, a natural citadel that spread itself across towering rocky outcrops where extensive bridges straddled the River Rhumnel. The city, the oldest continuously inhabited in Algeria, had held a key position within ancient North Africa. The Phoenicians settled it, rare such a hinterland choice for them, for its water. Scipio, at the Battle of Cirta, routed the Carthaginians and Berbers and secured the site for Rome. In spite of its cosmopolitan history, its occupants were and always have been predominantly Chaouia Berber.

I tapped my driver on the shoulder and requested he pull over. I stepped out, craning my head to take the city in, perched like a bird's nest on natural rock. Here was the hometown of Quashia, our gardener, a man I had always thought of as Arab. Quashia always claimed, and I had seen it on his family home movies, that the women of his household did not '*porte la voile*', wear the veil, but the city looked, as we skirted it, with its rocket-high, twin-minareted central mosque and renowned *madrasa*, hardline Muslim. When Quashia was growing up, close to sixty years ago, Algeria was unleashing itself from the French and the hand of Fundamentalist Islam had not yet squeezed. The city I was gazing upon was a living example of the shift, of the power of fanatical faith to change traditional ways.

I began to recall Quashia's tales as a boy shepherd in the mountains, of his sheepdog that had died, a creature whose cracked photo he still carried in his wallet almost fifty years on, of the firewood he had collected on his back from the mountainsides, selling it in the streets to feed his mother and siblings after the murder of his father at the hands of the French in 1949, the year after the Sétif Massacre, when Quashia had been fourteen, the shack-bungalow he had built with his own bare hands after theirs had been burned to the ground. His stories had a context for me now.

I pulled out my phone and dialled him, working in the grounds of our olive farm, holding the fort. Miraculously, I had a connection.

'Guess where I am?'

'The olive trees are in blossom,' he yelled. 'You should be here!

Weather's hotting up, though. We should think about that well you are always talking about. And the repair of the drip-feed pipes.'

'Are you a Chaouia Berber, Mr Quashia?'

I heard his laugh, knew that toothless grin almost intimately. '*Mais, bien sûr.* One hundred per cent.'

I also recollected how, while I was in preparation for this long voyage, he had requested time off to make the Hajj, the pilgrimage to Mecca. Spiritual a man though I have always known him to be, this had both surprised and unsettled me. I gave the city one more glance, wished Quashia and our farm a *bonne journée* and settled back to my travels.

A descent into softly sloping inclines, silvered by olive groves and wildly yellow mustard flowers, onwards through weed-infested vineyards, originally Phoenician, then Roman, later French. On past a colossal and perfectly grotesque cement factory, to Annaba. Annaba, nudging the eastern hem of Algeria, was a picturesque Riviera-style seaside resort frequented by French colonisers who had described it as their '*petit Nice*'. Ancient tracks for the trains that transported the wheat from the mills to the boats were still visible. The modern railway station was the colour of desert sand. From here, if it was safe, I would return west – 600 kilometres, over ten hours by train – to the port of Algiers in search of a boat to Sicily.

Finally, the rain had stopped and the clouds had lifted. I was welcomed by the first sunshine I had been blessed with since Morocco. Still within the core of Hamzoui's framework of beekeepers, my hosts Mostafa, a dead ringer for American actor Bill Murray who, not surprisingly, he had never heard of, and wife, Nadjet, with one peppermint-white glass eye, were a courteous, well-educated couple with a son living in Paris and an unmarried daughter who drooled day and night over wedding-photo albums. I was housed with Nadjet's sister, Saoud, who lived alone in a colonial bungalow in a pretty tree-lined street. It could indeed have been the suburbs of Nice. A shy and studious fortysomething spinister, Saoud was a professor of classical Arabic, a strict adherent of Islam and up before the light of day, praying. The women of the family, Saoud, Nadjet and daughter, waited on me hand and foot, which embarrassed me deeply. They did not wear veils but they were believers and saw me as a very different woman.

'Our lives are within the kitchen, but you have found a place out in the world and it is our pleasure to serve you.'

'Algeria,' said Mostafa, 'is producing one million barrels of crude oil a day. Unlike Morocco, our government doesn't need the revenue accrued from tourism but culturally, socially, we are worried. Algeria is closing down.'

As students, both Mostafa and Nadjet had studied in Europe and they harboured deep-seated concerns for Algeria's future. They were alert to the dangers of insularity, particularly for the young who had no exchanges with others abroad, who could not leave for the West because visas were denied them, who could only travel to neighbouring Islamic countries. Consequently, they lacked perspective, lacked a broader vision of the world.

I began to understand why Hamzoui had gone to such lengths to make my trip possible. I began to comprehend the hospitality that had been offered to me. I had put this unconditional generosity down to our mutual friends, our beekeepers from Provence. I had supposed that this varied collection of apiarists with their remarkably efficient network across this vast North African spread welcomed me because Marie-Gabrielle was Algerian and a mutual friend, but it was more complex.

These people were starved of exchange and I, somehow, represented a lifeline.

'The psychosis of terrorism runs deep here. Fear has raised its head again and everyone is anxious for the country's future. The aim of the terrorists is to close us off from the world.' Mostafa's words.

Concerned for my wellbeing as Hamzoui and his beekeepers were, they had not wanted my trip to be aborted. They needed a witness, a messenger to the world beyond Algeria. And the bombs, exploding during the opening moments of my arrival, had threatened to disrupt their well-laid plans. But I had not cut and run, and this meant a great deal to them. I had not understood any of this. In fact, my determination to continue along my loosely programmed itinerary had not been an expression of bravery or courage. Stubbornness was a more apt description. Ignorance. Beyond Blida, I had received little news. My mobile rarely picked up a signal. Michel and I had hardly exchanged a word since my arrival, and only once had I visited an Internet café.

Annaba. Once upon a time, the Phoenicians' Hippo Regius, rechristened by the Romans, Hippone. Under the Romans, it grew into an early cradle of Christianity guided by Saint Augustine whose mother, Monica, had been a Berber. It was invaded by the Muslims in the twelfth century and from that date onwards the local Berbers had been Islamised. Souvenirs of that epoch lay within the winding labyrinthine medieval heart built by the Muslims in patterns of blue and white, like famed Sidi Bou Said neighbouring Carthage.

To reach what remained of the ancient Phoenician harbour, once set within a well-protected bay where fresh river water had supplied the eastern sailors' needs, proved problematic. A national demonstration had gridlocked the seaside resort. Sétif had been preparing theirs, too, as I drove away. An '*anti-terrorisme*' march, with white banners falling like chutes of snow in the streets. Algeria was vocalising its outrage, its determination that the country did not regress to the violence of the nineties. The modern port, constructed by the French in 1912, bombed by the Germans during World War II, had been cordoned off and the police turned us away. We were obliged to climb back up through the town and approach from another direction, but nobody complained. The demonstrators represented an essential step. Free expression had been denied to Algeria for too long. It was heartening to weave through streets surging with all generations. Predominantly in full Islamic dress, yes, but voices cast against extremism. Ringing through squares and avenues of decaying colonial elegance were booming, unified cries of '*Non!*' '*Non!*' to violence and repression, '*Non!*' to Fundamentalist Islam and its Holy War.

My final trajectory inland, in a dinky yellow taxi with sinking seats, was in search of the oldest Roman mill in North Africa and then, ever southwards, to El-Oued, a late addition to my schedule, pasted in after my visit to the Olive Institute. Mostafa had organised the driver, Mohammed, and insisted the man stay with me for the duration because I was moving towards the mountainous portals of the Sahara and from there, desert-bound. The trip was calculated to take six days, and it was deemed dangerous.

From Annaba, on a winding road that ascended towards the modern town of Souk Ahras situated along the higher plateaux, the clear blue sky was studded with swallows. Beyond the rattling windowpanes, the acrid yet seductive scent of blossoming asphodels. One of the excitements of these journeys was the new information gleaned along the way; the downside was that I inevitably ended up having to make choices. El Tarf, to the east, beyond sight, bordering Tunisia, I learned about during my last evening in Annaba, too late to include a stopover. There, grew 'ten million' wild olive trees. I wished I'd known sooner. The government's regeneration pro-gramme was actively encouraging the husbanding of these forests. Five euros paid for every tree pruned, so much for a graft executed, another sum for a water basin constructed, irrigation aids, so on and so forth; scaled tariffs for each stage of the work. A massive redevelopment scheme to transform those wild forests into thousands of hectares of fruit-bearing groves, an attempt to return Algeria to its former agricultural glory. I wondered about the origin of those trees. Numidian? Phoenician? Roman?

Instead, first stop Souk Ahras. Souk Ahras, originally Numidian, had been known as Tagaste in Roman times. Towards the village's summit, Saint Augustine's olive tree, purported to be 2000 years old, still grows. Beneath the tree, Augustine, later Bishop of Hippone (Annaba), had prayed and meditated. Compared to the Methuselahs from Lebanon, this was not such a remarkably aged fellow, but it warranted a salute of respect nonetheless.

Augustine was born in Tagaste in AD 354. At that time, Rome's dominance stretched unimpeded the entire length of a North African coast that today is Libya, Tunisia, Algeria and Morocco and extended with diminishing influence inland towards the Sahara. The coastal regions were fertile and remunerative for the Romans, producing crops of grain and vegetables in the river valleys as well as massive forests of olive trees on the hillsides and high plains. Augustine quit his natal village to study rhetoric in Carthage, a mere 150 kilometres east of here, travelling overland through those endless groves. By that time, Phoenician Carthage had long been levelled by the Romans, but in 29 BC Emperor Augustus rebuilt it. During the years of Augustine's studies there, it was the second largest city in the Western Empire. Only Rome outclassed it. A convert to Christianity, Augustine's literary output was prodigious. He was judged to be one of the finest philosophers of his time, arguing always for the purity of man and the fallibility of the human condition. During his years in Tagaste, before he settled in Hippo, he lived the life of a penniless recluse.

The settlements we were passing through were peopled by rough-hewn, emaciated mountain types where the women wore full-length robes and headdresses if not always the veil. Every village, no matter how humble, had a mosque with minaret and displayed the unsmiling faces of politicians on posters. I could not equate politics or religion with these remote landscapes where storks waded in mudflats and solitary shepherds stood guard over less than a handful of beasts. Occasionally, we drove through deserted stone hamlets, ghost settlements, and I learned they had been inhabited by Jews, French, Spanish, even Turkish Jews, who had upped sticks swiftly after Independence and fled to Israel.

On the hillsides surrounding Souk Ahras, holm and cork oak forests had flourished and in these naturally wooded habitats had roamed lions and panthers. These big cats had been hunted with nets and shipped off to Rome for entertainment in its amphitheatres. Today, our route was flanked by dense olive groves. In these regions, many had confirmed it, though I found no evidence of it, women pressed the olives with their feet.

'This region wants for nothing,' I remarked to Mohammed.

'Except honest men to govern it. It serves to allow the people to remain in a backwater state of mind. Then Islam extremism can pick and choose its youth for its own ends.' I had not expected such a response, but it confirmed my thinking. Surely, our role in the West was not to close down but to open up communications, to offer access, to broaden the Algerians' spectrum of choice?

The outskirts of the town itself were unpromising: industrial activity, cement works, road blocks, the overwhelming smell of boiled meat, avalanches of black refuse bags with rotted rubbish spilling forth, swarming with a film of black flies. A filthy entry. The late morning hung with pigeon-grey clouds. Brightly coloured blankets and sheets had been draped from the balconies and windows of semi-constructed, inhabited homes. We found no directions to St Augustine's tree. Enquiries returned only suspicion. Eventually, a toothless codger in a check jacket, a frayed rag of a man, offered to lead us to the 'Christian spot'. We parked up. I followed him while my driver slipped off to a mosque for a few swift prayers. Was I Italian, my shuffling guide enquired. Pilgrims came regularly from Italy, arriving via Tunisia. He was carrying a newspaper. The front page was taken up with a photograph of military tanks.

'Where is this?' I asked him.

'Algiers.' He shook his head. 'Not good news. Troubles not far from here, too.'

Through a locked and guarded gate, climbing a curved flight of immaculately clean, newly laid steps, I was now in the hands of the *gardien* of the chapel and guide for the site as well as a small, incessantly yapping white dog. The spreading multi-trunked olive tree, undoubtedly of venerable years, stood alone; its roots entombed within a circular stone wall and low iron fence. It was in full flower. At its base were its black winter fruits, shrivelling. Overhead, a flock of storks in flight that seemed to hover moment- arily above the Christian site. I climbed another short flight up into St Augustine's chapel, a recent addition, and its privileged crowning views out across the city. Figs, vines were growing wild out of the walls of crumbling, abandoned properties, birds were nesting on terraces and rooftops within arm's reach. Birdsong abounded. I spied a four-minaret mosque, a holy shrine, some way across the town. Then the recorded *muezzin* cranked into lugubrious life and the hum of everyday business settled into stillness for a moment or two. Returning to the taxi, no one requested money. Half a dozen colourfully attired women sat cross-legged on the steps of a doorway cawing and gossiping, photo-shy but willing. Even the local policeman shook my hand and kept company with me while we awaited the return of the driver.

What would Augustine have made today of his alpine retreat?

There is an Arab saying, *Yesterday never existed*. Aside from August- ine's olive tree, here I could have believed it.

*

The road, as such, to Tébessa had vanished, or it had never existed. Dust tracks we bumped along, rattling through mile after mile of untenanted high-altitude plains where the sole signs of life were a small eagle that made an appearance, a thin man in blue uniform holding up a furled red flag by a barely visible rail track and another fellow sleeping on his side close to half a dozen olive saplings pushing upwards in arid desert. The track had been laid by the Algerians between Tébessa and Annaba. Horizontal to it could still be seen the uprooted, rusting remnants of an earlier line, possibly a French legacy. We passed through a village, dusty, dry, godforsaken. Sheep grazed on – what? The women were either in full chador or had covered their faces with white handkerchiefs, protection against the winds and dust as much as for God's sake. The buildings were one-storey, biscuit-baked huts. The intermittent olive grove was a relief, a pleasing verticality in a horizontal void. How did these Chaouia Berbers survive? At El-Aouinet, an inconsequential nowhere, we found a substantial wheat factory. From here the basics for couscous and flour were produced and despatched by train, a seven-hour trajectory, to Annaba. From there the tons were shipped to other ports, other markets. Then came whistling tablelands of wheat backdropped by distant ranges of terracotta mountains, twisted and fretted like chewed sweets. It was empty, lonely, monotonous, yet lovely, but I was puzzled as to how the plains were irrigated. Water piped from where?

The director at the Olive Institute told me this region had been one of Rome's most bountiful granaries, a remarkably fertile spread with nothing but golden wheat. Closer towards Tébessa, where stood the oldest olive mill in North Africa, acre upon acre of silvery olive groves had been farmed. But as the parched desert conditions had crept further north all had been lost. Today, it was hard to believe that the land had ever been otherwise.

The crippling effects of desertification.

'Do the locals live off these wheatlands?' I asked the driver.

He shook his head. Some were hired hands at the factory but the bulk of their pittance incomes was generated by cigarettes.

'Cigarettes?'

'Contraband. We're less than a hundred kilometres from the Tunisian border. The cigarettes are smuggled in and sold on.'

My first response to Tébessa when we eventually, mid-afternoon, pulled into its dustbowl of a marketplace and bus station was to turn round and go straight back out again. Ali was the beekeeper in situ here, but connecting with him had proved difficult. He spoke little French and seemed incapable of settling a fixed rendezvous. Mohammed, who had been at the wheel since seven that morning, was exhausted and his temper was growing short. We sat in the car and waited. I stepped out to stretch my legs and take in the scene. Even at 1100 metres, a hot, gritty wind was blowing. Papers, bags, soles of shoes, cuts of cloth were flying here and there. Empty tins rolled and skittered. The poverty was shocking; women with bawling babes-in-arms covered in flies, three-legged dogs, buses that were not fit for the breaker's yard, hobbling old turbaned men with rust-coloured skin. And chaotically busy. When Ali eventually pulled up, he was Arab-dark, handsome, robust; swashbuckling in a hinterland fashion. At every available opportunity he attempted to rid us of Mohammed. Ali was in the process of an acrimonious divorce, I learned within minutes, which in this Muslim nowhereland was rare. Having not understood what I was after – the whole subject seemed to puzzle or confuse him – he dragged me off to the museum. It was Thursday afternoon, closing for the weekend, Friday being the Muslim sabbath. The curator with a clanking set of horror-movie keys in hand was locking up. She was from Tizi and happy to assist, openly admitting that she was bored and had no work to be getting on with. Her office was piled high with files. Its odour was of mildew. The walls were stained with rivered patches of damp. On her desk, an old-fashioned computer, an Algerian flag and a small bronze head of Nefertiti.

'*Hélas, le Directeur* was mistaken. The oldest mill in Africa? No.'

'Oh.'

'But we have the largest.'

'That'll do.'

But the mill was not in Tébessa. It was another fifty kilometres south, on the outskirts of the Sahara. Mohammed was still at the bus station looking dust-filmed and fed up.

'This extra hop calls for a renegotiation of my fee,' he pouted.

I agreed and off we set. Finding no shops, we pulled in at a one-pump garage where I purchased sweet black coffees, crumbling wafer biscuits, a stick of bread and a packet of utterly tasteless, plastic-wrapped, livid orange cheese. The provisions kept him fuelled and on we went. Back at base, part-time beekeeper Ali was arranging a hotel and dinner.

Along the way, bitumen was being laid to improve the route and water pipes were being sunk into roadside trenches where donkeys pulled the loads. I wondered again at the transformation since the Romans had ruled this territory. The processes that had caused such drastic desertification. Was it reversible? Or was I staring the future in the face?

Mohammed was growing irritable, moaning that we were lost, that we had no clear directions.

I was attempting to brighten his mood. 'There is only this one route, Mohammed.'

He harrumphed and bitched about the cost of fuel, which I was paying for. Eventually, a man standing in the middle of nowhere, looking as though he was trying to decide whether or not to cross the road. We pulled over. The two shook hands and fell into discussion, talking fast in both Berber and Arabic. The desert man was wearing a bobble knit hat and a very bedraggled, faded French military jacket. His face was etched with desert hardships. On the horizon, a cargo train appeared from nowhere and chugged slowly north. Dalíesque in this windblown emptiness.

'Up from the Sahara,' our local informed us, 'beating a path to the coast.'

'Transporting what?'

He shook his head. Crude oil, perhaps.

Within my imaginings, I pictured camel trains trekking this immense African journey transporting tradeable riches and black slaves. I thought of legionnaires who marched these routes to protect and conquer, overseers of the slaves working the groves and wheatfields. Soldiers on horseback. Millennia later, French Foreign Legionnaires would have set their feet here. So, too, the Algerian resistance fighters. Berber warriors. For such an isolated desert spot, its history was busy.

The wind was howling like a hyena. We were inching forward again, hailing every passing car – a total of three – all of which stopped. Hands were shaken, niceties exchanged, God's blessing offered and returned. I was peered at, spoken of, as though I did not exist, but none knew the *huilerie* until finally one fellow provided the location. It involved turning off the road on to a sand track. Springs clanking, a descent into a dried-out wadi, riverbed, and seconds later, jammed wheels, spinning, and the rising smell of burning rubber. Mohammed bustled me off to retrieve any dried sticks I could find. These he laid beneath the tyres like straw matting and on we continued. And there, ahead, were the ruins. A magic castle rose up before us like a stupendous sandstone Phoenix in the middle of nowhere: the largest Roman olive mill in North Africa, El Ma el Abiod. This was its Arabic name, of course, not its Roman appellation, which I failed to find. What I did discover later was that El Ma el Abiod was the name given to this entire vast plain and beneath it lay a substantial sandstone aquifer, slowly being contaminated by surface pollution. The aquifer was at least five million years old.

I scooted from the car to the mill's faded green gate. The site was fenced and protected, locked with a substantial padlock. A herdsboy with small flock and four barking dogs watched on. There was one habitation, drystone walled as though built of sandbags. An orange tractor, a few chickens offered a notion of domesticity. Mohammed ran, calling for the occupant. A Berber woman, ruddy-skinned, pronounced aquiline nose and startlingly clear eyes, with the largest, most pendulous breasts I had ever seen, waddled towards us in burgundy, crushed-velvet robe belted with string, brandishing the key.

'These people never get sick,' remarked Mohammed. 'They just die of hard work, of old age. Living up on these high windy plains with the desert on their doorsteps and life with the elements, you cannot be hardier.'

Within the site's grounds, a few straggly sheep were grazing on a yellow-flowered ground plant. The ruins were fascinating and entirely forgotten. I had rarely felt so excited, so triumphant. Algeria had unveiled a cache, a real jewel. There were settling tanks, pressing wheels, chunks of stone jars, carved ingresses where wooden beams would have been inserted ... This may not have been the oldest *huilerie* in North Africa, but it was certainly Herculean. Roman mills lay scattered and forgotten everywhere. Here, when operational, immense olive activity had taken place, whereas now it was nothing more than a wind- and sand-blown portal to the not-so-distant Sahara. Here, more than anywhere, I understood the scale, the magnitude, of the commerce that had been developed and deployed by the Romans. Others, too, before them, perhaps. Myriad stone pressing wheels had turned here, crushing innumerable tons of olives and had brought forth more litres of green-golden oil than I could have envisaged. The riverbed that had trapped our tyres, today as dry as dead skin, would have been a flowing vital water source; it would have fuelled the mills. Lost within centuries and layers of sand and stones had lain this vital clue along one of the main east–west, north–south arteries of the Olive Route. At this lonely, evocative spot, I began to comprehend the extent of the olive tree's history, as well as its potential for tomorrow. All across the Mediterranean had been these to-ings and fro-ings, these cross-fertilisations. The olive tree, like the mulberry in China with its silk offerings, had spawned not only a series of fruit products but trade, cultural exchanges, civilisations, marriages that had shifted the world's perception of itself.

I closed my eyes, wind whistling sharp round my head, and pictured an apocalyptic, what-if scenario that had been haunting me since Spain. The desert beating at our Western, twenty-first-century doors. In decades, centuries to come, if I were to climb those Andalucían olive groves, might sand, wind, soil-eroded nothingness be the scene that greeted me? Will that monster mill in Baena become a forgotten relic of a mismanaged past, just as this solitary, undiscovered skeleton, whose name I could not find, was today? Or was there another, arboreal forecast? Reforestation. Olive trees are an excellent water pump – hadn't I discovered that during these travels? – they stimulate humidity. Can the olive tree contribute? Forests of olive trees feeding the soil, regenerating deserts, generating water, turning the wheels once again? I was confident that in El-Oued, with its programme to plant a million olives by 2010, I might encounter such a picture.

*

Tébessa was seductive in its desolate bleakness, its unrelenting layers of sand that gnawed into me, that shifted and turned. It was limbo, a backwater with a Roman town nestling at its heart, a town that civilisation had turned its back on. At my hotel, Ali had left a message to say that he would collect me at eight to dine with his family. In Tébessa, women were forbidden out after dark and dusk was falling fast as I scooted through the unmade, windswept alleys towards a cybercafé. Mistrustful eyes followed my every move but I was on such a high that I barely paid them attention until I noticed I was being followed by a half-wit, stooped, with splayed fingers, moaning to himself. For just a moment I felt a shiver of fear.

The Internet point was, of course, not a café at all, but it was the first I had ever visited where I was directed into a separate room. Women in Tébessa were segregated, forbidden to use the same com-puters as the men. One other female was present, cowled in her robes and scarves, booting up her screen. I set to work. Suddenly, the music of Jacques Brel playing from the speakers of her computer. I turned and the woman did too, smiling.

'Does it bother you?'

'Not at all.'

She was a student of sociology who lived locally and passed here every evening to study, but most of all to listen to music. When I quizzed her about being out alone, I learned that she had a special dispensation. Her college could not provide the necessary research material, so she found it online.

'I love Jacques Brel,' she confessed.

The lyrics of 'Ne Me Quitte Pas' were still circling in my head when I strode back into the lobby and found Ali spruced up, ready to go, and cross. In his van, I was politely chided for wandering the streets.

'We don't allow our women out. We like them shut up indoors,' he stated.

Beyond the van's window, the sidewalks were paved with men, crouching, walking, leaning, smoking but not a single female in view.

'Why, if I should be indoors, have I been invited to dinner?'

'Because you are a stranger. A stranger is always made welcome, even a woman. It is our tradition.'

Ali left me seething.

The faceless high-rise set in a bomb site of a plot at the town's edge promised a desultory soirée, but, as was so frequently the case, the interior of the apartment was sprucely clean with floor-length white curtains, hand-embroidered with giant scarlet flowers. I was ushered into the sitting room where two daughters and a very shrivelled old lady awaited me.

'Enjoy your dinner,' said Ali.

'Where're you going?' I snapped.

He was bound for the neighbouring room to dine with father and brothers. I was to eat with the women. On a coffee table sat two cooked chickens, numerous heaped bowls of salads, fruits, home-made breads, a veritable feast. And no couscous. I was delighted. I was couscoused out. The women directed me to the sofa. The laden table was lifted and placed at my knees. I was the only one eating. We lacked knives, forks and plates. Their burnished faces watched me like hawks, smiles broke open, golden as egg yolks, while I struggled with fingers to do justice to the delicious offerings. Linda, one of nine daughters, seated beside me, suddenly suggested to her mother that a plate was required. A sideboard was opened and one of only two plates was handed to me. Linda's mother who, shockingly, was only sixty-two, the result of having borne eighteen children, bemoaned the woman's lot, listing woes and chores while beautiful Linda, soon to marry, had forewarned her fiancé that she would give him but two offspring. Gossip and chatter. We had a very jolly evening.

Linda spoke '*cassé*' French and with that broken language and her translations, we managed admirably.

'*Who* was my age?' they asked repeatedly.

A cabal we were of female secrets and exchanges. So much so that when Ali returned and saw our merriment, he grew suspicious.

'What are you laughing at?' he barked.

My sole distress was when I learned from Linda that she covered up and wore a veil not because her mother had ever insisted – here, the mother shook her head – but because she had read in an Islamic medical book at the school where she taught kindergarten that the cells in a woman's brain were feeble and less resistant than a man's;

therefore head and face coverings were essential to protect health, preserve life. I had come across this argument in Syria and had dismissed it as nonsense, but hearing it a second time troubled me profoundly. Such misinformation fed to women, to herd them, to keep them powerless and ignorant.

'Look again at that book,' I said to her *sotto voce*, as I was leaving, Ali rattling keys at the door, itching to get me on my way. 'I think you'll discover that it was written by a man.'

One more day at Tébessa. With Ali, I visited another out-of-town, long-disused mill site from where a secret, three-kilometre underground passage led back to Tébessa's Roman and Byzantine ruins within the town's centre. Two local Berbers thought, though no one knew for sure because theirs is an oral tradition not a written one, that the passage had been used to hide persecuted Christians.

'But the stories are being left to sleep, to fall into distant memories in the sand,' one herdsman remarked to us.

The whole region was a veritable picture book, an anthology of a thousand legends, tales, buried epic dramas.

Back at Tébessa, within the Byzantine walls of the old town, we wandered round a stupendous herb market. I tried 'pulverised tobacco powder' for the first time, sniffing and coughing, a form of snuff. Ali bought a twig – he could not identify the tree – from a vendor for twenty dinars. He borrowed a well-used knife from a passer-by and split the twig.

'This is for women to clean their teeth,' he said.

'Why women?'

He brushed away at his own set until his lips and tongue turned scarlet, like a whore's make-up. I was offered the second split but I found the taste too bitter. He made me offerings of postcards, books in Arabic I could not read. Within the classical city, at the Byzantine cathedral, we met a man of ninety-six, dressed in white with big black cracked sunglasses. His nickname, 'The Shark'. He had spent time in 'the coal mines of northern Belgium labouring for the French'. He proudly presented the identity tattoos on his wrist and the underside of his arms. He had never joined the Algerian resistance, the *maquis*, because the French had treated him well enough. When he returned to Tébessa after his years in France he had been foreman of an estate here, farming olives. In those days the drupes were taken all the way to Guelma to be pressed. During French rule, olive farming was an important crop in the environs of Tébessa but no one, as far as he knew, had ever considered reinstating the old Roman presses or utilising those sites. The old man whiled away his days at these ruins, sitting within the skeleton of the basilica, talking to strangers, pondering life. His best friend, long deceased, had been the gardener here, back when the archaeological site had been in better repair.

'Temples converted into churches and then mosques,' he growled.

He was a Muslim but he liked sitting in the frame of the great church that had never made it to mosque. His sepulchre it was, he said, from where he could contemplate the centuries of bones and civilisations disintegrating in the sands.

El-Oued, the City of a Thousand Domes, lay at the centre of an area of oases in the northern Sahara. A back-breaking drive south of Tébessa, it was to have been my final port of call before returning to Algiers to make my way to Sicily. Up at first light the following morning, the weather had grown exceptionally cold. A sharp wind cut through us as a greyish blanket of sand rose up out of the desert, closing out the horizon. It reminded me of flocks of herons in flight. Mohammed was unhappy, fearful of the journey that lay ahead. The surrounding mountains began to disappear as though a metal grill was closing in around us. We inched on southwards for over an hour in sombre silence along what must once have been a road and was now little more than a narrow track. The challenges of harsh desertlands in such a vehicle made the going sufficiently arduous without the added pitfalls of a full-blown sandstorm. Eventually, we reached a roadblock. Two wind-fatigued police officers, looking like a pair of exhausted *rammaals*, sand porters, flagged us down.

'The road south is closed off due to storms and flash flooding,' they informed us. Inundations had washed away entire tracks. Herds of goats, 'numbers reaching two thousand', had been killed, drowned in landslides. 'Two drivers drowned.'

'Is there any way round it?' I begged.

They shook their heads. 'You must turn back.'

'How long before it blows over?'

'Days, could be weeks.'

I had been hoping to meet up with a hydrologist from El-Oued whose expertise was water management. El-Oued offered a vision of the future that was positive, constructive. At the end of the late fourteenth century, Sidi Mastour, an Arab, arrived in El-Oued from the eastern Sahara. He brought with him date-palm seedlings. He believed that even in this arid region the trees could flourish if the subterranean water source was tapped. He taught the locals to carry off the top level of sand and create sunken farms, craters known as *aghwaat*. Into these were planted the palms. The trees' roots were able to reach the water and so they flourished and became the foundation of the Algerian date industry. Today, the water table lies much deeper. The challenges are to keep the sand managed and to irrigate the plants, drip by drip, and to choose crops that can survive. The olive fits the bill better than any, I had been told. I had dearly wanted to see how this operated, this vision for the future. To learn of the olive's root systems. To see in what way, if any, I could put this knowledge to use on our farm, too. Had it been a day, even two, I would have sat it out but an indefinite length of time was not feasible. I needed to move on to Sicily. Turning back was a blow, a bitter disappointment. Still, Mohammed was happy, returning home a few days earlier and still getting paid. He swung his boneshaker about and retraced our route to Annaba.

At Algiers airport, landside, I was browsing in the bookshop when a strangled, blood-curdling ululation broke out. It stopped everyone in their tracks, causing a restrained panic. Resonances of the recent bombings still lingered in the hearts of people. I hurried with my bags to see what it was about. Standing before the sliding doors at Arrivals was a short, pear-shaped Arab in long beige dress and grey headscarf. She was holding the lower palms of her hands over her eyes, her wrists covering the lower part of her face. The sound she was emitting was a low-spirited chirruping. Others who had come to look moved on, no longer interested as the distressed woman slumped on to a bench. Another woman seated there, also in full dress code, stared straight ahead, ignoring her new neighbour, determined not to engage with the other who was now howling dry tears. I inched forward and took her hand. Limply, she accepted the warmth without registering it. I looked about for a security officer, beckoning someone who could take control, assist.

'What do you want?' he snapped.

'Can you help this lady, please?'

He shook his head. Her son had been killed in France. They were bringing in the body, the coffin, off the recently landed plane. By now, a small huddle of women had gathered round the grieving mother, babbling in Arabic. I released my hand and slipped out of their way.

The officer looked at me and said: 'She shouldn't have come here. Her place is in the house. Not here.'

I walked off without responding through passport control, into the no-man's-land of travellers, onwards to my next destination, Sicily. The woman's heart-rending cries were still audible, accompanying me all the way. It was my last image of Algeria.

The five-times-a-day *muezzin* calling the faithful to prayer, yes, that would abide in my memory, as well as the dust, the desert sands, the aridity, the weeks of torrential rains. But this woman weeping sank deep into my bones. Weeping for Algeria, it seemed, for a country snagged up in transition. A country with dreams, plans, possibilities, full of generosity and welcomes, caught somewhere between violence, turmoil and repression, between poverty and ignorance, with little time for its past and a future not even sketched.

Sicily

What struck me when I landed in Sicily and began to penetrate the island's countryside from the Falcone-Borsellino airport to Palermo was the vibrancy of nature's colours, the clean and cared-for roadsides, fields, the young women in their skimpy outfits expressing an easy sexuality. And pigs. I smiled to myself. It had been a while since I had seen pens of muddied pigs gathered round troughs gorging happily. It was almost the end of April and I had left the world of Islam behind me, though not entirely. Two centuries of Arab occupation of Sicily had left many traces. The dialect abounded in archaic Arabic words and Arab blood flowed through Sicilian veins.

Ziz, Paleopolis, Panormus, Palermo. The coastal city of Palermo assumed many identities and saw many conquerors. Its geographical location, a strategically perfect transit port right at the heart of the Mediterranean, has always given it great allure. In its heyday, Palermo was judged to be one of the grandest and most luxurious cities in Europe and the Palermitans of today still regard it as such. Palermo was established around a natural harbour on the north-western coast of the island in the eighth century BC by Phoenician tradesmen from Tyre. They called it Ziz, 'flower'. It is tucked into the centre of a wide bay enclosed to the north by the Pellegrino Mount and to the south by Capo Zafferano.

The Greeks, who had known the island as Trinacria, or 'three tips' because of its shape, occupied the port city some one hundred years later and rechristened it Panormus, which is 'all harbour'. They lived in Panormus, established settlements at various points on the island and traded, skirmished and fought with the Carthaginians. During the First Punic War, Palermo was conquered by the Romans and, when the Roman Empire split, it fell under Byzantine control until the Arabs arrived in AD 831. Under Arab rule, until 1072 (when the Normans took the reins), Palermo enjoyed a period of prosperity and creativity and became a jewel in the Islamic casket.

After several weeks of travelling in the world of Islam, I was out of step with the calendar of Christian Europe. May Day was upon us and the island was overrun with vacationers from the Italian mainland. For my first night, I booked a hotel on the north-western coast just outside the capital, near the city's commercial port. It proved to be a sumptuous mansion, constructed at the end of the nineteenth century and designed in the Art Nouveau style – when Liberty was all the rage – for a powerful Sicilian family. The Florios were members of the rising class of rich merchants. They had amassed fortunes through several businesses, the most important of which were Marsala wine and the canning of tuna fish. In the lobby hung a painting of a graceful woman sporting a magnificent rope of pearls set against a black cocktail dress. This was Donna Florio, a renowned beauty in her day. Wife of one of the two brothers who had founded the merchant dynasty, she had been the empress of fashion and her lavish dinner parties at their city residence, Villino Florio, were legendary.

This hotel, set on a low bluff at the foot slopes of Monte Pellegrino, had been for the Florio clan a weekend seaside retreat. It was way beyond my budget, but I had found nowhere else and its history offered me a starting point for my travels. Where there was canned tuna, there was certainly olive oil.

Two perennial images of Sicily are its Mafia and its olive oil, and they were not unrelated. The fame of Italian olive oil worldwide, particularly in the United States, was born when Sicilian Mafia families based in North America began to transport it across the Atlantic. Those Mafia families needed an honest business to cover for their steeped-in-vice dealings and olive oil suited them down to the ground.

The island was swimming in it and it came cheap. Why not turn it to their advantage?

I asked the concierge whether he could assist me in contacting a member of the esteemed Florio family; one who could tell me something about their heritage.

'They're all dead, lady,' was the surprising reply.

I knew the house had long since been sold on but I had not expected the Florios to lack survivors.

'No one living?'

'*Tutti morti*, lady. Like I tell you, all dead.'

Everyone addressed me as 'lady': 'You wanna order, lady?' 'Hey, lady, you got bags?'

'What happened?'

The porter shrugged. 'Let's just call it a decline in fortunes.'

Palermo was like a conglomeration of everywhere I had visited round the Med and yet it was very much its own personality, if not its own master. The past, a thousand pasts, lingered everywhere. Still, somehow, it was difficult to grasp. It was theatrical, had a grandeur about it yet its character slipped like oil through my fingers, but I loved wandering its streets, its stylish quarters, peering into its shockingly decaying slums, its historic centre.

Two uniformed *polizia* leaning against a blue and white police car; a young woman, garishly attired, pressed up against one of the men, rubbing her hand up and down his gun, caressing it as though it were his member. Slickly attired, iron-grey men, resembling retired lawyers, judges, bankers, sat perusing *Giornale di Sicilia*, the island's daily paper, at outdoor cafés. Fleets of red Ferraris – more Ferraris than I had seen in my life – snarled up the streets. Handsome buildings blackened by fumes and pollution; classical buildings dripping with hanging plants; the high-pitched wail of police sirens, *carabinieri* on the move, possibly escorting judges, prisoners or witnesses linked to yet another episode in the *scandali di mafioso*. The decaying quarters alongside the loud displays of wealth were hard to stomach. The Vucciria food market stretching through the streets of the city's historic heart with a mix of Arab and Latin faces, men with coppola caps, naked light bulbs dangling from tarpaulins, the cries of the hawkers, crates of olives and capers. In the Sicilian dialect Vucciria means noisy, vociferous cries. This outdoor market has existed for seven centuries. An expression in Sicilian says: *Quannu s'asciucanu i balati dà Vucciria.* Loosely translated: When the streets of Vucciria run dry . . . or It could never happen. But the fears among the stallholders I chatted with were that the market could disappear. The Mafia were moving in, levelling the crumbling tenements, handing out construction contracts to friends.

Unable to afford an extension on my luxurious if cupboard-size accommodation, I decided to set off round the island and hired a car for the purpose. I had instigated two meetings. The first was with a Sicilian American. Let us call her 'La Signora'. She was the granddaughter of a Mafia mobster who had made his living, until he was bumped off, working as an enforcer for Joe Profaci and his 'family' in Brooklyn during the 1940s and 1950s. Born in Sicily outside Palermo in 1897, Joe Profaci was a New York Mafia racketeer. He was 'Olive Oil King' because he had fronted his activities by running a legitimate olive oil and tomato paste import business.

Before checking out of the hotel, I left a message to say I was on my way to Scopello and suggested lunch. From our brief, rather oblique conversations I deduced she lived somewhere close to this seaside village. Driving out of the city along the coast road, it was easy to see very quickly how this seaside capital had thrived, perched as it was at the edge of a fertile plain called Conca d'Oro, Golden Shell or Horn of Plenty, with protective mountains either side falling directly to the beach. Passing through Mondello – seafront promenade and bathing establishment with huts dating from the beginning of the twentieth century. Three-wheelers everywhere along the coast road selling fruits and fresh fish. An ice-cream mood abounded on a soft day with louring clouds. An earlier spit of rain had ceased. As I approached the tongue of land where Scopello lay, my phone rang. It was La Signora. She was cancelling.

'I cannot meet you.'

'But?'

'Talk to Coldiretti.'

Months I had been working on this contact. She refused to reconsider and the line went dead.

My second meeting was with an organic olive producer over on the south-east side of the island, outside Ragusa, not far from Siracusa, but I had several days to kill before that rendezvous. Coldiretti was the Italian Farmers' Union. I had no contacts there. In any case, it was May Day weekend: all offices were closed.

I pulled over and dialled the home of a writer I knew of living close to Palermo. Maybe she could help. Her answer machine informed me that she was off the island for two weeks.

I had originally envisaged approaching the south-east by cutting right through the centre of the island and stopping en route at the small hilltop farming town of Corleone. I had hoped La Signora might accompany me. If Corleone was not the birthplace of the Mafia, it remained the location most closely associated with their nefarious carryings on. The novelist Mario Puzo took its name for his most celebrated characters, Don Vito Corleone, the boss of all bosses, *il capo di tutti capi*, in his book *The Godfather*, portrayed in the films by Marlon Brando and Robert De Niro, and son, Michael Corleone, played by Al Pacino. The fictitious Corleones ran their businesses behind the cover of the Genco Olive Oil Company. Coincidently, Al Pacino's grandparents hailed from Corleone and had emigrated to the States at about the same time as fictitious Don Corleone had set sail.

I shoved the gear stick back into first, deciding to cut inland.

Long before the birth of the Mafia, the town of Corleone had been of strategic importance. It controlled an arterial route that intersected Sicily. For two centuries it was dominated by Arabs who knew it as Qurlayun, pronounced *kerleon*. I found no translation for this Arabic word, but it was easy to hear how the name had transmuted over the centuries to Corleone. As elsewhere round the Med, two particular agricultural gifts brought to the island by the Arabs were a skilled knowledge of irrigation systems and the farming of citrus fruits.

In real life, several Mafia bosses had hailed from this rural town and from its altitudinous position these criminals ruled over the greater part of the island. Bernardo Provenzano, a recent real-life 'boss of bosses', son of peasant farmers, was born a Corleonesi in 1933. He was also arrested there on 11 April 2006. Said of him by a fellow Mafia member: 'He shoots like a god, pity he has the brains of a chicken.'

Today, the State of Sicily is confiscating much of the Mafia-owned lands and handing them over to small cooperative groups, such as Libera Terra, who are planting up the acres with wheat, wine and olives. I wondered whether the neatly kept groves all around me were these. Libera Terra have olive groves on what was Bernardo Provenzano's private estate. Another coincidence: Provenzano is also the name of a variety of local olive.

The birth, and the ascendance, of the Mafia came about during the long and bloody years of Unification, known in Italian as *Risorgimento*, or the unifying of all states of the country and its islands into a single nation, Italy. Loosely speaking Unification began in 1815, after Napoleonic rule, and began to cohere around 1860, though multiple outbreaks of insurrection continued right up until the end of World War I. Sicily was brought into the new Italy after the arrival of Garibaldi and his thousand-strong Redshirts who took the independent island and declared it part of the new mainland power, in 1860. The peasantry supported this move; they hoped to rid themselves of the landowning classes and the *mafiosi* and share in the profits of the earth.

After decades of struggle, in 1860 Italy became unified. Still there remains, both in mind and spirit, two Italys: the more prosperous, industrialised upper half of the country, and the south, the *Mezzogiorno*, Land of the Midday Sun. Sicily and the foot of southern Italy are a distance from Europe. Here, in this poorer fraction, where crime and unemployment figures are double, lies a tempestuous sea-girt world where earthquakes, volcanic eruptions and Mafia are ever-present ogres.

During its Roman occupation, Sicily fell victim to the latifundia system. Expansive estates, producing wine, grain and olives, were owned by noblemen or senators and operated by slave labour. This practice of land reallocation had proliferated throughout Magna Graecia (the Greek states in southern Italy), Sicily, Andalucía and North Africa. Pliny the Elder reported that at one stage only six landowners possessed more than 50 per cent of Roman North Africa. These estates had been confiscated as war spoil, but once inherited the farms stayed in the hands of the entitled few and, what is more, these privileged paid no taxes, so their wealth accrued. Most were involved in the long-distance shipping of wine, garum (fish paste), cereal and olive oil. The latifundia paved the way for the European feudal systems.

By the nineteenth century Sicily found itself oppressed by feudal law, where the great estates were owned by absentee landlords. Bailiffs, known in Sicily as the *gabelotti*, leased large tracts of land from rich property owners and then divided up the plots and rented them on to struggling peasant families who toiled what little they had in a struggle to survive. From these smallholders the bailiffs extracted exorbitant ground rents. To assist the *gabelotti* in the collecting of their rents, they enlisted the help of local gangs who took on the role of arbitrators. Self-appointed intermediaries, they regulated the bailiff's affairs, frequently through the use of violence. These individuals became known as *mafiosi*. They operated in small territorial gangs drawn up along family lines. Out of this rural role of fixers and rent collectors grew the Mafia, mini crime cartels, gangs of men who took the law into their own hands and snatched what they believed was rightly their due or the due of those who had gun-hired them.

Since that time, of course, the Sicilian Mafia, operating under the infamous sobriquet the *Cosa Nostra*, has spawned extensively, creating both urban and rural 'families' and has infiltrated itself into politics, governments, importation, exportation, extortion rackets, drugs- and arms-running on both sides of the Atlantic. Today, the Mafia in its various incarnations holds power over a great deal of the *Mezzogiorno*. The *Cosa Nostra* is exclusively Sicilian while in Puglia there is the *Sacra Corona Unita*, in Naples they are the *Camorra* while the Calabrian network is the *'Ndrangheta*.

The Italian olive oil business may no longer serve as a screen for money laundering, but it remains clouded by corruption. I had hoped that La Signora, the deceased mobster's granddaughter, whose identity I had promised to keep secret and who had, before I landed on the island, seemed willing enough to meet, would help me to understand how and why olive oil had been chosen as the 'clean' product and how Sicily and its oil businesses had changed, moved on. But without her to connect the dots, I was a little lost. I feared that whoever I tried to approach would not speak, would protect themselves behind walls of silence and suspicion. In any case, I doubted whether I could instigate introductions at this late stage. It had taken me months to track her down.

So engrossed was I by my dilemma and the beauty of the surrounding nature – it was full-blown spring and the immaculate sloping fields and hillsides were carpeted with yellow and pink flowers – that I found myself not on the road to Corleone, but somewhere around Salemi, pootling along a pretty lane in the direction of Marsala. Without La Signora, I had given up on Scopello, much as I had been looking forward to seeing its converted *tonnara*, tuna canning factory, a fishing station where writer Gavin Maxwell had lived a while. And as Corleone was these days the main point of interest on the American *Godfather* trail, I decided then to continue along in my present direction and make an anti-clockwise island circuit.

It meant that I was also to miss 3000-year-old Trapani. An important port even today, it had been an entrepôt for the Phoenicians, known back then as Drepanon. Drepanon, meaning sickle, describing the shape of the little peninsula upon which it sits, had held a key position for defence of the island against the Romans, who eventually captured it in 241 BC and allowed it to drift into a long, slow decline. Today, it ships salt to Norway.

There was not a soul on the roads, more an assemblage of rambling bridle paths. I pulled over at a lane's edge, listening to the almost inaudible hiss and buzz of insects foraging the wild flowers all around me and refilled my water bottle at a roadside source. Green lizards, bigger and greener than ours at home on the farm, darted to and fro, in and out of the terraced walls. Even a snake slithered in between the stones, shy of me, not looking for trouble or confrontation. The day promised all the heat of summer. Even then, at the tail end of April, there was a tangible sense of the desiccation that lay ahead, burning up these sandy, winding paths and prickly weeds, of the blistering heat of the months to come. In this season, though, it hid its sunburned ferocity. I sipped the water; it tasted good. All around me were flowering olive groves, exquisitely pruned, each tree a work of art. These groves were clean, cared for but, unlike Spain, the soil had not been denuded. Wild flowers sprouted insouciantly at their bases.

Italy, right across its peninsular mainland and islands, farms 250 million olive trees and, after Spain, is the second largest producer in the world. However, due to its international reputation carried to the States and nurtured by the Mafia, the demand for Italian olive oil far exceeds its 600,000 metric ton production. Recent figures published suggested that 50 per cent of all olive oil sold worldwide under the label Italian Olive Oil had been grown and pressed outside Italy, usually shipped in, in tankers, from Tunisia, Spain and Greece. And the net was widening . . .

Was this the issue La Signora had been referring to when she advised, 'talk to Coldiretti'? I was still smarting from her change of mind.

After the silent beauty of the countryside, my arrival into Marsala, thirty kilometres south of Trapani, felt disappointing. Everywhere was closed up and it seemed that I was penetrating a decaying ghost town to reach its port. I headed directly for the Cantine Florio, its Marsala wine outlet, founded in 1833. I was hoping to find a living family member who could fill me in on their 'decline in fortunes', but unfortunately it had closed its gates and would not be reopening until Tuesday of the following week. I parked the car and kicked my heels down by the water. Still frustrated by missing out on El-Oued and now La Signora, I was wondering where to go next.

Marsala was founded by the Carthaginians in 379 BC. Their colony was relocated here from the small offshore island of Mozia when Mozia was destroyed by the Siracusans. Under Carthage control, Marsala, or Lilibeo as it was known then, quickly grew into an important and vital naval base. It was the last Punic stronghold to fall to the Romans who rechristened it Lilybaeum. When the Arabs arrived, it re-emerged as Marsa-el-Allah, or Port of God. It was here that Garibaldi landed with his thousand-strong army to take the island. I decided, after a spot of lunch at a restaurant converted from a waterside home once inhabited by an Englishman, Charles Gordon, who had sailed here to manage the Florios' wine businesses, to go in search of the archaeological museum. I had noticed a sign to it on my way through town.

Fish couscous was the dish of the day. A thread to Sicily's Arab past. Still, I ordered pesce spada alla Siciliana. Sicilian swordfish.

Carlo, who served my lunch, told me that the Florio family, 'due to a lack of male heirs', had sold its wine interests in the twenties to Cinzano and that today the business was owned by a consortium. I was disappointed not to take their story a little further.

'But if you are interested in that family you should make a trip to the island of Favignana and witness the *mattanza* first-hand,' he suggested. 'It's not far off this coast.'

The slaughter of the bluefin tuna (*Thunnus thynnus*), which takes place in the spring when the huge fish swim by these western Sicilian waters, was about to get under way.

'These days it's a dying tradition, still played out but it's principally for tourists.'

On this western coast of Sicily, tuna fishing, the most lucrative of all Mediterranean fishing concerns, had been dominated by the Florio family, I was learning. They had owned the island of Favignana as well as its water's fishing rights and, having dedicated the island to this purpose, had also constructed its *tonnara*.

I asked the waiter if he knew anything of Favignana's history.

'During the Punic Wars, Carthaginians and Romans fought for its dominance, but it was the tuna fishing that gave the island its notoriety.'

Hunting the bluefin dates back to the Phoenicians and those eastern navigators were almost certainly responsible for an earlier style of trapping and slaughtering of the huge fish, though this annual event was eventually perfected by the Arabs in the ninth century. The Arabic word *rais*, meaning head or boss, the name given to the chief fisherman, is testimony to their involvement in this ritual pursuit during their Sicilian years.

Mattanza grew out of the Spanish *matar*, to kill, though in Spain the killing ritual is *almadrába*, also the Andalucíans' name for the nets. *Matar*, in turn, is a derivative of the Latin *mactare* meaning to honour or kill. A perfect example of the mix of Mediterranean cultures.

Favignana's position was ideally situated close by the breeding grounds of the man-sized creatures which migrated in large shoals from the Atlantic Ocean, swimming through the Strait of Gibraltar to these warmer waters, for the purposes of reproduction.

The fish were trapped within a complex atrium of underwater nets. Each grew smaller and more restrictive until the creatures found themselves bumping up against one another in *la camera della morte*, the death chamber. Once sufficient tuna had been imprisoned – and this could take days – the *rais* called for the *mattanza*, the slaughter, to begin. The colossal nets were hoisted – each fish can weigh in excess of 200 kilos (bluefins are the world's largest tuna) – and hauled aboard the boats by the manpower of the *tonnarati*, the specialised fishermen, under instructions from a hollering *rais* who remained in a separate boat. The fish were then slaughtered with harpoons and iron hooks while the fishermen chanted and sang songs of ancient superstitions, the *scialome*, and the sea turned red with the beasts' spilled blood.

'Even today,' said Carlo, 'the lyrics are a mix of Sicilian and Arabic.'

The entire ritual followed strict practices and was very much a team effort. The vessels had no engines, gave off no sound to alert the prey.

'In 1874,' he continued, 'the Florio family introduced a method for conserving tuna fish in olive oil and thus created a vast production process that made the Favignana tuna fishery the only one of its kind in the world.'

I smiled at this. In fact, antique jars, possibly Phoenician, were discovered by archaeologists in Benidorm. These were believed to have been used for the storage of chopped and filleted fish conserved in olive oil.

The Florio tuna fishery shut its doors in the 1970s, closing down with it a way of life. Since antiquity, the tuna hunt had provided work and sustenance for thousands of Mediterranean families. Today, organisations such as Greenpeace are calling for a halt before the bluefin becomes extinct. Overfishing and illegal fishing are fast depleting the Mediterranean of its tuna schools.

Beyond the restaurant, I considered what I had just learned. It seemed that I was fortuitously in the right place at the right time, if I wished it. Should I search out a boat and go to witness the slaughter of these tunas, be a silent party to the historic *mattanza*?

Aristotle had described the migratory habits of the bluefin tuna.

Homer had written of it in the *Odyssey*, Pliny had prescribed various parts of the tuna as homeopathic remedies for humans. The fish carried a wealth of Mediterranean material in its wake. Like salmon, bluefins return annually to their original spawning grounds and for many this is the southern Mediterranean, either here in Sicily or through the Strait of Gibraltar along the African coast of Spain. Within the annals of olive-oil history, this would represent a page or two and a ferry across to the Egadi Islands, conquered by the Romans from the Carthaginians in 241 BC, was an inviting option. I strolled alongside the sea, the breeze playing on my face. I had time to spare now, but I decided that I would not go. Tradition it might be, but I could not face its gruesomeness and settled for the museum instead.

In 1969, Diego Bonini, a citizen of Marsala, captain of a dredger that was supplying glassmakers with sand hauled up from the local seabed, began to notice splinters and cuts of wood in his scoops – vestiges of an ancient vessel. He was working north of Marsala, off the seaward side of an islet, the Isola Lunga, which faced out towards the Florios' Favignana, the closest of the Egadi Islands. His modest findings led to an archaeological haul that stunned the world.

And was about to stun me.

Standing in front of the Phoenician galley that was disentombed piece by piece from the seabed and then reconstructed, pinned together on land, was a mind-blowing moment for me. More so because I had not been expecting it. There were bits missing, of course, but the boat was remarkably intact, even down to the Phoenician writing chiselled into several of the 3000-year-old hull planks. These boats were put together almost on a production line back in the Levant. From Tripoli to Tyre the Phoenicians were renowned for their boat-building skills. So, too, the inhabitants of Byblos long before the Phoenicians had reached the coast from Canaan. The cedar forests of Lebanon, today the centrepiece on the country's flag, were eventually denuded, the soils eroded, because their timbers were so in demand by every seafaring nation. Even the Romans modelled their shipbuilding techniques on vessels such as the one I was gazing upon. This galley I was standing in front of had traversed the Mediterranean, had played its part in the development of the Mediterranean top-ography and personality. In the founding of the olive routes.

I wandered off to have a look at the objects, also from the seabed, found aboard this ship. Hundreds of jars, amphorae, were on display. Used for the transportation of olive oil, olives and wine, they came from locations as far-reaching as Andalucía, mainland Italy, Greece, Corinth, Tunisia, Tripoli: all olive-producing regions. These tall terracotta pots gave substance to my journeys, to my quests. I saw the arteries unfold before me, the back and forth crossings, the business and production; it all sprang to life. I found rusted anchors, corks to seal the capacious amphorae, the shrivelled remains of olive drupes, granite olive presses and one unexpected contribution that caught my attention: cannabis leaves, still intact. Were the Phoenicians farming cannabis? Today, in the Beqaa Valley, cannabis is produced by the ton and sold illegally to fund the training and purchase of armaments required by Hezbollah to fight its war, but it had never occurred to me that the land we know today as Lebanon had historically been a grower of hashish.

An elderly chap in a suit, loud scarlet tie, glasses and oil-slicked hair came over to greet me, to offer assistance. I had noticed him earlier acting as guide to a small group of Italians. I did not need a guide but the cannabis fascinated, puzzled me, and I asked him if he knew anything about it.

'Consider how it must have been for those oarsmen,' he smiled. 'Rowing hour upon hour in all weathers. The cannabis was given to them as a muscle relaxant.'

This *signor* had been a member of the original archaeological team who had itemised all the dredged articles and he had been coming to the museum every day for the past thirty years.

'I'm voluntary. I just like being near that ship.'

A lady, head round the door, called to the guide and he excused himself. I returned my attention to the glass case, and then I spotted it. An OLIVE SPRIG. That it had survived seemed incredible. Why was it aboard? Was it possible that this cutting was a peace offering, a Phoenician calling card? 'We are traders, merchants, this is not a war ship.' Had the notion of the olive as the tree of peace already been currency round the Med? I think so. The tale of the monumental flooding and the ark was an old one, in circulation before it found its way into the Old Testament. Had the story travelled beyond the eastern Mediterranean? Possibly. I was not sure, but the presence of this twig, this olive cutting, helped to substantiate my personal theory that in many of the coastal locations where the Phoenicians set up trading posts, they had not, as I had originally supposed, delivered sapling trees. They did not introduce the olive tree to the western Mediterranean, because the wild trees were already growing in vast forests close to many shorelines, and inland, too. How far north the tree had spawned by that stage, I did not know. Probably not to the cold environs of Altamira, but along the littoral of southern France, yes, across Italy, definitely, and in southern Spain. Tartessus, for example.

I would also hazard a guess that the sprig I was staring at was one of clusters brought over to graft the wild trees. I was beginning to believe now that it was the spread of *knowledge of cultivation* rather than the plant itself that had been introduced and traded. They taught grafting. Does it make any difference? I think so. The topography was not altered, interfered with. It was the ability to husband what already existed that the Phoenicians, the sailors on these galleys, offered. Of course, they also bartered, sold other produce including ready-pressed oil, home-produced, or from other regions where they were trading – witness all the amphorae in this museum. Thinking about it, they might very well have been responsible for the earliest grape-growing here in Marsala, today a renowned region of viti-culture.

I suppose I was trying to find out at what stage agriculture had stopped working with nature. I swung about looking for the old man to discuss these thoughts, but he was nowhere to be found.

Exiting the museum, right across the street from the sea, I spotted dolphins swimming close to the rocky shore. I set off at a lick, running in the road the length of the curving esplanade, following them in their northerly trajectory. A car pulled up outside Eno, one of the government-run wine shops. Three people got out. I yelled to them as I charged by, 'Dolphins, *delfini, delfini!*' But they paid me no attention, probably thought I was mad. I hugged the coast, listening to the slap-and-lick of waves against brown rocks, until I was panting, out of breath, and the sleek mammals had slipped beneath the gentle swells and did not resurface. Then I returned to my car, still thinking about the Phoenicians and set off again, hoping to reach Selinus, the most westerly of the ancient Greek colonies in Sicily, before nightfall.

After a stop at the ancient quarries of Cave di Cusa, which I only found at the very tail end of the afternoon – the silent, empty place had an eerie vibe about it and struck me as more Neolithic temple, more sacrificial site, than a quarry – I searched in vain for a hotel. Bank holidays, no room at any inns. I continued making for Selinunte, travelling by lanes and not the main route. Passing through a seaside town, Tre Fontane, where the sand swept the streets like a snowdrift and everywhere was boarded up. Nobody about save three plump men sitting on white plastic chairs on the beach, silently watching the sea, waiting for the sun's fall. And a remarkable sunset it proved to be even though I was driving away from it. Signs to Castelvetrano Selinunte, *Città dell'Olivo*, City of Olives. At some point around eight thirty, darkness upon me, I resigned myself to a night in the car and opted to continue on to the fishing spot of Marinella where I hoped to find a car park and possibly a bite to eat. A lovely old building set back from the road drew my attention. I slowed and decided to pull in to its gravelled courtyard. It was a hotel and, even more fortunate, it was a converted olive mill. A sprightly chap probably in his late sixties wearing a Panama day and night, inside and out, was both proprietor and renovator of the establishment – every room, situated off an upper quadrangled terrace, bore the name of a classical Greek personage. I was in the Dionysus suite.

After breakfast the following morning the boss escorted me up on to the flat roof with newly tiled terrace to show off his 1300 olive trees in the surrounding groves and 360-degree view, with a soft, clear light in every direction. It was a view like no other and offered an exceptional perspective on ancient Selinus with its principal temple and the lapping Mediterranean at its feet.

My companion confessed a passion for olive trees and was clutching a book written in both Latin and Greek, which he offered to lend me. Alas, I read neither. He eulogised the olive tree, '*olivo bellissimo, bellissimo*, with its fruits the colour of Athene's eyes'.

Back downstairs, as I was checking out, the receptionist asked the proprietor, 'Who is that woman?'

He replied, 'I've no idea, but she loves olives and speaks good Spanish.'

I laughed, taken aback, thinking I had been conversing in Italian. I realised then that I had been on the road for so long, engaging in a babel of tongues, that I no longer knew one from another!

The city of Selinus, today Selinunte, was founded by Greeks around 650 BC. Separated by a shallow valley, where in lusher times had flowed a river, also known as Selinus, the city was divided into two distinct parts. The name Selinus was derived from a broad-leafed wild celery (*selinon*) that covered the hillsides hereabouts and still grows around the locality.

The eastern section, where I began, was situated outside the ancient city on a broad, open-faced eminence. There, three remarkable Doric temples had stood. Today, they are known as Temples E, F and G and only E, the second largest of the three, has been reconstructed. The trio of temples seen together, when all were standing, must have presented a spectacle unrivalled in antiquity. Only the Temple to Artemis at Ephesus was larger than Temple G and that by a mere five metres. In his second volume of *Travels*, the English poet Algernon Charles Swinburne described this immense rubble of stones as the 'most gigantic and sublime ruins imaginable'.

In its heyday, Selinus was hailed as rich and magnificent. Climbing around these massive solid stones, wondering at the skill of transporting each stone unit, none smaller than a family car, the nineteen kilometres distance from the quarry at Cave di Cusa, I could not doubt it. In its fallen state, it resembled a game, a puzzle, tossed from the heavens, of gigantic proportions, precious, dazzling as gold coinage, from a universe more sublime than any we mortals have ever looked upon. And lay incomplete, awaiting assemblage.

In 409 BC, Hannibal, the Carthaginian general, mustered an army of Iberians out of Spain along with his own fellows from Africa, put them aboard 'three-score-long galleys' and provided them with 1500 transport ships to convey provisions, weapons, engines, battering rams, everything required for a plotted incursion. Crossing the

African sea, the troops landed at Lilibeo (Marsala) and from there marched to Selinus, where, during a nine-day siege and sacking, 16,000 citizens were slaughtered. By any standards, that was a barbarous week and a half. Hannibal awarded the plunder to his soldiers who sailed back to Africa victorious.

What struck me as deeply tragic about this invasion was that until that time the Greeks had sided with the Carthaginians in other local wars on the island and it seems that this attack had taken them completely by surprise. I thought back to the raised galley I had wondered at the day before. That boat would have been a Phoenician forerunner of those that Hannibal's army had docked at Marsala.

The sun was hot. I had lost my hat somewhere. Wild flowers perfumed the morning. Buggies and minibuses were transporting the few tourists present from the temples across the dried-up riverbed, westwards to the city site. I decided to walk it.

Those Greek citizens who had fled the Carthaginian invasion of Selinus began to slowly drift back and there were attempts to reconstruct their fabulous metropolis, but it never regained its former glory and eventually a massive earthquake razed its monumental architecture to the ground.

Along my promenade I found a copse clearing where I sat and ate Sicilian oranges so sweet and sticky they honey-stained my fingers. In all my travels I had found no story of Phoenician violences such as this one, no treachery such as the sacking of this city, and I wondered what genetic or circumstantial sea change had caused their descendants from Carthage to conduct themselves with such monstrous inhumanity. What shift might have taken place? Had the battle for control of the Mediterranean grown so vicious?

At the acropolis, rising up on a distant promontory with its panoramic views over the sea, I spied several ancient olive mills and settling tanks set right in front of the area marked Sacred Punic Site. I wondered whether here the Carthaginians had buried their soldiers lost in the fray. After I had seen everything and was aching with exhaustion, I took a stroll to the fishing village of Marinella, where I sat at the waterfront in a wood-framed café and drank lemonade and ate ice cream, watching the weekenders playing with their kids and dogs on the beach. Spring, *primavera*, in Sicily was magical. An island of secrets, of cover-ups, a bloodied earth it might be but, at its rural heart, it was enchanting.

Still, I failed to engage any Sicilian in a conversation about the recent past, about the organisation that continued to hold the infrastructure of the island in its grip. Everyone brushed it aside, claiming that their patch had never been tainted by the Mafia, that they and theirs had somehow been exempt. I telephoned La Signora one more time, hoping for a change of heart, but she was on answer service.

Agrigento, a World Heritage Site thanks to its Valley of the Temples, much of which stood on a rocky scarp not in a valley, made an ideal overnight stop. The ruins were closed by the time I arrived but I wandered up the road anyway and found five policemen standing by the ticket booth, receiving keys from a sixth officer who was holding a white paper bag doling them out. They told me I could go in for half an hour if I wanted to.

I wandered about in the gloaming light, dazzled by the looming shapes and shadows. The hotel I had chosen, a kilometre or two from the modern town but within sight of the illuminated temples, had a garden full of flowers and bushes where I sat and drank wine and listened to, not a chorus, but a full-blown orchestra of nightingales. Pindar once described this place as 'the most beautiful of mortal cities' and after two glasses of white wine, the warmish southern Med air with its scents and symphonic birdsong, I was close to concurring. In fact, I found this the loveliest of all mortal islands. After the light had faded, I took my car and drove into the town of Agrigento to grab a bite. Little was open but I found a decent pizzeria and afterwards wandered aimlessly in this city that had been one of the leading lights of Magna Graecia during the golden age of ancient Greece. The architecture that remained was a mix of modern bland intermingled with a few examples of Baroque. Earlier, while searching for somewhere to eat, several cars had crawled the kerbside, as well as one or two pedestrians, all males, each trying to attract my attention. I had not responded. During my post-dinner meanderings the same happened and I decided it was more prudent to return to the car. As I was crossing the square, there approached a mean-looking young bloke, face tessellated by scars, and I determinedly avoided looking his way. Only when I had fired up my engine and started to reverse was I aware that I had been hemmed in by two cars, one driven by Scarface.

I had been having problems with the locking system on the VW since Marsala and I was suddenly panicked. I shot the gears into reverse, gunned the accelerator, executed a bizarre snake movement round both vehicles and roared off. Gloomy street lighting, lack of familiarity, one too many glasses of wine, I overshot the hotel turning and found myself ascending a steep, winding hill. I checked the mirror. At least one of the cars was directly on my heels, headlamps beaming. I felt a cold sweat break out. I had no idea where this road was leading until I landed in a grubby estate of seventies high-rises. Lines of laundry and satellite dishes its meagre decorations. I was in it before I knew it. The scene became a film chase as dustbins went flying and tomcats bolted for their lives. I skidded from one narrow lane to the next, each spilling with rubbish and looking identical. I checked the mirror. The pursuer had mysteriously vanished, but I was alone in an unlocked car on a Sicilian housing estate – swirling fears of petty *mafiosi* gangs – at close to midnight. As I swung the next left I found myself blocked in a cul-de-sac, stacked with dozens of spilling rubbish bags, staring at an iron-gated hydraulic something or other. With little space to manoeuvre, I reversed to the crunch of broken bottles beneath my tyres, found an exit by good fortune and began a more measured descent, eventually locating the hotel. By the time I locked myself securely within my ugly little room, I was trembling all over.

I awoke to the Valley of the Temples glistening with rain, water gurgling over the pebbled tracks. Across the hills and dales of temples I squelched where I found broad-trunked, barrel-chested *oliviers*; hunchbacks and statuesque oleasters blossoming between fallen stones and lopped monuments. Some were possibly seven, maybe eight hundred years old, but once I had chanced upon the Garden of Kolymbetra, I abandoned the soaring Temples to Vulcan, Hercules, Juno and Concord and their bell-bottomed, grey-skinned groves. The garden had been a water reservoir for the ancient Greeks. Kolymbetra was, said the pretty dark-haired girl selling tickets, packets of seeds and membership to Italy's National Trust, a Greek word meaning 'large water tub'. The gardens were located within a fissure, a long, open-to-the-skies cleft within the valley, where a profusion of Mediterranean plants and irrigation systems had been planted and restored. Like Alice descending, I strolled within this fertile cavity for several hours and found a treasure trove of botanical legacies.

The carob tree bears a fruit which is thought to have been the locust that John the Baptist survived on during his sojourn in the desert. It is sweet and nutritious and was a vital component in the diet of rural populations in the southern Mediterranean, including Sicily. In ancient times, its lentil-shaped seeds, nestling within the pendulous chocolate-brown, husk-hard pods, were used as a unit for measuring gold. The seed's Arabic name, *qirat*, meaning bean pod, gave us the measure carat. A *qirat*, or a carat, of gold.

Another throwback to the Arabs: citrus plantations were known as 'gardens', to celebrate the ambrosial scent of orange blossom. Aside from their fruits, the orange gardens were to be enjoyed, dallied in.

The irrigation systems within the valley were ingenious. Interlocking conical terracotta tiles, unchanged since Roman times, used on roofs all round the southern Mediterranean in an under and over fashion, had been upturned and dovetailed one upon another, in linear chains. In this way they created open channels, conduits for free-flowing water, similar to the clay canals used by Lahrcen's in-laws in Morocco. I took dozens of photographs to show Mr Quashia in the hope that he could set up the same arrangement for us. Cheaper than a plumber and possibly more efficient. Elsewhere, rainwater was gathered in mud tanks known as *gebbies*. Also a design inherited from the Islamic world.

Wheeling a barrow along one of the sand tracks, a gardener, a retired local man, stopped at my side. He seemed fascinated to know why I was snapping the tanks and seemed ready to pass a little of the drizzly morning in conversation with this lone stranger.

Had I known that the European Grand Tour had ended here at Agrigento, and that the region was as renowned for its almond blossom as its temples? From December to March, they flowered and they were the reason for Sicily's eternal spring.

'We have as many almond blossoms as stars in the Milky Way,' he boasted, waving a stubby black-fingered hand about.

From my new Sicilian friend, Tommaso, I also learned that the country people had grown their vegetables in the citrus and olive groves and they carried their loads to market in *coffe*, bags made from woven Mediterranean palm leaves. Once upon a time, these gardens grew mulberry, plums, medlar fruits, myrtle, pear, pistachio, figs and almonds as well as varieties of olives that have since disappeared from the island altogether. The olives and almond fruits used to be beaten from the trees with long, dry canes cut from cane thickets. I asked Tommaso about the Mafia and its hold over the island's olive industry, but he shook his head vehemently. 'Not in this region.'

When Bernardo Agostini eventually found me in the centre of Ragusa waiting for him in the rain outside a lingerie shop, it was late in the afternoon on the eve of the public holiday weekend. The municipality was closing down and he was leaving for his country estate, to spend the next few days with twenty members of his family. He had called on ahead to his wife to make up one more bed, but the request had not gone down well.

'*Basta!*' she had cried. 'Enough!'

'We'll talk at my town house,' he said apologetically, ushering me into his four-wheel.

He had telephoned a cousin in Siracusa to come over and translate for us. Bernardo had fallen for olive oil, 'quite literally', he told me as he negotiated the slow-moving traffic while everyone waved, hooted, called out to him or peered in through his open window to shake his hand, when, as a boy, he had watched his father decanting olive containers. He had badly wanted to taste the golden liquid and had stooped in over a vat and tumbled into it. The memory caused him to laugh out loud.

Bernardo was 'wickedly gorgeous', I had been warned by Julia, a mutual friend from Malta who had put me in touch with him, 'a real Italian charmer'. With his open-necked check shirt, gold chain, slacks and quality leather loafers, he was not quite the olive producer I had been expecting. I had pictured an older man, not the fellow at my side who was possibly mid-thirties.

What were his thoughts, I ventured, on the Mafia opening up American awareness to Sicilian foods, particularly olive oil?

'It was good,' he felt, returning the attention of a group of pedestrians calling to him. I was puzzled. It was rare, outside the world of entertainment, to come across anyone with such a high profile.

'What can you tell me about Coldiretti and olive oil?'

'The Farmers' Union. They fight for standards.' He shot me a glance, then shoved his arm out of the window, squeezing someone's hand.

'You seem to be very well known, Bernardo.'

'Of course.' He slowed the car and leaned over to open the rear door behind me. '*Ciao*, Rafael! *Vieni qua, vieni con me!* He can help us,' he said as a whippet-thin, bearded individual in glasses and corduroy cap climbed in, bringing with him a stench of alcohol that almost turned my stomach. Rafael had the fear of the hunted in his black beady eyes, puffing on a roll-up that looked as if it was about to collapse.

'Rafael speaks French and English,' explained Bernardo.

In fact, the poor fellow was so drunk he could barely articulate his mother tongue. What came out of his mouth was little better than gibberish.

Bernardo's oil was organic and its label carried a DOP, the Italian equivalent of an AOC.

'How many trees do you have?'

Rafael behind me seemed to be engaged in a conversation, half sung, with himself. He was wittering away while my contact was trying to park outside an ice-cream parlour.

'There's someone I want you to meet. *Andiamo*, Rafael, let's go!'

Out we piled, or staggered, into the coffee shop. Bernado was on his phone again while Rafael, who had ordered himself two beers, was firing slurred questions at me in a French that made little sense and I was beginning to think I'd better drive on to Siracusa and find a hotel.

We sat and waited.

'Have many trees do you have?' I persisted.

'Seventeen hundred but farming is not my business. I am a transformer. Ah, *Dottore, Dottore*! Carol, please meet Dottore Carini.'

Into the establishment walked a short, dark Sicilian, elegant, handsome, preoccupied and seemingly not too pleased to have been called to the meeting.

'I've just flown in from Sardegna,' explained the doctor, shaking my hand with barely a glance in my direction. 'What is this about?'

'Carol is making a study of Sicilian olive oil,' explained Bernardo. This, albeit untrue, aroused the interest of the *dottore* who, it transpired, was the island's leading specialist in oil tasting. It was upon his recommendation that a farmer was or was not awarded the coveted DOP.

'Ah, I have been in Sardegna judging at an international olive oil competition,' he explained while Rafael called for another beer.

'Who won?' I asked.

'Sicily took first prize. A producer from this region.' The *dottore* pulled out a bottle from his briefcase and passed it across to Bernardo who nodded, making hand gestures that suggested he was impressed.

'Bravo,' cried Bernardo. 'Ah, but wait! Carol, now I see who you must meet. There is a man, the finest olive producer in our region. Well, now we have many – me among them – but old Bernardo, a saint of a fellow, was the first.'

After a telephone call, it was settled that we would continue on to what I understood was the prizewinner's farm and that the farmer, another by the name of Bernardo, could tell me everything. Rafael was to accompany us and translate. The poor fellow could hardly stand but both men indulged his weakness and acted in a kindly, almost fatherly manner towards him. We piled back into the black four-wheeler and set off out of Ragusa into the hills. The cousin up at the town house who had driven from Siracusa was cancelled. Both men were telephoning their wives every few minutes to pacify them and explain their delays.

'It's a big holiday here,' explained the *dottore*. 'Where will you be spending it?'

'I'll drive to Siracusa.'

'But no, you must stay here. You must see Noto, it is exceptional. You must see the tuna factories down at the coast.' The doctor was now on the phone to his wife. 'We have an extra guest, please make up a bed.'

'Who is it?' I heard from the other end.

'A woman, a journalist. I have no idea. She is writing an article on award-winning Sicilian olive farmers.'

'No, I'm not and I'm not a journ—'

'Have you ever heard of the London *Sunday Times*?' he asked, palm of hand over the phone. His wife was still begging for some identification or reason for the late arrival of 'a woman' to their family weekend.

'Yes, of course, but please, I'm not a journalist.'

'It doesn't matter. Our country home is simple. I reconstructed it with my brother on land that has been in our family for several generations. We have olive trees. You must stay the night with us. Do you have a car?'

I nodded.

'We will drive to my country house in your car.'

By now we had arrived at a very humble abode in the middle of an olive grove. A bent old man in slippers with nobbled face and a true Sicilian *mamma* of a wife, rotund in black dress, black rolled-down stockings with her plump arms folded across her apron, were waiting outside in the fading light for us. The *dottore* and Bernardo embraced the veteran and his lady. Rafael was tolerated while I was ushered, as though royalty, into a small office with a fax machine, many pencils, stacks of labels with an olive sprig design and more holy statues and burning candles than the Vatican. I was given a rush-matted chair while everyone else stood congregated around the desk and stared at me. I felt guilty, a shocking fraud. A conversation was rattling on in Sicilian. I could not understand any of it until I caught the words *Sunday Times* and all heads turned to me and nodded in that traditional peasant way that means mightily impressed.

'Translate, please, Rafael,' commanded Dottore Carini. He had taken on the air now of the professional, the mighty olive taster, pulling from his briefcase once again the award-winning bottle, which had not, as I had originally understood, come from this farm. This producer, though, old Bernardo, was south-east Sicily's first and most accoladed patriarch.

Rafael looked bemused. He had not followed any of what had been said. 'Do you have any questions?' he slurred, peering at me, popeyed.

'Could you explain, please, that I am not from the *Sunday Times*?'

'No, you are from France. You write in French? They know that. When you write the article will you give my parents a mention? My father was an author and my mother a concert pianist. I want the world to remember them.'

'I am not writing an article,' I insisted.

The others were growing impatient now and confused. *Mamma* was sitting back against the far whitewashed wall beneath her holy statues, clutching rosary beads and, judging by her almost imperceptible lip movements, reeling off a few prayers.

'What is being said?' snapped the *dottore*. 'Translate, Rafael, if you will.'

Rafael began a rush of speech, spitting all over the place, mainly at me, hysterical nonsense. He was glistening with sweat. Nobody could follow his reasoning.

'This won't do. I will contact my cousin.' Young Bernardo then telephoned the forgotten woman who had journeyed from Siracusa to meet us. She was driving home. The phone was passed to me. Rafael grew petulant, rejected. He was almost slobbering, teary-eyed.

'What do you want?' sighed the young woman as though bored with us all.

Hastily, I cobbled together a question, requesting the history of this old farmer and his rise to international fame.

'In 1968, I began working with olives when I bought a plantation with two hundred and eight trees.'

His father had owned about forty trees but he had never learned to farm them. 'It's all down to God,' was his explanation. 'God, in his wisdom, led me to olive farming.'

His wife was nodding proudly, shifting her sausage fingers along the beads while the small metal crucifix swayed.

'And now I am the most famous olive farmer in the world,' he boasted. He claimed to have a 'sympathy with olive trees' and received letters from all over the planet complimenting his oil.

The *dottore* was sneaking glances at his watch, worrying about his wife. Rafael was begging a glass of water while the rest of the assembly watched me expectantly. I thanked everyone for their time, assured them that it had all been most informative and wished them a pleasant holiday. The old couple seemed deeply relieved but first we filed through to an adjoining room containing stacked cartons of bottles, all ready for shipment. I was given a bottle, as a sample. Which I would have preferred not to accept, then Rafael insisted that he wanted one and, finally, we were on our way.

Returning to Ragusa to collect my vehicle, I learned that Bernardo, the one at the wheel, was vice chief of the region's police squad. This explained his popularity, or notoriety. He was a 'transformer' in the sense that he transformed olives into oil. Or in my terms, he was a miller, albeit on a very large scale. His state-of-the-art machinery could press up to 2700 kilos of olives per hour. He ran a syndicate of organic olive farmers and he assisted them in making contacts abroad, to sell and promote their oil. He was selective. He did business only with those who had been awarded a DOP (Protected Denomination of Origin), and this was where the *dottore* came in. It was he who put in the recommendations for the local farms to the Italian governmental body based on the mainland and it was he who frequently travelled abroad to sit on panels where olive oil was tasted and graded, and awarded. It struck me as neat, but I kept that to myself.

'Each of my farmers targets a market and does not tread on the toes of his fellow producers. We sell to California, France, Sweden, Malta, Canada and mainland Italy.'

'Mainland Italy?!'

'Predominantly Tuscany. Tuscan oil is the most famous in the world and they cannot produce sufficient quantities to meet their markets so they buy from us and sell it as Tuscan.'

I had to contain my amusement. The entire world bitched about the Italians selling on foreign-produced olive oil and here was a Sicilian admitting that elsewhere in Italy the scam was operating.

'But the experts have declared that Sicilian oil is better than Tuscan,' he crowed.

I looked to the *dottore* who was on the phone in debate with his wife. Was he the 'expert' in question?

Bernardo and I were now at the rear of his jeep, the door open. He dragged out a carton of a dozen bottles of his oil. It was a gift for me. 'You'll see how excellent it is.' I had no idea how I was to transport all these bottles but I accepted the present graciously and thanked him for his time.

It was late, night had fallen.

'I'll drive,' announced the doctor, now my host, as we piled into my car, thirteen bottles rattling in the boot along with both our suitcases. Off we shot into dark, Sicilian rurality. He was roaring forth, penetrating lanes narrow as pencils with stone walls on either side but an inch from the car with wild rose briars and brambles scraping the bodywork. I could not help but reflect upon the moment. I was in *my* hire car, a complete stranger at my side, going I had absolutely no idea where except that it was some country location south of Rosolini and he was at the wheel and punishing the vehicle as though it were a Ferrari. His telephone rang. *Pronto?* He was now steering with the palm of one hand. I took a deep breath.

It was his wife again. 'I don't know who she is,' he was repeating. 'She works for the *Sunday Times*. It's good publicity.'

'I DON'T!' I muttered between clenched teeth.

He leaned over and whispered, 'Don't be nervous. I know this route like the back of my hand. I could drive it blindfolded.'

'Please don't,' I mumbled.

The country estate was no real distance, thank heavens, and we were parked up behind two other cars and pulling out our luggage in no time. The world was perfumed with blossoms and tranquillity, not a sound, though I could see little if any of it, save for an expansive starlit sky.

'Quite a spot, eh?' bragged my host as a swarm of women, daughters and mother, charged out of a door and hung themselves about him. I felt awkward, an intruder, and saw that his wife was eyeing me with suspicion. She showed me to my suite, a private apartment attached to the main house. It was a no-frills arrangement, unpretentious but perfect. The double bed had been made up, soap and towels laid out for me, water at the bedside; generous consideration given to the arrival of the unanticipated stranger. His wife, thick-hipped in denims, full-lipped, sensual with lovely green eyes, accompanied me, explaining the workings of the rudimentary shower.

'How do you know my husband?'

I shrugged. 'I don't. I met him in an ice-cream parlour a couple of hours ago.'

This did not please her. 'Come through when you are ready. Dinner has been waiting for over an hour.' And with that she was gone.

The family meal in the kitchen consisted of a variety of pasta dishes followed by Sicilian goat's cheese and home-made bread. It could not have been simpler. There were two other guests at the table: a heavily made-up young woman, friend of one of the daughters, who lived in Palermo and was visiting for the weekend, and an avuncular bald-headed fellow who had arrived with half a dozen unlabelled bottles: consecrated wine purchased on the quiet from a church in Noto. The man, a close companion of il *dottore*'s wife, though I failed to understand the precise nature of their friendship, was drinking heavily and talking incessantly, explaining that because he preferred to drink wine that had been blessed he had struck up a deal with his resident priest, who kept him well supplied at a very reasonable price.

'Holy wine is better for one's health,' he declared.

Il dottore pooh-poohed such a notion and with pantomimic flourish reached into his briefcase and pulled out the prize-winning oil.

'Now this *is* good for your health.'

Instantly, he began to play act a display of professional tasting insisting, after he had shown us all how, that we give it a try. Everyone assented, rolling a spoonful of the oil round their palate and offering suitable compliments until from the far end of the table the young girl from Palermo screwed up her face and said, 'Ooh, I think it's 'orrible. Real sour.'

Dottore Carini, it transpired, was a man of steadfast vision. The region of Mont Iblei, south-west of Noto, south of Rosolini, but still five kilometres from the sea as seen from the flat roof terrace of the doctor's country residence, was the setting for our talk and not one to be easily forgotten. After coffee the following morning, he invited me to ascend, up through the family's unmade bedroom, to the roof where the view was a 360-degree spectacle. The doctor was in navy slacks and a short-sleeved hugging T-shirt. He was a handsome, sexy man but, though more casually attired, one who maintained a level of formality. He had called for a family relation, a young nephew, to drop by and translate for us. He wanted to be sure that the information exchanged between us was accurate. Chairs were arranged in a circle. The swallows were flying so low they swooped and tacked beneath the empty laundry lines. So close were they, it would almost have been possible to catch them in a butterfly net.

Il dottore's wife, with youngest daughter and smallest son, sat silently listening. This Doctor of Agriculture had given up state-salaried employment to set up in business on his own as an adviser to olive farmers from his region. Spain had scooped first prize with its production levels, but Sicily was determined to compete. These local farmers could not produce the same quantity of oil or olives but they could offer quality. The doctor saw his role as one of mentor. He could open doors internationally and guide the smaller producers towards standards they had never realised before. He had chosen olive oil because after he had become a taster, originally as a side interest, he grew impassioned by the shades and depth of flavours and perfume. Like good wine, it was a witness to its territory. This had been an awakening for him. His grandparents, who had built the original farm on this site, had been humble agriculturalists working in grain, cheese, almonds and a few livestock. Their olive oil had been for family consumption only. He remembered it from boyhood years, its crude aftertaste. In those difficult days, olives did not bring them an income and so eventually, when his father took control of the land, he felled the trees and erected plastic greenhouses for intensive vegetable production, which was more remunerative; the *plasticultura* revolution that I had seen all over southern Spain had taken hold of Sicily, too. They had dug for their own water, irrigated extravagantly, recklessly, and they made a very decent living selling to town and city markets. Also, back then, the mid-sixties, the European Union gave support to vegetables but precious little to olive oil. Olive oil was out of favour, unfashionable. *Il dottore* rose and beckoned me to follow. He drew the shoreline with his fingers. On three sides we were lapped by the southern Mediterranean, and in the other direction mountains and plains.

'Look, see there,' he said. 'Only that one small pocket of plastic greenhouses remains, but if you had come here ten years ago, you would have been hurt by what you were looking at.'

Thirty years ago, and more recently, the view to the sea had been obliterated by plastic.

'Farmers, indeed all Sicilians, are island people. We understand how precious our territory is. We are slowly coming to our senses and have pulled those monstrosities down. *Plasticultura* is on its way out. Folk are realising that they can make a living working with indigenous trees by producing top-quality products and with such a mindset our tourism is improving too. Eco and agrotourism will be our future.'

His vision was to transform his land as well as that of other producers within the region back to what his grandparents and those before them had worked with, except there was to be one remarkable difference: knowledge.

'Sicilian oil was not special because we had no technology. The oil was crude and usually mixed with oils from other regions in Italy. It was good for the family or for canning tuna. Now we have the knowledge, expertise and the technology to compete internationally. We, in Mont Iblei, in fact, all Sicily, are a small participant in the international market but we intend to be an exceptional one.'

'Do you use pesticides?'

'All the farms Bernardo works with are organic.'

His vision, he confessed, was receiving resistance within certain circles in Sicily but, beyond the island, the reaction had been very positive.

Who were resistant? Why? Was this a Mafia connection?

The very mention of the word Mafia brought a grimace to the doctor's face. 'Yes, they took oil, pasta and tomato paste to the States. It proved to be one of the best marketing campaigns in history, but it had nothing to do with us here. All the business was with Corleone or Palermo. There was no Mafia here, not on the east side of the island.'

'So what was here?' I asked him.

'Feudalism. Noto had been dominated by three aristocratic families. They owned all the lands as far as the eye could see and the people worked for them. It was so poor here under this feudalist arrangement.'

'But feudalism was what bred the *mafiosi*?'

'No, from this eastern quarter the people preferred to leave. They fled the island in boatloads . . .'

'To the States?'

'No, on this side of Sicily they emigrated to Canada and Argentina. It was only when Mussolini came along, divided up the land, gave it to the people and provided them with agricultural machinery that matters improved. Mussolini is a hero here.'

'What happened to those three families?'

'They are gone. Dead. The inheritors of one remain.'

This had overtones of the Florio story. 'Gone, in what way?'

'Those that were willing to accept change and work with the ordinary people . . .' he stopped.

'Are still living?' I urged.

'As I said, the descendants of one family have survived.'

'And the others?'

'They died' was his bald response. Neither *il dottore* nor any of his family would elucidate.

The doctor and his wife offered to guide me to the road that would lead me to Siracusa. Before we set off, I found myself alone for five minutes with a couple of younger members of the family, cousins, nephews, a boyfriend of one, who had dropped by when they had heard there was a guest from 'off the island'. The boyfriend, shoulder-length hair, on crutches due to a football accident, was hoping to open up a modest hotel with spa but he was having tremendous difficulties with planning permission, he confessed. 'My uncle is well known. Not everyone favours his dreams . . .'

'And?'

'There is a great deal of corruption.'

'Mafia?'

'They're everywhere. Don't let anyone persuade you otherwise.'

'Are they still involved in olive oil?'

'Sure.'

'What's Coldiretti's involvement?'

'Food products are big business for the Mafia these days. Coldiretti claims the Mafia is cutting the oil with colza and selling it inter-nationally as Italian olive oil. Or worse, they just add flavouring to the colza oil. It's a big scandal.'

'Colza? Rapeseed oil. It's used to lubricate machinery?'

'It's also a lesser cooking oil. They're not poisoning people, just cheating them. Listen, my uncle is wise. He understands what counts and he's fighting to protect it. We Sicilians have olive oil in our veins, not colza. It's in our blood.'

After fond farewells, before Siracusa, I made a brief detour towards Capo Passero where the remains of the tuna fishery at Portopalo still stood. Here, the waters of the Ionian Sea meet those of the Sicilian Channel, on a southerly cape more frequented today by surfers than fishermen. It was a flourishing centre for bluefin tuna fishing right up until the 1970s. A hundred years ago there were dozens of tuna canneries all around the island's coastline but due to overfishing and huge demands from Japan, resulting in depletion of stock, the fishing rights were regulated and much of the twenty-first-century activity takes place out at sea on Japanese factory-boats, many of which are illegal. (A single bluefin fetches a hundred thousand dollars at the famous Tsukiji fish market in Tokyo, so prized is its meat.)

Today, the Portopalo fishery lies idle, a monument to a past and a fishing method that has lost its place. Everything was closed up, due no doubt to the holiday, but *il dottore* had told me that on an ordinary day it was still possible to visit the factory. Before it had shut up shop, the factory with its storehouses, furnaces and fishing fleets had sprung into life each spring in early March to begin seasonal reparations: maintenance of the machinery as well as the great oak boats that a couple of months later would be setting out to sea to catch and slaughter the fish. The heavy chambered nets needed attention, too. When the *mattanza* was over, the boats returned to shore and the slaughtered fish were transported on trolleys to the factory where they were cleaned and gutted. The next stage was the boiling of the flesh and afterwards its conservation in olive oil. As in Favignana where the Florios created the tuna fisheries, here the factory was built by one of the princely families from Noto, who owned vast olive estates that provided the required gallons of oil. The factory closed its doors almost half a century ago, leaving unemployment and depleted seas.

The *mattanza* had been a vital source of work for the local population, for the small settlement that had sprung up around the Portopalo fishery. Today, those inhabitants, men with the sea in their veins, earn a meagre living off low-key tourism, and, to a smaller degree, the neighbouring saltpans, while their women continue to tend the family lands alone, bringing in the harvests of olives, almonds, carobs, medlars and citrus fruits. Olives, modest harvests, transformed to oil that, when the fishery was operative, could have been sold, ensuring their income. A way of life that had existed since the Phoenicians.

I found an *albergo* overlooking the water on the island of Ortigia, an island within an island attached to the mainland by three bridges. Within this historical heart of Siracusa, during my first hour, after a stroll round crumbling streets as narrow as zips, medieval palaces, Baroque churches, the mind-blowing columned Duomo and its piazza, I had been irretrievably seduced. I lost my heart to Siracusa's decaying beauty and I threw my schedule to its eastern winds. I stayed on because I wanted to. I wrote up notes, ate ice cream in the hot sunny afternoons, read and settled to being a foreigner, a tourist who longed to see all that was on offer. I telephoned Michel, wishing he were with me. Having seen Sicily, I told him, having traversed its coasts and mountainous interior in springtime, I could easily contemplate selling our own, very special olive farm to settle here where there were olives aplenty, organic, too, a burgeoning awareness of the riches their fruits contained and a sense of history that imbued every brush stroke of the island.

'It's time for you to come home!' he retorted jovially.

I paid a visit to the catacombs where Lawrence Durrell concluded that a coalmine would have been as spectacular, but I did not care. I was deeply content just to wander, to study the wild flowers and natter with or observe the Siracusans. The May Day festival was over and the city, the island, had settled back into itself. People had gone, tranquillity returned, disordered order. The waiters laying the tables or sweeping the terraces were humming or singing softly in this miniature Venice where the lagoon waters lapped the salmon-coloured walls and played percussion to the activity, where the hotels and street cafés had laid out brimming baskets of oranges, for the taking. I whiled away hours in a local bookshop where the exquisitely painted frescoes on the ceiling might have been an adjunct to the Sistine Chapel. So, too, the car hire office where the mundane business of extending my rental agreement was elevated to a joyful interlude while I stood in the queue, lost to time, drinking in the ceiling's fading artwork. I watched two cars screech to a halt by an open-air bookstall. Six ruffians, thugs, stepped out and harangued the bookseller, threatening to close him down for an offence that I could not follow. Unpaid protection fees? I found a London bus, a red double-decker, parked at the waterside, number 85a to Stamford Bridge, converted into a Snackeria selling *pizze* and *patatine*. At dusk, after following the *passeggiata*, on this occasion a mere handful of grannies in black idling along the ramparts of the old city overlooking the waterfront, I drank a glass of crisp white wine grown at the sooty feet of Etna. It was accompanied by a saucer of green olives, a pair of grissini in a sealed packet and a little dish of anchovies. Beneath me, high stone walls enclosed the Fonte Aretusa. Here, ducks paddled serenely surrounded by papyrus. This freshwater spring dated back to antiquity and was said to be the living embodiment of the nymph Arethusa. It had been an important water source for Siracusa's earliest Greek settlers, the Corinthians, who dropped anchor around 734 BC and soon turned the island-city into a glory that rivalled, indeed equalled, Athens. Then came the Carthaginians. This attracted the attention of the power-grabbing Romans who did everything to squeeze Siracusa's influence until in 213 BC they sacked the city and proclaimed it a part of their Province of Sicily. Hundreds of years later, during the sixteenth and seventeenth centuries, its Spanish period, much of the city's fabulous architecture was destroyed by an earthquake.

After failed negotiations with a trio of seadogs, salt encrusted into their crow's feet, getting quietly sozzled at the water's edge, captains of ageing, tethered tour boats, I cut a deal with Giuseppe for a *mezzo giorno*, a half day of his time, with his freshly painted emerald-green boat. He was a Siracusan fisherman. His work completed before I had even digested my breakfast, he promised to take me on a tour of the surrounding waters, in and around Ortigia island, beneath its bridges so that I could get a better sense of its aquatic layout and the generous harbour waterways that encompassed it. From this perspective, it was certainly a miniature, sweeter-smelling, slower-paced Venice and for the first time since I had arrived in Sicilia, I had the sense that I was in Italy. Business was not brisk and Giuseppe had nothing better to do with his day so I was given a generous outing. Although his accent was thick and we had difficulties understanding one another, he was more open to conversation than any other islander I had passed the time of day with.

Siracusa was strangled by Mafia, he said, spitting overboard to express his contempt. 'You do what they tell you.' Fear of the Mafia had kept organised tourism off the island until recently and for that the place had remained unspoiled. Crumbling, poor, lacking facilities but quite its own Sicilian self, he felt. As we circuited, he pointed out to me ornate palaces, a high-security prison, hospitals; all dark and empty, staring lifelessly out towards the open sea. Each had recently been sold to undisclosed purchasers for sums of money not even breathed. And the city's prison had been relocated forty kilometres into the countryside.

I took a walk to the Parco Archeologico della Neapolis, to the Greek theatre first where rehearsals were in progress. Music, lights, electrics, actors limbering, then drum rolls and a scene began to unfold. Evening was falling. In the distance beyond towering pines and cypresses was the milky glint of the Ionian Sea. I pictured the arrival of fleets of Phoenician galleys, Greek warships, sun-crusted men disembarking on to these pebbled shores, and then I caught the word 'Graecia'. A Greek drama, the words of mighty Aeschylus, performed in Italian, here in what was once the pulsing heart of Magna Graecia. Finally, a marriage of two great empires. I recalled my visits in my twenties to the Odeon of Herod Atticus, situated on the south slope of the Athenian Acropolis. This city of Siracusa with its vast Teatro Greco cut directly into the rock was built half a millennium earlier. I sat down on the curved stone bench and watched the players enact their drama, intoning, prancing and playing dead operatically. For a short while, it made me long to be that young actress again, a life before olive oil, who had slept illicitly at Epidavros, had woken at dawn and trilled out voice exercises, running up and down scales, playing with the acoustics, puffed up with the promise of the future. Fleetingly, I felt saddened by the passage of time. I recalled aspirations, loves lost, continents crossed, the transformation of broken dreams. In reality, I was already pining for this island with its interweave of civilisations and the fact that it would soon be time to leave.

As with my first sighting of the Sierra Nevada, I longed for Michel at my side to share Etna. Etna, from the Greek 'to burn'. To the Greeks also, 'Pillar of Heaven', was this seething cone. As I approached its cracked, purpled feet, like the scaled tentacles of an octopus where great clods, deformed aubergine rocks, lava from its ruthless fallout in the 1960s, threatened to overrun the *strada*. I pulled over, heard a donkey bray its lonesomeness, and sat watching the red giant smoke. Wispy exhalations, but this was a deceit. Fissures striate its muscled skin, threatening to expel hot fury. On its upper north side, snow fell; pistes of ice cream melting. Three-thousand-metred Etna, the wicked witch, the fabled home of the Cyclops where today scruffy olive trees were growing alongside burned-out shells of properties, classical façades high up above the sea, blackened, dry-throated, gutted.

The careful agricultural techniques which had transformed the lower slopes of Etna into an arable garden must be attributed to the Arabs. Nature throws up its promises everywhere.

I spent my last night in Taormina, ancient Greek Tauromenium, dramatic, magnificent and dripping in high-priced tourism. It could have been the South of France. I drank a heady red wine from the slopes of Etna, listened to dogs barking beneath the stars, the roar of a Ferrari or two descending the steep tracked cliff face, and felt my heart crack. Across the Strait of Messina, the toe of the mainland lay waiting and Michel would soon be arriving into Milano to greet my arrival into the grey industrial north, but I could have stayed forever. Forever on this island, crammed with feasts and festivals celebrating traditions of agriculture. Artichokes, medlars and mulberries, ears of corn, wine and, of course, olive oil, all were celebrated. I loved its wheaty springtime hues, its soft, steep or jagged surfaces, was intrigued by its sulphurous secrets, its midnight profiteering, its generosity. Oh, it was hard to say goodbye to this volcanic isle of the *Mezzogiorno*, but, *andiamo!*

Mezzogiorno

The spring went away. Along the strip of land where the road by the sea had been drawn, the beaches grew black and then blacker as though Etna was casting its shadow upon me, clawing me back. An angry louring sky greeted my arrival into Messina. Busy town, grey as pewter, fast-paced honking Italy – not the laidback Sicilian approach of lemon groves and olive trees pruned to perfection – battered by rattling winds that grounded the ferries. I kicked my heels till evening, then proceeded aboard with a dozen other cars. The sea, this measly strip of a strait with its swells, glared back at me with a seismic fury. I watched the crossing from an upper deck, clouds hanging low, wrapped like skirts around the mountains. Beneath me, beside my hire car swimming in bottled olive oil, was a heavily armed and guarded navy-blue prison van, belonging to the *Polizia Penitenziaria*. It was surrounded by police officers, some paunchy, others lean, and men in khaki uniforms all wielding machine guns. Who was their cargo, I wondered. Mafia to the mainland?

Once on the Italian peninsula I stopped to buy petrol and a map and learned that the drive to my destination in Bari was close to six hours. It was now pitch dark and after nine. As I pulled away from the pumps, wind dust gritting my eyes, I saw the same *Polizia Penitenziaria* van and another, a black saloon car with smoked windows alongside it. Dozens of fellows, twice as many guns, four more men in dark suits and one sallow convict whose features in slashed shadow

I could not see, but chained, both ankles and wrists, encircled by the law. Was he off to incarceration on this leg of land or was he to be exchanged? I hit the accelerator and shot away, reluctant to find myself witness to any incident. Rain began to splotch the windscreen. I hurtled forward along the *autostrada*, anxious. I had not planned to drive on the mainland but the inaccessibility of trains to Puglia from this dark toe of Calabria – my destination was Bitonto where no railway line existed – and the rattling gifts in my boot had altered my decision and now I felt ill-prepared and afraid, irrationally so. The officialdom and the notion that someone, whoever, was clanking about in irons in the twenty-first century, soon to be interned, had unsettled me. And this, Calabria, was the domain of the *'Ndrangheta*, the deadliest of Mafia set-ups.

I was not planning on driving all night. I would stop when I found somewhere, when I felt tired, but I was on an *autostrada* hundreds of giddying metres above sea level in the darkness with Italian cars racing at my rear and flashing me furiously. The landscape was threatening, Junoesque with its precipices, peaks and pointed mountain summits, dragon shadows draped in starless night, and my mind whirled wildly with thoughts of *'ndranghetista* bandits waiting to ambush.

Reality was less dramatic but scary all the same. A long stretch of roadworks had filtered the traffic into one lane; all the others closed off. The wind was spinning furiously, the car vibrating. I glanced down alongside the viaduct, staring into a plummeting abyss and was gripped by panic, by vertiginous horror. I slowed, clutching at the wheel. Cars were banking up behind me. I felt sure that I was going to make a mistake and nose-dive off this neverending bridge. A flashing sign informed me that the roadworks would end in ten kilometres. TEN kilometres! I feared I could not continue but there was no way out or back, no other lane, no turnoff, nothing but a death drop. Eventually an exit arrived, and I followed directions to Bagnara Calabria; a painstaking snaking descent, mile after mile to the craggy coast, arriving into a seaside municipality of illuminated Virgin Marys and fishing boats. The place was dead and a dead-end. I stopped and asked a young man, the only soul about on the blustery esplanade, if there was a hotel, *un albergo, per favore*. Fortunately, the town possessed one, and I eventually found it. Even better, across the street was a makeshift pizzeria, empty, Il New Yorker. Although it was now gone ten, the family seemed happy to serve me. Alone with a glass of wine, the tarpaulin roof beating like a carpet sweeper above my head, I tried to calm down and understand what had spooked me so. Two young men, late twenties, entered, glancing constantly, curiously, conspiratorially in my direction. One unshaven, vulpine-featured, in a slick blazer and revealing, figure-hugging jeans; his companion round and soft, long-haired, glasses, sneakers and baggy, ill-fitting denims with dozens of zips. They ordered plates of chips and beer. A call from a girl to one of them seemed to be their evening's amusement. Both leaned in to the mobile, giggling like schoolboys behind cupped hands, masking their lasciviousness.

How do people entertain themselves here, I wondered. How easy is the relationship between the sexes? How rigid the mores of Catholicism? In the Islamic countries, with the women locked indoors before sunset, the males kill time at Internet points. Catholicism here might be equally constricting, equally narrow. I could not follow their conversation. They spoke a Calabrian dialect, thick and lazy.

It was raining, raining hard. After such marvellous days with laundry-blue skies and spring flowers! I traipsed in the downpour, wet-haired, wet-shouldered, back to the *albergo* where I must have been the only guest because a striated *mamma*, the chef and one scrawny waitress stared at me with rural watchfulness, stipulating *documenti* with stabbing fingers as though I were a criminal. I fell into bed exhausted, bereft, and left after an early breakfast of dry *biscotti* and coffee so strong I could have stood my pen in it. As I drove out of town, the catch was being dragged ashore: nets tangled with silvery swordfish as big as children. Who could say if there was not a body or two tangled within the bloodstained cargo? Bagnara Calabria was, as I gave it my final glance, like a town nobody had ever left, so remote and inbred did it appear to be.

Rugged was the nature, the way of life as I ascended through untouched, stony villages where rotund widows still passed their lives plumped on steps, preparing vegetables and knitting, and groups of ruddy-faced, worked-to-a-bone men in caps sat smoking together, playing cards. It was hard to believe that the Romans referred to the calabresi as Sybarites who slept on beds of roses. More accurate was the fact that cocaine- and weapon-smuggling gangs inhabited these mountains. Born from the dire poverty that had ruled over this area for centuries, the 'Ndrangheta's drug operations were believed to have surpassed both Sicily's and South America's.

Onwards to the precarious perches, crowned with clouds, that were to lead me through Calabria to the coastal instep of Italy. I passed goat-faced pensioners filling entire crates of plastic bottles with crystal water free-flowing down the mountainsides. Families were out working in their modest olive holdings where a few peaches added a vibrant verdancy and young vines climbed hand-cut canes. They cocked an eye my way whenever I pulled over to shoot the scene, but no more. So many industrialised olive businesses had I encountered over the last months that the simplicity, the rude rurality of this Calabria, lacking the classical beauty or design of Sicily, touched my heart. When the peaks opened to the distant sea, even with brewing storms on the skyline, the views were quite remarkable. Without the skilled engineering of viaducts and suspension bridges – each giraffe-legged, kilometres in length, traversing impenetrable valleys – these peasant peoples must have been entirely cut off. Save for sea access, the ingress of conquerors. Still, coastal Calabria was hardly dizzy with activity, whatever the crime reports logged, and I wondered just how profoundly modern Italy had impacted here. It seemed to me during this briefest of first encounters that their exist-ences literally hung off the cliffsides and had not altered in a mil-lennium.

Before leaving this forgotten corner of old-world Italy, I drove by statuesque olive forests with trees as lofty as eucalypts and canopies spreading like oaks. I had to stop to reassure myself that these were olives. Were these wild oleasters, growing to such a measure? If not, could it be possible that here in Italy, the historical olive capital of the world (whatever position Spain might currently hold in terms of production), such vast tracts of trees could be left uncultivated, unpruned, unharvested? There was not a soul to be seen anywhere so my question remained a puzzle.

The Gulf of Taranto, a 140-kilometre stretch beside swelling turquoise waters and deserted windy beaches. Magna Graecia was here. Four

Greek colonies were founded: Croton, Heraclea, Thurii and Sybaris (home to the Sybarites. In the sixth century BC, Sybaris was the richest and most envied city in the Hellenistic world. Nothing of it remains today). I dawdled by, Ry Cooder on the radio. To my right, sparse constructions fringing the gulf waters of the Ionian Sea, to my left, an extended cradle of olive trees sweeping all the way to the distant mountains. From my map, I guessed these were the Appennino Lucano ranges.

Taranto, touching the stiletto of Italy, western-side, which I did not enter, once an ancient city on an island attached to the mainland by two bridges. An ideal placement for the Phoenicians, thought I, but it seemed that it was the Spartans who first staked their flag here in 707 BC and christened it Taras. Today, it is a military port, specialising in the construction of warships; all offshore islets are off-limit and strongly fortified.

I parked close to the exit of a busy bypass beyond Taranto's suburbs and got out. The weather had cleared up and it was spring again with small birds chirruping and feeding in the grass. All around me olive trees, but these were extraordinary and new to me. My contact, Francisco, was running late so while I stretched my legs in the sunshine I photographed them, their silhouettes; thick, woody limbs reaching heavenwards and then tumbling from on high, putting me in mind of witches or crazed big birds with wings extended, ready to alight or swoop.

Suddenly, I remembered the obnoxious fellow in Cádiz, weeks and weeks back, who had spoken of the passion, creativity with which the pugliesi tend their farms. I could see it. The pruned shapes gave the groves a vigour, a sense of life and movement.

'Fantastic trees,' I grinned as Francisco pulled up in a small Fiat.

'They are unique to this region,' he told me as we, strangers, embraced.

Francisco was a virologist specialising in vines and olives. His wife, Dora, was a laboratory scientist who ran her own olive oil business. Her family, I learned later, were wealthy landowners. I had never met anyone who studied plant viruses before and I was not certain in what way this man could help me. Also, I doubted whether I would know the right questions to ask of such a formidable scientist, but he was yet another colleague of my miller friends from Malta, Nat and Julia, and they had insisted I should talk with him. It was Francisco who had recommended a nursery in Bari where Nat's slender young sprigs plucked from the only Roman grove still surviving in Malta, near the tiny hamlet of Bidnija, could be grafted, and the grafting had proved an enormous success. The potted saplings had been fruiting when I visited Malta, sweet olives they were. After I returned from my eastern Mediterranean travels, I stayed in touch with Nat and Julia and we invited them to spend New Year with us at the farm, bottling oil, making marmalade, cooking endless mouthwatering meals. I was eager to learn about grafting and Julia had been adamant that Fransciso was a man I should meet when I made this western Med circuit. Fortunately, he had agreed to be my guide and had arranged a visit to the specialists for the following morning.

After checking me into a hotel in his home town of Bitonto, before our olive tour began, Francisco wanted to show me a very special sight, a '*pugliese* originality'. Passing through the Valle d'Itria, where a red olive grew, our first port of call was Alberobello.

'*Albero bello*, beautiful tree?'

'That's correct.'

'Does the name originate from one particular tree?'

'I think not. It probably refers to the forests of bizarrely shaped, towering olives that grow beyond the small town. Or the oaks. There remain a few stands of an oversized oak that exists only here and in the Balkans and no one knows how they first arrived in the area. But the groves later, Carol. First, let us visit the *trulli*.'

A *trullo* was a traditional drystone dwelling with a conical roof. It resembled a giant white beehive.

'Their original purpose has not been discovered but it is probable that they were used as simple habitations or possibly storehouses.'

Each *trullo* was round, constructed without cement or mortar, and lime whitewashed. Drystone, like the walls surrounding the fields in which they had frequently been erected. Atop each domed roof was a pinnacle, decorated with a symbol. Many of the roofs themselves also had symbols painted on them in white. No two were the same. The symbols were to ward off evil spirits, the evil eye, *malocchio*.

'Amazing, I've come across evil-eye superstitions in Turkey, Malta, Tunisia, Greece . . .'

Such idolism might have originated with ophiolatry, snake worship, in Egypt and was carried west with the Phoenicians. Other roofs were daubed with stars and crescents and I wondered if these might have borne an Arabic influence.

'These mortarless, limestone *trulli* can be found nowhere else in the world,' Francisco claimed. 'Based on prehistoric building techniques, erected before architects existed, they offer examples of "vernacular architecture".'

I was ignorant of the term 'vernacular architecture'.

'Ah, buildings constructed purely to meet man's requirements, when local traditions ruled, when no thought was given to design. Before "noble architecture",' explained my learned guide. 'Here, for example, the *trulli* walls are drystone and the roofs are an assembly of grey stones. No cement, nothing permanent. They could be taken apart in minutes. When enemies approached, the residents just dismantled their homes and secreted themselves in deep wells until danger had passed.'

They were not entirely dissimilar to the cruder drystone huts I had seen in northern Spain or the less conical *bories* in the Luberon. *Borie* is a Provençal noun meaning 'ox stable' and was frequently a refuge for the shepherd and his flock.

'Well, these *trulli* might also have been for storage of wine, grain, olive oil or used by shepherds and farmers as temporary accommodation, shelter from the heat.'

We wandered through cobbled, whitewashed-walled lanes in this small town of one thousand *trulli*. It genuinely was a unique sight.

'Many of the *trulli* have been sold off to foreigners or transformed into hotels.'

To protect those that remained Alberobello had been designated World Heritage status.

The place was a touch wedding-dress touristy for my taste, but it was remarkable that the dwellings were not only intact but occupied. Alberobello was a prospering community, albeit with dozens of trinkets shops and southern Mediterranean types standing in doorways offering to show us their home, a '*trullo tipico*', for a few euros.

Once out on the open roads, we spotted many more *trulli* abandoned in fields. These I found more pleasing, more authentic.

While we drove, Francisco, a physically small man, in his mid-thirties, early balding, rimless spectacles, features that were not memorable or remarkable but sensitive, spoke to me about his life and work. He lived in Bitonto, one of the 'most important centres for the production of extra-virgin olive oil in Italy'. His grandfather had graduated in agriculture in 1927 in Napoli. Oil was in the blood. When he, Francisco, was a child he had worked on the family's farms. He studied at Bari University. Having specialised in entomology, he took his doctorate in virology. While he was a student, he had bolstered his grant with a small income from the Puglia agricultural department by taking on thirty olive farmers in the Murge Hills, advising them on the health of their trees.

'A vet for olive trees,' he joked.

His laboratory was in the historic port city of Bari, lying on the Adriatic Sea, housed within the university, though he was employed by the state and not the municipality. As a viral specialist, he researched existent diseases as well as potential threats to vines and olives.

A scientist, I judged silently, whose work could be a gift to the major chemical companies.

Puglia produced 10 per cent of Europe's wine, which surprised me. Until recently, the majority of it had been for local consumption or sold across Italy to cut with more esteemed labels. The same was true for its olive oil. Pugliesi oils had been a dilute for oils from elsewhere, particularly Tuscany. Tuscan oils were renowned for their soft sweetness. They were judged the finest in Italy and they fetched the highest prices abroad, but a behind-the-scenes problem existed: 'They had no shelf life. Just months after being pressed, the oils were losing flavour, oxidising.'

'Why?'

'They are low in polyphenols,' explained Francisco.

Polyphenols created a pungent oil, the best. Tuscan farmers with their sweetish crops looked to Sicily or Puglia to redress the balance. From the farmers of the *Mezzogiorno*, they purchased olives. These they combined with their Tuscan harvests. This gave them two advantages: an oil with a gutsier palate and one that corroded less swiftly.

'Polyphenols also give protection against heart diseases and cancers, correct?'

The man at my side nodded.

'Are these mixes sold as Tuscan olive oil?' I wanted to know.

I felt Francisco elusive. He stated that the identification of produce for the international market was strictly regulated. If a label read 'Italian olive oil', then its provenance was strictly Italy.

'But if the oil is not 100 per cent Tuscan, not 100 per cent Italian?' I pressed.

'Every olive oil is improved by being mixed with another,' he added a little testily.

'Not ours,' I countered. 'In order to maintain our AOC, ours must be of its single variety and pure,' I explained. We cannot add any fruits from any other variety. 'Only the *cailletier* olive gains the "Olive de Nice" ticket.'

What was Francisco's response to the accusation that Italy was involved in fraudulent olive practices? Oil that is not 100 per cent olive?

He frowned.

And what of the possibility that oils with higher acidic levels were being sold on the international market under the guise of Extra Virgin?

He knew of no such malpractices. European regulations stated clearly that to meet 'Extra-Virgin' coding, the oil must have acid levels of 0.8 per cent or less. He was sure this was adhered to.

What of the local Mafia, the *Sacra Corona Unita*? Did they have fingers in olive pies? Was it not true that modern Mafia organisations were spreading beyond drugs and protection to embrace the food industry, cutting fine quality comestibles with barely edible ingredients?

He had never heard of such Mafia involvement.

By now we had climbed inland to the apex of a hill that overlooked a valley forested with the Ogliarola Barese variety. These were the weird big fellows I had been photographing earlier. It was a remarkable sight with, occasionally, in the far distance, the peaked dome, all askew, of a tumbling *trullo*. This was agrarian Italy, scenic, at its loveliest.

Puglia was a surprise. It was an area that had been invaded and conquered on countless occasions over the past 2500 years and I was beginning to glimpse both in its nature and its architecture the diversity that had unfurled beyond such a cosmopolitan battlefield. We wound down into the valley. Here, my new acquaintance showed me how the trees were farmed. At the foot of each, a wide circumference of earth was tamped until compacted. Nothing grew on this rich, brown-red circle of soil. The trees were so tall that even with the assistance of every modern Italian harvesting appliance, reaching the branches growing out from the apex proved challenging. The firm earth solved the problem. When the fruits fell they were gathered swiftly, with ease.

'Why not just lop the crowns, keep the trees shorter?'

They were pruned in such a way because experience and study had taught the pugliesi that for this variety, their vertical form produced the finest fruits and bumper harvests. The olives, big bitter drupes, from these upstanding oleasters possessed the highest polyphenol content in Italy.

Bitonto was quite a famous little town, I discovered from Francisco, clearly a loyal inhabitant. Guide on our evening stroll of its Romanesque heart, he was exalting its rather lovely cathedral. Bitonto's nomenclature, 'City of Olives', was born from the density of groves in the surrounding countryside and the ninety olive mills operating within the town itself. During the pressing season the noise through the busy streets had been untenable until, under duress, the city council shut down a number of the mills and moved the oil businesses to the countryside. Francisco's father-in-law, whose machines had operated in a basement, had been a victim of this Quieter Town policy, but he was intending to launch a spanking new enterprise elsewhere.

Bitonto was the first district in Italy to open its mill doors each autumn, ten to fifteen days ahead of anywhere else. As in our Alpes-Maritimes area, there was a time-honoured date for the commencement of pressing. For us, it had always been the third week of

November, but with shifting weather conditions our millers were grudgingly being forced to reconsider this tradition. Here, the doors were unlocked the day after the second feast of *I Santi Medici*, the Healing Saints. Their principal feast day was 26 September, but they had been designated a second one, the *esterna*, which fell on the third Sunday in October. This enabled the completion of the harvests before celebrations. The labourers were then relaxed and spruced and ready to party and pray.

I was interested to know whether this region was suffering from fruits ripening too early. Francisco had noticed a week or two's shift, yes, but he did not seem unduly concerned.

'Do you know the cult of the two Healing Saints?' he asked.

I did not.

Cosmos and Damian were twins who had practised their skills in Arabia and Roman Syria. In AD 303, they were tortured, beheaded and martyred. News of their courage and miracles – their most renowned was the transplanting of a black Ethiopian's leg on to a white patient! – spread fast to the Byzantine east and via the Roman trading routes reached this Adriatic coast. Bitonto was the final stop along the pilgrim's route. The saints' relics were held in a reliquary in Bitonto's cathedral.

Fascinated, I looked their history up later and found that their two skulls are kept in Munich. I also discovered that the same two skulls (unless they had two heads apiece) were housed in Madrid. But wherever various bits of their bodies rested in reality, the candlelit procession through the streets of Bitonto, with the local women barefoot and praying, on *I Medici*'s second feast day was, according to Francisco, a spectacle to be savoured.

I countered his saints' story with one of my own: a more gruesome, less holy, tidbit that I had come across by chance, also with its roots here. It concerned a family of princes from northern Puglia, the Sangro family, one of the most illustrious dynasties in southern Italy. One of their clan, Raimondo de Sangro, the seventh Prince of Sansevero, who claimed kinship to the Bourbons of Spain, the Dukes of Burgundy and, on his father's side, was a direct descendant of Charlemagne, was the subject of my tale.

'Are you acquainted with the *peranzana* olive?' I asked Francisco as he led me into a cavernous candlelit taverna in a very pretty town, Palo del Colle, neighbouring Bitonto.

'*Ma certo*, of course.'

The Provençal olive tree known in Italy as *peranzana* – *peranzana*, in the local dialect, is the adjective for *provenzale*, Italian for provençal – has all but disappeared from France. In fact, I could not find one mention of its existence anywhere in my own country.

'As far I know, it grows only around Daunia in northern Puglia,' offered my scientist friend.

'Well, it was introduced here from Provence towards the middle of the 1700s by the prince, Raimondo de Sangro. Raimondo was a philosopher, an alchemist, a leading Freemason and gifted celebrity of his time who loved to challenge the moral codes of the day, and he was feared for his secret, rather creepy experiments. Gossip whispered that he was a murderer who saw seven cardinals off to heaven and produced chairs from their skin and bones.'

Francisco was laughing.

I asked him if he had any idea why an aristocrat, who was anything but a man of the soil, would trouble to bring a French olive to a region already heavily planted with many of its own cultivars.

He shook his head.

'Might properties from the oil of the *peranzana* olive have been a necessary component for one of Raimondo's alchemistic experiments? Might Raimondo, who was infamous for his experiments in his search for the secret to eternal life, have believed the olive, this Provençal variety in particular, with its low acid level, might aid him? Raimondo had famously boasted that when he died he would rise again.'

Francisco knew nothing of the prince's story. He knew that San Severo called itself Olive Oil City, even though its production was far inferior to Bitonto's. It produced some quality oils, my host confirmed, and the *peranzana* variety was one. How or from where it had arrived into Puglia, my dinner companion would not hazard a guess.

'Italian researchers and biogeographers are working with tree DNA in an attempt to discover and log the parentage and origins of every Italian olive. It is a long-term challenge because Italy boasts close to three hundred different varieties and Puglia has the densest concentration of trees on the peninsula, from which comes 40 per cent of the country's entire oil production. On a global level that represents about 20 per cent.'

'Perhaps Raimondo was ahead of the game. Perhaps he had discovered the advantages of the Mediterranean diet long before anyone else had conceived of such a notion,' I smiled, lifting a glass of the very excellent local red wine Francisco had ordered for us. 'I read that when Raimondo's grave was opened up, it was empty. His body had disappeared, and has never been recuperated. True to his bluff, he had risen from the dead.'

The following morning, we set off from my hotel early to drive out beyond Giannoccaro to the renowned nursery Nat and Julia had worked with. In the passing groves around us were mixed varieties of trees pruned in a selection of styles. It was like staring into an agricultural jewellery shop. Francisco pointed right, towards the middle hilly distance.

'Over there, there are stone mills still operating in the caves where they have turned for centuries.' He did not specify the precise location. 'Unfortunately, your programme is too short to visit them,' he chided. 'You should stay longer.'

A warm sunny day was breaking. I wanted to learn from scratch, the rudiments of grafting.

'It's the act of causing two cuttings or parts from different plants to grow together; the insertion of scions or small shoots from one tree into another.'

'But why, with so many varieties in existence, would nurseries bother?' I demanded.

'For the purposes of developing hardier stock.'

From Roman times, grafting has produced effective results with olive trees and the Italians, or the Romans from Pliny the Elder onwards, mastered the skills better than the rest of the olive world put together.

And I was keen to learn a few of their secrets.

'What I would like is to see the process of grafting from a cultivated tree on to a wild *olea*, to try to understand how this might originally have come about.'

'Carol, there are no wild olives left anywhere in Italy' was Francisco's response, 'but there are possibly a few examples of very ancient cultivars.'

'Any in this region?'

He doubted it. At some date, post-War World II, when olives became modish, many of the venerables were uprooted and sold for fabulous sums; the equivalent of two thousand euros per tree.

'Ha! They fetch much higher prices in the South of France,' I laughed. 'Proprietors of stylish gardens and chic hotels and restaurants will pay above market value for a centenarian *olivier*, if they can get their hands on one. They buy them in from Spain.'

Such botanical trafficking had since been outlawed in Puglia. It had made a handful of canny farmers wealthier, but it had scarred the landscape and impinged upon heritage.

'To protect the trees, the regional Puglia Park of Secular Olive Trees—'

'Such a municipal title!'

'—was inaugurated. All trees older than a certain age,' Francisco could not recall the precise age, 'must by law be registered, maintained and protected.'

What did he know of the towering stands I had come across in Calabria with crowns as expansive as oaks?

'Their custom is not to prune, care for the trees or gather fruits on an annual basis. The calabresi are a rough bunch,' spoken by the scientist at my side. 'They prefer their oil bordering on rancid. It is a peculiarity of theirs. In the south of Puglia, some of the villagers follow the same practices.'

South of Lecce, the trees were not left to grow quite as tall as the Calabrian forests, nor did they become so unruly, but the fruits were gathered directly from the earth whenever the population felt the mind to do it. Those pugliesi southerners also preferred a rancid oil.

'Such country folk have deeply embedded opinions. They don't alter their habits to suit modern fashions.'

*

301

I spent several days in Francisco's company and we talked olives non-stop. There was so much to learn! Much of what he spoke of was beyond my comprehension: protoplasms, germplasms, molecule markers, cell structures. I don't have a scientific bone in my body so, on the whole, we avoided viral matters and stuck to farming or Italian history. I spoke of the labourers I had seen in southern Spain gathering mounds of fruits with automatic sweepers. Francisco conceded that occasionally it was practised in Italy but the tonnages were less, so it was not really necessary.

I recounted much of what I had learned about the abuse of water and resulting pollution in southern Spain and my fascination with the olive as a desert regenerator.

Francisco confirmed that Puglia suffered acute water shortages. Aside from three small rivers, the region lacked surface water. In past times, exceedingly deep wells were sunk; some said that the earliest *trulli* were well covers, he explained, but whenever possible these days it was the habit to cultivate the orchards without irrigation. When water was required, wells were bored. Around the coasts, this was a less daunting prospect because the water stayed closer to the surface but inland it was necessary to drill to seven or eight hundred metres.

In the orchards as we drove by, occasional figures, solitary or working in small groups, were threading their drip-feed piping through the trees' crowns.

'All Italy has taken up this method. It conserves water and protects the earth.'

'Protects the pipes from the wild boars, eh?'

'Not only. When the pipes were placed round the feet of the trees, farmers stopped working the soil. Lifting the pipes, moving them out of the way, was too time-consuming, too much hard work and when the weeds shot up, it was easier, quicker, just to spray pesticides all around the roots. Pipes in the trees like electricity wires are unattractive, I agree, but it means the soil is cleared without impediment and no toxic products are used for the purpose.'

'You favour organic farming?'

'Of course. The Israelis have come up with a method of feeding the water pipes underground.'

'That sounds like a good idea.'

'Yes, but the technology is still being worked on.'

I could not see why it would be so difficult.

The evening previous, over an aperitif with Francisco and his wife who did not join us for dinner because she was babysitting, I had recounted my experience in Palestine, of planting trees with Israeli peace activists.

'Why are you doing all this?' Dora had demanded, as others had.

'It began as a quest, to seek the historical roots of the olive tree.' I told them about Lebanon, described the 6000-year-old oleasters, the emotions standing alongside them. I showed them photographs. 'They are possibly the oldest living beings on earth.' Then I spoke of the Roman mill in Algeria, talked of the olive sprig in Sicily . . .

'I have been tracking traditions, myths, trade routes.'

Francisco shook his head. 'We have nothing like that here.'

'But now that I have come almost full circle, my interest has shifted to the future. There is so much I think we are in danger of losing.'

'Some of our nurseries and the more experienced farmers are grafting their oldest cultivated specimens with younger varieties, to give them new leases of life. There's a future that might interest you?' Dora again.

'This has nothing to do with genetic modification,' emphasised the grey-haired proprietor of the nursery, with his half-moon glasses, worried face and tweed hat. 'The birth of grafting was organic, a natural development. In nature, plants do on occasions come together, bonding to create a strain that might have a better chance of survival. Perhaps prehistoric man observed this and decided to give it a try himself.'

I asked whether he thought it possible that from the Middle East came the knowledge, the know-how, of olive cultivation, brought by navigators to a western Mediterranean already abounding in forests of wild oleasters.

He had never given it any thought.

'Basic plant propagation – seeding, rhizomes, bulbs, layering, cuttings, grafting – has existed since almost time immemorial,' he explained. 'Long before Mendel and the birth of modern genetics. Most of the changes and improvements on the earlier methods have been developments in techniques caused by scientific progress in plant physiology, biochemistry, environmental influences.'

Had I known that every tree grown from a stone is in essence a new variety? I had not. 'But the market insists on knowing the provenance of its produce. From where came its mother and its father? Rather like people.'

We proceeded to the first of a series of tunnelled greenhouses. I was about to witness the grafting process from beginning to end.

'First, an olive stone is planted in a shallow bed of soil. The shoot that grows from that stone is known as the rootstock.'

We strolled by row upon row of tiny pots, hundreds of them, each with a slender shoot hardly firmer than a short piece of string.

'Within the world of grafting, the rootstock is the mother. The tree that grew the fruit from which we took the stone must be known, identified. Its variety must be declared and it must be a plant that is virus-free.

'Once planted, the stone is left for three years to develop into a sapling.'

'Why three years?'

'That is the time the tiny tree needs to attain a certain width – about that of a finger – before it can be slit gently open and receive its other half, the father, its partner in the grafting process.'

We moved to another of the elongated greenhouses.

'Three years later, in the progress report!'

Here, for me, was where the skill really came in. The tender bark of the three-year-old was gently incised and into it, like an act of coitus, was inserted a snip of a twig, about two inches in length, plucked from a different variety of olive. The provenance of the twig, the scion, must also be declared and be virus-free. The two were then bound together, to close the join, with a spill of heated wax.

'The wax seals in the juices: the sap of the baby tree and the water content.'

Now, the two parts, held as one, were left to fuse. Looking at them, newly mated, leafless, just a basic woody state, they reminded me of newly hatched bald chicks. Ninety per cent of these grafted juniors would survive, but it would take another two years before these saplings were sufficiently strong to be sold on to farmers, to oleiculturalists. I walked the rows of, quite literally, thousands of minuscule trees within the carefully thermostated conservatories and thought back to the summer Michel and I had made our outing to choose the young trees for our farm. The two hundred youngsters we finally ordered arrived the following spring. Once they had found their places on our hillside, they soon began to fruit, sooner than I had expected, and it is a fact that the drupes produced are larger and more oleaginous than those of the gnarled warriors who have lived on our farm's inclines for centuries.

'Graft hybridisation is an asexual process. It involves no pollenisation, no bees, no organic intercourse, only the skills of man. It offers the possibility of creating plant varieties, olive trees in this instance, with improved inherited genes which give the young plants carefully chosen properties. Do we require a tall tree, short tree, sweet fruit, a faster growing plant? The opportunities are endless.'

I stared silently upon these rows of babies. What, if any, were the moral implications of this form of plant breeding? Where was it leading us? Could these ever-more sophisticated methods of propagation help us survive climate changes, save our future? If an olive tree were bred that could withstand drought stress to an even greater degree than the average olive, could such a hybrid save our deserts, reforest the entire Sahara? Could armies of these mass-produced infants halt desertification? Could they turn climate change around? The questions were as numerous as the pots I was gazing upon.

Italy produces 1.5 million grafted trees a year. They are the leaders in the industry.

In Spain, according to these southern Italian propagation and disease specialists, all new olive orchards were grown from branch cuttings sown directly into earth. The roots that are produced from cuttings are shallower in the early years and not drought resistant so they need to be regularly irrigated, which is a very heavy burden on water resources. Plants that were self-seeded from stones, transported by nature or birds, for example, also needed more water because they, too, are shallow-rooted.

Later, when I reached Tuscany, I was told that trees grown from stones or cuttings take fifteen years to produce fruits whereas the grafted plants can yield within eight years. The growth cycle could be halved.

Here in Puglia every new orchard was planted up with grafted trees. Here, it had always been the tradition. It was vital in a region where lack of water was a critical issue. The root systems on grafted trees burrow much deeper and produce one, even two, extra long taproots that seek out deeper levels of moisture.

'Water conservation. The Romans grew from grafted plants. They understood the root systems.'

For a self-taught olive farmer such as myself, this was all new material. I had walked into the science of olive farming and it was causing me to reflect. I had been seeking history and an alternative method of combatting the olive fly. Other than our escalating water bills, due to the excessively hot recent summers, I had not given these irrigation issues a thought. And I had never considered the looming possibility of a waterless world.

This trilby-hatted owner of the conservatory had been responsible for transforming Nat's Roman sprigs from Malta into healthy young, fruit-bearing trees. I congratulated him and asked him whether, during the process of working with cuttings from trees that were 2000 years old, he had found any difference. He shook his head.

Had he encountered any difficulties?

Yes, the Maltese Romans had not been pruned in decades, perhaps a century, so the best young shoots were sprouting right at the very top of the trees. Accessing them was no easy feat. Beyond that, transporting them from Malta across the foot of Italy without damaging them, had been a challenge for Nat.

How had this specialist chosen the stone, the mother variety, the rootstock, to marry with the Roman scions?

He had undertaken a long search for a progenitor, contacting colleagues all across Europe. Eventually, a variety of tree almost identical to the old Roman groves had been found growing in Turkey. From these trees, he had taken the fruit, the stone, which became the rootstock.

Towards the end of my stay, Dora sent a message inviting me to her offices, a block of converted warehouses including massive storerooms where her oil for export was sealed and packed. Up a winding staircase to the atelier, her laboratories and modern, well-equipped offices. Dora, mother of two tiny children, was a slender, dark-haired, pretty woman, poised, discerning, to the point. This couple welcomed me into their home, a high-ceilinged, postmodern flat that covered the first floor of two adjoining town houses owned by her parents. It was bright, with delightfully imaginative furnishings and fixtures and clinically pristine, as I might have expected from two scientists whose families had considerable land and wealth. Dora cooked delicious pastas, made crunchy salads and I brought wine purchased from a supermarket in the new town not far from my faceless, perfunctory hotel. A wasted exercise when I learned that her parents owned substantial vineyards. Afterwards, out on the spacious, marbled terrace cluttered with the children's toys, we sipped home-made basil liqueur in the spring sunshine. Another speciality of the region, which Dora had run out of, was a laurel liqueur.

On my final day, before I set off, Dora presented me with a crate of her olive oil, a dozen bottles. I was embarrassed. It was too generous and the boot of the hire car was already tightly packed. I had nothing to offer in return so I took out the award-winning bottle from old Sicilian Bernardo and gave it to my kind hosts, warning them that God probably accompanied it.

Car packed, a last glass of basil liqueur together on their terrace, I took photographs to send back to them and we said our farewells. Then I set off again with Francisco for our final outing. My last hour with him, possibly the most fruitful, revealed the poet within the scientist. He took me to fifteen hectares of exquisite, immaculately cared-for olive groves, romantically situated on a slight incline with views back towards the Murge Hills.

'Here is my personal project,' he confided a little shyly. 'It is an organic grove. I am working here with many of my ideas. For example, instead of feeding the soil with fertilisers or nitrogen, at the onset of winter I am going to sow chickpea seeds. I will leave them till spring. Once they have flowered and seeded, I will turn the earth. The seeds in the soil will regrow the following year and generate natural nitrogen. The variety to buy is not the edible chickpea but another used for animal feed.'

'I have been trying unsuccessfully to run our farm organically but the olive fly defeats us.'

My companion talked of how he combatted our pest with a copper-based solution, though he admitted the insect was less destructive, less invasive in this part of southern Italy. 'We have a lower level of humidity.'

Our farm, Appassionata, closer to the coast offered ideal conditions for the fly.

'Keep the ground clean, leave no stray olives on the earth after harvest. The fly infiltrates them and resides within them until summer.'

The mid-afternoon was perfectly still. We strolled and circled the trees, admiring them, brushing our fingers gently against their white lacy flowers in full blossom, remarking bees nectar-gathering on a profusion of poppies, dandelions and clovers flowering in the fields. There was no irrigation used here, only rainfall fed these fields.

'Water is becoming the most coveted, expensive commodity on earth. And as the earth gets hotter and soil degenerates, we will look to the olive tree. It has several fascinating methods of preserving itself during drought-stressed periods.'

'For example?'

'Do you know why the underside of the olive leaf is silver?'

I was rather ashamed to admit that I had never asked myself the question.

'The leaf is covered in tiny, all but invisible hairs. They attract sunlight and turn its underside silver while the upper remains green-ish. The function of these hairs is to reflect sunlight and regulate the evaporation of water. The olive tree transpires through its leaves. Remarkably, it has a shoot-to-root signal, a message service between the roots and the leaves, alerting leaves of the need to decrease transpiration, protecting against water loss. And it is in direct relation to the lack of water in the soil.'

A man with a dog and wooden walking stick passed by at the extremity of the lane. He threw a wave with his cane when he spotted us.

'But there is something else.'

A pair of butterflies in love-play fluttered by.

'The olive tree not only conserves water, it has the ability to create it.'

'How can that be?'

'Put crudely, the olive root burrows deep for water, which is why over-irrigation damages the long-term health of the plant. While excavating, the root creates channels that allow rain to seep into the soil and infiltrate groundwater levels, thus regenerating underground water deposits. With the work of the olive root, it is possible to remedy desiccated soil conditions. Sow olive groves in the desert, feed them prudently and they will, over generations, reclaim the terrain. It is a remarkably resourceful tree.'

I recollected the Roman mill lost at the high doors to the Sahara and my twin visions for the future.

'These groves are not mine; they belong to my uncle,' Francisco added a little wistfully. 'But I am the one who is always here. Let us walk, we can see his summer palace.'

We traced the contours of the lane, until we stood outside imposing, ornate gates and stared through the bars like children towards a rather overgrown driveway and beyond a magnificent eighteenth-century property. Out of season, not even a gardener or guardian cared for it. 'When I am not studying diseases, I like best of all to be here, walking these orchards, sitting in the summer palace gardens reading, thinking up schemes to lend nature a hand.'

On my solitary Saturday way, once through legions of pugliesi olive groves, I crossed the narrow ankle of Italy, through undulating, soft-toned countryside that seemed at peace with the world, but who could say? Beyond the quietude of the early evening and the glorious peach-ripe sunset ahead of me, I was unprepared for the cut-and-thrust onslaught on the outskirts of Naples, once the capital of the Bourbon Kingdom. I lost my way in and around terminally decrepit backstreets where lean-faced fixers, messengers, pimps, busy with petty missions ran to and fro or stood on street corners smoking. I got caught up in a yellow and blue flagged municipal street party of drums, gunshots, drunks and traffic jams and arrived into Pompeii, frazzled, at close to midnight with nowhere to sleep. Eventually, I found what I was told was 'the last room in the town'. No doubt, an exaggeration.

The sun had risen on a beautiful day, filling in the spaces between the charred stones with a kindly, diffused light, as it must have done on that mid-summer morning almost 2000 years ago, August AD 79, when the people of this Amalfi coast city awoke, oblivious to their gruesome fate. Pompeii. Such a living and dead place! So many sweet scents and perfumes and delicate living touches pervading a city perished, a charcoaled image of itself. I sat within an olive grove planted with twentieth-century trees beside a fountain whose water stopped flowing 2000 years ago. There were a couple of fresh-leafed apple trees in blossom, too, while, not twenty yards away, laid out in a glass case, were several small, frozen bodies: terrified citizens attempting an escape from the streets flowing with red-hot larva, faces pressed against the ground, faces shoved into another's long-rotted flesh, incredulous at what was befalling them, caught up in the stampede while overhead the black, billowing clouds cloaked the sky, plunging them into a darkness darker than any night. Stiff, brittle corpses, a diary of a day, a record of nature's monstrous capabilities.

Alongside, tender young petals.

And then I sniffed a lingering, sulphurous aroma. Burning. At first I thought it was my imagination playing tricks on me, but it never relented, never let up. It was possibly caused by the continuing gun-shots or perhaps fireworks, elsewhere. I heard the cracks throughout my day at Pompeii, reaching crescendos every couple of hours, but I did not see anything. They must have been an accompaniment to whatever the neighbouring civic celebrations were in honour of. I found it freaky, as though the stones told their story and the perfumes in the air, too, had never let go. At Porta de Nola, I sat in the shade and listened to crows, blackbirds and small songbirds. I overheard an American ask her husband: 'Did they serve pizza and beer back then?' The air was perfumed with flowers but it was also tinged with a damp, decaying odour. I heard in the distance a train passing, a horse neighing and cantering, and then it was back to the lacklustre stones. Time present, time past.

I walked the ruins for nine hours, always shadowed by the threat-ening silhouette of Vesuvius, which had given no warnings that day, that afternoon, 2000 years ago, of the fire in its throat ready to roar, ready to blow its top.

Modern Pompeii was an altogether different proposition. No ghosts here, just the flesh and blood shove of armies of hawkers and tourists, the eternal union, and flocks of nuns parading the streets like penguins, and the incessant pealing of church bells. I was exhausted, drained after the blackened city, but was bucked up when, sitting drinking a well-earned cappuccino, I observed three whiskery biddies, fat as butter, dawdling in the square eating crumbling pastries out of paper tissues. They were whispering conspiratorially, throwing glances at an imposing door with a large brass knocker. Gingerly, one of the old girls eased herself up to the door, rapped hard with the knocker and then the trio hot-footed it out of the square, lickety-split, like naughty children, giggling. That evening, I ate dinner in an *osteria* where the paunched but kindly Neapolitan proprietor reminded me that Vesuvius still boils at its centre and, unlike gently smoking Etna, according to him, it could erupt at any moment without warning.

I made a brief stop on the coast at Positano, because I wanted to, because I had not visited it since I had lived fleetingly, intermittently, in Rome in my twenties and because I needed to take stock, to log in my head the many images of the *Mezzogiorno* before I left. Positano had been a fishing village until the sixties when the hippy chic discovered it. Potted hydrangeas, all blue, lined the marble stairway at the entrance to my hotel that looked out across the steep cliffside to the sea, and the balconies were overhung with scarlet flowering geraniums. Fruits were in season: freckled apricots, egg-shaped tomatoes, medlars. Packed tight in wooden boxes, like the poor relative of an apricot, I knew this fruit, its dark-leaved tree, from home. It grows in every garden in the South of France though we don't have one. Whenever I have asked I was told, *nèfle* from the tree, *néflier*. Here in Italy it was *nespola*, but I had never known the English name before.

'Best eaten when the skin has wrinkled and become patched with brown,' the old woman in the shop across from my hotel advised. And lemons, remarkable knobbly, thick-skinned lemons the size of melons, served with every dish.

'The Mediterranean dream of earth's plenty and the quiet satisfaction of those who gather and live this life is an illusion. It is *hard*,' said Domenico, an olive-farming waiter whose family had one hundred trees on one hundred and twenty ragged hillside acres close to nearby Praiano, the fruits of which they pressed at a granite-stone mill in Sorrento. Yes, it was hard, but he would never sell. 'The olive trees are our currency.' His father had been a farmer-fisherman, like so many here. They grew tomatoes, potatoes and olives and he fished. Since his father died two years earlier, Domenico had taken over the responsibility for the groves, pressing sufficient oil for his three brothers, two sisters and their families. During the last war when his father had been posted in Taranto and then sent overseas to Ethiopia, his mother had run the farm single-handed with a little assistance from the very small sons. But tourism had changed the fortunes of these *Mezzogiorno* natives.

'We live within the shadows of volcanoes, one foot in Europe and the other in Africa, but the tourists love it and they pay handsomely. Further south in Calabria, they are less fortunate. Their oil is poor, too.'

I walked to the beach with an armful of books, sunk my feet in the sand and settled. Instantly it began to rain, wildly, throwing up deckchairs as though they were of papier-mâché. Spring storms. They were thrilling. I watched them through the windows of cafés and I whiled away the evenings in a bar listening to a Neapolitan tenor sing his heart out; Neapolitan melodies. 'O Sole Mio'.

People lived here; they did not exist. Their lives were lived in, inhabited with an intensity which reached right into the marrow of their bones. Still, it was time to move on to Sardegna, then north. Time to whisper *arrivederci* to this sunburned elsewhere. The days to my rendezvous with Michel in Milan were lessening, and to the meeting I had scheduled with another propagator, in Tuscany, land of sweet oil and the mother tongue of the Italian language. I dawdled along the coast because it was too glorious to race through, stopping at every second roadside spot that commanded views down upon the distant emerald-blue sea, wanting to dive from the belvederes, lingeringly. Passing through Campania, where the first water buffalo were bred for the ploughing of the fields, I avoided Rome because it is insane. It invades. Rome is impossible simply to pass through or overnight. Rome demands attention, Rome demands commitment. Its lived-in, dense, eternally decadent past and its frenetic, cracked-at-the-vocal-chords, modernistic energy reaches subtly into the core of you, lusts after you, seduces and insists with a stroke of the tongue that you stay. *Vieni qua, vieni qua.* I knew it. I had lived there. I knew, too, that if I sailed in there was an old story – Babingtons, two rooftop terraces overlooking the Spanish Steps, Cinecittà, Trastevere, the banks of the Tiber – a young love story in an antique city that I would want to haunt. I suddenly recollected his black eyes; cocaine highs; his shy silences. It remained a wound, a desire that still occasionally stung bitter-sweet, so I turned the wheel north-west and my thoughts, away from a man who had long preceded Michel, bypassing Roma, and took the starlit ferry from fortressed Civita Vecchia to Olbia. Penultimate stop, Sardegna.

Sardegna and Northern Italy

Sardinia, Sardegna, took me by surprise. Had I said the same of Sicily? Two islands both with autonomy, both Italian, both dealing in the euro currency yet worlds apart. Sardinia took me over, almost as soon as I drove off the boat. I disembarked into the port of Olbia soon after dawn, intent upon Santa Teresa de Gallura at the very northern tip of the island where the ferries departed for Corsica. Corsica! I was nearly home. This was my fifth month on the road. I had not been paying attention to time. But now that I had paused to consider the date for the first time in a while, I realised that I had missed Michel's birthday. I called him but the phone was switched off. He was probably working outside somewhere on the land. My head was a rush, a flood of olive farm images. Images that I had kept aside in one of the trunks in my mind. It did not do to allow my thoughts to wander home too frequently because it made me aware of my aloneness, my loneliness, whereas, when I stayed in the present, I was perfectly content, excited by my journeyings and the discoveries along the way.

It was not yet 8 a.m. when I took a right turn off the Olbia highway. I had not eaten breakfast and was in need of a cup of coffee. I followed the shoreline hoping to discover a beachside shack and found myself at the sea's edge passing by a chic yachting resort along the Costa Smeralda. During the sixties and seventies, this whole area was developed by a consortium of businessmen headed by Prince Karim Aga Khan IV, stepson of the late Rita Hayworth. Film star and heroine of mine, Ms Hayworth was Karim's father's second wife. She was pregnant with their only child, a daughter, Yasmin, when Aly Aga Khan married her in the South of France in May 1949. The marriage lasted two years, but Rita stayed on in the Alpes-Maritimes and lived out her later, lost years in a village not too far from our farm.

Elegant, fashionable though this resort might be, I did not stop to find out; this was not the Sardinia of ancient olives.

I had ample time to spare before my meeting with Antonio and decided, as I had been unsuccessful in hunting down a cup of coffee, to flip off the beaten track. Soon lost, I pulled up in a small village and requested the best route to Santa Teresa. I did not specify 'de Gallura'. The man, a maintenance gardener, the only soul about, stopped digging and thought for a while – clearly not in any rush – and then pointed out a road, left and then right, that seemed to promise north. Either there was a miscommunication – the Sardegnan language is closer to Latin than to modern Italian; it has also been hugely influenced by Catalan, due to centuries of occupation by both the Spanish and the Catalonians – or I miscalculated the left/right turnings. Whichever, I found myself climbing a winding, dusty track that within no time led me to a high, deserted zone of pines, cacti and boulders. It was a wilderness landscape of *maquis* and stones, many of the latter resembling megalithic dolmens; curious, strange, prehistoric. Less than two hours off the boat and I already had the notion that this was a land with mysteries where flora and rocks possessed lives, spirits of their own. The higher I climbed the less accommodating the sand path became and I began to question whether the tyres of the hire car were up to it. Once or twice they skidded, refusing to grab, but there was nowhere to turn round. When I eventually reached the end of the road, with stupendous views down to a cobalt-blue sea clustered with islets, I found myself at a meteorological station where iron steps wound to the summit, to mounds of smooth, round, pinky-granite stones upon which the base had been constructed. There was no transport, no signs of a presence. I called out, wandered to the entrance, but the place was locked, deserted. And such a silence, save for a high-altitude, wind boom.

I was obliged to turn the car on a sixpence and retrace my steps all the way back to where I had asked directions of the fellow working in the street. He was gone and I was lost. Eventually, having found my way on to a more public road, still hoping for coffee – it was now after nine thirty – I passed a garden centre where nothing but olive trees were on display. The gates were locked. As in Puglia, the pruning was unique, but here the plants took the forms of primitive beasts or their thick, ringletted trunks looked like colossal barley sugar sticks; lopped branches reshooting, turned full circles, resembling magnifying glasses. I pulled over and took some shots but beyond a shallow ditch the grassed area had been enclosed with barbed wire so I could not approach.

After the mainland, all was eerily silent and deserted. It was tipping the third week of May. I would have expected to see more travellers. Next to Sicily, Sardinia is the second largest island in the Mediterranean, but its population is only 1.7 million compared to Sicily's over five million.

Santa Teresa was an arrival spot, a stepping-off point for sea travel and an easy-going, manageably sized town with yellow and orange houses and few signs of resort tourism. It had a sixties feel about it, which rather endeared it to me. I knew nothing about Antonio, my contact. His name had been given to me in Positano as a fellow who 'knew the geography of his island'. He was late. I hung about in front of the WWF offices, a temporary looking wooden establishment that, though bearing a Closed sign on the door, was actually unlocked. I had been inside twice, calling into absence. Chaotic piles of books, papers, posters and disks lay everywhere. Anything could have been stolen and I liked the idea that whoever manned the place trusted their material would not be going astray. Outside, I settled on a wooden bench beneath a tree reading up history of the island. My mobile rang. It was Antonio.

'I was wondering if you would like to meet up today,' he said.

'I am waiting for you,' I replied, surprised, and confirmed my position.

The twentysomething who stepped out of a battered old car clutching fast to a mobile was sheepish and frowning. He did not strike me as a ranger, more a civil servant. He suggested coffee and led me to a local bar where he shook hands with just about everyone. He listened politely while I gave him a swift résumé of my journeys so far and what I might be looking for: historical trees, Mediterranean olive links, folkloric tales connected to the olive tree . . .

'I am an accountant,' he apologised after several moments of reflection. 'You should meet my grandfather, perhaps, but he is very old, eighty-four. Or Andreo, he fights for trees.'

We began with Andreo though Antonio had no number for the conservationist. I suggested we try the office of the World Wildlife Fund. It was now occupied by a woman who put me in mind of someone who had been left behind at Woodstock, years after the concert, an ageing spinster with beads and flyaway hair. She knew Andreo and telephoned him immediately. After a series of calls it was arranged that I would go to Andreo's farm later in the afternoon. In the meantime, Antonio invited me to lunch and called his parents to ask permission! Over an excellent pasta and glass or two of Sardinian white, my new companion spilled the troubles of his broken heart: a feisty woman in Rome. The patron and chef was introduced to me because he had run his own business in Stoke Newington, north London, while Antonio was still fretting about love and how best to assist me.

'I very much want to help,' he repeated anxiously, as though his life depended on it. He was still trying to reach his grandfather who lived some distance from Santa Teresa, but concluded that the old man was probably out in his fields. Even at eighty-four he worked the land from dawn till dusk.

My guide shook his head, clutching and staring at his phone as though begging it to ring. The woman in Rome had promised to contact him. There was to be a family party the following weekend. She had promised to fly over. Poor Antonio's woes felt insurmountable and I was concerned that I was burdening him, making his situation worse.

'Look, why don't we meet Andreo as planned and then I'll head off,' I suggested, without wishing to give offence.

'But where will you go? Where will you stay?'

I assured him that it was not a problem. I had not been expecting him to organise hotels or my itinerary. The situation was settled. After the tree-guardian, I would move on, so Antonio's remark, spoken almost as an apology, nearly knocked me off my feet.

'I don't suppose you'd be interested in a three-thousand-year-old olive tree? I know it's not as old—'

The tree was growing some distance across the island. Antonio's car would not make the journey, he feared.

'But the hire car will,' I cried excitedly.

We had no time to make the excursion and be back before our meeting with Andreo. In any case, Antonio was not sure where this venerable was situated. He had never seen it. We decided to set off directly afterwards.

'But what about my grandfather? I want you to meet him.'

'You haven't managed to contact him yet. The tree first.'

Andreo's croft, on sun-drenched farmlands, was in remote country-side, far off any beaten track. We bumped along a winding stony lane until we reached a crooked, wooden gate. Dangling from it were horseshoes and a rather spooky goat's skull. Alongside it, an assort-ment of curled horns nailed to a flagpole. From there we continued by foot. The man I was about to meet, I learned, had saved a peach tree from extinction, the sole remaining example of its species growing anywhere in the world. Long-haired goats were grazing in a neigh-bouring field. Cairn configurations of local stones were piled two or three high, resembling phalluses or sacred totem poles. Renato, Andreo's son and only child, big and gawky, came pounding up the lane to greet us. His hair was as black as a gypsy's and he had buck-teeth. He pointed out a rare flowering wild gladioli, spoke to the lizards, fell upon a tortoise nestling in the undergrowth and lay at its side, whispering. Richly coloured wild flowers were in blossom everywhere. The afternoon had turned embracingly warm and I knew by the fluttering silences and the perfumes that I was deep within the Mediterranean.

Andreo, with an olive-wood cane, came to greet us, waving us onwards into a garden that was organically chaotic and lush with life. Painted hand-made chairs, a wooden swing that could seat a family, string ladders climbing overgrown trees, butterflies, an amphitheatre of nightingales singing their hearts out. In mid-afternoon!

'They must be in love,' grinned Andreo.

Nothing had been pruned, nothing seemed structured. In spite of the heat, our host, late sixties, wore a thick-ribbed brown wool cardigan. He spoke as though his tonsils had been sandpapered and had a carved face like one of his poled effigies. It was an eccentric free-for-all environment with tiny inventive arrangements made from barks, stones, sticks, skulls, bones, dotted everywhere. Fringed hammocks hung beneath the spread canopies of trees.

'I have no time,' growled the man. He wore a wedding ring on a leather strap round his neck. 'You must speak about water shortages. It is as dry as a bone here,' he yelled while his son, who had left the tortoise and joined our tour, continued with the fabrication of a bow; his arrows were of bamboo shoots.

'Yes, of course, *ma certo*, I know the millennia olive tree. It dominates a wild olive forest, near a tiny church.' He danced from language to language, rattling away in a local dialect to Antonio who seemed a little less down in the mouth since we had arrived here, then on to Italian, then another Sardegnan dialect peppered with a few words of English and French. Antonio's English was stilted so I was constantly lost and begging for explanations. A rare lizard was spotted scuttling in the undergrowth, '*Ziricuccu! Ziricuccu!*' cried both father and son at once and shot off after it.

'I built my house,' announced Andreo, 'without plans, following only the spaces without plants.'

It was the craziest, quirkiest of homes, more like a series of shacks piled one upon another, with plants climbing everywhere.

'What do you want to know? Our language comes from the Phoenicians and then a cross-fertilisation from every other invader who has walked our soil. You know, in the coastal town of L'Alguer over on the western side of the island, face to the Balearic isles, Catalan remains the spoken language. A thousand different peoples have left their mark here. It is a chain that they say began with the Greeks and Phoenicians, but it is also older. Much older. Pagan settlements, traces of life, exist here that reach back hundreds of thousands of years.'

Andreo bemoaned the fact that the Sardegnans don't love their land, that they have not been educated to respect it and protect it.

'This is a mysterious, magical island,' he claimed. 'Each year around thirty-two million acres of natural forests are lost worldwide through illegal logging and bad management. On this island, we have some of the oldest Mediterranean specimens of olives, oaks and cork trees but does anybody care? Ogliastra, the name is born of the wild olive. It is a magnificent region in the south but are there wild olives? Precious few. Do you know about Santa Maria Navaresse?' He was almost shouting.

I shook my head. 'A fishing village in the south?'

'Go there!' he cried dramatically. 'A dozen giant olive trees survive but the town's tradition is to cut one down every year and burn it on a ritual fire.'

'But why?'

Andreo lit another cigarette – for an ecologist his habit surprised me – and shrugged. 'Every year, I battle with their mayor but he tells me it is a pagan tradition to chop the biggest surviving tree in the neighbourhood. Have you ever heard anything so foolish?'

I scribbled the town's name in a notebook.

'You can't go there,' interrupted Antonio. 'How will you get there? It's very far and there are bandits, shepherds everywhere. It's famous for kidnappings.'

Andreo waved young Antonio silent with a dismissive arm. The wind was picking up. It was the *Punenti*, a westerly force, I learned, whistling through the bamboo shoots growing along the banks of a brook that ran through the property. Alas, the stream was drying up; its bed nothing but mud and stones.

'Our water shortage is critical,' Andreo muttered. 'Our harvests are ending up shrivelled, undeveloped. I collect rainwater in this barrel for washing purposes. See for yourself. It's dregs only. Week after week of dry skies.'

'Climate change?'

'We fell the forests and shower the razed grounds with pesticides, what do we expect? Go to the three-thousand-year-old olive tree and then move south.' Andreo was banging his fist against a wooden table where his wife had just served up a pot of green tea and a plate of cream biscuits. 'Do you know what is happening on this island of remarkable, mystical stones?'

I shook my head, no inkling where this new turn in the conversation was leading.

'Granite quarries. Everywhere, the talk is of *cemento*. The young men are not being reared to work the land but to go into the cement businesses. More lucrative. At Monte de Messudi there was a piece of granite, a monster specimen, which used to light up. How would you say? It brillianted itself through the sunlight at midday. It was famous the island over and there were many traditional fables about it. In Sardegna, our predecessors believed that every stone, rock and tree was imbued with a spirit, a god-like life force. Some of us still believe it. Well, this piece of granite was chosen for someone's kitchen by a local architect and he ordered it to be cut up into pieces. God knows if he had the right to do so, still he did it. But when the architect saw the mutilated offerings, he decided against it. The quality was not good enough for the blasted kitchen he was designing. Today, those drilled fragments lie on that hillside. The dull remains of a massacred spirit. Gone is that once brilliant stone that inspired stories and poetry.'

The island was too large to cover in the short time that remained to me. The Phoenicians had created some excellent trading stations here, both in the south around Cagliari where they had mined salt and in the west on the Spanish side, but I would have needed weeks to cover so much ground. Better to concentrate my energies and, in that respect, Andreo's suggestion seemed as good as any.

It was close to four when we said our farewells.

'I never wear a watch. It destroys harmony with natural time,' he warned when he glimpsed me checking mine.

Antonio had finally made contact with his grandfather who had agreed to welcome us on our return leg from the olive tree, which was due west, somewhere off the road to Sassari. We returned to Santa Teresa to change cars. Antonio suggested cutting through the interior, off the beaten track, to afford me the opportunity of glimpsing the majesty and authenticity of the island.

Our meandering route brought us, eventually, to Tempio Pausania, capital of the Gallura province, and from there the landscape changed. We were entering extensive wild forests of *Quercus suber*, cork oak trees, many of which had recently been harvested, stripped of their lower barks. Brown-legged cork trees. From young, heartbroken Antonio at my side whose phone had not rung all day, I learned that there remained about 120 cork-oak stations on the island. The cork harvest traditionally took place between May and September. Once stripped, the lower trunks were left naked with a reddish, almost raw-flesh look to them. The harvest had been achieved early this year because the spring had been unseasonably hot and dry. I had not known that each tree can only be stripped once every six to nine years. Sardinia's hinterland, rocky and infertile, has the ideal soil for these trees and the best cork comes from wild trees rather than those grown on plantations.

I knew precious little about the production of this crop. Antonio was not an expert, but he was able to tell me that after the bark had been stripped off the tree, it was taken to the factory where it was left for up to two years to drain, releasing almost all its moisture. Only about 25 per cent of all harvested cork is of a sufficiently high standard to be used as bottle stoppers. The rest is sold off for industrial concerns. The cork forests are vital for birds because they are organic, never are pesticides used, but the drought conditions, a direct result of global warming, were causing deep concerns. And two other as yet inexplicable threats had occurred to damage these trees: recent infestations of gypsy moths and an unidentified fungus. No one was sure yet whether these were also caused by the environmental changes taking place.

This oak is native to the western Mediterranean. The South of France has plenty of *Quercus suber* trees though it is the lowest producer of cork in the Med basin and I had no idea where any of their cork stations were.

Who had discovered such an ingenious use for this bark and what had they used the product for before stoppers were required? Of course, the millions of terracotta jars, the amphorae that I had come across everywhere, required a sealing component, a stopper, both for safe transport and for storage, so cork would have come into its own at a very early stage in the story of Med agriculture. Cut marginally larger than the inner diameter of the neck of the amphora and then squeezed into it, the cork sealed the wine or olive oil, protecting the liquids from air and contaminants. Antonio had no answers to my out-loud musings but he had an uncle who owned one of the island's most productive stations. He offered to telephone him but I sensed that what he was really desirous of was to kick-start his blasted phone into action in the hope that the Roman girlfriend would pick up the vibes, his energy.

And then he took me completely by surprise.

'The Greeks called the tree *phellos*,' he said. 'They soled their theatrical boots, *kothornos*, with cork for their Greek dramas. These elevated soles raised the stature of certain actors so that they were Greek gods in the company of their fellow players.'

'Any idea what the Phoenicians or Romans called the cork?'

'Phoenicians?' He shook his head, but the Romans knew the tree simply as *suber* and their women – here he paused and sighed, clearly recalling his own unfaithful Roman lynx – wore shoes of cork to keep their feet warm in winter.

Cork was also employed to float fishing nets and sailors attached cork buoys to the draglines of their anchors. I hazarded a guess that these were either Phoenician, Egyptian or Minoan inventions but Antonio suggested Babylonian.

'Mmm, they lived by rivers.'

'They had an important influence on the Greeks.'

Because the cork tree was native to the western Med rather than the eastern, it would have involved trading the crop this side of the sea.

Later, after my travels, I discovered that the French, until the Middle Ages, had hived their honeybees in cork, keeping them cool in summer and warm in winter, similar to those I had seen along the banks of the Guadalquivir in Andalucía. Another fascinating tidbit that came to my attention was the discovery attributed to the French monk Dom Pérignon, of champagne fame. When he was running the monastery cellars, wine bottles were plugged with rags or hemp soaked in olive oil but these were found to pop out during fermentation. Whether or not it was Dom Pérignon who personally came up with the idea of changing the oil-soaked rag for cork, it was ingenious and revolutionised the champagne industry from that time onwards. The Greeks had employed it for wine stoppers thousands of years earlier. A wine jar from the first century BC was found in Ephesus. Sealed with cork, it still contained its liquid.

Michel collects drawn corks. I have always been rather baffled by this eccentric habit of his. All around the olive farm are stacked straw shopping bags brimming with them.

'What are you going to do with all these?' I have begged on more than one occasion.

'Cork is a limited commodity,' he responds.

Dare I confess that once when I was clearing out the cabin up behind Mr Quashia's home-constructed hangar I came across kilos of them and I burned them on a bonfire? When Michel found out he was not only cross but profoundly upset.

'One day,' he said, 'when I am less taken up with professional commitments, I intend to build a cork sculpture in the garden. A monument to a dying trade.'

It is a fact that today wine bottles are frequently plugged with plastic or screw tops.

Dusk was inching down upon us. I glanced at my watch. It was well gone six.

'Is it much further?'

Antonio seemed weary, poor broken-hearted fellow. 'I have no idea,' he sighed. 'We should ask. Shall I call my grandfather? Who should we ask?' So desperate to use his phone.

There was no one. We were in the middle of nowhere. The island had the feel of being shipwrecked, lost at sea, north of the heart of the Mediterranean and drifting. Hills, forests and distant jaggedy blue mountains. I had the sensation that nature was watching me with curious eyes, peering out of itself, wary of strangers. We descended into a long valley. It could not be described as a plain. I wondered to myself when we had last passed any habitation. Where were we? And then a woman riding her bicycle.

'Shall we ask?'

She knew the tree. 'But you still have some way to go.'

I was concerned for the light and when Antonio returned to the car I picked up speed a little. Eventually we drove into forest country again.

'These are wild olives,' I stated, incredulously. Hectare after climbing, hilly hectare of silvery forests, burnished by the sun descending in the western sky ahead of us. And then a sign, a handwritten, wooden arrow directing us to a track on the left. The light was fading fast now.

'I hope we don't drive by it,' the fretful man at my side.

'We'll know it.'

'How?'

'It's three thousand years old. It's an olive tree. I'll spot it.'

We were approaching a stone chapel, just as Andreo had described. Ahead was a gate, chained.

'Look! There, beyond the fence, there it is.'

'We cannot go in. It's too late. It's closed. Better not to.'

'Then you wait in the car.' I grabbed my camera and made for the gate, ready to climb, but as I pressed my hand against it, it swung invitingly open. I stood a moment in the fast-fading daylight, angular slants of beams falling across circular canopies of foliage, and took in the scene. Jumbo olive trees dotted about a field, knee-high in grasses and wild lavender flowers, ascending the gently sloping hillsides like African game grazing at sundown. The companions to the chief of the pack were younger, but were not adolescents by any standards. I paced slowly towards my destination, the oldest I had encountered anywhere in the western Mediterranean. What did it mean a wild tree of three thousand years old? It was growing here before the arrival of the Phoenicians to the island. Had its stone been carried from afar by a bird? If so, from how far? Surely not from the Middle East? Or could it be that the arrival of the Phoenicians, or other foreigners from the east, predated the archaeological facts that we hold true? Could it be that it was neither the Phoenicians nor the Greeks who brought the olive tree to the western Mediterranean?

Or was it possible that this tree was one hell of a survivor, the sole survivor from forests of uncultivated oleasters that had been growing wild since prehistory all across this island, all across the western basin of the Mediterranean? And that the cargo transported from the east on those fifty-oared galleys was not the tree itself, but knowledge, knowledge of cultivation, plant care and nutrition.

I lifted up my camera and took a first shot. Its crown was too extended, its trunk too solid, too broad, to capture its entire silhouette in one frame. I began to circle its base, shooting up into its branches, but the light was against me now. I snapped once more and then let the camera hang loose. Instead, I began to study the tree, communing tentatively, a step at a time.

Antonio was at my side. 'She rang!'

'Bravo. Look at this, Antonio.'

'Well, actually I rang her and then she called back, but I don't think she's coming for the party.'

Unlike the cultivated trees in Lebanon, this relic had been left to its own undomesticated devices. The trunk had split, but it had not disintegrated. It had not a central void with suckers grown into substantial trunks flanking the original. Its principal torso was studded with knots and knobs, topped by an unruly dome. And then I stopped, looked and then looked again. The tree, unquestionably a female to my mind, had two oval hollows and a twisted, bulbous eruption, between those hollows. I lifted my camera and began to shoot again wildly, snap-snapping.

'Antonio! Come here! What do you see?'

'She's very big, very old.'

'Yes, yes, but look *here*. Can you see anything over on this side?'

My young companion came scampering round and looked up into the tree. His face broke into a broad grin of amazement. '*Mamma mia*. She has a face.'

'Yes, she has a face. She has eyes, an elephantine nose and expressions.'

In Italian, *albero*, meaning tree, is masculine, yet Antonio had described this primitive, pagan *olivo* as female. I, too, perceived her as female.

I took a step to my left to study *her* from another angle, and the eyes appeared to follow me.

'She's watching you,' called Antonio, laughing skittishly. His observation seemed accurate. Wherever I moved, the tree's gaze appeared to follow. I moved in close and the 'eyes' seemed to realign, to refocus. What did its expression tell me, telepathically communicate to me? Bewilderment? Sagacity? Concern? A sense that this spirit was trapped, had been left behind, had no one to commune with? I wasn't sure. It certainly did not strike me as a malicious spirit, but nor did it seem to be happy. The baggy 'face' had a rheumy-eyed, worried expression.

I have for most of my adult life experienced plants as living beings. In scientific terms of course they live, but whether they possess a spirit is open to hot debate. The early occupants of this island about whom almost nothing is known, not unlike the Stone Age peoples of Mallorca and elsewhere, saw their world as filled with spirits. Many spirits, not just one. Plurality. Spirits that took up residence in trees and stones. They believed in the divine presence in existence, not exclusively within us but within everything.

If you live your life surrounded by nature, working with it, looking at it in every mood and light, this is not such an extraordinary concept to take on board. As far as I am concerned our olive trees have always possessed a divine presence, as has everything else that lives on our farm and beyond, but I had never until this moment come face to face with a tree spirit and so visible, tangible. Without wishing to demean *her*, this 3000-year-old energy force could have been incorporated directly into a Disney film and given a voice. The character was so present, so animated, alive.

It was eight thirty, growing dark. Antonio, elated by his communication with the Roman woman, was now worrying about his grandfather. 'We must go, we should be on our way.'

'Yes, yes, I'm coming.' It was exceedingly difficult to walk away from that tree, from a spirit that I felt profoundly had been attempting to express itself. I spoke a few private words to *her* and returned to Antonio, agitating alongside the car. I drove in silence while Antonio chattered light-heartedly.

His grandfather lived in the historic heart of Tempio Pausania. We pulled up in a cobbled, typically Mediterranean narrow street and walked the half-lane to the farmer's home. As Antonio rapped on the door's wooden surface, a dog began to yap. Moments passed and a stooped old man of eighty-four with cadaverous features and tanned skin, Piedro, was welcoming us. He led us with slippered feet through to a rear dining room-cum-kitchen where two hunting rifles hung from a wall alongside a large wooden armoire. Hooked up to one of the ceiling beams were long, looped strings of sausages, made by Piedro. Since his wife died five years earlier – he crossed himself whenever he mentioned her – he had taken charge of the house as well as the vineyards, olives and livestock. Occasionally, a daughter or Antonio dropped by, but it satisfied him to be self-sufficient. He shuffled to a corner, lifted out a bottle of his own wine, a Moscato, and drew the cork.

Glasses poured, I took a sip . . .

Through serendipity's blessing and the graciousness of good Lebanese friends, I had found what I believe are the oldest cultivated olive trees on the planet, perhaps the most ancient living specimens of any plant in existence. I had had a fair crack at understanding the comings and goings and the cross-fertilisations of Mediterranean peoples, the trade exchanges of oil and olives, all of which had played a mighty part in the creation of what today are the Mediterranean nations, and I was satisfied, excited, by all that I had found. I am not a botanist, after all, nor an archaeologist or historian. Merely a woman who had set out on a journey alone, determined to find a decent, constructive way to live in harmony with her surroundings and who loves olive trees with a passion. What I had been hunting for this time, on this western tour, had been a path forward, constructive pointers that might assist us to alleviate the destruction of the earth's surface and atmosphere. I now knew that the olive tree had much to offer as a paradigm for drought tolerance, as a major contributor to the reforestation of desert areas . . . all this was positive material that I could take back to the farm and work with. But an ancient spirit, a perplexed old girl living within a tree seeded 3000 years ago? No, this had not been on the agenda. It was even difficult to grasp. But I could not ignore what I had found even if I was thrown off course . . .

'What do you want to know from my grandfather?' Clearly this was a repeat of Antonio's question but I had not been paying attention, lost as I had been in my contemplations. To gain time, to find balance, I requested a potted history of the old man's life.

He had been labouring the land since a child. Back then they had worked with wooden implements; they seeded by hand, toiling from dawn to nightfall. He only attended elementary school and sometimes skipped those classes, but he could read and write. Horses, donkeys, bulls had transported everything.

'At seventeen, I went to be a soldier, but only on Saturdays. I had a problem with my throat and used it as an excuse. The Germans were camped close by several of the fields my father worked, but they were always decent and paid for whatever they took. Life was very hard due to the *syndicos*. Sixty per cent of everything earned went back to the landowners. If we didn't pay, we could be kicked out of our home on San Giovanni's Day.'

'When is that?'

'The feast of John the Baptist, 24 June.'

Piedro was a decent old bloke, counteracting his loneliness and the ongoing grief he felt at the loss of his childhood sweetheart and wife for more than half a century by the addition of a sandy-haired puppy whose picture he insisted I take. He wanted to speak, was keen to share his lifetime experiences from Mussolini onwards.

'Mussolini was good to us, for us, the peasants, in the early days, until he joined forces with Hitler. After that, life was terrible.'

He talked of the defunct feudal system, which had taken much the same form as had existed in Sicily. The Mafia had maintained a stranglehold here, too, within the *syndicos*, but Mussolini had done his best to stamp it out.

'Had he succeeded?' I asked.

Piedro shrugged and popped an olive in his mouth with a glint in his eyes. For the puppy on his worn corduroys or the past, I could not tell.

This island, lost somewhere between Europe and Africa, had been slow to move into the twentieth century. However, in 1946 things had started to improve.

'In 1948, I bought the land my grandfather had been renting at exorbitant prices since 1919 and began to make it productive for myself and the family.'

Today, according to Antonio, his grandfather was land-rich. He had sufficient for his needs and that of his grand- and great-grandchildren. His story was one of success, a redemption from the shackles of the landlords.

I studied him as he talked, slicing ham, sausages, cheeses, all made by his own sweat, with a substantial horn-handled knife worn in a sheath attached to his leather belt. The knife, Antonio said to me later – 'did you notice my grandfather's knife? It is an island speciality, a *sa pattadesa*.' It was common, explained the grandson, for country men to work on the land well into their eighties, tilling, husbanding the beasts, making wine, foodstuffs, getting about on their three-wheelers. Piedro must have been a handsome man in his youth. He was still resilient, still fighting fit with big, arthritic hands and stubby fingernails, stained like dying leaves. He represented the vestiges of a passing peasant class.

I had hoped to make a start on my journey south that same evening, but it was late by the time I dropped Antonio back at his car outside the WWF shack. I decided instead to find a *pensione* in Santa Teresa, which I did with little difficulty, and I was off at daybreak with a great deal of ground to cover. By lunchtime, because I had spent a while at the Giant's Tomb, I was still north. I had reached a sign for Santa Lucia and decided to turn off for a quick bite. The bay offered one bar, one restaurant plus a stone lookout tower facing towards Italy. There were several groups of cyclists sitting on the breakwall knocking back gallons of water. I ordered the set lunch. The only other table occupied was the proprietor's, eating with his family, the chef and the fisherman who had brought in the catch that morning. It was a typical Italian affair, plenty of laden plates punctuated with uninhibited outbursts of laughter. Gone, it seemed, were the days of Sardinian poverty, of hen-scratched existences. After I had eaten my fish I was invited to join them, offered a glass of *crema di limoncello*, a thick and tartly sweet digestive, and then handed a bottle of their own vineyard wine from nearby Siniscola. A dessert was placed in front of me, a paste of almonds and goat's milk and honey. Delicious. Then was poured a glass of *crema di milto*. A myrtle liqueur. Now, I was protesting; I was replete; I was driving! Along came a fellow, a *capitano*, yellowing, bloodshot eyes, broken capillary vessels, grey stubble and British naval captain's cap. A man who had been born at sea. This called for another bottle of vino. He, too, was a local fisherman. There were nine altogether plying their trade in this tiny community. From a nearby house appeared a wizened corn straw of a woman dressed in colourful local costume. She, too, idled a moment at the table. Her clawed hand was clutching a hand-painted seashell.

'It brings good fortune,' bayed the old girl at me.

Maria, generous-hearted wife of the proprietor, took it and handed it to me: '*occhio di Santa Lucia*'.

Protection, once more, against the evil eye.

Maria offered to make up a snack for me to enjoy along my way. Their generosity was large, bordering on incomprehensible. It was only after I had settled my bill and I was about to get on the road that it became clear that a mistake had been made. For a reason to do with the label on my car-hire keys and something about my T-shirt they had mistaken me for a rep from Europcar. I offered to give back the bottle of wine and pay for the extra delights but they shook their heads, embraced me, hoping to see me back again soon.

After a fabulous drive through some of the loveliest of mountain scenery of red granite cliffs, Bob Dylan crooning, high-ranging forests, desolate moorlands, scrublands known here not as *maquis* but *macchia*, I came to the conclusion that Sardinia was quintessential, unadulterated Mediterranean. While Sicily was rich with elegant cities and architecture, Sardinia exuded an untouched, virgin air. It was prehistoric. Exhilarated, I pelted up hillsides, climbing the long spurs and then swung a bend, looking out across miles of untouched scenery, free-falling down into extended curves that seemed to wind forever. Where there was intermittent habitation, the island's natural boulders were used as meadow walls and gateposts. Rock formations rose from the mountain's surface like rockets, still-life artwork, almost as unsettling and enigmatic as my lady friend olive tree. Almost. These had a name: *tacchi*. I had climbed up into the impenetrable province of Ogliastra, seas of olive trees, a silver and green sea-ness of foliage, and was surrounded by ranges including the highest point on the island. Up near Baunei, towards journey's end for the day, some women were clad in traditional black, others in local costume.

Santa Maria Navarrese, where the neighbouring limestone mountains fell dramatically, abruptly to the sea, was settling into its out-of-season evening when I rolled in as the sun was setting. I found a hotel for twenty-five euros. The night receptionist, Luca, was a teacher by day working with acutely handicapped children. He pulled out a map of the town and drew crosses to mark the ancient olive trees. None of which, he assured me, were in danger.

'We respect them.' The following day was his free time and I engaged him to give me a tour of the region. He smiled, 'Every bay, inlet, rock and tree has its tale to tell.'

I decided that I would spend my last couple of days here and took a walk before the light disappeared to tour *gli olivastri* and get a brief sense of this sleepy fishing village waking up to tourism. I passed a café where a bunch of red-faced Brits, burned by the sun, were drinking beer and loudly discussing the prices of local properties. The olive trees were groved in a central, public square and encirling a white medieval church set metres from the beach. And, indeed, they told a legendary tale.

Once upon a time there was a princess, the Princess of Navarra, whose marriage in Spain had been arranged by her father. She was not happy, did not wish to marry the man chosen by the king, but no amount of pleading would change his mind so at the eleventh hour she set sail in the dead of night with a small band of Basque sailors. Their navigations were due to take them to the foot of the peninsula of what is today Italy, but they were driven off course in a terrible storm, along this eastern coast of Sardinia, caught up in the maelstrom of the Bentu de Soli wind. Their ship was all but destroyed near the Monti Insani. But they did not lose their lives and once they were safely ashore they took refuge beneath a wild, centenarian olive. To offer up her thanks to God for saving her life and that of her sailors, the princess requested that her able-bodied seamen build a humble church that stood within the shade of the olive that had given them shelter. After the church had been constructed, in 1052, the remaining olive trees were planted. Each today stands a proud thousand years old. And perhaps there had been others, too, that have since been felled for the pagan rituals Andreo had spoken of? After, I walked the bow-shaped esplanade, enchanting in the crimson light, looking out upon a turquoise-turning-purple sea in which a series of islets lay.

This was a region of olives, figs and carobs. The Sardinians of this oriental coast prided themselves on a way of life that had always been lived in harmony with nature. That was until the nineteenth and early twentieth centuries. Until that time, these monumental limestone cliffs had been carpeted in holm oak, *Quercus ilex*, and heathen olives but they fell foul of the *carbonari*, the charcoal-burners, who demolished thousands and thousands of acres of trees. Luca had borrowed a jeep from his brother which allowed us to climb up into the Gennargentu National Park to a barren plateau, the Golgo, where wild animals, horses, boars and pigs, survived on little. We trekked along stone paths laid down by the charcoal-burners who carried their charred, porous produce directly to the shores, descending to inlets where they themselves loaded up the boats bound for Italy. We sighted several long-haired goats scaling cliffsides and Luca took me to see a couple of abandoned shepherds' huts alongside their beasts' pens. They were ingenious. Circular bases of shaly limestone upon which stood the conical hut fashioned like a wigwam out of long, slender juniper faggots. One had a door taken from a shipwrecked boat. Somehow or other, the shepherds lit fires within them to cook and keep warm and they made their cheeses there, too, from the milk of their herds. We crossed small bridges, flexible not solid, also constructed by the shepherds from juniper wood.

'There are no sheep here any more,' explained Luca. 'The deforestation caused by the *carbonari* as well as the acute water shortages due to changes in the climate have made it impossible for them to feed and survive.'

The few shepherds that remained lived in towns, no longer for months on end in their juniper huts. They kept herds of goats on the mountains now, not sheep. The goats could access underground springs that flowed from beneath the seabed into coastal caves.

'But surely, it's salt water?'

Luca shook his head. Along this Mediterranean coast there were sweet water springs beneath the seabed that found their way up on to the land within the cave formations.

The limestone cliffs were potted with caves, many still to be discovered. One had housed a gargantuan fig tree at the water's edge, gone today, but its roots still bore witness to its original stature. Here was where the monk seals used to take refuge from the storms. They were hunted along this coastline by fishermen who came over from the island of Ponza. Today, they have disappeared altogether from these waters.

The area was a living library of myths, legends, rare old tales, forgotten pasts set against an undisturbed dark, fairytale heart; the striped hues of the water, the unusual formations of rocks, soaring pinnacles, rocky pencils, outcrops, heads, creatures. The Gulf of Arbatax had been a sheltering harbour in Roman times, inland were the remains of Stone Age settlements, the *nuraghi*, scattered every-where across the island; elsewhere was a hidden harbour that could not be detected from the sea. It was occupied over the centuries by pirates or else by native vessels determined to keep the looters at bay. Tales of prehistory, of corsairs, bandits, shepherds taking to the gun, kidnappers ... Young Luca, who loved his land with a quiet and dignified passion, was a repository of romances, *contes*, folk tales and secrets.

'And Saint Peter was here.'

He came to Baunei – the town's name can probably be traced to the Phoenicians. *Baun*: 'fortified place' – because the townspeople were in fear of their lives. A giant was terrorising them. The Lord's Shepherd stalked the giant and banished it into a bottomless pit from where it could never return. The pit really exists. Su Sterru, one of the deepest chasms in Europe. A church was built up on the high plateau, San Pietro del Golgo, in honour of the saint who saved these people from the destructive forces of the giant. No sighting of the monster has been claimed in many a century. Still, the farmers and villagers go to Peter's church once a year, end of June, dressed up in local finery, to give thanks to him for saving them and their harvests.

I asked Luca whether he believed in giants and magic, whether he was a practising Catholic and what he felt about spirits.

'I believe in God's goodness,' he said. And, yes, he believed in the power of spirits. 'When you work with youngsters as physically and mentally disabled as those I spend my days with, the spirit is the driving energy, the light.'

'Do you think that such energies inhabit trees and stones?'

'On this island, myths abound. Stone rings here, burial sites there. Nature and spirits have always been linked.'

I did not doubt it.

It was time to leave, time to cross back over to the mainland and make for Tuscany, my last port of call. I took the motorway north and rode back into Olbia to find that the evening ship had been delayed. It was a beautiful late afternoon. Breaking the surface of the water were smoothed, round granite stones, underbelly pink, resembling whales' backs. Occasionally, with the water's sway, they looked as though they were surfacing and diving. I whiled away the time by the dockside reading and staring at my photographs of the olive tree. The face was there, no doubt about it.

Tuscany, to the province of Pistoia, to Pescia, the town where Pinocchio was born. Gone was the intense dry heat of the *Mezzogiorno*, gone were the pagan mysteries, prehistoric forests and tree spirits of Sardegna. Tuscany was a softer land, genteel with its pencil-thin cypresses and tumbling geraniums. Men rode bicycles in country lanes where scarlet poppies grew from the flanking stone walls, the occasional ochred palazzo, usually converted into a hotel, could be glimpsed on hilltops, *osterias* were everywhere. The air was powerfully perfumed with the scent of freshly cut laurel which hedged the properties and roadsides. This was not really the rural Tuscany I remembered from my twenties. The authenticity of the region had been compromised, overwhelmed by its commercial success, but it remained pretty nonetheless, particularly in late springtime.

My directions, received from the horticulturist by email, were to meet him on the road between Lucca and Pescia outside a garden centre (not his) where bonsai olive trees were being propagated. He was a contact of a contact given to me by Francisco. He would be in a sky-blue car, *celeste*, not just blue. A man of precision, of details, then. Attilio was a nursery owner, an olive-grafting specialist who created and patented new varieties. His, unlike the centre I had visited in Puglia, was a family-run affair but one that had gained distinction and a reputation throughout Italy and beyond. He (like every other Italian I had arranged to meet with) was late. I hung about outside a mechanic's yard, opposite courtyards of miniature olive trees until eventually a sky-blue car with a grey-haired man in royal blue shirt and a toffee-coloured cocker spaniel pulled up.

'Sorry, lady, to be late. Two centres with the same name. Let's go, you follow.'

We wound down lanes of olive groves, then more olive groves, past Pinocchio parks, restaurants, gardens and garages, got caught behind an exceedingly fat couple wedged in a Piaggio three-wheeler that had broken down and driven the tailing traffic into apoplexies of hooting and screaming – I was back on the mainland! – until eventually we pulled into Attilio's nursery where the grafting was in full progress with a team of locals who looked as though they had not had a break in a hundred years.

'What you have to know is wherever else you have been, whatever they have told you, we, here, *we* created grafting. Think of Cato, Pliny, Columella, book five of *De Re Rustica* . . . all agricultural geniuses, all Italian, before and around the time of Christ. In Pescia, we have perfected a system that is exclusive to us. Others in Spain, Greece, Turkey, even Puglia, copy us. We graft in the spring and by autumn the trees are already beautiful. My teams consist of three, usually one man and two women. They work from sunup till sundown and they graft three and a half thousand trees a day. We keep the grafted stock in seedbeds, not outside in pots. Let them tell you what they like elsewhere, they come *here*, to me, to Attilio's nursery, for their required grafted rootstock.'

All the while Attilio was talking at me his two teams were cutting and splicing behind us, on their knees or on tiny stools, beavering away. I had never seen a group look so exhausted. Attilio, who with his aquiline nose had the head and shoulders of a Roman Caesar, was clearly driven.

'The Romans planted the rootstock further apart . . . we bring them closer.'

'How many trees or potential trees here?'

'Seventy thousand in every thousand square metres. None are *potential* trees, lady. We rarely have a failed graft here. And these trees will be out in the farms at five years old and delivering fruit the next season.'

'But I understood that olive trees take up to fifteen years before they fruit.'

'Don't you understand, lady, that is one of the joys of this business. A stone or sucker planted directly into the earth takes fifteen years. As it has done throughout history. It has to learn the process of flowering and fruiting. It teaches itself. But a grafted tree has the genes of knowledge within it. There's the beauty. It does not need to

336

take a decade beyond its initial growth stage to teach itself to propagate. It is born with that knowledge. Think of it this way: a child born in the wild must fend for itself, but those with parents are taught what the adults have already acquired. That is a part of the genius of this form of plant propagation. Did no one tell you that? The French know nothing about growing trees!'

'In Sicily and Puglia, I . . .'

'The Sicilians are Africans,' he dismissed with a wave of the hand. 'And as for the *Mezzogiorno*. They call it midday but it's not. It's midnight down there. They live in the Dark Ages. The Mafia would not make a living up here. We are cultured people.'

I was a little taken aback by this very tall gentleman's lively opinions.

'Do you eat lunch? Let me show you my trees, my treasures, and then we'll have some lunch. Leave your car here.'

I slipped alongside him, followed by his docile spaniel, into the sky-blue car and we shot off, leaving the teams hard at their graft.

His own groves were all young examples, varieties that he himself had created.

'This is an improved clone of a variety of *lecchino* olive. I have called it Minerva. And here, a created variety known as Diana. She gives excellent oil. From a *pendolino* came Zeus. And so on. I have baptised them with classical Greek names to honour Athene, you see.'

At least he had a good word to say about the Greeks. 'Do you think of yourself as Roman, Tuscan or . . .?'

'My family has been here around the hills of Lucca for five centuries; I am an Etruscan, I hope. Italy is a pretty country but not serious. Now, let me introduce you to Urano, Uranus! With Urano I am creating a new variety. The trees are small, so easy to harvest, no climbing up ladders or investing in expensive picking machines. Finish with the *bacchiatura*!'

'*Bacchiatura?*'

'Beating down, olive gathering with the use of poles. Picking, though, is not the problem. With tall trees, it is the pruning. It is a time-consuming nuisance. And Urano will give large quantities of fruits from a small, manageable crown. It used to be in Tuscany that the trees were taller, pruned to a goblet shape, but *finito*. Now we create shorter trees.'

It was midday. The sun was shining, the dog was scampering in and about the flowering daisies at the heels of Attilio. I stood and looked at the trees. Every one of them an original, a new variety. Attilio was also gazing, hands clasped behind his back like a member of royalty.

'This is a beautiful garden filled with young olive trees. It is not a Spanish factory,' he sighed. 'Small trees are the future,' he mused. 'Dwarfed rootstock. Intensive farming and gathering. Spain has changed the mentality of olive farming. Super-intensive, that's the way it's going.'

'And quality?'

'We can achieve that, too . . .'

'But?'

He threw both arms in the air as though finished with the subject.

'What do you consider, Attilio, will be the lifespan of these trees? Do you think they will live forever or almost forever? An enhancement to the landscape, knobbly elders, round the Mediterranean basin?'

He turned and drilled a look into me. I caught a glint in those fierce blue eyes. 'There you have it! Twenty years and then we'll dig them up and plant again with the next newly invented variety. If the shelf life of the oil is short, dig it up, marry it with another rich in polyphenol. These trees are children to me. I am sixty-eight.' (He did not look it.) 'If I am still around in eight years' time, do you know what I dream of?'

I shook my head.

'I dream of seeing the children of these crossings. The future is the new system.'

'And the statelies, the trees from the traditional methods of growing?' My mind flashed back to Sardinia, to that face. Was it perplexity, incomprehension, I had read in the expression of that three-thousand-year-old girl? An instinctive, visceral understanding that factory farming was destroying a method that respected and fed the land? Had she a sense of the magic and truth of things . . .?

'I hope there will be room for traditional farming as well as the call that comes from competing with Spain. Tradition alongside superproduction. But you don't have to be a traditionalist to love your trees. I love these trees. I come here every day, even Sundays, to check on them, my children. Now, *basta*! It is time for the restaurant. What do you think, lady? *Andiamo mangiare!*'

Across the table in the Osteria di Pinocchio, Attilio cut a more mellow figure. He drank his red wine and asked me about my travels. When I mentioned the olive laboratory in Algeria, he laughed.

'My father sold that place half a million trees.'

I told him that I had been sorry to cancel the last leg of my Algerian journey due to weather inaccessibility.

'You know, lady, this is what I do for a living; I followed my father into agriculture. My dream had been to be an explorer, but I was bidden home to run the nurseries. Here in Tuscany we produce twenty thousand tons of pure Tuscan olive oil a year but we sell eighty thousand!' He laughed and poured more wine. 'We are in the land where Pinocchio was born. Telling lies here is a regional occupation.'

'Have you been lying . . .'

'No, no, but people cheat. Italy is corrupt. Tuscany, too. If I were young I'd start again elsewhere but my wife would never leave the grandchildren. So, I stay and make the best of it.'

'Don't you have a dream left?' I dared, considering as I said it that it was perhaps indiscreet.

His emperor's face cracked into a wrinkled smile. 'You speak of Algeria. Have you heard of Tassili N'Ajjer, way down in the southern Algerian Sahara?'

'Yes, of course. I had wanted to see the cave art. In prehistory, that desert was a savannah. I had been fancying that perhaps olive trees grew there, back in those lusher days.'

Attilio nodded. 'They did, and they still do. In spite of the desert conditions there are mountains down there that still support certain examples of Mediterranean flora including myrtle, a variety of cypress and, most importantly, a wild olive variety known as *Olea laperrini*. It needs next to no rainfall and it is the sister of *Olea europaea*. It could be a good rootstock for our *europaea*. I want to go there, take cuttings and fruits. In Ethiopia, there is *Olea chrysophylla*. Another sister of *europaea* . . .'

'Ethiopia, way down south along the Rift Valley!?'

'Yes. I want to find those wild virgin strains, bring them back to Italy, graft them with *europaea* and create an olive tree that is desert-resistant, drought-sturdy.'

'But isn't that already true of the olive, its roots can descend . . .?'

'Yes, yes, but I want to take a strain of tree that has lived all its life, all its genes, in that aridity. A tree that will instinctively know how to survive, how to fight back when the waters of the world run dry. Because the planet is hotting up, lady. Over one hundred countries are already suffering water deficit. Here, in Europe, a third of Spain is in trouble. Cyprus, too, as well as Sardegna, Sicilia and mainland Greece. The wars that will be fought will be fought over water. We will need those new olive trees.'

I was speechless.

My travels were done. It had been almost two years since I had landed in Beirut. Two years, with short breaks at the farm, in quest of the olive tree and its stories. I had set out looking backwards digging into its history, its journeys across the Mediterranean, but it seemed that after everything, perhaps the most mind-blowing discovery was that I was looking at its future.

Michel's plane was due into Milan the following afternoon. I had one night free, for myself. I said *arrivederci* to Attilio, thanked him for our enlightening lunch and set a course for Florence.

The city was bursting at the seams, of course, not a room to be had anywhere. It was Saturday evening. Eventually, I found a suite in one of the palazzos and decided to take it. I had been in cargo pants and hiking boots for almost six months. This was Florence. After a shower I went shopping, returning to my totally luxurious pad with two pairs of new shoes, strappy and satin, a silk skirt and three sleek Italian T-shirts. I ate dinner out on the terrace and watched the Florentines unwind, strolling the streets hand in hand. Tomorrow, I would be meeting my husband again for the first time in months. And I would recount to him what I had found. The olive tree as a model, a tool for a future . . . that could possibly stem the onslaught of climate change and drought.

A New Beginning

It was nudging June when Michel and I drove up the winding, badly-in-need-of-resurfacing tarmac that is the entry to this farm of ours. Stubby-nosed little green fruits on the trees in the old orchards greeted my arrival. I was both delighted to be back and a little disoriented. I learned on the journey from Milan that Michel had already been calling in quotes from *forage* experts, the drillers for wells.

'We will also need to install new pipes for the drip-feeding,' I sighed, considering the work of the boars.

And we were one dog short, laid to rest with past companions in the shade beneath the spreading boughs of one of our fruiting cherries. Our hunting hound, Bassett, had been poisoned during my travels by – what irony! – a slug pellet.

'An insecticide used on lettuces.' Michel had decided not to break it to me until journey's end.

'On our grounds?'

'No, the vet thinks that the pellets were bought by another landowner, a neighbour, and hidden within food to destroy the wild boars. Bassett found it.'

Distressing as it was, it somehow seemed to fit the tune of things. One more mark on the postcard I was painting to send to the giant chemical companies.

I embraced smiling Quashia and handed him a couple of Bernardo Agostini's Sicilian bottles. The following day he said, 'We're getting better at this olive oil business. This batch is excellent.' He cannot read our alphabet. I had to confess it wasn't ours, but he was right about its quality. There was definitely no colza cut in with those litres.

I did not unpack my bag for several days and while Michel and Quashia were at work repairing walls damaged by boars and shoring up the garage roof that had begun to cave in during my absence, I strode slowly up and down the slopes of our hillside trying to reacquaint myself with its geography. Like a sailor after months at sea, I was attempting to find my legs, my equilibrium. I settled myself within the hollow of one of our biggest fellows. For two years, with breaks, I had been travelling. In search of the secrets of the olive tree.

Starting right here I had begun to delve into the past, but among the many questions I was returning with was: where does this lead me? After all this travelling, what, if anything, had changed?

Who the original people were who took cuttings from the family of the *Oleaceae*, genus *Olea*, the wild olive tree, known also as *Olea africana* or *Olea chrysophylla*, and grafted it with another to give us the *Olea europaea*, our cultivated Mediterranean olive tree, I had failed to identify. Or, rather, these olive trees had retained their secret. The location, time and ancestry of that original cultivar remained their protected mystery.

I breathed in the perfumes of the mountain-growing *garrigue* plants, the tranquillity, the routine normality of an agricultural environment while I recalled that wild Sardegnan tree. Three thousand years younger than the ancient twisted colossi I had found two years back in the Lebanese mountains behind Beirut. I rose again, restless, clambering across our terraces. The soil beneath my sandalled feet was crumbly and dry. Nothing had been watered, but the cherries were ripe. I picked a few and ate them in the sun. In my journeyings to find the spirit, the mysteries, of the olive tree, the great gift-giver, I had crossed war zones, calm seas, thousands of years and many cultures. I had gazed upon prehistoric cave art, marvelled at the secret of a golden Minoan ring, stood in the deserts alongside a forgotten Roman mill, stared upon a 3000-year-old sprig transported from the eastern Mediterranean to Sicily. All, save for the cave art, within the lifespan of the 6000-year-old living beings, still flowering, still fruiting, that I had encountered in Lebanon.

But somewhere there was a piece that was missing.

I had hoped to dazzle with figures. To set down the miles I had covered over the sixteen months out of twenty-four, but I had hopped back and forth, changed course so many times, that I had dizzied myself with calculations and so had abandoned the idea. What does it matter? Throughout all of those miles, those days on the road or sea, the olive tree had left clues, fed me, come to me in stories, snippets, treasures, puzzles, but it had retained for itself the answers to my principal questions: Where do you come from? Who first cultivated you?

Do the answers to these questions matter? Well, I remain curious.

Looking backwards at these journeys, I felt immense gratitude for all that had been shown to me, but what I was left with was not the questions about the past, though I will continue to search, but the future. The present and the future. The face of the Sardegnan tree looking out at me in the present. If these beings, these magisterial survivors, have held their own for such a monumental stretch of time, unimaginable to us short-lifers, don't they deserve a little respect? A pause for awe? The olive's longevity, its duration of service, had always impressed me. So, too, its grace and metallic beauty, but only during these last few laps had I begun to comprehend what a masterful organism the tree is and, in particular, the olive tree.

The earth is hotting up, the ice is melting, wars are annihilating homelands, flattening heritage, breaking apart communities, groundwater is drying up, is being polluted, and we are killing ourselves off at an alarming rate due to the cancers triggered in our systems by build-up from the pesticides in our foods. Who can we turn to, to assist with these almighty calamities? Might the tree have a role to play and again, in partciular, the olive tree?

It was early December. I was descending the hillsides, looking out towards the glinting winter sea, returning from the olive mill, where the gossip had been fast and the farmers were gloating. Word was out that the EU had recently fined Italy a sum exceeding seventy million euros to be deducted from their upcoming agricultural grants for 'unfulfilled commitments within their olive sector'.

'You're a traveller. What do you think of such a disgrace, Carol?' Gérard had called out to me. I had shrugged, laughed silently to myself, recalling Attilio and the frankness with which he had admitted that 'Here, in Tuscany, we produce twenty thousand tons of pure Tuscan olive oil a year, but we sell eighty thousand.'

'I think I know a few honest Italians,' I shouted back.

The farmers had hung their jowls. 'There's no such animal' was their united Provençal response. The last time I received a communication from Attilio he was planning his trip to the Sahara. 'There's no time left to dream about it,' he had written. 'I have to act. The future depends upon it.'

Swinging a hairpin now, I heard the swish of heavy liquid. The back of our old bus was awash with empty olive crates and close to seventy litres of the finest oil, pressed not an hour earlier. The sun was shining. This was our last load of the year. We had pressed a little over a ton, or 1000 kilos, of fruits this season. Soon it would be Christmas and our annual gatherings of friends invited to celebrate and decant all the fine juice.

I was thinking about inviting silver-haired René, our first olive guru, over for a glass along with his business partner, Raymond, the water sorcerer.

Coincidentally, during my previous mill visit, in late November, I had bumped into them, not seen since the year before.

'This season,' they boasted, talking over one another like a couple of schoolboys though the total age between them was 170, 'we have been pressing a ton of olives a week!' They were beginning to metamorphose into an old married couple.

'With so many private wells, your production and water expenditure must be second only to Andalucía,' I joked, recounting light-heartedly some of the concerns I had discovered throughout my days on the road.

René was opening a fine bottle of *cru classé rosé*. He was a man of substance these days and revelled in his exalted position.

'Carol, you are getting as bad as that bloke who wants to change the world,' he reposted, as he handed me a beaker of wine, calling over to Gérard, our miller, to enjoy a glass with us.

'Who's that, René?'

'That fellow who lives up behind Nice who reckons he's found the answer to the olive fly. A dreamer, he is, a Utopian. You're two of a kind, Carol.'

And that was how we found out about Luke.

While I had been trekking the Mediterranean, ironically, a *petit* turn of events had been digging its heels in back here at home. The organic farming revolution. In France, they call it L'Agriculture Biologique, abbreviated to *bio*, which means organic. The movement was fast taking hold in a small-scale way. Alas, one of the only sectors to be dragging its heels was the olive, due to Dacus, the blasted olive fly, our friend the *mouche*, who was still refusing to go away unless plastered with pesticides. This was until Luke, modest vegetable and olive farmer, had made a little experiment on his own groves. But no one seemed to be shouting about it from the rooftops, no Stop Press had arrived from the olive bodies to inform us of this extraordinary turn of events.

I tracked him down, this 'Utopian', and he confirmed that he had just completed his first, highly successful harvest, his first outing with *Psyttalia Lounsburyi*.

'A tropical beauty and a natural enemy' was his description for the fly that preys on Dacus.

'How does this work?' I asked Michel. 'Do we buy the fly by the box or by the dozen and then let them loose in the garden? Will they prey on other creatures?'

'Let's invite him to lunch and find out.'

I smiled.

'I've made the decision,' he said. 'I'm with you. No more pesticides.'

Luke had agreed to visit, to tell us all about *Psyttalia Lounsburyi*, the fly that stalks the olive fly.

I pulled up the drive, hooting. Three dogs came storming down to greet me. An old white van was parked up alongside one of Quashia's untidy heaps of sand. I spotted the two men further up the grounds, standing beneath one of our four-hundred-year-olds. The stranger, dressed in denim, a hand's length shorter than my husband, was waving his arms about, talking heatedly. I glanced swiftly through the window into the back of his van, wondering whether it might be packed tight with boxes of tropical insects. Disappointingly, there were a few gardening tools and pair of boots. Little else. Little to suggest that the proprietor of this vehicle was offering a radical alternative to the way we and others are running our farms, feeding our families. I called out and the men turned. Michel beckoned me up. I climbed the stone steps alongside the stables. Luke, smiling, stepped to offer his hand. He could have been any age from forty to fifty-five, slender, fit with a presence that was calm but an energy that was determined.

'Two per cent of French farmers have shifted to *bio*, Luke has been telling me,' said Michel. 'It's very exciting. This new fly, *Lounsburyi*, the predator of Dacus, is originally from Kenya. Come on, let's go inside. Lunch is ready. This is a whole new departure for our olive farm.'

The men stepped on, talking enthusiastically. I held back a moment. Turning my gaze round the garden, up into the groves, images from my journey flooded back. At the caves of Altamira I had read that the wild olive had been in existence in prehistoric times and had grown along the Rift Valley. Syria and Lebanon, the north of the Rift, I had been thinking, not Kenya way down in the south. I began to smile, appreciating the irony. From where the earliest traces of wild olives have been found we are seeking assistance, reaching out towards a less tainted tomorrow.

Your origins remain your secret, I mumbled to the groves. But the past and the future are irrevocably linked and time is perhaps not of your making, but ours.

Index

Visit Carol Drinkwater's online photo gallery

If you have been captivated by Carol Drinkwater's travels make sure you visit her online gallery of photos at
www.caroldrinkwater.com/gallery
<http://www.caroldrinkwater.com/gallery> The vast array of photos were taken during her trips around the Mediterranean Basin as featured in both *The Olive Route* and *The Olive Tree*.

www.caroldrinkwater.com <http://www.caroldrinkwater.com/> also includes information about all of Carol Drinkwater's previous books and audiobooks, a seasonal newsletter and details of upcoming events that Carol is attending.